Programming of

Embedded Systems

Programming of Embedded Systems

Applications to SM32F10x μControllers

Vincent Mahout
Thierry Rocacher
Guillaume Auriol

iSTE

WILEY

First published 2026 in Great Britain and the United States by ISTE Ltd and John Wiley & Sons, Inc.

ISTE Ltd
27-37 St George's Road
London SW19 4EU
UK

www.iste.co.uk

John Wiley & Sons, Inc.
111 River Street
Hoboken, NJ 07030
USA

www.wiley.com

Library of Congress Control Number: 2025946209

British Library Cataloguing-in-Publication Data
A CIP record for this book is available from the British Library
ISBN 978-1-78630-951-8

The manufacturer's authorized representative according to the EU General Product Safety Regulation is Wiley-VCH GmbH, Boschstr. 12, 69469 Weinheim, Germany, e-mail: Product_Safety@wiley.com.

Contents

Preface

The writing of this work is the result of more than 25 years of teaching experience at the *Institut National des Sciences Appliquées* (INSA) in Toulouse within the department of electrical and computer engineering.

It concerns itself with embedded computing and hardware architecture, a field that lies along the interface of two other areas: electronics and computer science. It involves an impressive number of useful objects that includes more than just the computers and smartphones we use every day. From the smallest household robots that populate our kitchens to the airplanes that criss-cross our skies, embedded computing can be found everywhere in our daily lives, both at home and at work. A poor grasp of the techniques used in embedded computing can result in minor annoyances for the user, as well as major disasters.

There are several approaches when it comes to programming a μcontroller. One of them, proposed by Arduino©, for example, consists of working with consumer-grade circuits and providing "off-the-shelf" libraries, which allow for a particular application to be developed very quickly and that is supported by a large community. This first approach is completely suitable for personal applications that are not very demanding in terms of performance.

These solutions are designed to hide how complex low-level hardware really is by providing software libraries. However, these libraries do not necessarily exploit the full performance of the peripheral units that a μcontroller can use (ADC, PWM, etc.).

The approach that we describe in this book forms part of another one whose aim is to acquire the greatest possible range of skills related to this field. To do so, some knowledge of digital electronics is therefore required to master the hardware concepts so that the peripheral circuitry can be exploited to its full potential. This also involves so-called "low-level" computing (i.e. close to the hardware) in the C programming language, which allows for simple and efficient code to be used. This coding will also be approached with suitable software structuring that emphasizes portability and reusability.

In the age of artificial intelligence and automatic coding, we consider it essential therefore that future engineers should be trained with the knowledge of what is happening inside the box. We get to the core of the circuits and systems so that the student can understand the fundamental mechanisms, which enable a computer program to successfully carry out the task for which it was designed.

This teaching experience, and the work offered to you, are based on a family of μcontrollers manufactured by STmicro©. However, our experience has been built over the years on other architectures (Intel, Motorola, Infinéon, etc.). This book is obviously therefore targeted in terms of program implementation, but has been designed to remain generic when describing the different components (both hardware and software) encountered in the world of embedded systems by as much as possible.

Finally and above all else, this work is the fruition of an immense collective effort. Three of us co-signed the drafting, but there are many other colleagues who contributed greatly to enriching our knowledge. Of course, we cannot name them all, but we would like in particular to thank Sébastien Di Mercurio, Pascal Acco, Pierre-Emmanuel Hladik and Jean-Louis Noullet for the quality of their work and the richness of our exchanges. When it came to putting our pen down to paper, we cannot forget that Michel Castan, Pascal Chargé, Michel Bonnet and Didier Le Botlan also knew how to contribute their fair share of ink.

October 2025

1

Aims, Context and a Guiding Thread Example

1.1. Aims of this book

The programming of any kind of μcontroller is a relatively complicated job when starting from scratch. The first task is to gather together all the documentation related to the equipment and tools you are going to use. Between the *datasheets*, reference manuals, user manuals, etc., it is normal to find yourself faced with several thousands of pages that will have to be reviewed and cross-referenced before any information relevant to the task can be extracted.

However, one simple alternative is available to those who might become discouraged by this abundance of documentation. It consists of using prewritten examples that can be found on the Internet in abundance. Reading such "source" files allows you to acquire the knowledge required to implement basic functions at a lower cost.

This book aims to follow an intermediate approach. Throughout the various chapters, we aim to provide the reader with the information needed to start programming an application on a STM32-type architecture from the very beginning and/or to understand the examples more easily and quickly than they would have gathered on their own. We also aim to be as general as possible. Thus, each chapter that deals with a specific peripheral unit will begin with a section explaining how the peripheral operates, without any programming considerations nor its particular version for the μcontroller being studied.

We hope to shed a methodological light on programming. Whether it be via the chapter on general programming principles (see Chapter 2) or via different program examples, we will try to apply coding and structuring techniques that offer both rigor, safety and readability.

Finally, let us point out that this work is based on a particular version of the STM32 μcontrollers from the STmicro© product range, namely, the STM32F10x family.

1.2. What this book contains... and what it does not

This book cannot be exhaustive. Indeed, the family of STM32 μcontrollers is particularly vast. It would therefore be unrealistic to claim that every particular subtlety or limitation for a specific μcontroller version will be presented. The reader will therefore necessarily need to consult the documentation specific to their μcontroller in order to ensure the existence and compatibility of the functions presented in this book.

In addition, we have chosen only to deal with peripheral units that seem to be the most widespread when controlling embedded systems to us. Without minimizing either their importance or usefulness, certain units, although present in μcontrollers, will not be discussed in the chapters of this book. The beginner programmer will find plenty to engage with in the units we will cover in detail. The more advanced programmer will be able to find clarifications on the electronic structure of the peripheral units that cannot be obtained simply by reading the reference manual STMicroelectronics (2011).

These large units that are “absent” in our discussion are:

– any circuit related to the debugging unit DBG connections;

– units linked to external memory access:

  - FSMC (*Flexible Static Memory Controller*)-type units,
  - SDIO (*Secure Digital Input/Output interface*)-type units;

– digital/analog (DAC) units;

– communication bus CAN units;

– USB and OTG_USB port management units;

– units supporting the Ethernet ETH protocol;

– cyclic redundancy check (CRC) units;

– the electronic signature of the circuits.

After a reminder on the elements of C for embedded systems in Chapter 2, this book is then divided into chapters, each explaining one of the main functionalities required in the creation of the vast majority of embedded applications:

– Chapter 3 presents the general aspects of the STM32F10x architecture. We will also discuss some important concepts such as internal clocks, *watchdogs*.

– Chapter 4 is dedicated to everything related to managing the μcontroller at the pin level, in particular detailing the binary input/output aspects (GPIO).

– Chapter 5 explains the crucial aspect of embedded system programming, namely, interrupts and their management as well as the principles of using a DMA.

– Chapter 6 explains everything related to time management via Timer units.

– Chapter 7 focuses on an important functionality of Timers which allows for PWM (*Pulse Width Modulation*)-type signals to be generated.

– Chapter 8 studies everything to do with analog/digital converters.

– Chapter 9 is dedicated to communications peripherals: serial communication via USART (*Universal Synchronous and Asynchronous Receiver Transmitter*), SPI (*Serial Peripheral Interconnect*) communication and lastly the industrial I^{2}C (*Inter-Integrated Circuit*) bus.

– The final chapter addresses the various energy-management modes offered by the STM32.

– The appendix is a reminder on the technological foundations of digital electronics.

1.3. About the code examples

This book is intended to be primarily practical. Unlike what is provided in the manufacturer's documentation, commented examples can be found throughout this book to concretely illustrate the steps one can follow to set up a particular configuration or simple application example. Chapter 2 is dedicated to the key implementation principles when adopting methods and structures suitable for one's needs.

The examples provided are written to be as readable as possible for educational purposes only. We want the reader-programmer to perfectly discern between the different actions they can take when setting up their own application. However, we also invite them to inspect the efficiency of their code and therefore to optimize the instructions accordingly.

1.4. Choosing your μcontroller: the STM32 family

The family of STM32 μcontrollers is available in many versions. What is more, as they are recent technologies, this family undergoes regular developments and additions. Consequently, this book cannot claim to be up-to-date and the information presented[1] in this chapter will necessarily be incomplete. However, it is important to us to draw up a quick portrait of the STM32 family, so that the reader can realize one of the first difficulties when it comes to implementing a μcontroller: Which one to choose?

1 The information used to write these sentences dates back to October 2012.

1.4.1. *Criteria when choosing a μcontroller*

The question of which μcontroller to choose can be complex. Rather than trying to answer it, we propose a list of a certain number of technical criteria:

– the number and nature of the inputs/outputs required to control the system in which the μcontroller will be used;

– the number and nature of the peripherals that will be useful to the application. A system-oriented design must therefore be carried out;

– the μcontroller package. This may seem anecdotal, but this choice is important and will depend on several factors:

- the need to miniaturize as much as possible or not,

- the production equipment: it is not the same skill, nor the same equipment, that will be required to assemble a LQFP, QFPN nor even a BGA case on a *printed circuit board* (PCB);

– memory capacity: this is often what determines the price of the component. This includes the RAM, as well as the flash memory. Depending on the application, the ROM or RAM requirements can be very different. Among the indicators that can help us choose are:

- a system analysis allowing for any particular RAM requirements to be anticipated,

- the libraries used: depending on their complexity, the use of flash memory in particular can be increased as opposed to programming with custom libraries that meet a particular need (the method presented in this book);

– operating speed: a high operating speed ensures that the processor can function quickly enough for a given task. However, good programming that is simple and efficient makes it possible to obtain high operating speeds with a reasonable processor frequency. This is the path that we propose in this book again. There are very powerful cross-platform libraries (HAL *[Hardware Abstraction Layer]* by STmicro©), which offer the advantage of an apparent ease of development, but at the cost of making multiple calls to generic and nested interrupt routines, which extend processing times. Here again, the objective of this book is to go against the grain of using these generic libraries so that the programmer is able to optimize this or that critical functionality in terms of speed when necessary;

– electrical consumption: this has been a very important area of improvement for all μcontroller manufacturers over the years, and STmicro© is very well established in this area. Most of the controllers offered include a so-called *low-power* mode.

This list of criteria is certainly not exhaustive, but it states the main elements to be considered by the user so that they can make a suitable choice.

1.4.2. *STM32 family*

Just by browsing the STmicro© website, we can see that the STM32 μcontrollers are available in more than *1,200 different versions*. Considering the scale of this range, it becomes clear that understanding the choice of circuit is not quite so straightforward.

The STM32 range is initially divided into four large families:

– the *high-performance* family which, as its name indicates, brings together the most efficient versions within the catalog;

– the *mainstream* family which constitutes the most standard versions on offer;

– the *ultra low power* family which benefits from optimized technology to reduce electricity consumption;

– the *wireless* family, the latest addition to the range, which is equipped with peripherals dedicated to wireless connectivity.

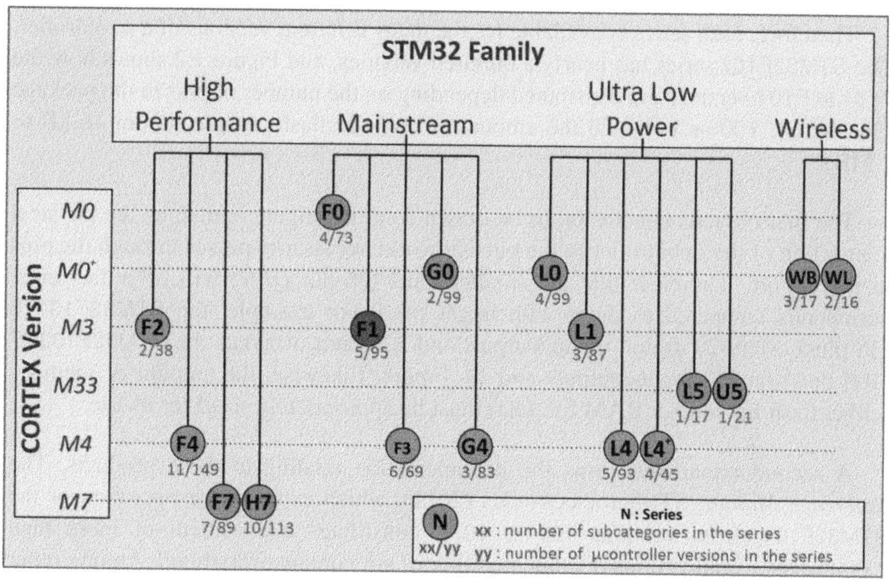

Figure 1.1. *Distribution of the different STM32 families*

These families are then further subdivided into different series (Lx, Fx, Gx, etc.), depending on which version of the Cortex core the μcontroller possesses. Figure 1.1

illustrates the breakdown of this range, all while indicating the number of versions that are currently being marketed[2].

1.4.3. *STM32F10x line*

This book is essentially based on the STM32F10x series. We chose this mid-range series to represent the STM32 μcontrollers because it is not possible to provide concrete and illustrated explanations without referring to a specific architecture. As one will see in the various examples, this restriction still remains relatively broad. In fact, many features are not present on each version within this series.

Nonetheless, it is true that the 1,200 different μcontroller versions all share a common basis. What is presented about the Timers for the STM32F10x series remains valid for the vast majority of the STM32L4xx series, for example. The main difficulty will perhaps be ascertaining what is different so that an adaption can be made.

Therefore, each series is available for the many different versions of a μcontroller. The STM32F10x series has nearly a hundred versions, and Figure 1.2 shows how the F101 to F107 versions are distributed depending on the number of pins in the package (38, 44, 64, 100 or 144) and the amount of onboard flash memory (from 16 kB to 1 MB).

The first obvious conclusion to be drawn from this figure is that, as the physical connection of the μcontroller to the outside world necessarily passes through the pins in the circuit, it is clear that the smaller units (36-pin *QFN*) will offer far fewer peripherals compared to those with larger ones. For example, the STM32F101T8 (36 pins) offers 28 digital inputs/outputs and 3 Timers, whereas the STM32F103VF (100 pins) has 80 inputs/outputs and 14 Timers. Likewise, the amount of memory (either flash for code or RAM for data) must be appropriately sized for its use.

A second remark concerns the documentation relating to these products. The *Reference Manual* STMicroelectronics (2011), which explains the operation of the STM32F10x (from versions 101 to 107), constitutes a document of more than 1,000 pages..., and yet this document still does not contain everything! Among other things, it is also necessary to have access to the Cortex *Programming Manual* STMicroelectronics (2013) to find the details on interrupts, for example, and of course the specific *datasheet* for the μcontroller version in question to obtain its precise specifications (number of pins, number of peripherals, electrical characteristics, etc.).

2 This information was obtained in March 2022. There is no doubt that it will soon need to be updated.

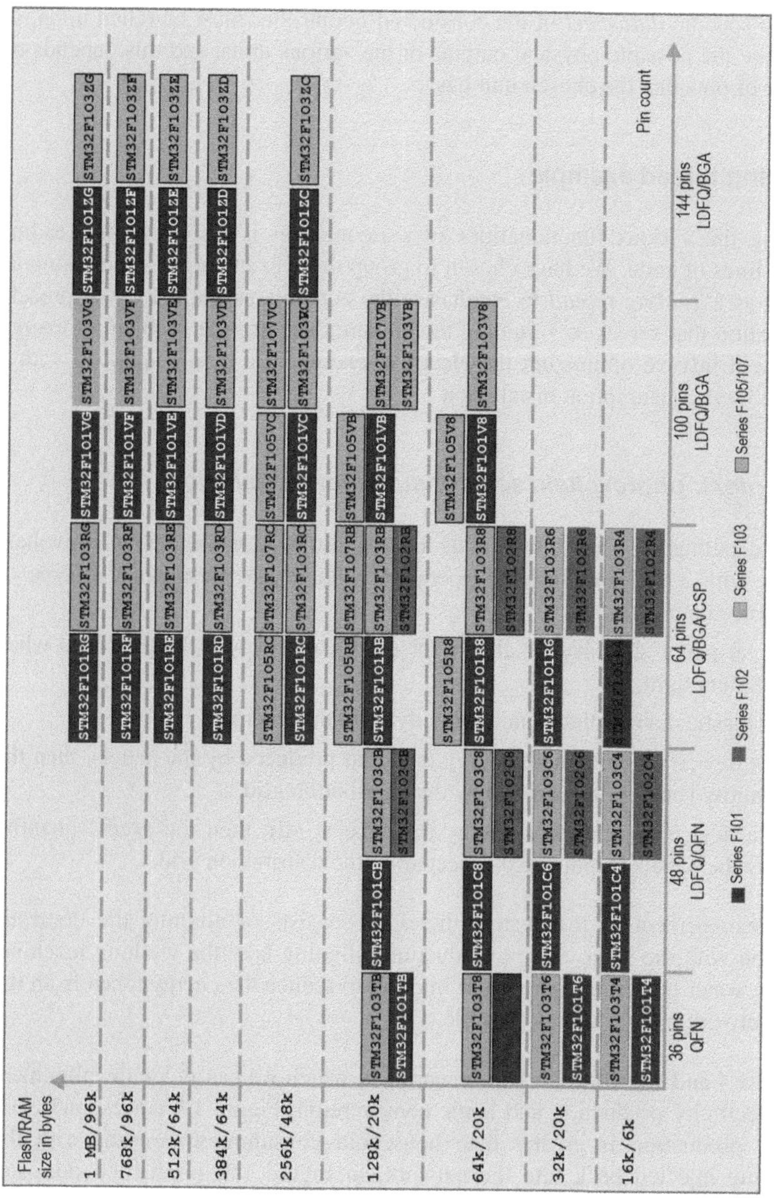

Figure 1.2. *F1 line of the STM32 family. For a color version of this figure, see www.iste.co.uk/mahout/programming.zip*

As not all peripherals are available on every version, it is important to note that the *Reference Manual* is recalled at the start of each chapter and, depending on the μcontroller family, the presence or absence of the device in the corresponding chapter. Second, the specific *datasheet* of the considered μcontroller must be relied upon, so that we know the possible physical outputs of the various units, and this depends on the number of pins that the chosen unit has.

1.5. Guiding thread example

Learning the various functionalities of a μcontroller is also done by reading illustrative lines of code. We have chosen to group these examples together using an application as a *guiding thread* to emphasize the concrete aspects of our approach. The application that serves as a guiding thread here concerns the problem of energy saving. It will involve optimizing the electrical energy of a home equipped with a photovoltaic self-consumption installation.

1.5.1. *Context: photovoltaic self-consumption installation*

Before detailing the application, let us first explain what makes up a photovoltaic installation with a self-consumption operation. Figure 1.3 illustrates this type of system; we see that:

– the solar panel *AC* inverter allows for electrical energy to be produced when there is sufficient light;

– the domestic devices that benefit directly from this energy:

- if a device requires more energy than that produced by the panels, then the missing quantity is naturally supplied by the distribution grid,

- if a device requires less energy (or none at all), then the excess quantity produced by the panels is redirected (injected) to the distribution grid.

Good management of the system therefore consists of aligning the domestic consumption with the solar energy production (aligning how the washing machine, dishwasher, water heater, etc., are used) in order to reduce the energy taken from the electrical network by as much as possible.

Figures 1.4 and 1.5 illustrate two scenarios in which we can judge the alignment between electricity production and home consumption. Figure 1.4 corresponds to a case when production is greater than household consumption overall, with the surplus being injected back into the network. In Figure 1.5, production does not cover consumption, particularly toward the end of the day; the alignment is therefore less optimized.

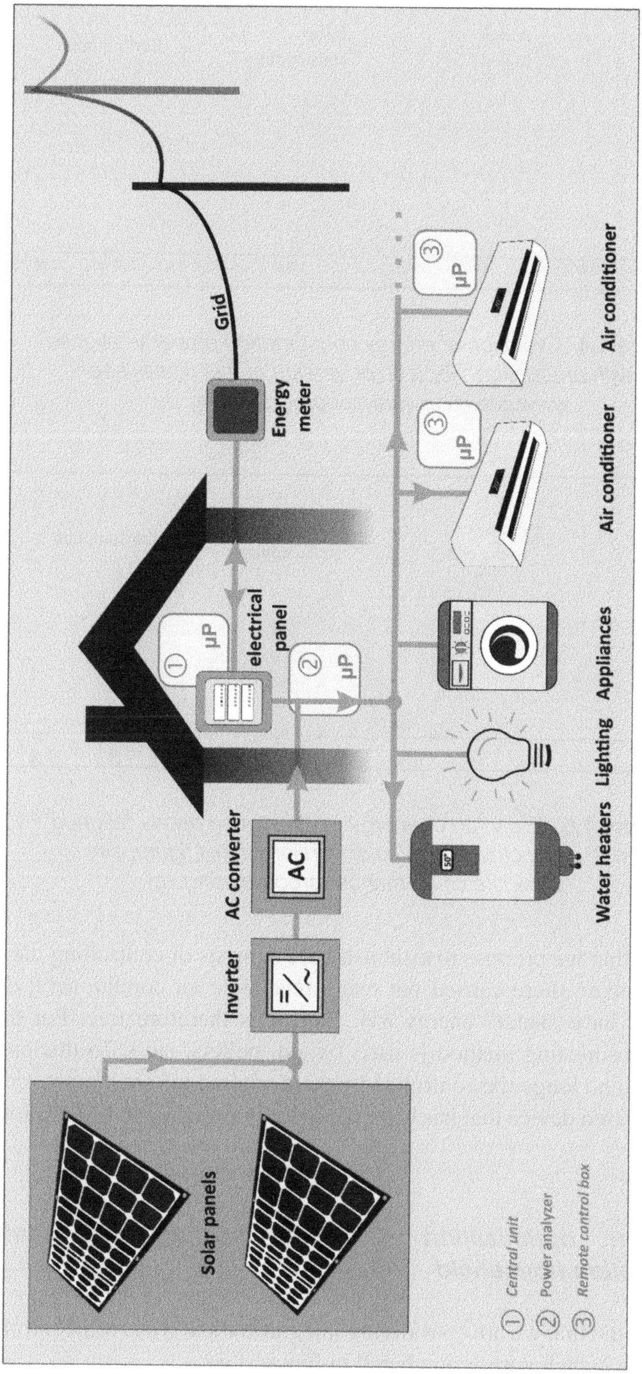

Figure 1.3. *Principle of a self-consumption installation*

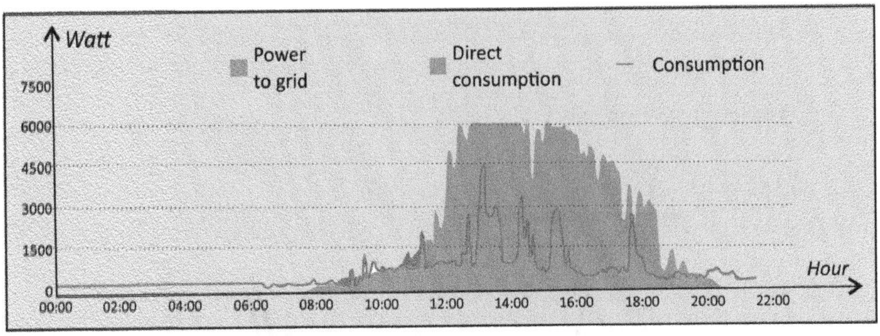

Figure 1.4. *Evolution of energy consumption properly "aligned" with production. For a color version of this figure, see www.iste.co.uk/mahout/programming.zip*

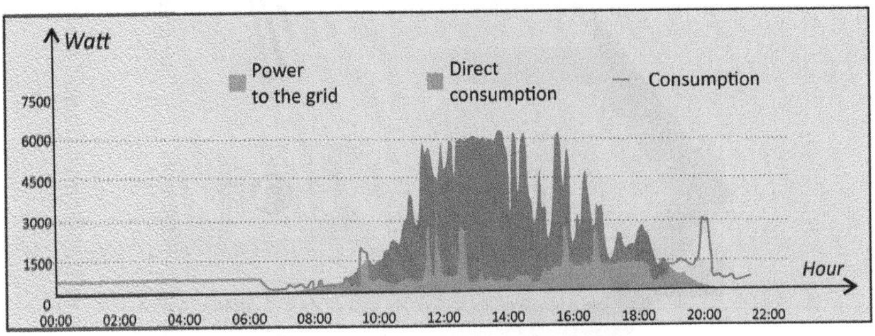

Figure 1.5. *Evolution of energy consumption poorly "aligned" with production. For a color version of this figure, see www.iste.co.uk/mahout/programming.zip*

The system that we propose to establish here consists of controlling the electrical heating of the home (here carried out using reversible air conditioners) during the times when we have "solar" energy kW, and it is therefore free. For the rest of the time, another heating method is used (wood, pellets, etc.). To this end, the air conditioners will no longer be controlled by their original infrared remote control, but rather by an infrared device that has been specifically designed to be used for this new operation.

1.5.2. *System: optimization of electric heating in a photovoltaic self-consumption household*

The installation that we are considering integrates three types of μcontroller-based control elements, which appear numbered in Figure 1.3:

1) The *power meter*: this is located at the electrical meter. Its role is to measure the power coming from both the inverter and the grid, so that the available energy can be measured.

2) The *central unit*: this is the brain of the system. It receives power information in real time. It is able to communicate wirelessly with the *remote control boxes* and request them to change the air conditioning settings.

3) The *remote control boxes*: there are as many such boxes as there are air conditioning units to control. These are battery-powered communicating remote controls. To save energy and avoid changing their batteries too frequently, they go into sleep mode and wake up every 30 min. Then they connect to the *central unit* to update it with the current temperature and also wait for any orders. If necessary, they also modify the air conditioning setpoint.

Let us now detail these three types of units that use a μcontroller and list the resources they will use. Figure 1.6 shows the functional architecture of these units.

1.5.2.1. *Power meter*

This unit must provide the following functionalities:

– measure three energy quantities: the grid voltage, the grid current and the current coming from the inverter;

– transmit information wirelessly to the *central unit*.

For this unit, we have opted to use a STM32F103RB μcontroller, which requires the following resources:

– a Timer to manage interrupt sequences of a real-time routine;

– a second Timer to drive the LED in the PWM;

– multiple-channel ADC to acquire analog input data. This function will be programmed with DMA access;

– an UART-type link for wireless communication;

– GPIO management for the LED and other input/output configurations.

1.5.2.2. *Central unit*

This unit plays the central role in the application as it must:

– retrieve power information from the *power meter*;

– implement the operating processes for the various air conditioning systems;

– retrieve information from each *remote control box* and send orders to them;

– provide the man–machine interface via an LCD screen, a rotary button for navigation, sound information, etc.

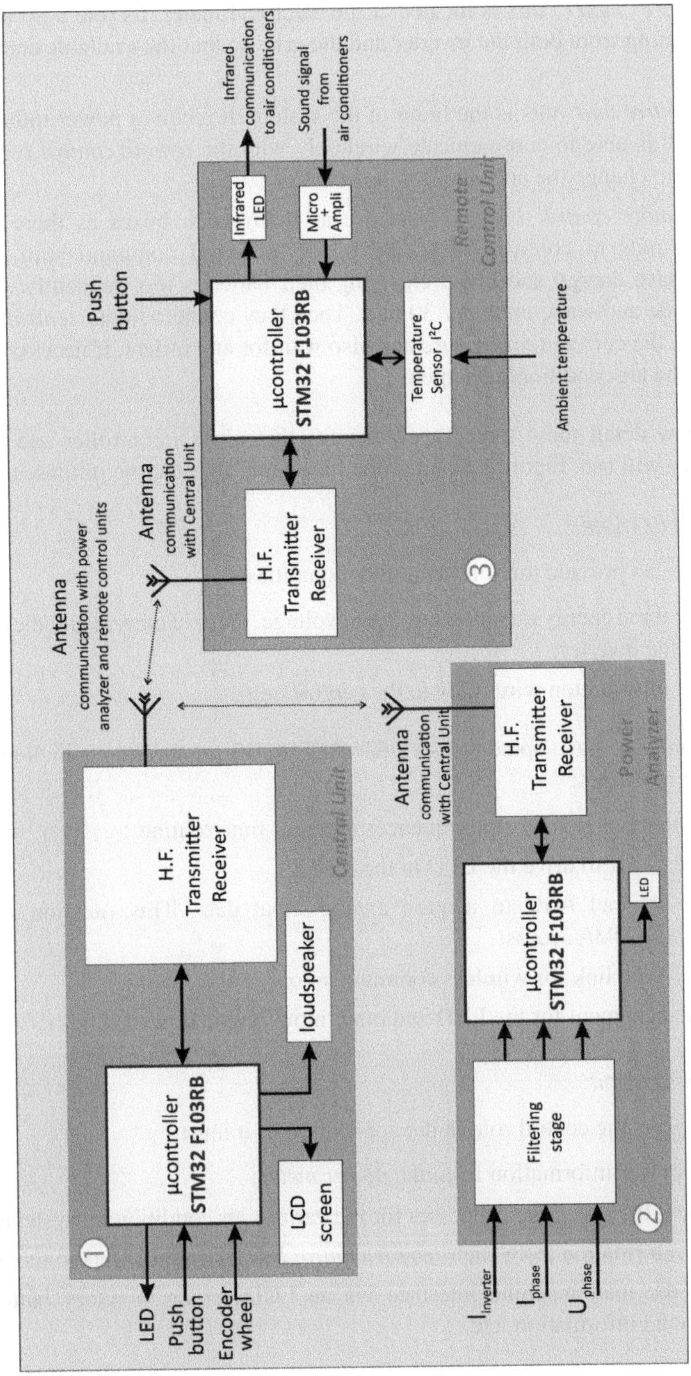

Figure 1.6. *The three types of application components*

As shown in Figure 1.6, this unit will be based upon an STM32F103RB μcontroller. The required peripherals are:

– a Timer to manage the interrupt sequences of a real-time routine;

– an SPI link for controlling the LCD module;

– an UART link for wireless communication;

– GPIO management for the push buttons and speaker;

– a direct external interrupt for the push buttons;

– a Timer in incremental mode for the encoder wheel.

1.5.2.3. *Remote control boxes*

These "small" units, which are more advanced than simple remote controls, will have the following tasks:

– to measure the ambient temperature;

– to control the air conditioning via infrared communication;

– to transmit (and receive) information to (and from) the central unit;

– to capture the sound emitted from the air conditioner so that it knows whether the air conditioner has received the intended order or not.

Each *remote control box* will be equipped with an STM32F103RB μcontroller, whose functions will use:

– a Timer to manage interrupt sequences of a real-time routine;

– an I^2C connection for the temperature sensor;

– a UART link for wireless communication;

– GPIO management for the infrared LED;

– direct external interrupts for the push buttons;

– an ADC to capture the sounds emitted by the air conditioners.

1.5.3. *Summary of the peripherals seen in the guiding thread example*

Chapter	System element	Description of the example presented
4 **Binary inputs/outputs (I/O): parallel ports**	*Remote control box* All the I/O	*Study*: all I/O remote control box configurations *Code*: generic GPIO driver

Chapter	System element	Description of the example presented
5 Interrupt and DMA management	*Central unit* Push-button management, HF transmission	*Code*: complete application: interrupt caused by menu navigation buttons (external interrupt) *Code*: complete application: sending messages *via* the UART using the DMA
6 Timer units	*Central unit* Encoder wheel management	*Code*: code snippet: configuring a Timer in incremental encoder mode
7 Pulse-width modulation (PWM)	*Central unit and power meter* LED activity indicator	*Code*: complete application: using a Timer for PWM and interrupts ("breathing" LED)
8 Analog-to-digital converter	*Power meter* Acquiring analog quantities from the EDF network	*Study*: ADC configuration according to the electrical parameters of the quantities to be measured *Code*: complete application: implementing the ADC with three channels in *Scan* mode, DMA utilization, ending DMA interrupts
9 Some communication buses	*Remote control box* HF reception, temperature measurement	*Study*: UART configured in reception and interrupt mode *Code*: complete application: I^2C communication with AT7410 temperature sensor. I^2C in non-interrupt DMA mode
10 STM32 energy management	*Remote control box* μcontroller sleep management	*Code*: complete application: put in *Standby* mode for 30 minutes, wake up *via* RTC. Wake-up management differentiating between wake-up from *Standby* or *Reset* mode enforced by nRST or power recovery

Table 1.1. *Peripherals seen in the guiding thread example*

2

General Programming Principles

This chapter aims to provide some important reminders about programming in the C language. It refers to elements of a μcontroller for application examples but understanding the functionality of these examples is not the main intention here. Rather, it is just to understand the good usage and practices for the C language that seemed necessary for us to clarify. The experienced programmer will be able to skim through this chapter very quickly.

2.1. Pointers and registers

Due to the μcontroller architecture, it is often necessary to structure certain program variables to access the components of a particular unit within the μcontroller. Furthermore, the various registers are only accessible if their memory address is known exactly. Unlike variables created by the programmer, to which the *linker* assigns an address, the registers here are "hard-coded", meaning they have a fixed address by the circuit designer.

It is therefore quite logical and practical to perform these various access operations using pointers. Let us begin by recalling their usage.

2.1.1. *"Simple" variables*

A variable is a memory location. It thus has an address, a value and a type. The type defines how the value of the variable is encoded in memory and, consequently, the size that this value occupies in memory.

The instructions (code example 2.1) create and initialize a simple variable of type char. At this stage, it only has an address that we do not explicitly know. Its value can

---

For a color version of all the Codes in this chapter, see www.iste.co.uk/mahout/programming.zip

vary, but its size is always 8 bits since Var_Char is of type char. Recall that char is an 8-bit integer type.

```
int main(void)
{
  char Var_Char;
  /* The variable Var_Char is created – we say that it is defined
      */
  Var_Char = 0x14;
  /* The value of the variable Var_Char is 20 (14 in hex) */
}
```

Code 2.1. *Simple variable*

2.1.2. *Pointer to a variable*

Even if it may seem disconcerting at first reading, *a pointer is a variable* whose value will always be an address, and therefore 32 bits in size, regardless of the object it points to (in the case of the previous example, a char). Let us complete code example 2.1 by adding a variable Ptr_Char, which is a pointer to a char.

```
int main(void)
{
  char Var_Char;
  char *Ptr_Char;
  /* Declaration of a pointer variable of type char */

  Var_Char = 0x1C;
  Prt_Char = &Var_Char;
  /* The pointer holds the address of the variable Var_Char */
  *Ptr_Char =  0x2F;  /* i.e. the value 47 in decimal */
  /* The variable pointed to by Ptr_Char is assigned the value 0
      x2F */
  /* The pointer variable is thus modified by indirection */
  /* Var_Char now holds the value 0x2F */
}
```

Code 2.2. *Pointer to a simple variable*

As the previous example illustrates, the symbol & is used to retrieve the address of a variable. Indirection, that is to say, the use of the value to the pointer variable, is done using the syntax *PointerName. The memory representation of this example is illustrated in Figure 2.1, assuming that the linker has placed the variable Var_Char at address 0x20000000 and the pointer variable Ptr_Char at 0x20000004.

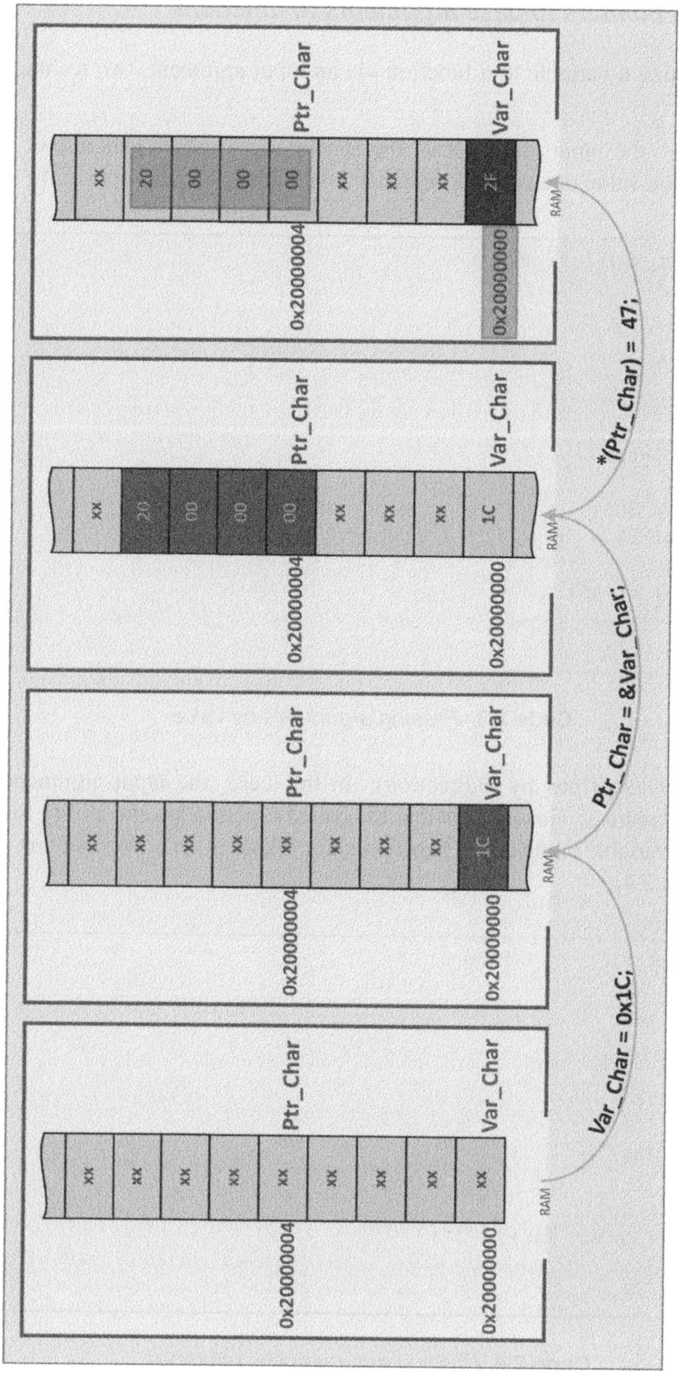

Figure 2.1. *Memory mapping of the presented example*

2.1.3. *Using pointers to pass arguments to functions*

When passing a variable to a function via an input argument, two techniques are possible:

– By *value*: the input argument of the function is a value. This allows passing either an explicit value or a copy of an existing variable (code example 2.3).

```
void  Funct_Val (int Param)
{
  .....
}

int main(void)
{
  int Var_Int;

  Var_Int = 2021;
  Funct_Val (Var_Int);
  /* Call with the value of an existing variable */
  Funct_Val (1965);
  /* Call with an direct explicit value */
}
```

Code 2.3. *Passing arguments by value*

– By *reference* (thus by indirection): in this case, the input argument of the function is an address. This implies that the called function has the ability to modify the value of a variable in the called function since it knows the address of this variable (code example 2.4).

```
void  Funct_Ptr (int *Param)
{
  .....
}

int main(void)
{
  int Var_Int;

  Var_Int = 2021;
  Funct_Ptr (&Var_Int);
  /* Call with the address of an existing variable */
}
```

Code 2.4. *Passing arguments by reference*

In code example 2.4, the input argument of the function Function_Ptr is no longer of type int, but rather int *. In other words, the internal variable Param is intended to receive an address and nothing else. *Param is therefore a pointer.*

Another example is provided in the code example 2.5 using a pointer in the calling procedure.

```
1  void  Funct_PtrChar (char* Param)
2  {
3    char LocalChar;
4
5    LocalChar = *Param;
6    /* LocalChar contains the value of the pointer element */
7    /* i.e. the value of the variable passed by reference */
8    *Param = LocalChar + 1;
9    /* The content of the variable passed by reference is   */
10   /* modified :it is incremented by 1 here since LocalChar */
11   /* holds its previous value */
12 }
13 int main(void)
14 {
15   char Var_Char;
16   /* The Var_Char variable is reserved */
17   /* It has an address, but no value yet */
18
19   char *Ptr_Char;
20   /* The variable Ptr_Char is reserved, */
21   /* 32 bits in size but unitialized. */
22   /* Ptr_Char does not have a value yet... */
23   /* ... but obviously it has its own address */
24   Ptr_Char = &Var_Char;
25   /* Ptr_Char is initialized as a pointer. */
26   /* It can only be assigned a char address */
27   Var_Char = 0x35;
28   /* Var_Char is initialized with a value of 35 */
29   Funct_PtrChar(Ptr_Char);
30   /* Equivalent to PtrChar(&Var_Char)                  */
31   /* The input argument is therefore the value of Ptr_Char. */
32
33   while(1);
34 }
```

Code 2.5. *Another example of passing by reference*

It is worth noting that on line 29 of the code listing 2.5 that Funct_PtrChar(Ptr_Char) is a *pass-by-value of Ptr_Char.* However, this value is indeed an address since the variable is an initialized pointer. This pass-by-value is equivalent to passing by reference the variable Var_Char.

The expressions Funct_PtrChar(Ptr_Char) and PtrChar(&Var_Char) have exactly the same effect. In both cases, the input argument of the function takes a 32-bit address as its value. Figure 2.2 illustrates this principle. The variable Param can be seen as a shared memory area between the two functions. In the vast majority of cases, this shared memory area is a processor register.

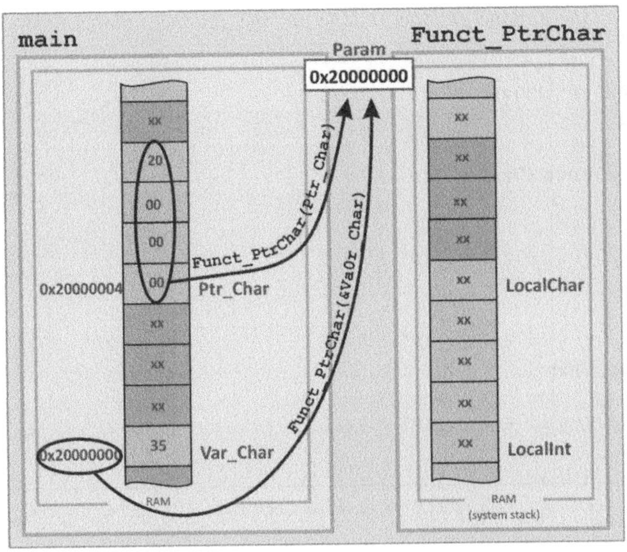

Figure 2.2. *Passing an input argument by address type*

Inside the function, it is possible to retrieve the value of *Var_Char* via the pointer (which is the main advantage!). In the presented example, the variable Var_Char is incremented by the function call. After the main procedure has been executed, the variable Var_Char will contain the value $54 = 0 \times 36$.

2.1.4. *When to use a pointer?*

Using a pointer in embedded computing is very common, especially when the argument to be passed is simply too large. The following two cases are the most common:

– an array (or a string): N bytes to pass, which can only be done by specifying the address of the first byte;

– a structure: this is an object containing several variables, and it is impossible to pass them all to a function. Here again, it is the address of the structure that must be passed (i.e. the address of the first variable in the structure).

Another requirement directly related to programming for the STM32 is the use of structures (and pointers to these structures). This method is used by the developers of the stm32f10x.h header file to access the various registers of peripheral units.

2.1.5. *Function pointers*

A function is a set of instructions that occupies a defined space allocated by the linker, therefore making it accessible to the rest of the program. When a function is called, the main task of the processor is to assign the program counter to the address where the function has been implemented. By definition, the manipulation of addresses involves the concept of a pointer. In the C language, it is possible to retrieve the address of a function and assign it to a pointer variable. When declaring this pointer variable, it is essential to account for the fact that only the "pointer" function will have a type. Therefore, the pointer variable can only accept the address of a function with the same type. The general form of declaring such a pointer is shown in code example 2.6.

```
type ( * ptrFct ) (type , type , ...) ;
```

Code 2.6. *Prototyping a function pointer*

The parentheses surrounding * ptrFct are necessary; otherwise, it would be a function returning a pointer. If the function takes no input arguments, then the right pair of parentheses surrounding the keyword void is also required. For example, a function takes no input argument and returns a byte: char (*ptrFct)(void).

The assignment of the pointer is done by using the address of a function with exactly the same signature (code example 2.7).

```
double (* ptrFct)(int , int , double); /* Function pointer */
double Root(int , int , double);       /* Function */

ptrFct = Root ; /* Assignment */
```

Code 2.7. *Initialization of a function pointer*

Once the function pointer has been initialized, it allows calling the function it points to using the syntax shown in code example 2.8.

```
*(prtFct)();
```

Code 2.8. *Using a function pointer*

2.2. C language structure and usage in the STM32

To configure and program the various units of an STM32F103 (GPIO, TIMER, SPI, etc.), STmicro© provides developers with a header file named stm32f10x.h, which consists of more than 8,000 lines. This file serves as an entry point for understanding how the memory of an STM32 is organized and allows access to each constituent component (external to the core) of the μcontroller. This section provides some key details to help understand the contents of this file.

2.2.1. *Structured type organization*

Among all the information contained in the stm32f10x.h file are the definitions of new structured types. Thus, each family of peripherals (GPIO, Timer, etc.) is associated with a particular structured type, and the fields of these structures bear the names of the registers that make up the corresponding peripheral unit.

As an example, let us consider the GPIO units, whose role is to control the electrical activity of the input/output pins. Searching in the header file for the term GPIO_TypeDef leads directly to the desired type.

This definition should be compared with the memory organization of a peripheral unit, information that can be found by cross-referencing the documentation from the μcontroller datasheet and the programming manual STMicroelectronics (2011).

Figure 2.3(a) shows the absolute positioning of the different *GPIO* units in the memory map chosen by STmicro© , whereas Figure 2.3(b) shows the relative positioning of each register that makes up the GPIO unit in relation to its base address. Clearly, we can deduce, for example, that the GPIOB_ODR is located at the address $(0{\times}40000C00 + 0{\times}0C = 0{\times}40000C0C)$.

A subtle point to note: the first line of the C structure will correspond to the first address it occupies in memory. However, in the memory representation shown here, the smallest addresses are at the bottom, which results in the order being reversed while reading.

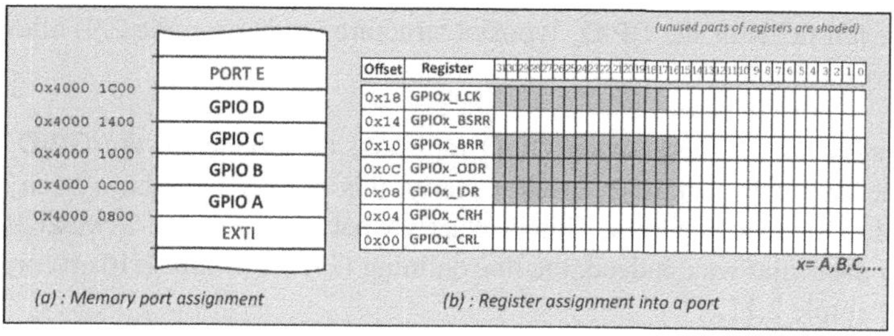

Figure 2.3. *Memory location of the GPIOs in STM32F10x*

```
typedef struct
{
  __IO uint32_t CRL;
  __IO uint32_t CRH;
  __IO uint32_t IDR;
  __IO uint32_t ODR;
  __IO uint32_t BSRR;
  __IO uint32_t BRR;
  __IO uint32_t LCKR;
} GPIO_TypeDef;
```

Code 2.9. *Declaration of a structure for accessing the registers of a GPIO unit*

The first remark to make regarding this structure declaration concerns the type of fields it is composed of. They are of type __IO uint32_t. The type __IO is defined in the core_cm3.h file and is equivalent to the C language keyword volatile[1]. Additionally, stdint.h redefines, among other things, the standard *int* types. The most commonly used ones in programs are:

```
/* exact-width signed integer types */
 typedef signed char        int8_t;
 typedef signed short int   int16_t;
 typedef signed int         int32_t;

/* exact-width unsigned integer types */
 typedef unsigned char        uint8_t;
 typedef unsigned short int   uint16_t;
 typedef unsigned int         uint32_t;
```

Code 2.10. *Excerpt from stdint.h*

1 Recall that the volatile keyword informs the compiler that the variable of this type can be modified by something external to the program, such as a peripheral unit, for example.

The seven fields of the GPIO_TypeDef structure (code example 2.9) allow access to 32-bit volatile integers.

To access one of these seven GPIO registers, the pointer to the GPIO_Typedef type associated with it must be used. Clearly, this pointer must have been properly initialized to the exact address. This is exactly what is done in the STM32F10x.h file, albeit in a particular way. Indeed, the line defining *GPIOA* in stm32f10x.h corresponds to code example 2.11.

```
#define GPIOA                    ((GPIO_TypeDef *) GPIOA_BASE)
```

Code 2.11. *Instantiation of a specific GPIO unit*

By examining the file, it is possible to see that GPIOA_BASE is defined, after several additions and other #define statements, by the value 0×40000800. This line is therefore unique since it defines the symbol GPIOA as being equivalent to a pointer initialized to the fixed address of GPIOA. When the compiler encounters the expression GPIOA, it will substitute it with the expression (GPIO_TypeDef * (0×40000800)).

2.2.2. *Accessing registers via a structure*

As we have just seen, each peripheral is associated with a group of registers organized into a structured variable. Management of peripherals can only be done through a pointer.

For example, GPIOA is a pointer to the structured variable of type GPIO_TypeDef, corresponding to the group of registers for the peripheralGPIOA. Therefore, GPIO is already an initialized pointer.

To access, for example, the IDR of GPIOA, you would write:

```
(*GPIOA).IDR
```

Code 2.12. *Accessing the IDR register of GPIOA*

where:

– (*GPIOA) allows access to the structured variable corresponding to the GPIOA peripheral;

– (*GPIOA).IDR allows access to the specific IDR field of this structured variable.

This rather cumbersome syntax is greatly simplified by using the indirection symbol –>:

```
GPIOA->IDR.
```

Code 2.13. *Alternative syntax for accessing the IDR of GPIOA*

This second syntax will be used exclusively throughout this book.

As we will see throughout this book, configuring and using a μcontroller device inevitably involves writing to or reading from registers belonging to that device. We have just explained how these registers can be accessed in the C language via pointers to structures. In the previous example, GPIOA–>IDR referred to the IDR of the GPIOA peripheral. Moving forward, and to align with the STmicro® documentation, we will refer to the Reg register of a peripheral of type Periph in the following manner: Periph_Reg. For example, the IDR of a GPIO peripheral will be referred to as GPIO_IDR.

2.3. Case of nested structures

In the embedded systems world, the variables exchanged in functions are often structures. This is particularly true for libraries developed by STmicro©, such as LL (*Low Layer*) or HAL (*Hardware Abstraction Layer*).

Let us break down this approach through a simple example of initializing an input/output port. As we will see in Chapter 4, for a given port (the GPIOA port, for example) and for a given pin (let us take pin 7 as an example), one of the two internal configuration registers (in this case, the CRL register) must be set to configure the pin as either an input or output, with a specific electronic technology (*output push/pull, output open drain, input pull up*, etc.). Therefore, three pieces of information are required to each pin. Using a structure to handle this leads, for example, to the following declaration:

```
typedef struct
{
  GPIO_TypeDef *GPIO;
  int8_t GPIO_PinNumber; /* pin number from 0 to 15 */
  int8_t GPIO_ConfPin;   /* type of configuration */
} MyGPIO_Struct_TypeDef;
```

Code 2.14. *Creating an initialization structure*

The declaration shows that the structure itself embeds another structure (GPIO_TypeDef). This nesting, while easy to understand conceptually, adds a slight layer of complexity. At the level of instantiation and assigning the initialization structure, it is enough to assign the values to a simple structured variable (without the need for a pointer at this level):

```
MyGPIO_Struct_TypeDef  My_GPIO_Init_A ;

  My_GPIO_Init_A.GPIO = GPIOA;
  My_GPIO_Init_A.PinNumber = 7;
  My_GPIO_Init_A.ConfPin = 0x0A;
```

Code 2.15. *Initializing an initialization structure*

The GPIO field of the MyGPIO_Struct_TypeDef structure is a pointer to a GPIO_TypeDef one, which is exactly the case for GIOPA, as we saw in the previous section. The other two fields expect a value encoded on a single byte. Here, we have used the specific value $0 \times 0A$ for the electronic configuration of the pin; it is clear that you need to understand what the driver expects in order to set a meaningful value (see Chapter 4).

Generally, the driver is designed with argument passing by reference into its functions. This is clearly not required if you are developing your own drivers, but this is the case for the libraries provided by STmicro©. Suppose our initialization function is named My_GPIO_Init and that it returns nothing. Its prototype would be as follows:

```
void MyGPIO_Init( MyGPIO_Struct_TypeDef *);
```

Code 2.16. *Prototype of an initialization function*

Let us finish this example by looking at how this routine will use the structure pointer to assign the registers of the GPIO in question:

```
void MyGPIO_Init( MyGPIO_Struct_TypeDef *GStr)
{
...
  if ( (GStr->GPIO_PinNumber < 8 ))
  { /* Using the CRL register => double indirection */
    /* Clearing the 4-bit field */
    GStr->GPIO->CRL &=~(0xF<<((GStr->GPIO_PinNumber)*4));
    /* Setting the bits one by one using bitwise OR mask */
```

```
9          GStr->GPIO->CRL |= ((GStr->GPIO_ConfPin)<<((GStr->
               GPIO_PinNumber)*4));
10     }
11   ...
12   }
```

Code 2.17. *Body of an initialization function*

This function must modify the "register" field, either CRL (or CRH), depending on the pin number and the desired configuration. When using the pin number or the configuration, a single indirection is sufficient (the targeted field is not a structure), GStr->GPIO_PinNumber.

On the other hand, the "register" fields form part of a structure GPIOStructPtr, which is itself contained within the MyGPIO_Struct_TypeDef structure. Therefore, access (line 7) is done via a double indirection: GStr->GPIO->CRL.

2.4. Masks usage

When programming a peripheral, it is often necessary to modify one or more bits in a register without altering the others. Let us take the example of the ADC_CR1 register (see Figure 2.4), which is used to configure the analog-to-digital ADC converter. Here, the purpose of these few lines of code does not matter in relation to the ADC unit.

To modify a bit or part of a register, logical masks must be used. In code example 2.18, bit 8 (SCAN) of the ADC_CR1 register is set to 1, and bit 5 (EOCIE) is cleared to 0 without affecting the other bits. The 3-bit field of consecutive bits [13:15] (DISCNUM) is also modified (lines 10 and 11).

```
1  /* Masks defined in stm32F10x.h */
2  #define ADC_CR1_SCAN  ((uint32_t)0x00000100)
3  #define ADC_CR1_EOCIE ((uint32_t)0x00000020)
4  ...
5  /* Enable continuous mode */
6  ADC1->CR1  |= (ADC_CR1_SCAN );
7  /* Disable EOC interrupt */
8  ADC1->CR1  &= ~(ADC_CR1_EOCIE);
9  /* Set the 3-bit DISCNUM field to 6 */
10 ADC1->CR1  &= ~(0x07 << 13);
11 ADC1->CR1  |= (0x06 << 13);
```

Code 2.18. *Masking example*

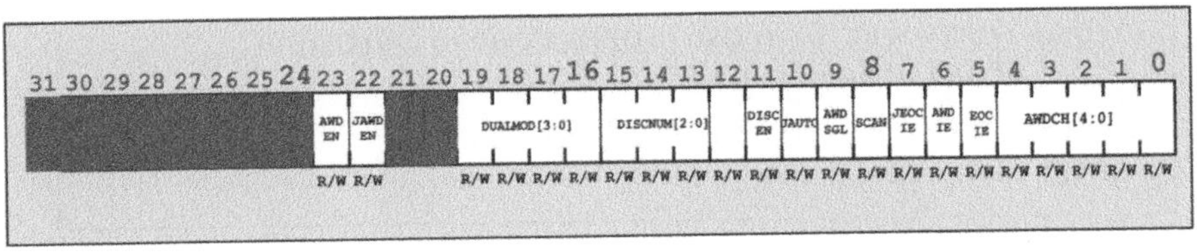

Figure 2.4. *ADC_CR1 register of the ADC unit*

2.4.1. *General considerations*

The technique relies entirely on Boolean algebra, and in the context used here, it is very approachable. Besides the inversion operator, only the three logical operators: AND, OR and XOR will be considered here, whose truth tables are provided in the Appendix.

In programming, however, and particularly in the C language, it is crucial to differentiate between logical operators and bitwise operators.

In C language, this difference is primarily represented by different syntax, as shown in Table 2.1.

Logical function	Logical operator	Bitwise operator
AND	&&	&
OR	||	|
XOR	none	^
NEG	!	~

Table 2.1. *Logical functions versus bitwise operators*

Logical operators treat operands (whether they are 8, 16 or 32 bits) as a Boolean value, considering them to be false if all bits are zero. Otherwise, the expression is considered to be true. This operation, therefore, provides a Boolean result: 0 if it is false and 1 otherwise.

Bitwise operators (third column of Table 2.1) perform logical operations on each respective bit of the operands (either 8, 16 or 32 bits). The value returned is therefore an integer value.

Code example 2.19 illustrates the differences between these two types of operator.

```
VarA = 0x1A; /* i.e. (00011010) in binary and considered
   ``true'' as it is not 0 */
```

```
VarB = 1; /* i.e. (00000001) in binary and also
    considered ''true'' */
ResuX = VarA && VarB;    /* returns 1 (true)
    as (VarA ET VarB) is true */
ResuY = VarA & VarB; /* returns 0: the AND between
    each bit of VarA and VarB is false */
```

Code 2.19. *Differences between the & operator and the && operator*

2.4.2. *Masks for setting bits to 1*

To set one or more bits at specific positions to 1, the OR operator is used with a binary value, called a mask, that has bits set to 1 only at the desired bit positions. Figure 2.5 illustrates this principle.

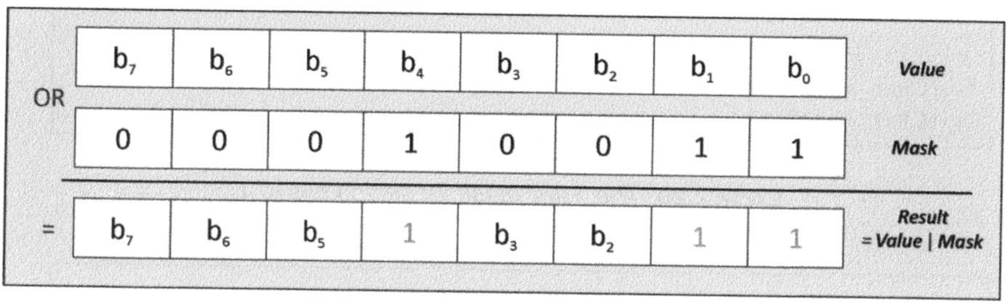

Figure 2.5. *Principle of the OR mask for setting bits to 1. For a color version of this figure, see www.iste.co.uk/mahout/programming.zip*

Thus, in this example, bits b_4, b_1 and b_0 are set to 1 without modifying the value of the other bits.

To apply this principle in the C language, the mask value would first need to be expressed in binary format as $(00010011)_2$, and then convert it into hexadecimal (0x13).

It is not very obvious to see that 0x13 corresponds to a mask targeting bits 0, 1 and 4. Additionally, it is very easy to make a mistake when doing the conversion yourself. It is be safer and more practical to use, as shown in Figure 2.6, the left shift operator <<x to place a logical 1 in front of the bit in position x and thus construct the mask.

Using this approach, code 2.20 becomes much more readable, and the risk of making conversion errors is greatly reduced.

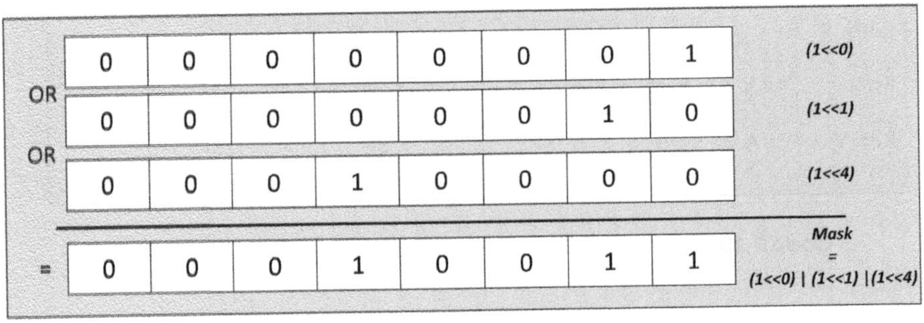

Figure 2.6. *Constructing an OR mask with the shift operator*

```
char TestChar;
...
/* equivalent formulations */
TestChar = TestChar |  0x13;   /* standard syntax */
TestChar |= 0x13;              /* ''compact'' syntax */
```

Code 2.20. *The "raw" mask for setting bits to 1*

```
/* Equivalent formulations */
TestChar = TestChar |  0x13;f
TestChar = TestChar |  (1<<0)|(1<<1)|(1<<4);
TestChar |= (1<<0)|(1<<1)|(1<<4);  /* Preferred version */
```

Code 2.21. *Mask for setting bits to 1 using the shift operator*

It is worth noting, for the sake of consistency and to improve readability, the use of a zero shift ($1 << 0$). While this has no significance for the language itself, it clearly indicates the setting of bit 0 to 1. Of course, this has no impact on code execution time, as the shift calculation will be handled by the compiler.

2.4.3. *Masks for setting bits to 0*

The *reset* of a bit is a little more complex. To do this, the AND operator is used with a mask that has 0s at the targeted bit positions (Figure 2.7).

Hence, bits b_4, b_1 and b_0 are cleared to 0 without altering the value of the other bits.

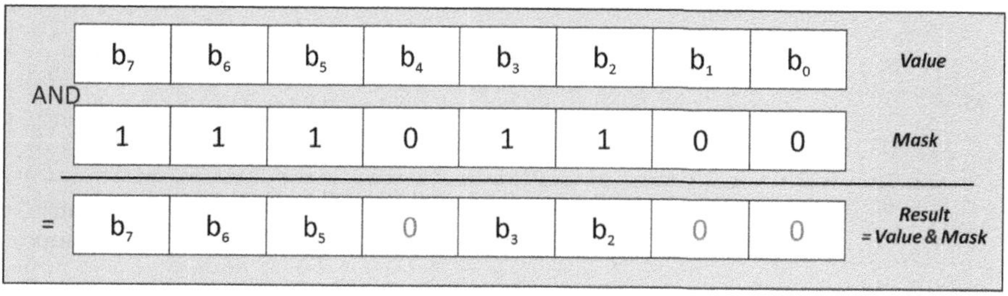

Figure 2.7. *Principle of the AND mask for setting bits to 0. For a color version of this figure, see www.iste.co.uk/mahout/programming.zip*

To construct the mask, you can manually perform the conversion, albeit with the risk of error mentioned earlier: $b11101100 = 0{\times}EC$. However, it is preferable to construct the mask based on the previous principle, using 1s in front of the bits to be cleared, before then inverting each bit using the logical inversion operator, ~.

By systematizing this approach, it is possible to produce code that is readable, safe and efficient:

```
/* Equivalent formulations */
TestChar = TestChar & 0xEB;
TestChar = TestChar & ~((1<<0)|(1<<1)|(1<<4));
TestChar &= ~((1<<0)|(1<<1)|(1<<4)); /* Preferred version */
```

Code 2.22. *Mask for clearing bits to 0 using the shift operator*

2.4.4. *Bit inversion*

To invert a bit without affecting any of the other bits of the operand, it is useful to remember the exclusive OR operator, XOR (Figure 2.8). It is enough to use this operator with a mask that has 1s only at the positions of the bits to be inverted.

Thus, only bits b_4, b_1 and b_0 have been inverted.

The construction of masks for this inversion is identical to that of the OR masks for setting bits to 1.

2.4.5. *Extension and generalization to bit field assignment*

A bit field is a group of contiguous bits that hold a specific meaning for the unit associated with that register. For example, DISCNUM is a 3-bit field within the ADC_CR1 register.

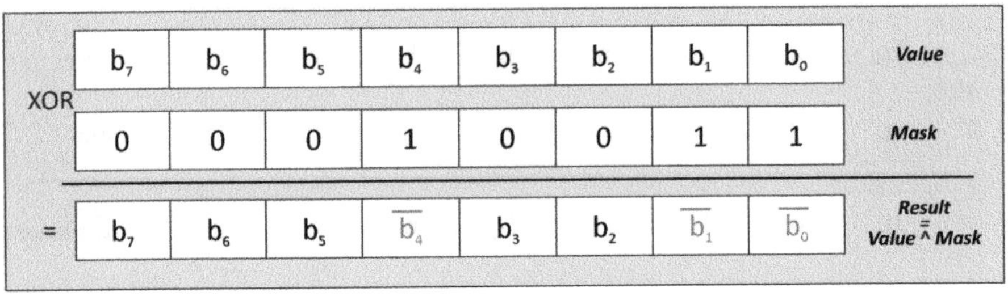

Figure 2.8. *Principle of the XOR mask for bit inversion. For a color version of this figure, see www.iste.co.uk/mahout/programming.zip*

An experienced programmer may wish to initialize a bit field of the TestChar byte with the value contained in the variable Number. To do this, it is useful and prudent to proceed in three steps:

– clear the 3-bit field in TestChar;

– copy the 1s from the first mask into TestChar using an OR mask.

In code example 2.23, the DISCNUM bit field of the ADC_CR1 register (Figure 2.4) is set with the value contained in the variable Number.

```
void set_discnum ( char Number)
{
/* Reset the DISCNUM field: 3 bits from position 13-15 in ADC_CR1
   */
  ADC->CR1 &= ~(0x7<<13);
/* Only bits 13-15 of the mask are set to 0 */

/* Initialize the bit field with Number */
  ADC->CR1 | = Number << 13
/* Copy the 1s from Number shifted to position 13 */

/* Warnining: if Number>7, it will overflow into bits 16 to 31*/
/* A mask must limit Number to values between 0 and 7: no more
    than 3 bits set to 1 */
/* This line ensures the limit */
  ADC->CR1 |= (Number & 0x7) <<13 /* Number is now limited */
}
```

Code 2.23. *Masking a bit field*

REMARK.– It is recommended, as demonstrated on line 14, to limit the value of Number to ensure that it does not exceed the maximum value that the bit field can contain and to position it correctly within the field.

2.5. Code structuring and the concept of drivers

When developing an application for an embedded system, the first fundamental choice arises: whether to use an operating system or not. This choice depends on the developer as well as the size of the project. Including an operating system (whether it be a *FreeRTOS* kernel or any other real-time OS) is costly by nature in terms of memory usage and CPU power. Furthermore, the features offered by an operating system may not necessarily be useful in the context of a small application.

Here, let us consider the specific context of what is known as *Bare-Metal* development. The term *Bare-Metal* implies that the main program runs directly "on the hardware", without any intermediary software such as an operating system.

As the project grows in terms of lines of code, dividing the application into different modules and/or different layers becomes essential. If the application is versioned multiple times or if there is a need to switch μcontrollers (introducing the concept of portability in software quality), then it becomes beneficial to adopt a rational and structured organization of the different components of code.

At a minimum, this organization involves writing *drivers* for each of the hardware peripheral components (GPIO, ADC, USART, etc.) that will be required in the application.

In order to implement the principle of portability in a project, we have chosen to divide the source files of a project into three distinct layers:

– The application layer: this is the highest layer, concerned solely with the functional aspect of the project. It does not deal with the implementation details of interfaces with the real world.

– The service layer: at this level, it is necessary to understand the physical reality of the target system, such as the type of signals that must be generated or the information to be conveyed over a communication channel, etc. This layer understands what the requests from the application layer correspond to, and how to translate them into specific processes for the driver layer.

– The driver layer: this is the lowest layer and the only one that directly interacts with and uses the μcontroller registers. It receives requests from the service layer and carries out the actual interfacing with the controlled system.

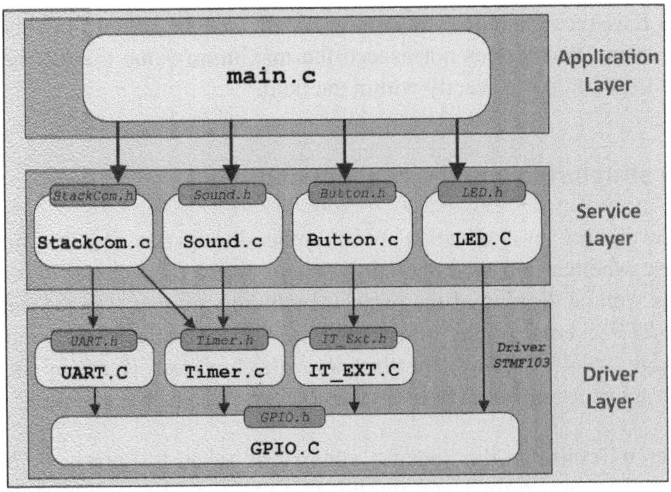

Figure 2.9. *Example of a layered software architecture*

It is quite simple to determine the boundaries of the driver layer since it is the only one that has access to the μcontroller registers. Thus, the portability of the application is directly influenced by this separation. If there is a change in hardware or if a new feature of existing hardware is to be used, the appropriate "drivers" must be utilized. The boundary between the application layer and the service layer is perhaps more difficult to define. It is not always easy to completely abstract the hardware implementation when designing the highest level of the software architecture for the application.

To illustrate this point, we will return to our *guiding thread*; more precisely, we will focus on the example of the *central unit* module, which is numbered as element 1 in Figure 1.6.

The software architecture could resemble that of Figure 2.5. In this diagram, the arrows indicate the inclusion of *header* files.

If, for example, it became necessary to work with a different μcontroller, then the application and service layers, as well as the *header* files for each of the drivers, would remain intact (with very slight adjustments, but the function prototypes would remain unchanged). Therefore, this project is portable.

Furthermore, if the programmer were to develop a completely different application while keeping the STM32F103 μcontroller, then the entire driver layer could be reusable.

In the deliberately simple code excerpt 2.24, note that the included *header* files only concern the service layer, and that no reference to the driver layer is needed.

```
#include "Sound.h"
#include "Button.h"
#include "LED.h"

int main(void)
{
  Sound_Init();
  Button_Init();
  LED_init();
  while(1)
  {
    if (Button_Push())
    {
      LED_On();
      Sound_Beep();
      /* ... continuation of the application... */
    }
    LED_Off();
  }
}
```

Code 2.24. *LED light example: application layer*

The designer of the service layer will need to know where and how the push button and LED are physically connected. In knowing this, they can call functions from the driver layer to actually perform the required actions. Let us take a quick look at how the LED_On() function could be coded, assuming that the LED is connected to pin 4 of the GPIO A port:

```
#include "GPIO.h"
void LED_On(void)
{
  GPIO_Set(GPIOA, 4);
}
```

Code 2.25. *LED_On() function: service layer*

Finally, with regard to the driver layer, it is a question of translating what this implies at the μcontroller register level. In the proposed code, we use an OR-type mask to set a given bit to 1:

```
#include "stm32f10x.h"

void GPIO_Set(GPIO_TypeDef * Port, uint8_t Channel)
{
  Port->ODR |= 1<<Channel;
}
```

Code 2.26. *GPIO_Set() function: driver layer*

This example highlights the pivotal role played by the service layer. It acts as the bridge between the fully abstracted application layer and the generic and hardware-specific driver layer, which has no particular meaning for the application. The driver layer remains exactly the same where, for example, it is used to toggle an LED or generate a serial data frame over a communication link.

As mentioned earlier, it is not always easy to abstract the implementation. In our example, the state of the button is polled by continuously reading the corresponding pin. However, it is also possible to imagine working through interrupts, meaning the application layer would no longer continuously check the button state, but rather this functionality would be implemented through an interrupt. In this case, the designer would need to include, *at the very least*, the initialization of interrupt services with the appropriate priority levels, eliminating the need for polling. This alternative approach would not only impact the overall software architecture of the project directly, but also its portability.

Clearly, there is no absolute truth in this domain. It is important to design the architecture based on the current constraints while also considering potential or likely future developments of the application. The idea of always maintaining, at the very least, a low-level driver layer seems essential. This is necessary, if only to ensure the ability to use the drivers typically provided by chip manufacturers.

2.6. Interrupt routines

2.6.1. *Handler routines concepts*

Chapter 5 will go into detail about what happens when an interrupt is triggered and accepted by the processor core. For now, let us clarify the basic principle: following a hardware event (an interrupt, an exception, or a software trap), the programmer wants a specifically written routine to be automatically and implicitly called.

These routines that handle an interrupt are called *Handlers*.

While there may be minor differences depending on the processor or controller, the mechanism for calling an exception handling routine is always the same. If the request is accepted, the CPU, after any performing any necessary saves, will “read” an interrupt vector table (IVT) to find the memory address of the handler routine written for this event. The IVT for the STM32 is presented in Figure 5.1, and example 2.27 presents an excerpt of the assembly code used to create it.

Although things may seem relatively straightforward on the processor side, a central question arises for the programmer: How can the address of the routine written to handle a hardware event be positioned correctly in the interrupt vector table?

2.6.2. *Interrupt routine implementation*

In the scenario where we assume complete control over the system and have access to all low-level programming resources, the simplest (and most direct) approach is to follow the conventions established by the compiler to construct the vector table. These conventions are visible in the standard startup file, written in assembly language, named startup_stm32f10x_md.s. In this file, the IVT is named __Vectors, and its creation consists of stacking the addresses of the routines that serve as handlers, that is, the software processes that are executed when an interrupt event occurs.

```
__Vectors DCD        __initial_sp
; Top of Stack
          DCD        Reset_Handler        ; Reset Handler
          DCD        NMI_Handler          ; NMI Handler
          DCD        HardFault_Handler    ; Hard Fault Handler
          DCD        MemManage_Handler    ; MPU Fault Handler
          DCD        BusFault_Handler     ; Bus Fault Handler
    .
    .
    .
          DCD        PendSV_Handler       ; PendSV Handler
          DCD        SysTick_Handler      ; SysTick Handler

      ; External Interrupts
          DCD        WWDG_IRQHandler      ; Window Watchdog
          DCD        PVD_IRQHandler       ; PVD (EXTI Line detect)
          DCD        TAMPER_IRQHandler    ; Tamper
    .
    .
    .
          DCD        USART3_IRQHandler       ; USART3
```

```
          DCD      EXTI15_10_IRQHandler   ; EXTI Line 15..10
          DCD      RTCAlarm_IRQHandler    ; RTC Alarm(EXTI Line)
          DCD      USBWakeUp_IRQHandler   ; USB Wakeup from suspend
__Vectors_End
```

Code 2.27. *Excerpt from the STM32 IVT*

Each routine is defined later on in the file. The 12 exception handling routines are all distinct, but only the routine corresponding to the Reset exception contains instructions (a call to a reset routine). The others are functions that contain only a single assembly instruction B ., which corresponds to a jump to itself, creating an infinite loop. These routines are, by default, "sinks" and only exist to prevent the program from going off-course and executing unintended operations.

The same B . instruction (and thus the same consequences) forms the body of the procedure that handles all the interrupt routines as well. These are the routines that we will rewrite. Upon examining the code of these routines, it is clear that it is essentially the same routine, renamed with as many names as there are entries in the interrupt vector table. However, it is also important to note that when these routines are made visible with the assembly directive EXPORT, they are marked with the WEAK "qualifier":

```
Default_Handler PROC

                EXPORT  WWDG_IRQHandler          [WEAK]
                EXPORT  PVD_IRQHandler           [WEAK]
                EXPORT  TAMPER_IRQHandler        [WEAK]
                EXPORT  RTC_IRQHandler           [WEAK]
       .
       .
       .
                EXPORT  USART3_IRQHandler        [WEAK]
                EXPORT  EXTI15_10_IRQHandler     [WEAK]
                EXPORT  RTCAlarm_IRQHandler      [WEAK]
                EXPORT  USBWakeUp_IRQHandler     [WEAK]

WWDG_IRQHandler
PVD_IRQHandler
TAMPER_IRQHandler
    .
    .
    .
EXTI15_10_IRQHandler
RTCAlarm_IRQHandler
```

```
USBWakeUp_IRQHandler
                B       .
                ENDP
```

Code 2.28. *The default single function for handling interrupts*

This declarative "weakness" informs the linker that if it finds a routine with the same name, the latter will override the "weak" one. Consequently, the address of this second routine will be used in the interrupt vector table.

Based on this observation, it becomes straightforward to construct an interrupt routine: simply create a void/void routine (since, by design, it can neither take arguments nor return values) and name it according to the corresponding interrupt. For example, if we want to implement code when the USART3 triggers an interrupt (e.g. after receiving characters on this serial interface), we simply write this code in a function with the following prototype and name:

```
void USART3_IRQHandler(void)
{
...   /* Processing code */
}
```

Code 2.29. *Example of overriding a Handler function*

2.6.3. *Redirection via dynamic programming*

Knowing the names of the routines and developing them at the service layer level is not truly compatible with the notion of portability. Therefore, we propose creating redirections through dynamic programming. This technique uses function pointers, which were discussed earlier in this chapter. The user can then write their own function with any name that they choose, as long as it adheres to the void-void prototype for the input and return arguments of the function. A driver function will then be available to the user, which will take the name of the function (or more precisely, its address) as an input parameter, to which the *handler* will be redirected to it.

To illustrate this principle, let us return to our previous *guiding thread* example, this time focusing on the StackCom.c part. This service should allow the user to retrieve a string of characters received byte by byte from the UART. We propose to use the UART with interrupts, and we will detail the mechanism by concentrating on the two modules, StackCom and UART (shown on the left in the service layer in Figure 2.5).

Code example 2.30 demonstrates the use of dynamic programming to redirect the interrupt of USART3. This section of code therefore forms part of the driver.

```
#include "stm32f10x.h"
void (* Ptr_Fct_3) (void); /* Function pointer */

void UART_Init(USART_TypeDef * UART, void (* HandlerIT)(void) )
{
  if (UART == USART3)
  {
  Ptr_Fct_3 = HandlerIT; /* Interrupt handler pointer initialization */
  /* UART initialization (see UART chapter) */
  /* ... continuation of code... */
  }
}
void USART3_IRQHandler (void)
{
  /* Clear the local UART interrupt flag (see UART chapter) */

  Ptr_Fct_3(); /* REDIRECTION: call the handler in the service layer */
}
```

Code 2.30. *Using a function pointer in the driver layer*

COMMENTARY ON CODE 2.30.– *The file begins with the declaration of a function pointer that will be set during the initialization of USART3. This setup must occur before any possibility of a UART interrupt. That is why the initialization Ptr_Fct_3=HandlerIT is performed first. If this is not done and if the USART handler is triggered before the pointer has been initialized, then a severe crash of the μcontroller would occur (from jumping to an invalid address).*

After the proper initialization and configuration of the UART, when an interrupt occurs, the USART3_IRQHandler *handler* is executed. The function in the higher layer (and therefore in the service layer) is then called via redirection.

Now, let us look at an excerpt from the *StackCom.c* module (code example 2.31).

```
#include "UART.h"
void Stack_Com_ByteReception(void)
{
  /* Construction of the character string */
}

void Stack_Init(void)
```

```
{
UART_Init(USART3, Stack_Com_ByteReception);
/* ... continued ... */
}
```

Code 2.31. *Passing the function name in the service layer*

COMMENTARY ON 2.31 CODE.– *At the application level, when the function Stack_Init() is called, the USART3 is configured. The function Stack_Com_ByteReception() is then associated with the specific handler for the USART3.*

This approach results in:

– giving the illusion that Stack_Com_ByteReception() is an interrupt *handler* (when, strictly speaking, this is not the case: it is a "normal" function called by the "real" interrupt *handler* buried in the driver layer);

– establishing a clear boundary between the driver and the service layers, and therefore, between hardware and the application/service software.

```
[illegible] Stack_Com_ByteReception() [illegible]
}
```

Code 1.31. [illegible]

3

General STM32F10x Hardware Considerations

A μcontroller is a complex semiconductor. It has a core, in this case a Cortex-M3, which handles the execution of the application and provides computational capabilities. This central part is then complemented by a set of peripheral units, whose primary role is to control the embedded process. We will begin this chapter by reviewing the key components that make up an STM32.

A μcontroller is, of course, a synchronous machine, meaning that it requires a clock to regulate its operations. While this seems simple, it hides a much more complex reality that the programmer cannot completely ignore: the multiplicity and distribution of clock signals throughout the circuit. Therefore, we will later detail the clock tree structure for the STM32F10x[1] family of μcontrollers.

3.1. Global STM32 architecture

To get an overview of what an STM32F10x contains, consider the block diagram shown in Figure 3.1. In this figure, there is the Cortex-M3 and the entire hardware environment added by STmicro© to design its μcontroller. Let us list[2] the different acronyms first before then defining them:

– DMA (*Direct Memory Access*) is a module, provided by ARM©, which allows peripheral units to access memory directly without going through the CPU, here the Cortex. This technique allows for significant time savings, for example, when acquiring N samples of an analog signal over a given period.

For a color version of all the Codes in this chapter, see www.iste.co.uk/mahout/programming.zip

1 Except for the *Connectivity line* series, which has a specific clock tree structure.

2 The units marked with ($\star$) will not be covered in detail in the remainder of this book.

– FSMC$^{(*)}$ (*Flexible Static Memory Controller*) and SDIO$^{(*)}$ (*Secure Digital Input/Output*) are two memory card standards. These hardware protocols make it relatively easy to add memory for more complex embedded applications.

– Backup registers provide a bank of registers that can be used, especially when the processor enters into sleep mode.

– GPIO (*General Purpose Input/Output*) handles the connectivity of the processor with external devices.

– ADC (*Analog-to-Digital Converter*) are units that convert an analog voltage into an integer.

– DAC$^{(*)}$ (*Digital-to-Analog Converter*) are the symmetric counterparts of an ADC and convert an integer value into an equivalent analog voltage.

– USART or UART (*Universal (Synchronous) Asynchronous Receiver Transmitter*) are units that manage standard asynchronous or synchronous serial communications (such as *RS232*).

– USB$^{(*)}$ (*Universal Serial Bus*) is a unit that manages this serial communication standard.

– Watchdog is a monitoring mechanism that must be periodically reactivated to ensure that the application it monitors has not fallen into a blocking procedure.

– I^{2}C, I^{2}S$^{(*)}$ and SPI are three serial bus standards that allow direct communication with external circuits (other μcontrollers, sensors, specific drivers, etc.).

– The CAN$^{(*)}$ bus is a serial bus protocol widely used in the automotive industry.

Obviously, this figure is based on a specific architecture, namely, that of an F103xE from the *high-density* line. However, the information it contains is quite general, and if you look at an equivalent diagram for other versions of the STM32F10x, the overall organization remains exactly the same. The main differences will be as follows:

– the amount of RAM and Flash memory natively present in the chip;

– the presence and, above all, the number of peripheral units (GPIO, Timer, ADC, etc.);

– some versions have only a single DMA channel;

– SDIO or FMSC memory card support is not present in all versions;

– the *connectivity line* versions have additional communication interfaces (notably Ethernet).

3.2. Cortex-M3 components

The STM3210x μcontrollers manufactured by STmicro© are built around a Cortex-M3 core, defined byARM©.

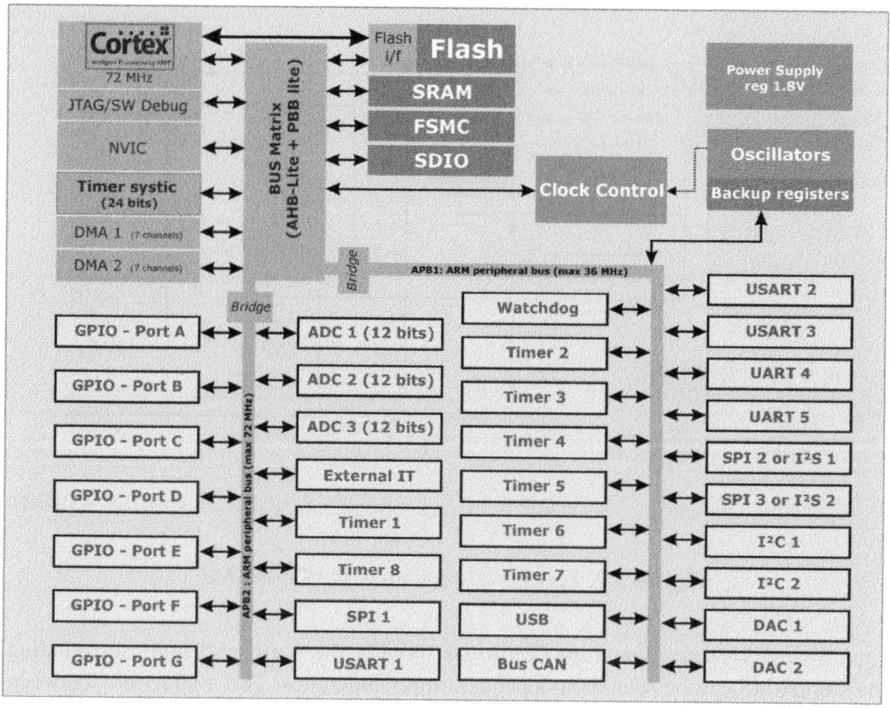

Figure 3.1. *Functional diagram of the STM32F103xE*

ARM© does not directly produce semiconductors; rather, it designs them and then licenses these designs to manufacturers, such as STmicro© or Freescale, who produce the physical chips.

This 32-bit processor core is specifically designed for embedded systems that require significant resources (particularly in terms of calculation) while maintaining low costs (in terms of product, development and consumption).

The first overall view (see Figure 3.2) of the Cortex, as found in the technical documentation of this product, is a functional diagram, simple in its representation but with each block potentially leaving the novice quite perplexed. It is relatively unnecessary to delve into the details of this architecture to program the μcontroller that hosts it properly. However, from the programmer's perspective, it is useful to understand the primary role of the following different components:

– CM3CORE: this is the core itself. This unit contains the various registers, all the mechanisms for reading/writing instructions and data, as well as the arithmetic and logic unit (32-bit only) for the actual execution of the different instructions.

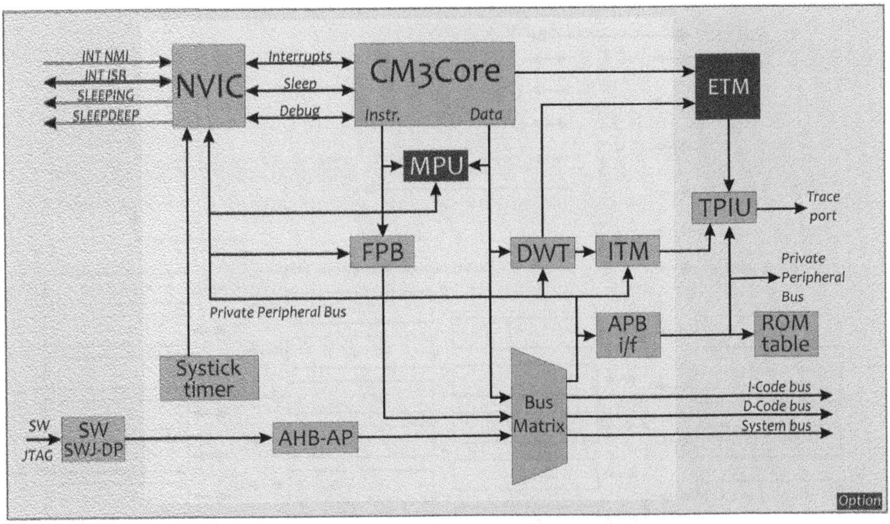

Figure 3.2. *Functional diagram of the Cortex-M3*

– *Nested Vectored Interrupt Controller* (NVIC): the peripheral units surrounding the Cortex-M3 can be seen as independent micromachines. The interactions between these units and the Cortex-M3 must be synchronized and organized in such a way that the task scheduling follows predetermined rules (priority levels) and determinism imposed in advance by the programmer. The NVIC plays this role of a "conductor". It is responsible for receiving, sorting and distributing the interrupts generated by the various STM32 peripherals. It also handles exceptions that jeopardize the proper execution of the current code sequence (*reset*, memory bus issues, division by 0, etc.). The operation of this unit will, of course, be detailed in Chapter 5, which focuses on interrupts.

– SYSTICK Timer: this 24-bit internal Timer was designed by ARM© to serve as a time base for designing of a real-time kernel independent of the μcontroller into which the Cortex is integrated. It will be presented at the end of Chapter 6.

– The other units, ETM, FPB, ITM, TPIU, APB, SW, DWT and AHB-AP, are all related to hardware debugging capabilities. This implies that, provided the corresponding hardware and software resources are available on the development system, the programmer has access to a full range of modern tools for observing and *debugging their application without modifying the code.*

– The memory protection unit (MPU).

3.3. Clock trees and RCC units

The first unavoidable difficulty when programming an STM32 is ensuring that the hardware function you want to control is properly clocked. By default, the different units are not connected to a clock signal, thus preventing unnecessary electrical consumption if the unit in question is not in use (see the Appendix). With this in mind, it is important to note that there is not a single clock driving the entire system, but a multitude, which allows for different frequencies to be distributed. This diversity is necessary to accommodate various technologies, which may operate at different speeds.

The various clocks form a tree-shaped branching network. For readability, we have divided this tree into two parts: a *primary tree* and a *secondary tree*.

3.3.1. *Generation of primary clocks*

To operate, the STM32F10x needs two clocks: a "low" frequency one (in kHz) and a "high" frequency one (in MHz). These two clock sources can either be internal to the μcontroller (LSI and HSI), corresponding to RC oscillators (which are relatively imprecise compared to what a quartz crystal can achieve), or they can be connected to external inputs designed electronically to receive quartz crystals (LSE and HSE). In this second case, the OSC_OUT, OSC_IN, OSC32_OUT and OSC32_IN pins will be used to connect the external low- or high-frequency crystal. It is also possible however to directly supply a clock signal via the IN pins.

As shown in Figure 3.3, four multiplexers guide the clock signals necessary for the μcontroller to operate. A PLL (*Phase-Locked Loop*) is also used to program the frequency of certain clocks. A PLL is a circuit that multiplies the input frequency in order to provide a desired and stable output frequency.

The primary clock tree therefore makes it possible to generate the main signal, *SYSCLK*, which is the source for the secondary tree. Four other signals are represented:

– *PLLCLK* is the clock output from the PLL. This clock can become the SYSCLK signal, and it is directly used for the USB interface.

– *USBLK* is a signal derived from dividing (by either 1 or 1.5) the previous signal. Since the USB unit requires a 48 MHz clock, the PLL must therefore provide either 48 or 72 MHz from the USB unit to function.

– *IWDGCLK*: the clock signal from the internal low-frequency LSI oscillator serves as the time reference for the independent *watchdog*. Using the internal oscillator ensures a sufficient level of security in case of failure of the external LSE signal.

– *RTCCLK*: the clock used for the RTC (*Real Time Clock*) unit.

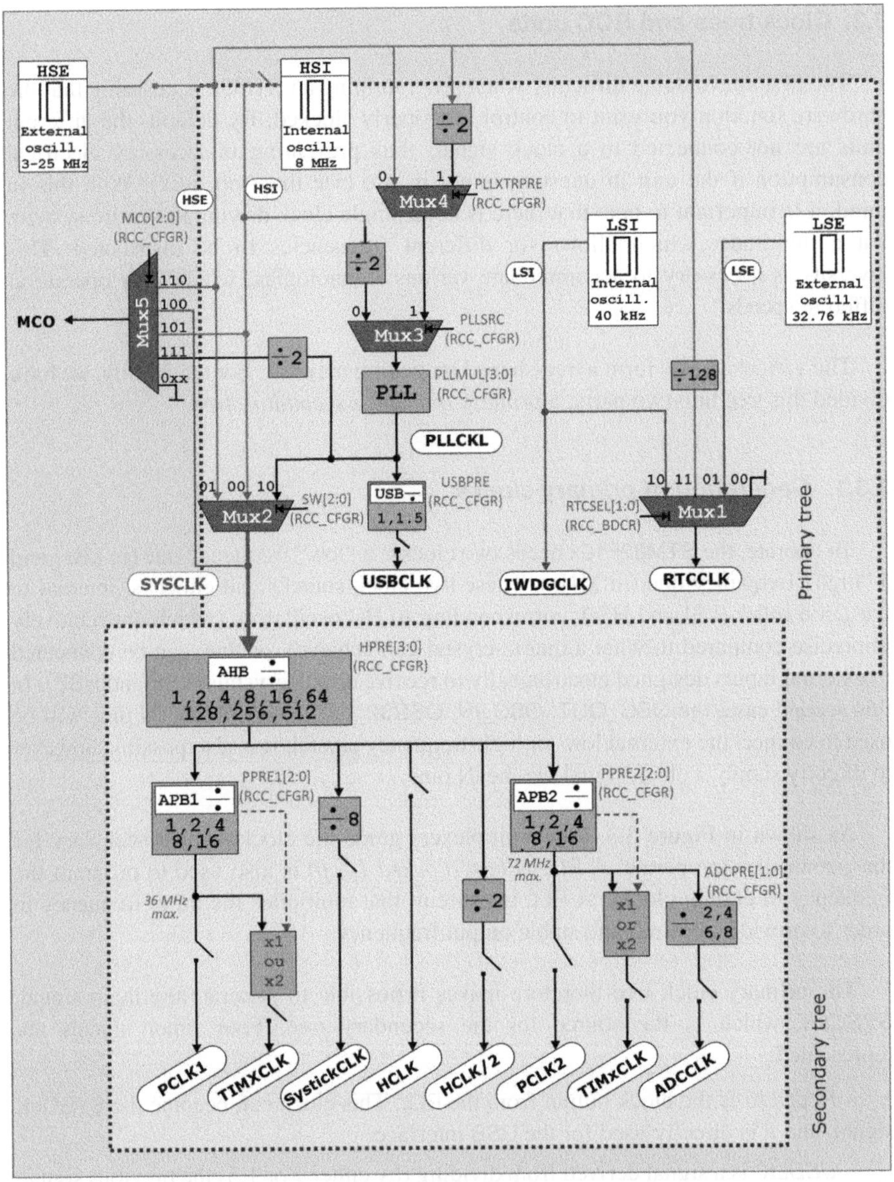

Figure 3.3. *Clock tree. For a color version of this figure, see www.iste.co.uk/mahout/programming.zip*

Each of these clocks can be activated or deactivated independently, with deactivation directly impacting the power consumption of the μcontroller.

The selection of the four multiplexers, as well as the frequency multiplication factor of the PLL, is configured through eight registers, typically at the very beginning of the software application.

However, it is quite understandable that changing the clocks driving the various units could cause serious stability problems for the processor. To address this, the designer can plan a security system (CSS) to prevent some of these inconveniences and to ensure the existence and stability of the external HSE signal. If necessary, it automatically switches to the internal HSI oscillator. The CSSON bit must be activated (see Figure 3.4) for this functionality to be effective.

3.3.2. *Generation of secondary clocks*

The secondary clock tree constructs the clock signals required by the various peripheral units. On the *low-*, *medium-* and *high-density* series circuits that we are considering here, there are nine signals potentially used by the different units (Figure 3.3):

– The clock paths must pass through an initial frequency divider, the AHB prescaler. This divider can take values from 2^0 to 2^9 (except for $2^5 = 32$), and the resulting signal is called *HCLK*. It feeds the AHB bus, in particular the Cortex-M3 core, as well as the internal memory. The *HCLK/2* signal is directed to the SDIOCLK unit.

– The Cortex-M3 core has an internal SysTick Timer, as we will see in Chapter 6. By default, this uses the signal supplied to the core (and therefore to the HCLK), but it can be programmed to use an external source to the Cortex, which we refer to here as *SysTickCLK*. In this case, the external signal is clocked at 1/8 of HCLK.

– Two additional prescaler stages generate the clock signals which feed the APB1 (max 36 MHz) and APB2 (max 72 MHz) buses. The clock signals for these buses, *PCLK1* and *PCLK2*, correspond to the output of the frequency dividers (1, 2, 4, 8 or 16).

– Time management is a key aspect of an embedded application. The STM3210x series offers up to 14 Timers for this purpose. Ten of them (TIM2 to TIM7, and TIM12 to TIM14) are fed by *TIMXCLK*, while the other five (TIM1 and TIM8 to TIM11) are fed by *TIMxCLK*[3]. In both cases, to create the clock signal, a multiplication by 2 is applied to the output of the APBi divider if the corresponding prescaler is set to a value other than 1. Thus, for example, if PCLK1 is 18 MHz with an APB1 prescaler of 4, the TIMXCLK signal will be clocked at 36 MHz.

3 Although it may not be very readable, it is important to note the distinction between the two names, which differ only in the capitalization of the letter x.

<table>
<tr><th colspan="3">Source, clock</th><th>Default frequency</th><th>Associated peripherals</th></tr>
<tr><td colspan="3">USBCLK</td><td>48 MHz</td><td>USB</td></tr>
<tr><td colspan="3">IWDGCLK (LSI only)</td><td>LSE or LSI
or HSE/128</td><td>RTC</td></tr>
<tr><td colspan="3">HSI</td><td>8 MHz</td><td>FLITF
(Flash Memory Interface)</td></tr>
<tr><td rowspan="23">AHB</td><td rowspan="10">APB1</td><td rowspan="9">PCLK1</td><td rowspan="9">36 MHz</td><td>DAC</td></tr>
<tr><td>PWR</td></tr>
<tr><td>BKP</td></tr>
<tr><td>CAN</td></tr>
<tr><td>I2C1 I2C2</td></tr>
<tr><td>USART2, USART3,
UART4 and UART5</td></tr>
<tr><td>SPI2 SPI3</td></tr>
<tr><td>WWDG</td></tr>
<tr><td>DAC</td></tr>
<tr><td>TIMXCLK</td><td>72 MHz</td><td>TIM2 to TIM7
TIM12 to TIM14</td></tr>
<tr><td rowspan="6">APB2</td><td rowspan="4">PCLK2</td><td rowspan="4">72 MHz</td><td>USART1</td></tr>
<tr><td>SPI1</td></tr>
<tr><td>GPIOA to GPIOG</td></tr>
<tr><td>AFIO</td></tr>
<tr><td>TIMxCLK</td><td>72 MHz</td><td>TIM1
TIM8 to TIM11</td></tr>
<tr><td>ADCCLK</td><td>12 MHz
(ADCPRE = 6)</td><td>ADC</td></tr>
<tr><td colspan="2">SysTickCLK</td><td>9 MHz</td><td>SysTick</td></tr>
<tr><td colspan="2" rowspan="5">HCLK</td><td rowspan="5">72 MHz</td><td>Cortex-M3</td></tr>
<tr><td>DMA1, DMA2</td></tr>
<tr><td>SRAM</td></tr>
<tr><td>FSMC</td></tr>
<tr><td>SDIO</td></tr>
<tr><td colspan="2">HCLK/2</td><td>36 MHz</td><td>SDIO</td></tr>
</table>

Table 3.1. *Clock distribution across peripherals*

– The analog to digital conversion (ADC) units, due to their technology, require adjustment of their clock frequency. The *ADCLCK* signal (divided by 2, 4, 6 or 8) from the APB2 output meets this need.

With the clocks available, it is then possible to connect the various units present on the STM32, independently of each other. Each of them is equipped with a switch that allows the clock signal to be transmitted or not to the respective unit. Table 3.1 shows the distribution of clocks across the different peripherals.

3.3.3. *RCC unit programming*

The management of the unit responsible for distributing the various clocks is done through eight registers. The first, RCC_CR (Figure 3.4), essentially controls the primary clock tree. With this register, it is possible:

– to set the *HSION* switch, which enables the activation of the HSI clock. This bit can be forced to 1 hardware-wise if the CSS security system detects a failure on the external quartz HSE input (1 = closed);

– to verify the stability of the HSI oscillator using the *HSIRDY* bit (1 = ready);

– to bypass the internal resonator by setting the *HSEBYP* bit to 1 when the HSE stage input corresponds to a direct clock signal instead of a quartz;

– to compensate for possible drifts in the HSI oscillator using the five *HSITRIM* bits;

– to read the clock calibration using the eight *HSICAL* bits;

– to connect the external quartz HSE input via the *HSEON* bit (1 = closed);

– to verify the availability of the HSE oscillator using the *HSERDY* bit (1 = valid);

– to activate the security system with the *CSSON* bit (1 = active);

– to start the PLL with the *PLLON* bit (1 = active);

– to test the hardware lock of the PLL using the *PLLRDY* bit (1 = locked).

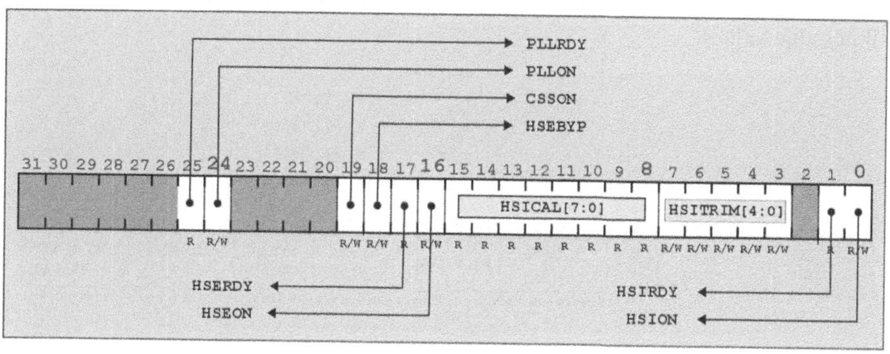

Figure 3.4. *Clock control register RCC_CR*

With the RCC_CFGR register (Figure 3.5), it is possible to adjust the various settings of the primary and secondary clock trees:

– The two *SW* bits act on the MUX2 multiplexer in Figure 3.3 as:

- $(00)_2$ selects the direct path from HSI.
- $(01)_2$ selects the direct path from HSE.

- $(10)_2$ selects the path coming from the PLL.
- $(11)_2$ is not allowed.

– The two *SWS* bits indicate which clock source is feeding SYSCLK. Therefore, it is possible to know (with the same values as above) the state of MUX2, which may be different from the requested SW state in the case where the CSS security system detected an error.

– The *PLLSRC* bit positions MUX3 (0 = channel HSI/2, 1 = MUX4 output).

– The *PLLXTPRE* bit positions MUX4 (0 = channel HSE, 1 = HSE/2).

– The *USBPRE* bit selects the USB divider (1 = no division, 0 = division by 1.5).

– The three-bit *MCO* field selects (MUX5) the signal to output on the MCO pin, namely:

- $(100)_2$ selects the SYSCLK signal (only works if Freq $<$ 50 MHz, the maximum speed allowed by the I/O ports).
- $(101)_2$ selects the HSI signal.
- $(110)_2$ selects the HSE signal.
- $(111)_2$ selects the PLL/2.
- $(0\times\times)_2$ no signal.

– The *SWS, HPRE, ADCPRE* and *PPREi* bit fields allow you to choose the value of the operators (divider or multiplier) that they control. Table 3.2 summarizes all possible values.

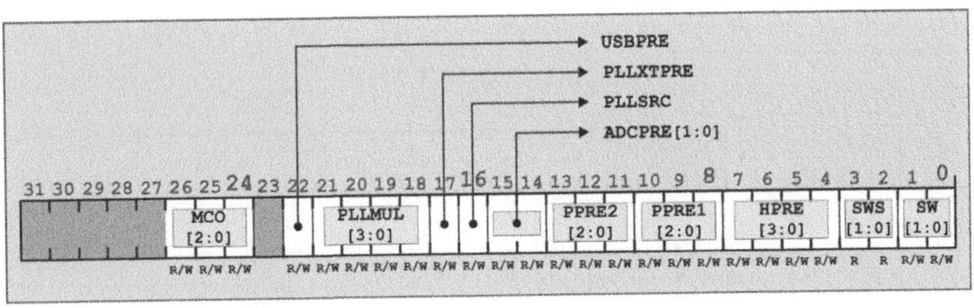

Figure 3.5. *Clock configuration register RCC_CFGR*

Once the clocks are configured, all that remains is to connect the various units. This goes through 36 bits distributed across the two RCC_APPB1ENR and RCC_APPB2ENR registers. When a bit is set to 1, the associated unit is fed with its clock; conversely, the bit to 0 disconnects the clock. Figures 3.6 and 3.7 indicate which bits control the "switches" for each unit.

<table>
<tr><th rowspan="2">Divisor or PLL</th><th rowspan="2">Signal affected</th><th colspan="3">Field</th></tr>
<tr><th>Name</th><th>Value</th><th>Operation</th></tr>
<tr><td rowspan="9">AHB</td><td rowspan="9">SYCLK</td><td rowspan="9">HPRE</td><td>$(0\times\times\times)_2$</td><td>No effect</td></tr>
<tr><td>$(1000)_2$</td><td>$\div 2$</td></tr>
<tr><td>$(1001)_2$</td><td>$\div 4$</td></tr>
<tr><td>$(1010)_2$</td><td>$\div 8$</td></tr>
<tr><td>$(1011)_2$</td><td>$\div 16$</td></tr>
<tr><td>$(1100)_2$</td><td>$\div 64$</td></tr>
<tr><td>$(1101)_2$</td><td>$\div 128$</td></tr>
<tr><td>$(1110)_2$</td><td>$\div 256$</td></tr>
<tr><td>$(1111)_2$</td><td>$\div 512$</td></tr>
<tr><td rowspan="5">APB1 or APB2</td><td rowspan="5">HCLK = AHB output</td><td rowspan="5">PPRE1 or PPRE2</td><td>$(0\times\times)_2$</td><td>No effect</td></tr>
<tr><td>$(100)_2$</td><td>$\div 2$</td></tr>
<tr><td>$(101)_2$</td><td>$\div 4$</td></tr>
<tr><td>$(110)_2$</td><td>$\div 8$</td></tr>
<tr><td>$(111)_2$</td><td>$\div 16$</td></tr>
<tr><td rowspan="16">PLL</td><td rowspan="16">MUX3 output</td><td rowspan="16">PLLMUL</td><td>$(0000)_2$</td><td>$\times 2$</td></tr>
<tr><td>$(0001)_2$</td><td>$\times 3$</td></tr>
<tr><td>$(0010)_2$</td><td>$\times 4$</td></tr>
<tr><td>$(0011)_2$</td><td>$\times 5$</td></tr>
<tr><td>$(0100)_2$</td><td>$\times 6$</td></tr>
<tr><td>$(0101)_2$</td><td>$\times 7$</td></tr>
<tr><td>$(0110)_2$</td><td>$\times 8$</td></tr>
<tr><td>$(0111)_2$</td><td>$\times 9$</td></tr>
<tr><td>$(1000)_2$</td><td>$\times 10$</td></tr>
<tr><td>$(1001)_2$</td><td>$\times 11$</td></tr>
<tr><td>$(1010)_2$</td><td>$\times 12$</td></tr>
<tr><td>$(1011)_2$</td><td>$\times 13$</td></tr>
<tr><td>$(1100)_2$</td><td>$\times 14$</td></tr>
<tr><td>$(1101)_2$</td><td>$\times 15$</td></tr>
<tr><td>$(1110)_2$</td><td rowspan="2">$\times 16$</td></tr>
<tr><td>$(1111)_2$</td></tr>
<tr><td rowspan="4">ADC</td><td rowspan="4">APB2 output</td><td rowspan="4">ADCPRE</td><td>$(00)_2$</td><td>$\div 2$</td></tr>
<tr><td>$(01)_2$</td><td>$\div 4$</td></tr>
<tr><td>$(10)_2$</td><td>$\div 6$</td></tr>
<tr><td>$(11)_2$</td><td>$\div 8$</td></tr>
</table>

Table 3.2. *Possible configurations of frequency operators*

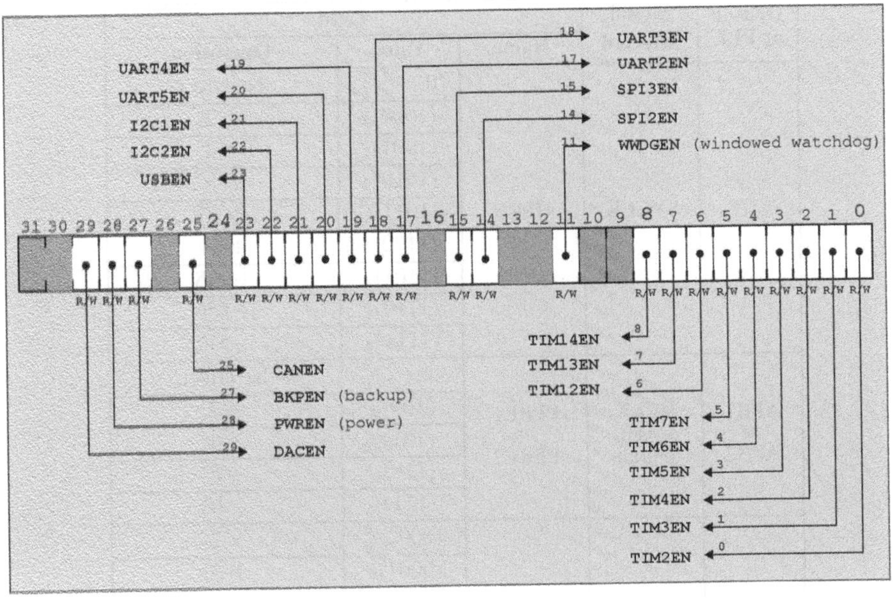

Figure 3.6. *Clock enable register for the APB1 units: RCC_APB1ENR*

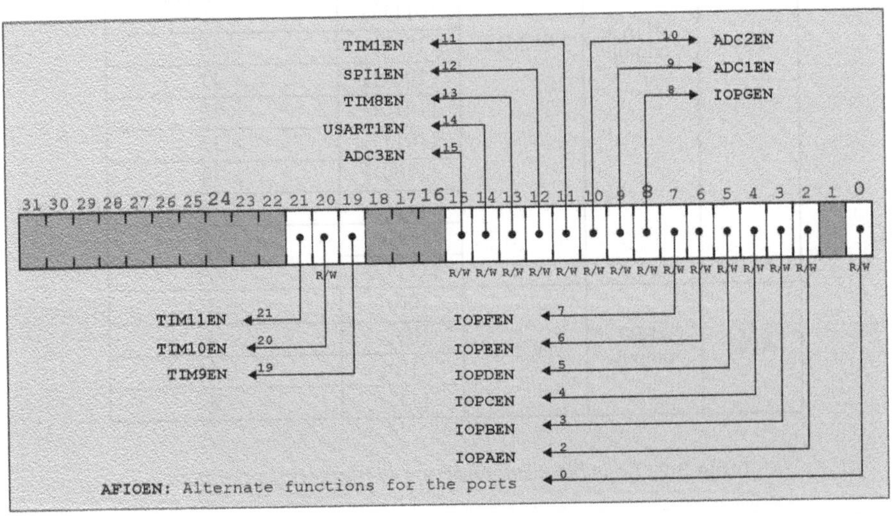

Figure 3.7. *Clock enable register for the APB2 units: RCC_APB2ENR*

Four additional registers complement this setup. The first two (RCC_APB2RSTR and RCC_APB1RSTR) enable a hardware reset for each unit to be triggered independently of one another. Each unit has a bit in one of these two registers, and when this bit is set to 1, it initiates a reset of the respective unit.

The third register (RCC_CIR) allows enabling and managing the interrupt of the RCC unit (interrupt No. 5). A typical example of an event that can trigger this interrupt is when the HSE signal becomes ready (HSERDYIE bit).

Finally, the RCC_BDCR is a register that defines the interaction rules between the RCC unit and the RTC unit when it is used. This topic will be covered in Chapter 10.

3.3.4. *RCC unit configuration coding example*

Code example 3.1 presents a typical RCC configuration, which can be observed in Figure 3.8.

```
/* Reset values of the main RCC registers */
#define __RCC_CR_RESET      0x00000083
#define __RCC_CIR_RESET     0x00000000
#define __RCC_CFGR_RESET    0x00000000

/**** __RCC_CFGR_VALUE calculation ****/
/* Definition of independent masks */
/* We want 72MHz starting from an 8MHz quartz, so mult=9 */
#define _PLLMUL 9
#define RCC_PLLMUL_VAL(mult) (((mult-2) & 0xF )<< 18)
/* Choose HSE for MUX4 */
#define _PLLXTPRE_MASK   (0<<17)
/* The source (MUX3) of the PLL is HSE (output from MUX4) */
#define RCC_PLLSRC_IS_HSE  (1<<16)
/* Choose PLCK2/6 for the divisor of the ADC */
#define _ADCPRE 6
#define RCC_ADCPRE_VAL(pres) ((((pres/2)-1) & 0x3 ) << 14)
/* At first, SYSCLK corresponds to HSI */
#define  RCC_CFGR_SW_HSI     0x00000000
/* Choose HCLK as SYSCLK/1 */
#define _HPRE 1
#define RCC_HPRE_VAL(pre) ( ((pre==1) ||(pre==32) ) ? 0 : (7+(pre
    >256)+(pre>128)+(pre>64)+(pre>16)+(pre>8)+(pre>4)+(pre>2)+
    (pre>1))<< 4)
/* Choose PCLK2 as HCLK/2 */
#define _PPRE1  2
```

```
#define RCC_PPRE1_VAL(pre) ((pre==1) ? 0 : ((pre/2)-(pre/8)
    -2*(pre/16)+3)<< 8)
/* Choose PCLK1 as HCLK/1 */
#define _PPRE2 1
#define RCC_PPRE2_VAL(pre) ((pre==1) ? 0 : ((pre/2)-(pre/8)
    -2*(pre/16)+3)<< 11)

/* Complete mask creation */
/* Finally, in our example, __RCC_CFGR_VALUE is 0x001D8400 */

#define __RCC_CFGR_VALUE (RCC_PLLMUL_VAL(_PLLMUL) | \
                          _PLLXTPRE_MASK |           \
                          RCC_PLLSRC_IS_HSE |        \
                          RCC_ADCPRE_VAL(_ADCPRE) |  \
                          RCC_CFGR_SW_HSI |          \
                          RCC_PPRE1_VAL(_PPRE1) |    \
                          RCC_PPRE2_VAL(_PPRE2)) |   \
                          RCC_HPRE_VAL(_HPRE)

void CLOCK_Configure(void)
{
    RCC->CR = __RCC_CR_RESET;
    RCC->CIR = __RCC_CIR_RESET;
    RCC->CFGR = __RCC_CFGR_VALUE;

/* Connection of the external HSE input */
    RCC->CR |= RCC_CR_HSEON;

/* Wait for the external oscillator to stabilize */
    while((RCC->CR & RCC_CR_HSERDY) == 0);

/* Start the PLL */
    RCC->CR |= RCC_CR_PLLON;

/* Wait for the PLL to stabilize */
    while((RCC->CR & RCC_CR_PLLRDY) == 0);

/* Switch MUX2 to the PLL input */
    RCC->CFGR &= ~(RCC_CFGR_SW);
    RCC->CFGR |= RCC_CFGR_SW_PLL;

/* Setting the divisor for the USB */
    RCC->CFGR |= RCC_CFGR_USBPRE;
}
```

Code 3.1. *Typical RCC unit configuration*

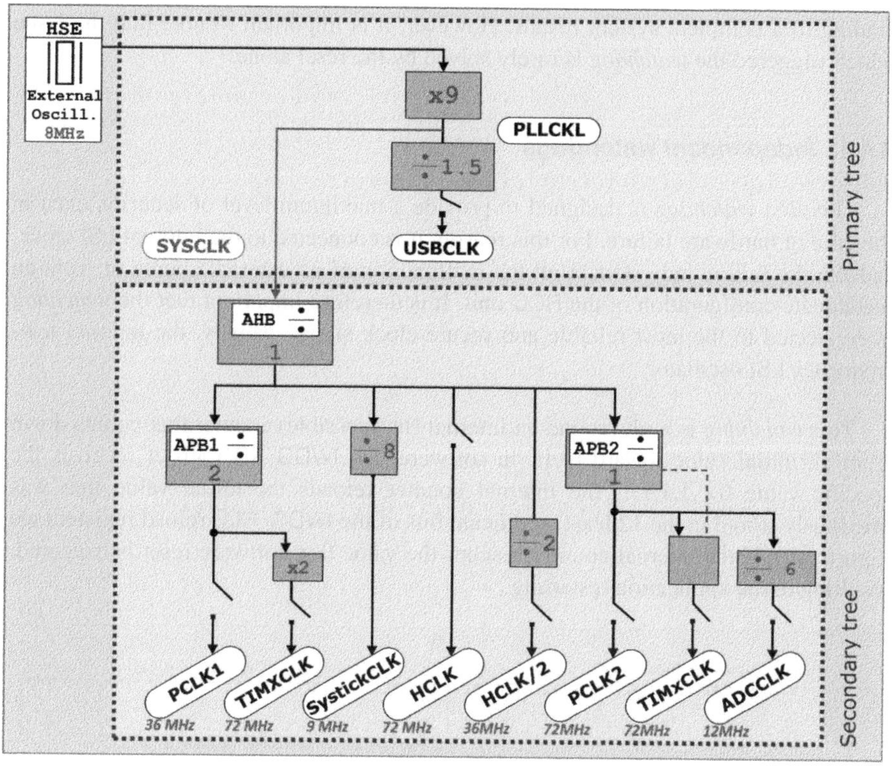

Figure 3.8. *Typical configuration of the RCC unit*

3.4. *Watchdogs*

When developing software for embedded systems, whether it be a simple gadget or a highly critical system, it is not always feasible to rely on external intervention to restart the system if it becomes "out of service". Among the reasons that could lead to such a situation, one can easily imagine an electronic failure, an unforeseen issue during software design leading to an infinite loop, or a peripheral unit monopolizing CPU resources, etc.

Watchdogs are therefore in place to provide necessary monitoring in order to react to abnormal situations. The example of the train driver perfectly illustrates the role of a *watchdog*: if they do not periodically press a dedicated button, the train switches to a safe mode.

For a *watchdog*, resetting is done by writing a bit or a register with a specific value (which is the case for STM32). If this reset does not occur, it results in a system reset, leading to a complete system restart. However, it is important to note that the issue which triggered the *watchdog* is rarely solved by the reset alone.

3.4.1. *Independent* watchdogs

This first *watchdog* is designed to provide a maximum level of security, even in the case of hardware failure. For this reason, it is connected to the internal LSI clock. Indeed, the failure may stem from the malfunction of an external source or from an inadequate configuration of the RCC unit. It is therefore important that the *watchdog* is connected to the most reliable and secure clock signal, namely, the internal low-frequency LSI oscillator.

This *watchdog* is built around an internal (inaccessible) counter that counts down from an initial value toward 0. If, in software, the IWDG_KR register receives the specific value $0\times AAAA$, the internal counter reloads the initial value that was previously stored in the 12 least significant bits of the IWDG_RLR reload register (see Figure 3.9). If the internal counter reaches the value 0, a software reset is triggered, resulting in the application restarting.

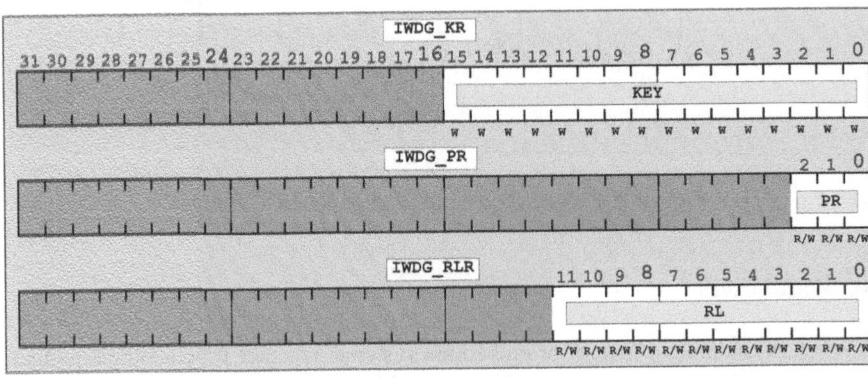

Figure 3.9. *Three main registers of the independent watchdog*

By default, this mechanism is not active. It is activated by writing the value $0\mathrm{x}CCCC$ into the IWDG_KR register.

A third register (IDWG_PR) is necessary for the complete configuration of this *watchdog*. Using the three least significant bits of this register, it sets the integer division that will apply downstream from the LSI clock, which oscillates at 40 kHz. Thus, the internal counter will decrement at rising edges clocked between 10 kHz (with the minimum divisor value of 4) and 156.25 Hz (with the maximum divisor value of 256). The eight admissible values of this 3-bit PR field (0–7) correspond to the 7 divisors: 4, 8, 16, 32, 64, 128 and 256, respectively. By combining this with the IWDG_RLR reload value, the reset time T_{reset} between the reset and the watchdog rearmament can be calculated as:

$$T_{reset} = \frac{Div_{PR}}{40.10^3} \times \text{IWDG\_RLR}$$

Considering the possible values for both the divisor and the reload value, the range of programmable durations for this *watchdog* spans from $100\ \mu s$ (PR = 0 and RLR = $0{\times}001$) to $26.2\ s$ (PR $=$ 6 or 7 and RLR $=$ $0{\times}\mathrm{FFF}$).

Be careful, the device is secured. It is only possible to modify the IDWG_PR and IDWG_RLR registers if the specific value $0{\times}5555$ has been written to the IDWG_KR register beforehand.

3.4.2. *Windowed* watchdogs

This second *watchdog* is more complex and addresses very specific needs, which is why we will not detail it here. However, let us highlight two essential differences that will allow the reader to determine whether this unit could be useful to them.

As the name suggests, the time interval used to prevent the *watchdog* from triggering is windowed. Therefore, this *watchdog* must always be reset before the maximum programmed time, but it must not be reset before the minimum duration has passed. The application must therefore ensure that certain tasks also have a minimum duration.

This *watchdog* does not necessarily lead to a reset. In fact, an interrupt vector is associated with this unit (*Window Watchdog Interrupt*). If this option is programmed, the internal *watchdog* counter reaching 0 will trigger an *early wake interrupt*, allowing the application to respond rather than immediately resetting.

4

Binary Inputs/Outputs (I/O): Parallel Ports

When a user takes hold of a μcontroller, literally and figuratively, the first reality they encounter is a physical one: it is a box with a potentially large number of pins. Semiconductor packages come in different formats: QFP, LQFP, DIP, SO, etc. Each of these boxes is mainly characterized by its geometry. The most easily observable characteristic is, of course, the number of pins on the chip. As seen in Chapter 1 (Figure 1.2), the same μcontroller can come in many different versions, particularly in terms of packaging, which leads to variations in the number of pins, among other things.

4.1. Concept of I/O ports

The pins of a μcontroller package form the physical interface between the μcontroller and the process it controls[1]. These pins provide a tangible and direct representation of the concept of input/output (I/O). As an illustration, Figure 4.1 shows the pin layout and distribution and nomenclature of the STM32F103RB, which we can use to understand some key elements.

Of the 64 connections on this pinout, a significant number are dedicated to receiving power supply voltage (V_{DD}_x) or ground (V_{SS}_x). While there is only one electrical power supply (all V_{DD} are connected to the same source), distributing the electrical input helps to divide the current carried within the processor. Additionally, two other power inputs are provided: voltages used as references for analog-to-digital conversions (V_{DDA} and V_{SSA}, discussed in Chapter 8), and a specific V_{BAT} input that can serve as a backup power supply in the event that the main power supply fails.

For a color version of all the Codes in this chapter, see www.iste.co.uk/mahout/programming.zip

1 With the exception of the power and external clock pins.

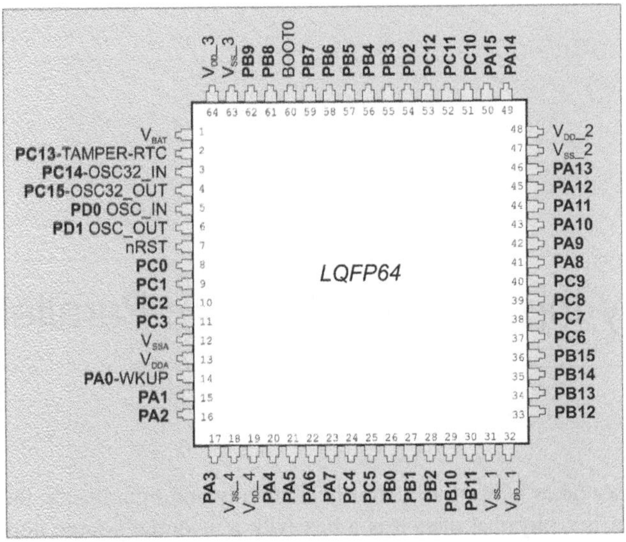

Figure 4.1. *Example of pinout in a 64-pin LQFP package*

A pin called Reset is also present in all μcontrollers to carry a reset command; in Figure 4.1, this corresponds to pin 7, labeled nRST (*not ReSeT*). Finally, as mentioned in the previous chapter, it is possible to provide a more precise external clock signal than the RC internal oscillators of the processor. The inputs designated for this purpose are numbered 3–6 here.

The remaining pins (PA0, PA1, ..., PB0, ..., PC0, ...) are available to the user. These pins correspond to the concept of *I/O ports* and are referred to as GPIO (*General Purpose Input Output*) in the STmicro© documentation. The I/O ports form the interface between the μcontroller and the outside world. For convenience and efficiency, designers group pins (in sets of 8 or 16, depending on the processor) to form what is known as a *port*. To access a particular bit of a port and thus a specific pin on the chip, the masking technique discussed in section 2.4 is used.

For example, PC4 is the fourth I/O pin of GPIOC, and thus bit no. 4 of the registers associated with this port. It corresponds to pin no. 24 in Figure 4.1.

4.2. Electronic aspect

A pin can be configured to receive a binary signal (input) or impose a binary signal (output). It can also be used to read an analog signal (and in some cases to impose one if a digital-to-analog converter is available). Naturally, these different functionalities are mutually exclusive, and the usage of each pin must be determined through configuration registers. Electronically, this is achieved through a specific internal architecture that allows the same pin to handle these different options.

4.2.1. *Global architecture*

Figure 4.2 illustrates how a particular pin of the package is accessed via registers, either from the core or a peripheral of the μcontroller. On this simplified diagram, the possibilities of pin input (reading) are illustrated using blue lines, and the output accesses (writing) are illustrated using red lines.

Several key points can be drawn from the careful reading of this figure:

– The pin is the physical interface between the digital inner world of the μcontroller and the external world.

– At input, the state of the pin is copied into a bit of the input register IDR (*Input Data Register*), here bit no. 5. The binary state is 1 if the potential applied to the pin is greater than $\frac{V_{DD}}{2}$ and 0 otherwise[2].

– Symmetrically at output, the corresponding bit of the output register ODR (*Output Data Register*) is sent to the pin via the multiplexer in Figure 4.2. The voltage is V_{DD} if the state is 1 and V_{SS} if the state is 0.

– The bits of rank k of the registers BSR (*Bit Set Register*) and BSRR (*Bit Set and Reset Register*) "drive" the kth bit of the ODR.

– Whether in input or output, the pin is also accessible by alternative functions that correspond to peripherals of the μcontroller (Timer, USART, SPI, etc.).

– At input, it is possible to force the default electrical state of the pin by connecting the internal *pull-up* or *pull-down* resistors.

– The output stage is disconnected when the pin is configured as an input, otherwise it controls an output in *push-pull* mode or in *open drain* mode.

– The input wiring is always active, so writing to the output (via the ODR, for example) will result in the assignment of the same rank bit of the IDR. This feedback is useful for software verification to ensure that "everything is going well" when imposing an output level on a pin.

2 To be more precise, and for $V_{DD} = 3.3$V, the input Schmitt trigger is such that if the applied voltage is above approximately $1.6V$, then the corresponding bit of IDR is set to 1. If this voltage drops below approximately 1.2V, the same bit switches to 0. Note that the μcontroller must operate with a maximum V_{DD} of 3.3V. The I/Os are therefore designed for this range of voltages, except for certain I/Os labeled *FT*, known as 5V tolerant (*Five Volt Tolerant*), which can safely handle 5V, in contrast to standard I/Os where applying 5V is prohibited.

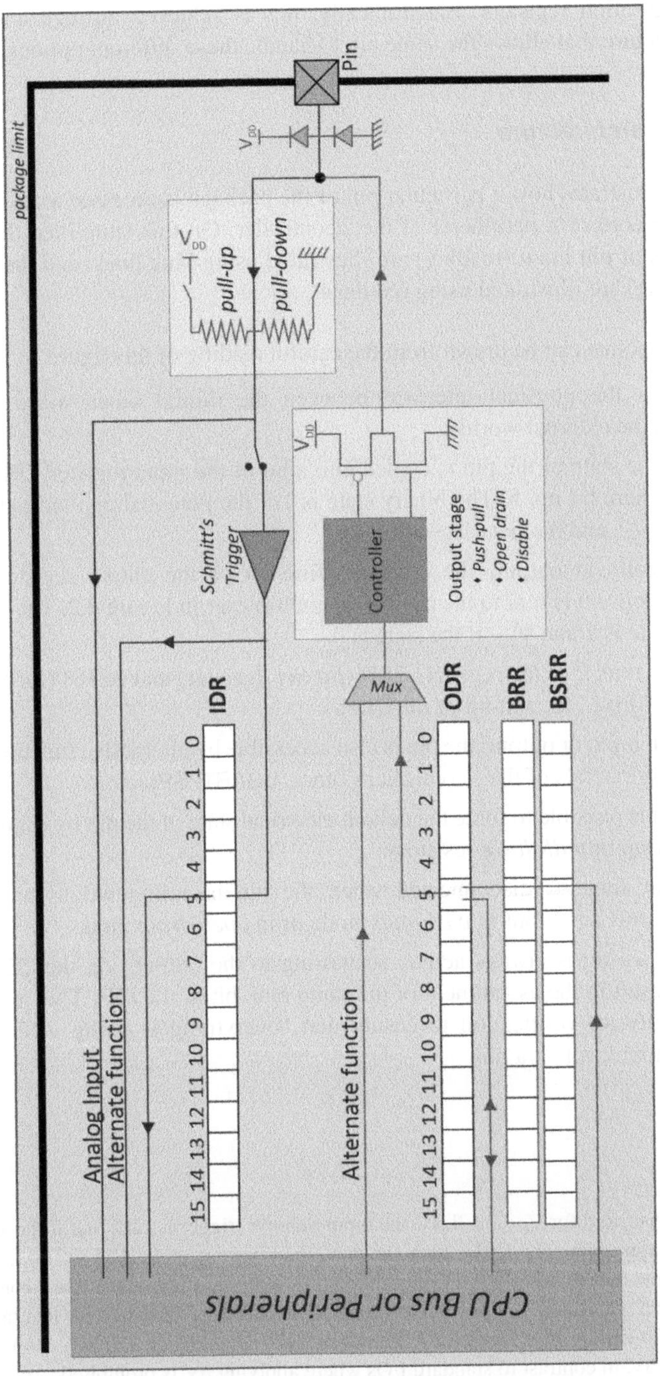

Figure 4.2. *Global architecture of an I/O pin. For a color version of this figure, see www.iste.co.uk/mahout/programming.zip*

4.2.2. *Input configuration*

As shown in Figure 4.2, the signal present at the input on the pin follows three different paths:

– It goes to the corresponding bit of the IDR, first by passing through a Schmitt trigger. This trigger has hysteresis to ensure that the transitions between the binary states 0 and 1 are clean and without oscillation.

– It is also connected to an alternative function (e.g. the capture input of a Timer). The alternate function of a particular pin is fixed; therefore, each pin cannot be used for each of the different existing peripherals.

– Finally, it is connected to the analog-to-digital conversion (ADC) units for the pins dedicated to these units.

Let us list the different configuration options available when configuring an input pin:

– The first is the so-called floating input configuration. The pin is then left floating, and the *pull-up* and *pull-down* resistors are not used. It is entirely up to the external part to impose the voltage. It is clear that in this case, the pin behaves like an antenna, and if the external wiring is incorrect, the information read (in the IDR) can be completely erratic.

– The second and third options allow setting the default voltage through *pull-up* or *pull-down* resistors connected to V_{DD} and V_{SS}, respectively. The values of these resistors are around 40 $k\Omega$.

– The last option involves taking an analog signal into account to convert it into a digital value. This path is specific because it must be exclusively directed toward the ADC and disconnected from the input of the Schmitt trigger.

It is therefore essential, when addressing the configuration of I/O pins, to understand how the external electrical circuit is made. If we consider the simplest case for a binary input, such as a push-button, four possible setups are shown in Figure 4.3.

From a configuration standpoint, push-buttons no. 1 and no. 2 cannot be set in floating input mode. Indeed, when the push-button is released, the pin is left floating, and the resulting binary value read in IDR cannot be guaranteed. Push-button no. 1 will need to be configured with a *pull-up* (default binary state of 1), while push-button no. 2 will need to be configured with a *pull-down* (default binary state of 0).

Push-buttons no. 3 and no. 4 correspond to a floating input configuration since the *pull-up* and *pull-down* resistors are placed in the external wiring. These two setups are symmetrical: pressing push-button no. 3 will cause a transition from binary state 1 to binary state 0, while the same action on push-button no. 4 will switch the binary state from 0 to 1.

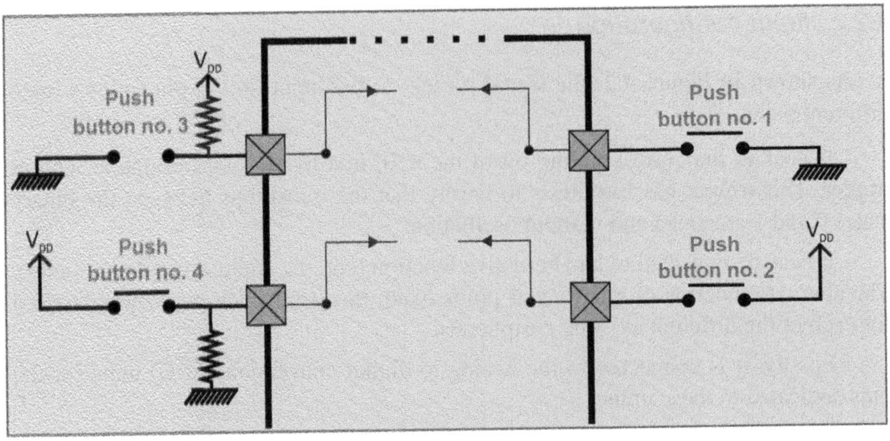

Figure 4.3. *Four possible connections for a push-button type input*

4.2.3. *Output configuration*

A pin can be set as an output through different configurations, and it is necessary to understand the electrical circuit connected to the pin to determine the appropriate configuration to program.

It is important to note that if a pin is configured as an input, the output stage is disconnected from the pin; therefore, there is no possibility of conflict between the external and internal sources when controlling the voltage on the pin.

The configuration is done in two distinct steps:

– a multiplexer that allows the selection of whether the pin is governed by the state of the corresponding pin in the ODR or by a peripheral of the alternative function routed to this pin;

– an output stage composed of two MOSFET transistors that allow the creation of either a *push-pull* or *open drain* setup. Without going into detail of these transistors, it is useful to understand the main difference between these two options (see Appendix):

- in *push-pull* mode[3]: both MOSFETs are active and work in opposition. The pin is therefore able to supply both 0V and V_{DD} with a maximum current of approximately $\pm 8mA$,

- in *open drain* mode: the MOSFET connected to V_{DD} is deactivated. The pin can only force the $0V$ (but not V_{DD}). The V_{DD} voltage must be supplied externally.

3 However, be careful, not all pins can simultaneously supply this maximum current, as there is also a global current limit for the μcontroller.

This configuration is useful, for example, for creating a multi-master bus (e.g. I^2C bus in Chapter 9) to avoid situations where two circuits attempt to impose different logic states simultaneously, which would create a short circuit.

Consider (Figure 4.4) two LEDs connected to two different pins. In this diagram, LED no. 1 is controlled by a PWM signal generated directly by a Timer. The multiplexer is configured to use this signal instead of the state of the ODR bit (in this example, bit 9). For LED no. 2, the multiplexer is configured to associate the output state with the state of the ODR bit (here bit 5).

Externally, LED no. 1 is connected to ground via a resistor. Clearly, since the LED is polarized, it is essential to connect the anode of the LED to the pin and the cathode to ground. In this setup, the μcontroller must be able to impose V_{DD} to turn on the LED and 0V to turn it off. Therefore, a *push-pull* configuration is mandatory.

LED no. 2, on the other hand, is externally connected to V_{DD}, always respecting the direction of current flow. The pin only needs to impose 0V to turn on the LED (inverted logic wiring) and switch to high impedance to turn it off. The *open drain* configuration can be used. A *push-pull* configuration is also possible but not mandatory.

4.3. STM32 GPIOs

STM32 μcontrollers can have up to seven I/O ports. Of course, this depends primarily on the type of package: a 32-pin package has far fewer GPIOs than a 100-pin package. However, not all pins are connected to a port, as some are used for other purposes, such as providing power. Additionally, some pins are connected to a port but are also designated for other uses, like connecting an external quartz crystal to generate the μcontroller's internal clocks (see section 3.3).

In STmicro©'s nomenclature, the different ports are labeled with letters, and the documentation refers to GPIOx (ranging from GPIOA to GPIOG). The individual pins are identified by a number (from 0 to 15) corresponding to the bit rank to which they are assigned: GPIOx.y. For example, GPIOB.13 refers to pin number 13 on port B, which is also labeled PB13 (Figure 4.1).

In particular, the STM32F103RB, on which we focus in the book, has four I/O ports (GPIOA to GPIOD) but only 51 possible I/Os. While port GPIOD exists, it only has three pins (on the LQFP64 package in Figure 4.1, pins 5, 6 and 54), and furthermore, GPIOD.0 and GPIOD.1 are intended for external oscillator signals. Therefore, when the board uses an external quartz crystal, these pins are generally no longer available.

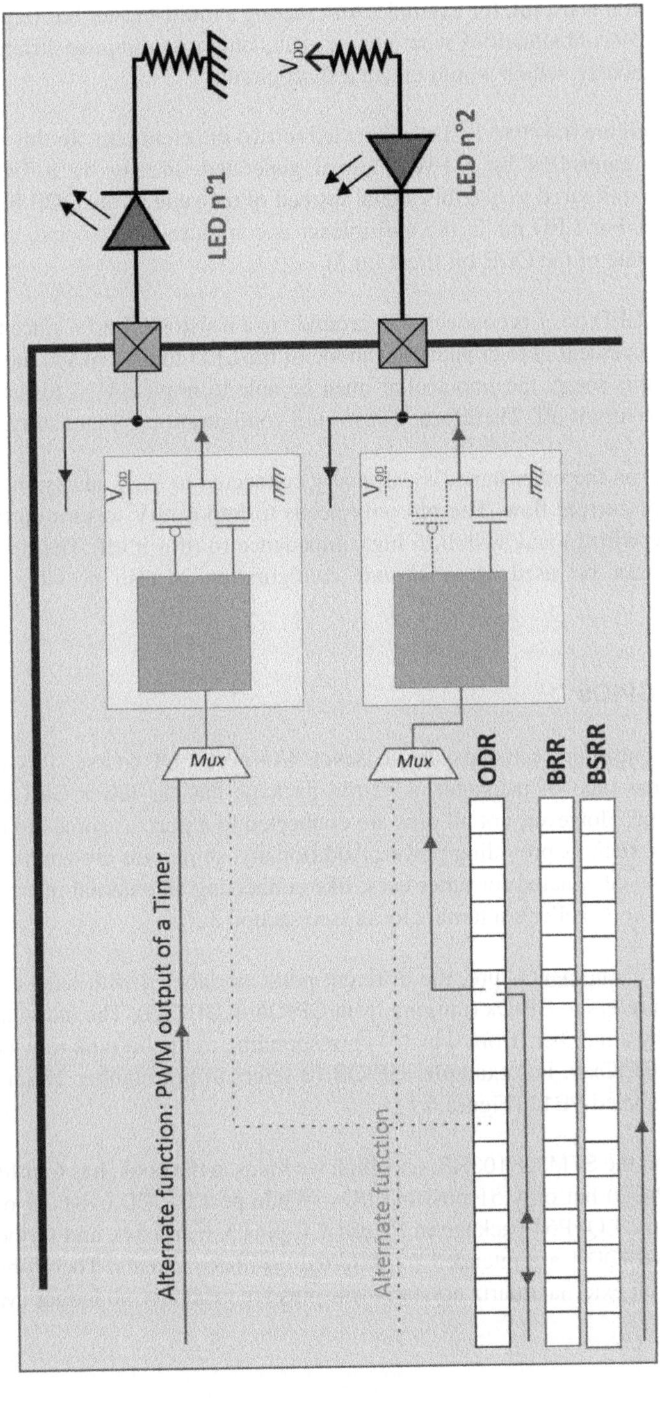

Figure 4.4. *Example of two possible LED output configurations*

4.3.1. *Configuration registers*

As we have seen previously, each pin can be configured independently on the same port. This configuration requires two fields of 2 bits each. In total, configuring all 16 pins requires 64 bits, which requires two complete 32-bit registers: the GPIOx_CRL register for pins 0 to 7, and the GPIOx_CRH register for the eight most significant pins (Figure 4.5).

The first 2-bit field, positioned as the least significant, is called MOD. It sets the direction. The pin will be an input if the binary value is $(00)_2$ and an output for the other three values, corresponding to three different maximum switching frequencies (2, 10 and 50 MHz). Indeed, when an output changes state, the rising and falling edges can generate high-frequency spectrum and cause oscillations as well as electromagnetic emissions that could disturb the environment and create malfunctions, for example, on neighboring I/O pins set as inputs. To reduce these phenomena, it is possible to slow down the edge (referred to as limiting the *slew rate* in $\frac{V}{\mu s}$). In STmicro©'s systems, there are three possible floating inputs. For any given application, the goal is always to use the gentlest edge slope, meaning the lowest output frequency.

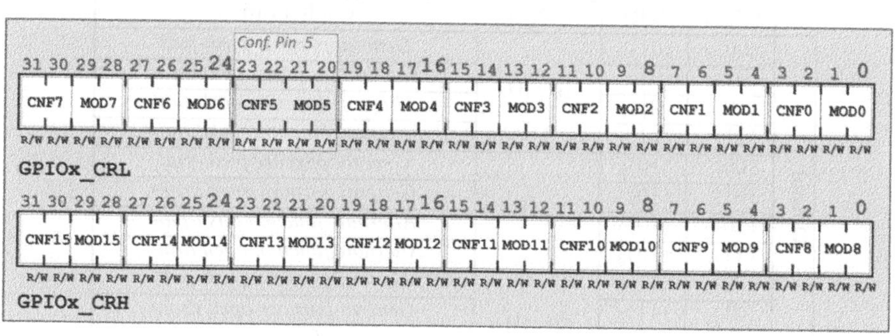

Figure 4.5. *Configuration registers of a GPIO*

The second field, CNF, depends on the first. If the pin is configured as an input, there are three possible configurations:

– With the value $(00)_2$, the input will be connected to the analog converter.

– With the value $(01)_2$, the input will be binary (connected to the Schmitt trigger) but electronically floating.

– With the value $(10)_2$, the input will also be binary but connected to internal *pull-up/pull-down* resistors. In this case, the corresponding bit of the output register (ODR) determines whether it is a *pull-up* (corresponding ODR bit set to 1) or a *pull-down* (bit set to 0).

If the MOD of the pin is different from 0, the output can have four configurations:

– With $(00)_2$, the multiplexer validates the path from the ODR with a *push-pull* configuration.

– With$(01)_2$, the multiplexer validates the path from the ODR with an *open drain* configuration.

– With $(10)_2$, the multiplexer validates the path from the alternative function with a *push-pull* configuration.

– With $(11)_2$, the multiplexer validates the path from the alternative function with an *open drain* configuration.

Table 4.1 summarizes this different information.

	Register			Configuration
	CNFx	**MODx**	**ODR.x**	
Input	$(00)_2$	$(00)_2$	/	*Analog*
	$(01)_2$	$(00)_2$	/	*Floating*
	$(10)_2$	$(00)_2$	$(0)_2$	*Pull-down*
			$(1)_2$	*Pull-up*
	$(11)_2$	$(00)_2$	/	*Unused*
	CNFx	**MODx**	**ODR.x**	**Configuration**
Output	$(00)_2$	$(01)_2$	10 MHz	*General purpose push-pull*
	$(01)_2$	$(01)_2$		*General purpose open drain*
	$(10)_2$	$(01)_2$		*Alternate function push-pull*
	$(11)_2$	$(01)_2$		*Alternate function open drain*
	$(00)_2$	$(10)_2$	2 MHz	*General purpose push-pull*
	$(01)_2$	$(10)_2$		*General purpose open drain*
	$(10)_2$	$(10)_2$		*Alternate function push-pull*
	$(11)_2$	$(10)_2$		*Alternate function open drain*
	$(00)_2$	$(11)_2$	50 MHz	*General purpose push-pull*
	$(01)_2$	$(11)_2$		*General purpose open drain*
	$(10)_2$	$(11)_2$		*Alternate function push-pull*
	$(11)_2$	$(11)_2$		*Alternate function open drain*

Table 4.1. *Possible configurations for pin x*

4.3.2. *Access registers*

Pins can be connected to alternative functions. If this is the intended use, the following chapters will describe the specific roles these I/Os play on the peripherals. From an application point of view, aside from the necessary configuration phase, the program does not need to worry about the state of these pins, as they will be managed directly by the relevant peripheral. In the case of binary accesses (typically a push-button as input and an LED as output), the program must manage the binary value associated with the pin. If the wiring and pin configuration are consistent, reading the state of an input pin is simply done via the IDR. For output, imposing a logical state is done directly via the ODR. It is important to note that the Cortex architecture does not offer bit-addressable instructions. Therefore, access is made to the entire GPIO port that is connected to the pin (Figure 4.6). Using masks (section 2.4) is crucial to perform these accesses properly.

Thus, if the programmer wants to set or reset a particular pin, the code must:

1) read the ODR;

2) modify the specific bit in the value read using the appropriate mask;

3) rewrite the result back to the ODR.

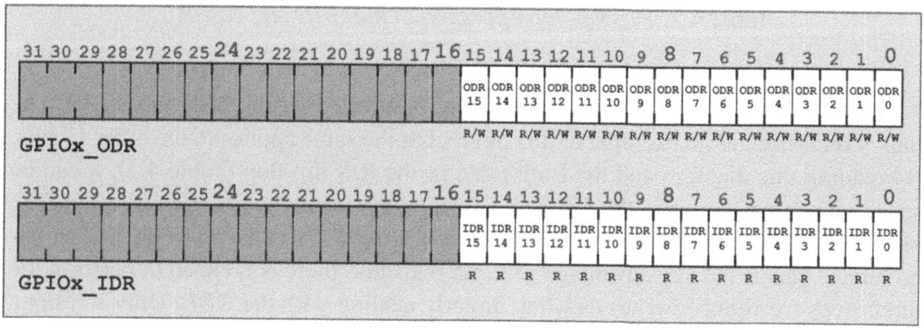

Figure 4.6. *Read/write access registers of a GPIO*

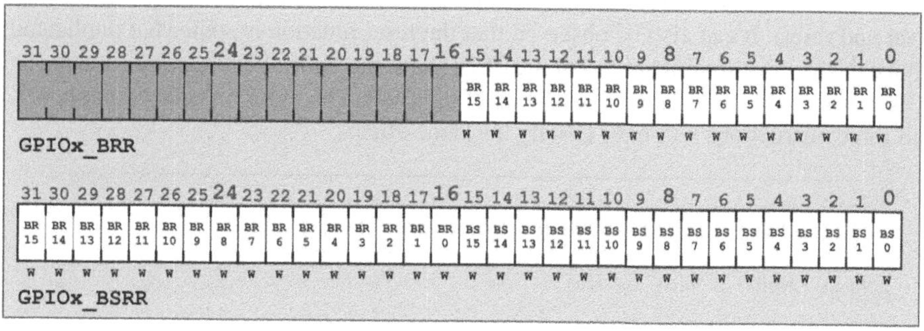

Figure 4.7. *Set/reset write registers of a GPIO*

The BRR and BSRR, which are write-only[4], behave like R/W flip-flops on the corresponding bit of the ODR. An R/S flip-flop has two inputs (R and S) that act on the output Q according to the truth table shown in Table 4.2.

Set **BRR.x**	*Reset* **BRR.x** or **BSRR.(x+16)**	**ODR.x output status**
0	0	Unchanged
0	1	0
1	0	1
1	1	Forbidden (priority set)

Table 4.2. *R/S flip-flop operation of the BRR and BSRR*

Figure 4.8 shows how an output pin can be controlled via the BRR and BSRR. The rank 9 bit is used as an example in this figure, but the same applies to the other 15 bits. By reading this diagram and the truth table of the R/S flip-flop (Table 4.2), it can be seen that setting the bit in the ODR to 1 is done by writing a 1 to the corresponding bit in the BSRR. It is important to note that writing a 0 to this bit in the BSRR has no effect. This is the key advantage of these registers: there is no need to perform the three steps (read/mask/write) as when directly dealing with the ODR. Only writing a 1 in these registers affects the ODR.

To reset a bit in the ODR, the same principle is applied using the BRR. For the beginner, this can be confusing since resetting a bit in the ODR involves setting a bit in the BSRR to 1. It is essential to think not in terms of states, but in terms of actions (set and reset). It can also be observed that the reset function is somewhat duplicated since the 16 most significant bits of the BSRR have the same effect (combined using an OR gate), as the 16 least significant bits of the BRR. Therefore, in code example 4.1, all three instructions will have exactly the same effect.

```
/* Reset by reading / masking / writing to ODR    */
GPIOA->ODR  = (GPIOA->ODR & ~(0x01 << 9)) ;
/* Reset via BRR access */
GPIOA->BRR  = 0x01 << 9 ;
/* Reset via BSRR access /*/
GPIOA->BSRR  = 0x01 << (9 + 16) ;
```

Code 4.1. *Zeroing an output pin*

4 These registers remain accessible for reading, but the information retrieved in such a case has no meaningful value.

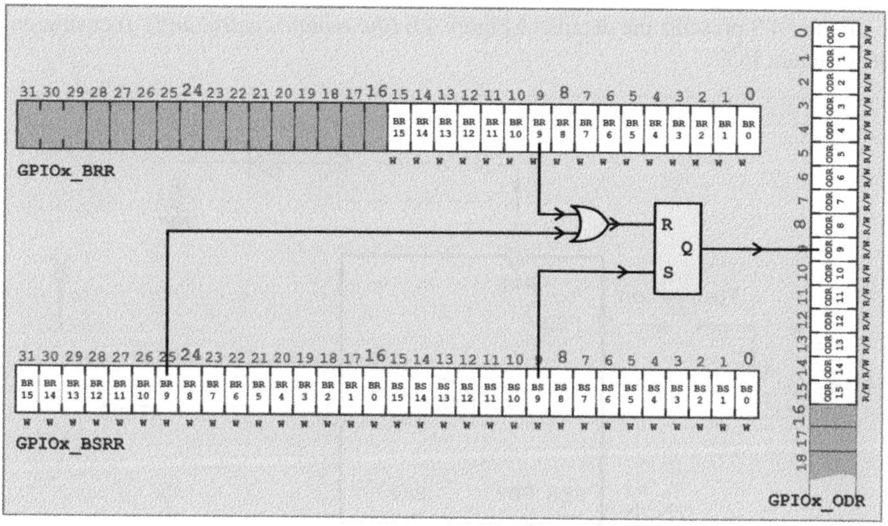

Figure 4.8. *Controlling an ODR bit via the BRR and BSRR (rank 9 pin example)*

If the program attempts to simultaneously set and reset a pin, it would not cause any issues, although this would not align with the typical operation of an R/S flip-flop. The set function would take priority, resulting in the corresponding ODR bit being set to 1.

The BSRR duplicates the reset functionality of the BRR. Therefore, it is possible to perform multiple set/reset operations on pins of the same port simultaneously with a single instruction. For certain applications, this synchronization is crucial.

4.4. Example

In the *guiding thread* example application, we will focus on the *remote control unit*. This unit requires a physical connection with:

– the temperature sensor, which communicates via I^{2}C;

– the HF transmitter/receiver, which communicates via UART;

– the infrared LED to control air conditioners;

– the microphone (via an amplifier) to receive feedback from the air conditioners;

– a *User* push-button for system reboot.

These various connections cover almost all possible GPIO configurations.

Figure 4.9 presents the details of Figure 1.6 (the *remote control unit*), focusing on the different I/O.

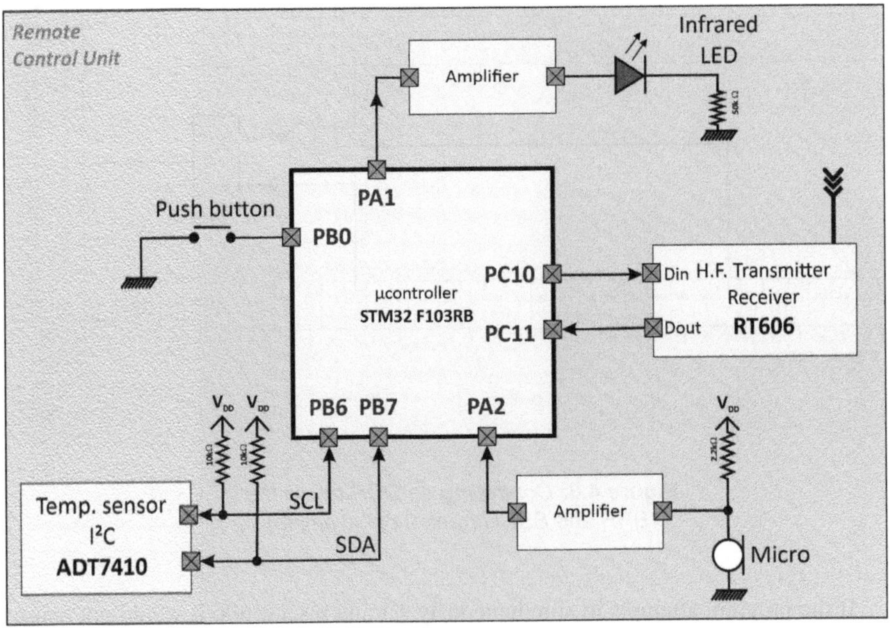

Figure 4.9. *Connections of a remote control unit on the STM32F103RB*

Let us list the different elements connected to this μcontroller:

– *The temperature sensor*: as we will see in Chapter 9, the I²C bus is a multi-master, multi-point bus. The SDA line transmits or receives data, while the SCL line transmits or receives clock pulses. To avoid any electrical conflict, as both lines are bidirectional, it is mandatory to use the *open drain* mode. In this application, we use I²C no. 1, with the SCL signal on the GPIOB.6 pin, and the SDA signal on the GPIOB.7 pin. These two pins must therefore be configured as *alternate output open drain* (CNF:MOD = $(11:10)_2$), since the I2C1 unit needs access to both pins. Note that, in this case, bits 6 and 7 of the ODR have no effect.

– *The HF transmitter/receiver via UART*: a UART unit (see Chapter 9) can be initially seen as a simple *Full-Duplex*[5] bus between two points. Two connections are used: Tx for transmitting data and Rx for receiving it. The Tx line can set a high or low logic level, and the UART receiver has corresponding reciprocal lines (Figure 4.9). The μcontroller has three USARTs, and we choose USART3. The *datasheet* indicates that

5 A *Full-Duplex* communication is a bidirectional communication that occurs simultaneously.

Tx is associated with GPIOC.10 and Rx is connected to GPIOC.11. The Din input of the HF transmitter/receiver does not draw any current and is floating type. Therefore, the configuration for Tx must be *alternate output push-pull* (CNF:MOD $= (10:10)_2$). Conversely, the Dout output can impose 3.3V or 0V, so the Rx input should be configured as *floating input*[6] (CNF:MOD $= (01:00)_2$).

– *Infrared LED*: the range of the IR LED must be sufficient, so the current passing through it is significant (typically 20 mA). An amplifier is required, and it has a high-impedance (floating) input. Additionally, the complex control of the LED is handled by software. Finally, the pin selection is not critical, we just have to check that the chosen I/O does not correspond to a specific function (like an oscillator or debug pin). We arbitrarily choose GPIOA.1. This pin will be configured as *output push-pull* (CNF:MOD $= (00:10)_2$) to impose both possible levels on the amplifier input. Thus, bit 1 of the ODR will control the LED.

– *Microphone*: it is connected to the input of an analog amplifier. The amplifier produces a continuous analog signal that varies between 0V and 3.3V depending on the sound level detected. To select the pin, it is sufficient to verify in the technical documentation that it is associated with an alternative ADC function. GPIOA.2 matches this specification, since it is connected to ADC input 2 and will be configured as an *analog input* (CNF:MOD $= (00:00)_2$).

– *User push-button*: this is a very simple configuration. The push-button is connected only to the input, and it can impose a level 0 when pressed. The choice of GPIOB.0 is arbitrary. To ensure a level 1 when the button is released, it is essential to configure the pin as *input pull-up* (CNF:MOD $= (10:00)_2$). The corresponding bit 0 in the ODR must also be set to select between *pull-up* and *pull-down* (ODR.0 $= 1$).

4.4.1. *Proposed solution*

To avoid making the explanation too lengthy, the proposed solution does not completely follow the recommendations from section 2.5. Only the driver layer and the application layer are included in the project to simplify the code.

For developing this example, the GPIO driver introduces six functions. The configuration part has been split into two functions: one for input configuration and one for output configuration. Additionally, a function has been added to toggle an output pin. Various constants have also been defined to list the different possible configuration options.

6 In this case, an *input pull-up* or *pull-down* configuration would also work, but it would be unnecessary.

```
void Port_IO_Set(GPIO_TypeDef * , int8_t);
void Port_IO_Reset(GPIO_TypeDef * , int8_t);
unsigned int Port_IO_Toggle(GPIO_TypeDef * ,int8_t);
unsigned int Port_IO_Read(GPIO_TypeDef * , int8_t);
void GPIO_Conf_In(GPIO_TypeDef * , int8_t , int );
void GPIO_Conf_Out(GPIO_TypeDef * , int8_t , int );

/* Techno for input pin (INPUT) */
#define ANALOG 0
#define INPUT_FLOATING 1
#define INPUT_PULL_DOWN 2
#define INPUT_PULL_UP 3

/* Techno for output pin (OUTPUT) */
#define OUTPUT_PPULL 0
#define OUTPUT_OPDRAIN 1
#define ALT_PPULL 2
#define ALT_OPDRAIN 3
```

Code 4.2. *Header file Pilot_IO.h*

The corresponding C file for this *header* is provided in code example 4.3. The comments in this example help to understand the techniques and programming choices made.

```
#include <stm32f10x.h> /* Peripheral registers of the stm_32 */
#include "pilot_IO.h"

/*********************************************/
/* Input configuration function for          */
/* a pin of a port                           */
/*********************************************/
void GPIO_Conf_In(GPIO_TypeDef * Port, int8_t Pin, int Techno)
{
  char CoNF;

  /* Enabling clocks for GPIOA, GPIOB and GPIOC */
  if (Port == GPIOA) (RCC->APB2ENR) |= RCC_APB2ENR_IOPAEN;
  if (Port == GPIOB) (RCC->APB2ENR) |= RCC_APB2ENR_IOPBEN;
  if (Port == GPIOC) (RCC->APB2ENR) |= RCC_APB2ENR_IOPCEN;

  CoNF = Techno;
  /* CNF field is identical in pull-up and pull-down */
  if (Techno == 3) CoNF = 2;

```

```
  /* Configuration according to the required techno and the pin
      */
    if (Pin < 8)  /* We must refer to GPIO_CRL */
      {
      /* We clear the 2 bits of MOD => Input */
      Port->CRL = (Port->CRL)&~(0x3<<(4*Pin));
      /* Writing the CNF value */
      /* Setting the 2-bit field to 0 */
      Port->CRL = (Port->CRL) & ~(0x3<<(4*Pin)+2);
      /* then setting the necessary bits to 1 */
      Port->CRL = (Port->CRL) | CoNF<<(4*Pin+2);
      }
    else /* We must refer to GPIO_CRH */
      {
      /* We must refer to GPIO_CRH */
      /* Additionally, shift by -8 on the pin number */
      Port->CRH = (Port->CRH) & ~(0x3<<(4*(Pin-8)));
      /* clearing the field */
      Port->CRH = (Port->CRH)&~(0x3<<(4*(Pin-8)+2));
      /* writing the value */
      Port->CRH = (Port->CRH) | CoNF<<(4*(Pin-8)+2);
      }
      /* Setting up the pull-up or pull-down option */
    if (Techno == 2)
        Port->ODR = (Port->ODR) &~ (0x1<<(Pin)); /*pull-down*/
    if (Techno == 3)
        Port->ODR = (Port->ODR) |  (0x1<<(Pin)); /*pull-up*/
  }

  /*************************************************/
  /*  Output configuration function (2MHz)    */
  /*  for a pin of a port
                                                 */
  /*************************************************/
void GPIO_Conf_Out(GPIO_TypeDef * Port, int8_t Pin, int Techno)
  {
    /* Enabling clocks for GPIOA, GPIOB and GPIOC */
    if (Port == GPIOA) (RCC->APB2ENR) |= RCC_APB2ENR_IOPAEN;
    if (Port == GPIOB) (RCC->APB2ENR) |= RCC_APB2ENR_IOPBEN;
    if (Port == GPIOC) (RCC->APB2ENR) |= RCC_APB2ENR_IOPCEN;

  /* Configuration according to the required techno and the pin*/
    if (Pin < 8) /* We must refer to GPIO_CRL */
      {
      /* MOD = 0b10 => 2MHz output */
      Port->CRL = (Port->CRL) & ~(0x3<<(4*Pin));
      Port->CRL = (Port->CRL) | 0x2 <<(4*Pin);

      /* CNF based on the chosen techno */
      /* clearing the field */
```

```
        Port->CRL = (Port->CRL)&~(0x3<<(4*Pin+2));
        /* writing the bits to set to 1 */
        Port->CRL = (Port->CRL) | Techno<<(4*Pin+2);
        }
    else /* We must refer to GPIO_CRH */
    /* Additionally, shift by -8 on the pin number */
        {
        Port->CRH = (Port->CRH) & ~(0x3<<(4*(Pin-8)));
        Port->CRH = (Port->CRH) | 0x2 <<(4*(Pin-8));

        /* CNF based on the chosen techno */
        /* clearing the field */
        Port->CRH = (Port->CRH)&~(0x3<<(4*(Pin-8)+2));
        /* writing the bits to set to 1 */
        Port->CRH = (Port->CRH) | Techno<<(4*(Pin-8)+2);
        }
  }

  /**************************************************/
  /*  Function to set a pin to 1                    */
  /**************************************************/
void Port_IO_Set(GPIO_TypeDef * Port, int8_t Pin)
   {
     /* Checking that the pin number is correct */
     if (Pin < 16)
     /* Direct by setting the BS part of BSRR */
     Port->BSRR = 0x01 << Pin ;
   }

  /**************************************************/
  /*  Function to set a pin to 0                    */
  /**************************************************/
void Port_IO_Reset(GPIO_TypeDef * Port, int8_t Pin)
   {
     /* Checking that the pin number is correct */
     if (Pin < 16)
    /* Direct by setting the BRR */
      Port->BRR = 0x01 << Pin ;
   }

  /**************************************************/
  /*  Function to toggle a pin                      */
  /*  Returns the state of the pin after execution  */
  /**************************************************/
unsigned int Port_IO_Toggle(GPIO_TypeDef * Port, int8_t Pin)
   {
     /* Checking that the pin number is correct */
     if (Pin < 16)
     /* Toggling by using an exclusive OR */
      Port->ODR = Port->ODR ^ (0x01 << Pin) ;
```

```
    /* The state of the pin is returned */
    /*  Filtering the bit with an & mask*/
    /*  Shifting the bit to the right to place */
    /*   => the result on bit 0 */
    return ( (Port->ODR & (0x01 << Pin)) >> Pin) ;
  }

/*****************************************************************/
/*  Function to read from a pin                                  */
/*****************************************************************/
unsigned int Port_IO_Read(GPIO_TypeDef * Port, int8_t Pin)
  {
    return (unsigned int) (Port->IDR & (0x01 << Pin) >> Pin);
  }
```

Code 4.3. *Pilot_IO.c file*

In the end, considering the functions of the driver, the application is coded with just a few lines, as shown in code example 4.4, first chaining calls to the initialization functions.

```
#include "stm32f10x.h"
#include "pilot_IO.h"

int main(void)
{
  /*********************************************************/
  /*   ==== IO CONFIGURATION ====                          */
  /*                                                       */
  /*      I2C temperature sensor                           */
  /*    PB6 (SCL): Alternate Output Open Drain             */
  /*    PB7 (SDA): Alternate Output Open Drain             */
  /*      IR transmitter / receiver                        */
  /*    PC10 (Tx): Alternate Output Push-pull              */
  /*    PC11 (Rx): floating input                          */
  /*      Infrared LED                                     */
  /*    PA1 (LED): Output Push-pull                        */
  /*      Microphone                                       */
  /*     PA2 (MIC): Analog input                           */
  /*       UserBP                                          */
  /*     PB0 (User_BP): Input pull-up                      */
  /*********************************************************/

  /* I2C temperature sensor */
  GPIO_Conf_Out(GPIOB, 6, ALT_OPDRAIN);
  GPIO_Conf_Out(GPIOB, 7, OUTPUT_OPDRAIN);
  /* IR transmitter/receiver */
  GPIO_Conf_Out(GPIOC, 10, ALT_PPULL);
```

```
    GPIO_Conf_In(GPIOC, 11, INPUT_FLOATING);
    /* Infrared LED */
    GPIO_Conf_Out(GPIOA, 1, OUTPUT_PPULL);
    /* Microphone */
    GPIO_Conf_In(GPIOA, 2, ANALOG);
    /* UserBP */
    GPIO_Conf_In(GPIOB, 0, INPUT_PULL_UP);

    /*******************************************/
    /*   ==== WAIT FOR USER BUTTON PRESS ====    */
    /*******************************************/

    while (Port_IO_Read(GPIOB,0) == 0x01)
    {}

    /*******************************************/
    /*   ==== SET TO 1 THEN TO 0 for IR LED ==== */
    /*******************************************/
      Port_IO_Set(GPIOA,1);     /* Turn on the IR LED */
    Port_IO_Reset(GPIOA,1);   /* Turn off the IR LED */

    while(1);    /* Infinite loop */
}
```

Code 4.4. *Main_IO.c file*

Next, the state of the push-button is detected[7]. This is determined by using the appropriate Port_IO_Read() function. The code is designed to wait for the button to be pressed, meaning the bit goes to 0, since the button is in *pull-up* configuration, making it active low. Finally, the program turns the IR LED on and off. Again, the goal here is to illustrate the simple control of an I/O, deviating from the expectations of the *guiding thread* example.

4.4.2. *Comments*

Here are a few comments regarding this proposed solution:

– The driver is, of course, largely incomplete. Additional necessary functions still need to be developed to account for all the possibilities offered by an STM32 in terms of the GPIO. However, it has been written with as much generality as possible to truly function as a driver. For example, the configuration functions are not specific to the application and can be used in any service layer since all configurations are considered.

7 It would be wise to configure this push-button with an interrupt, as we will see in Chapter 5.

– For the output configurations, the choice to impose the maximum frequency at 2 MHz is arbitrary, excluding the two other possibilities (50 and 10 MHz) for simplicity.

– The driver does not handle inconsistencies or errors in calls. For example, one could request the configuration of the GPIOB.47 pin with a technology value of 7, and the driver would not raise an issue. This could lead to execution with faulty results. In a more general framework, it would be prudent and useful to "lock down" the code.

4.5. Unaddressed points regarding GPIOs

There are still some aspects to explore to fully cover the topic of GPIOs. We will only briefly mention them here, as they fall under advanced usage of the μcontroller. We assume that readers who have understood the material presented so far will be able to find the necessary information in the documentation to implement these features.

Here are the points that would require further exploration:

1) A specific GPIO register has not been discussed: the GPIO_LCKR register. As its name suggests (LCKR for *LoCK Register*), the bits in this register allow locking the configuration of a pin, thus preventing any unintended or accidental changes to it.

2) There is also the topic of AFIO (Alternate Function Input/Output). Apart from a small part concerning external oscillators, these registers are involved in two distinct cases:

- Pin *remapping*: as previously mentioned (Chapter 3), each pin is connected to one or more alternative functions. For example, in the STM32F013, the GPIOB.8 pin corresponds to Timer 4 channel 3, and the GPIOA.9 pin corresponds either to the USART1 Tx transmission signal or to Timer 4 channel 2. All of this is clearly referenced in the *datasheet*, and readers will find the meaning of these signals in the upcoming chapters. *Remapping* involves choosing an alternative to the initial mapping for certain peripheral units. However, not all remappings are possible! Only a few rare possibilities, again clearly documented, are allowed. The AFIO registers enable these limited *remappings*, such as for USART1, which is by default on GPIOA.9 for Tx and GPIOA.10 for Rx, which can be remapped to GPIOB.6 for Tx and GPIOB.7 for Rx, as an example.

- Using GPIO inputs directly to generate interrupt requests. This point will be detailed in Chapter 5.

5

Interrupt and DMA Management

A μcontroller is equipped with peripheral units that enable it to control an embedded system. These units are highly specialized and possess a certain degree of autonomy in their tasks. Interrupts and direct memory access (DMA) facilitate this autonomy and significantly reduce the workload of the central processing unit. For example, it is unnecessary for the CPU to monitor the arrival of a character on a serial interface if an interrupt system can notify it of such an event. Similarly, why require the CPU to read and store the latest analog-to-digital conversion (ADC) in memory if the dedicated unit can perform this transfer directly to memory via DMA?

In this chapter, we delve into these two techniques in detail, starting with interrupts.

5.1. General exceptions and particular interrupts

What happens when a μcontroller is powered on? What does the processor do after pressing the Reset button? How does the architecture handle situations where the program attempts to execute an unfeasible instruction (e.g. when the memory address of the targeted operand does not exist)? How does the μcontroller process interrupt requests from a peripheral (e.g. generated by the USART after receiving a character on its Rx line)?

The answers to all these questions lie in understanding the concept of exceptions in general and interrupts in particular, interrupts being a specific type of exception corresponding to a request from a peripheral. Since interrupts represent the cases that need to be anticipated and programmed in an application, this is the only term that we will use throughout this book.

For a color version of all the Codes in this chapter, see www.iste.co.uk/mahout/programming.zip

The techniques used to handle interrupts are generally similar across processors. While the number and specific functions can vary significantly from one chip to another, the way that they are dealt with will always be similar. In this book, we focus on the specific STM32F10x case, but the fundamental principles presented here are broadly applicable and easily transferable to a wide range of other μcontrollers.

The core idea is to redirect the normal execution flow of the processor, when an interrupt-type event occurs, to a routine specifically written to handle that event. By definition, these events are asynchronous and, although it is often technically possible, it is impractical in general to call these routines programmatically. *Their triggering is hardware-driven.* This characteristic is what makes the development (and particularly the debugging) of a *Bare Metal* application distinct from standard programming. The concept of a routine being triggered without an explicit call from another part of the program can be confusing at first.

Interrupts are, therefore, a fundamental mechanism of a μcontroller. They are the only means by which various peripheral units can alert the core that their "state" requires a specific response or action.

5.2. *Resets* and interrupt vector tables

Let us begin with what happens when the μcontroller is powered on, which is the same process triggered by pressing the reset button[1]. The μcontroller must become operational as quickly as possible and achieve a deterministic state. This requires three things:

1) all registers must be initialized with a known default value;

2) the system stack pointer must be assigned to a valid RAM address;

3) the instruction pointer must point to a memory address containing the instructions for the initialization sequence.

The first requirement is fulfilled at every restart, and the default values assigned to various registers (whether for the core or peripherals) are detailed in the documentation. The other two requirements are slightly more complex. While it might be feasible to design the μcontroller such that it mandates a fixed memory address for startup, this is generally not the approach taken. Since memory configurations can vary across different versions of the μcontroller, the startup address is instead specified in the *Interrupt Vector Table* (IVT).

5.2.1. *Stack pointers and program counters*

Before delving into the contents and role of an interrupt vector table, let us first revisit the roles of the stack pointer and the program counter (PC).

1 There are, in fact, nuances in the possible reset sources, which we will discuss in Chapter 10.

A *system stack* is a *LIFO* (*Last In, First Out*) data structure located in RAM memory (and so is accessible for both reading and writing). A *LIFO* structure operates like a stack of plates in a cupboard: when adding a new plate, it is always placed on top of the stack and, when retrieving one, it is also the topmost plate that is taken. Thus, the first plate taken out (*First Out*) is the last one placed on the stack (*Last In*). Using this household analogy, it becomes clear that problems arise if the stack reaches the top of the cupboard or if one wants to set the table and finds the cupboard empty. In computing terms, these scenarios correspond to an *overflow* or *underflow* of the storage space allocated for the *LIFO* stack.

In its basic operation, this data area is shared across all application routines and serves three primary purposes: temporary data storage, the creation of local variables and the passing of arguments to functions. The *stack pointer (SP)* indicates the current address within the memory area reserved for the system stack. When an interrupt is triggered, the first of these three purposes comes into play. The processor saves a set of registers onto the stack to restore them later, ensuring it can resume its work in the same state as before the interrupt. Notably, it saves the current address of the instruction being executed before the interruption, so that it knows where to resume normal execution once the interrupt handling is complete.

The PC holds the address (in Flash memory) of the instruction currently being executed. During a redirection caused by an interrupt, this pointer must be updated with the address of the routine written to handle the specific interrupt.

Both of these pointers must therefore be initialized during startup. For the STM32F10x, the initialization values for these two pointers are found at the eight lowest addresses in memory. Recall that a memory address corresponds to a single byte of data, and that the registers are 32 bits wide. Initialization involves reading these 2–4 addresses[2]. Once these two assignments are made, the μcontroller is "ready for operation".

5.2.2. *IVT contents*

The ARM© architecture mandates that the IVT is located at the lowest addresses in memory, starting at 0×00000000. Upon a reset, the μcontroller reads from these low addresses. Given the Harvard architecture, these addresses correspond to code addresses and are thus stored in Flash memory.

For the Cortex-M3 architecture, as used in the STM3210x series, the IVT is structured as shown in Figure 5.1.

2 This process requires two clock cycles, as the processor can only read 32 bits at a time, which are stored across four consecutive addresses.

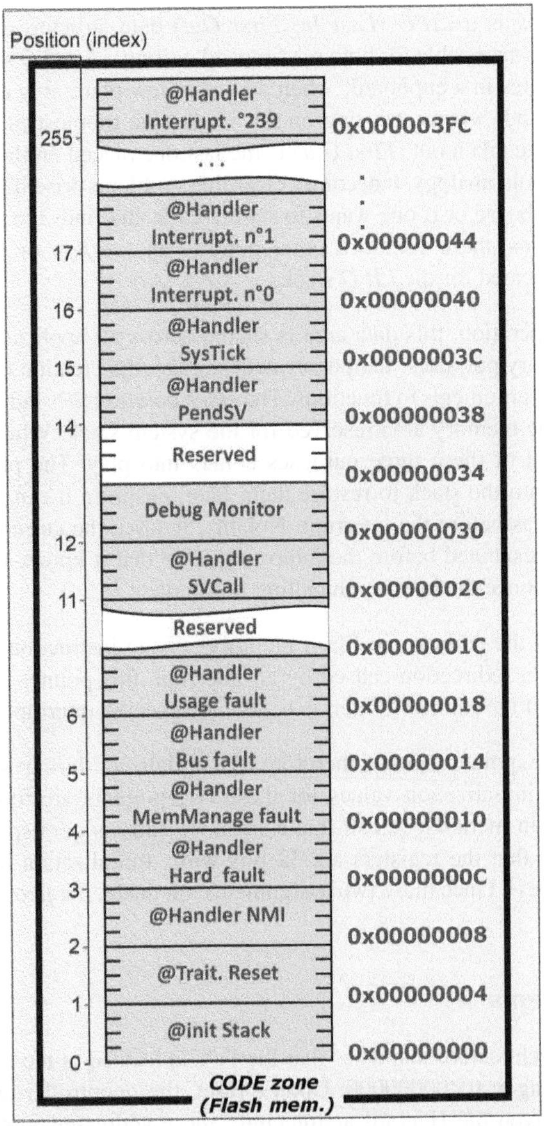

Figure 5.1. *Composition of the Interrupt Vector Table for a Cortex-M3*

Let us clarify the contents of this table.

The first two 32-bit integers contained in this IVT are the address of the memory stack that initializes the SP and the address of the reset handler routine.

Subsequently, it consists of *nine entries corresponding to various exception cases* with some slots set to zero (unused) to occupy a total of 14 memory locations, each holding 32-bit data. While we will not delve into the specifics of these exception cases here, we briefly remind readers of their general purpose; for those interested in a more detailed explanation, we recommend referring to Mahout (2011).

– NMI (2): an unmaskable interrupt, essentially a "super interrupt" with the highest priority. Its priority level is fixed and cannot be modified. In the STM32 case, it is directly linked to the reset and clock control (RCC) module to signal errors related to external clock signals.

– Hard Fault (3): this highly critical exception could also be called a *double fault* since it is triggered when a Memory Management Fault, a Bus Fault or a Usage Fault occurs, but the handling of the fault fails to resolve the issue.

– Mem Manage Fault (4): this corresponds to a memory management issue, but it can only occur if a Memory Management Unit (MMU) is present, which is not addressed here.

– Bus Fault (5): this fault, which sometimes arises during the development phase of an application, is triggered when the processor is unable to fetch an instruction or perform a data read/write operation. A typical trigger is an improper pointer handling.

– Usage Fault (6): this exception is triggered when the execution of the current instruction cannot be completed. The two most common cases are division by zero and misaligned data access[3].

– SVCall (11): a System Service Call is a specific functionality designed to create an operating system, enabling faster and more systematic deployment of various applications. A special assembly instruction, SVC no. i, triggers the interrupt with service no. i of the OS thus created. It is, in a way, a sort of software interrupt.

– Debug Monitor (12): triggered in an interrupt-driven manner to enter Debug mode. The exception routine must then handle various debugging requests.

– PendSV (14): similar to SVCall, but triggered by the pending state of this exception rather than through an instruction.

– SysTick (15): an interrupt requested by the internal Timer of the Cortex. Unlike the previous exceptions, which are related to issues or advanced processor usage, this one could be useful to the programmer. This Timer operation will be detailed in section 6.3.

The IVT, as initially designed by ARM©, can contain up to 240 possible interrupt entries, allowing for up to 240 different requests from peripheral units. The actual

3 R/W access must be aligned, meaning a 16-bit data access requires an even address, and a 32-bit data access requires a doubly even address (divisible by 4).

number of entries depends on the number of peripheral units present in the μcontroller. For the STM32F10x series, the typical number of utilized entries is "only" 59.

5.3. Principle of redirection and the role of the NVIC

Let us now examine the conditions required for an interrupt request to be accepted and what happens during the redirection process. It is clearly inconceivable for any peripheral unit to trigger an interrupt arbitrarily at any time or under any circumstances. Strict validation rules are necessary, if only to prevent erratic triggering. These rules and their implementation fall under the responsibility of the *NVIC* (Nested Vectored Interrupt Controller).

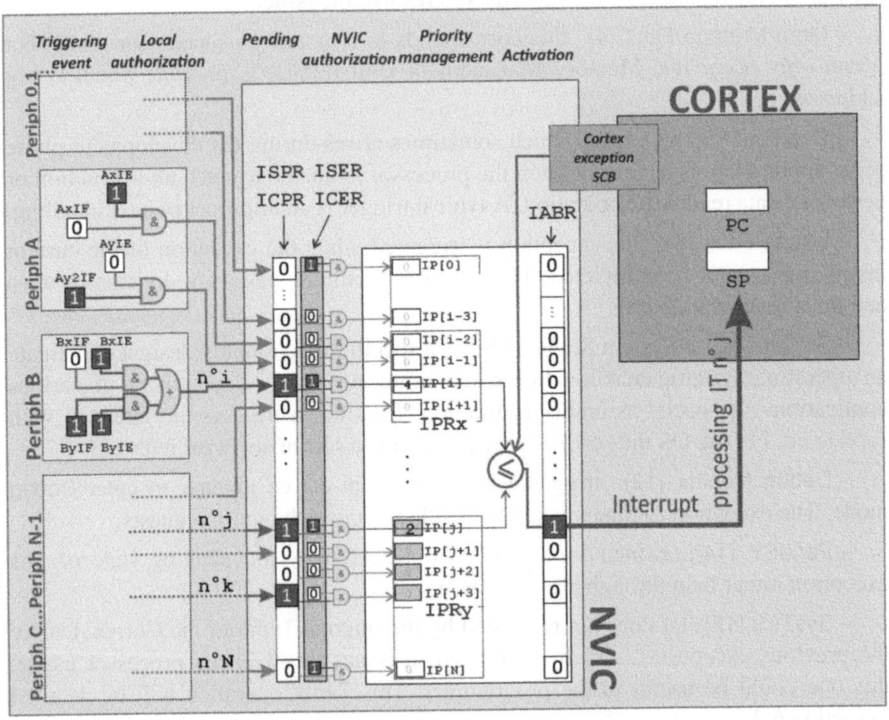

Figure 5.2. *Hardware processing of an interrupt request*

5.3.1. *NVIC*

First and foremost, it is important to note that this unit is specific to the Cortex, designed by ARM©. Consequently, it is present in all μcontrollers based on this core. Beyond this generic aspect, there are a few implications for the programmer. First, regarding documentation, while the *Reference Manual* STMicroelectronics (2011) mentions this unit, all the necessary details can be found in the Cortex documentation STMicroelectronics (2013). Another key point is that all the C structures and #define directives related to this unit are grouped in the *header* file of the core, rather than in that of the μcontroller[4].

5.3.1.1. *Its role*

The role of the NVIC is to receive, authorize and prioritize various interrupt requests, whether they originate from the Cortex itself or from peripheral units, and to initiate a redirection procedure if necessary. For peripheral units, it acts as an intermediary between them and the Cortex, as illustrated in Figure 5.2.

5.3.1.2. *Its main registers*

The NVIC registers are organized into six tables and one register. The structure declaration that provides access to these registers is shown in the code example 5.1.

```
typedef struct
{
  __IOM uint32_t ISER[8U];   /* Interrupt Set Enable Register    */
        uint32_t RESERVED0[24U];
  __IOM uint32_t ICER[8U];   /* Interrupt Clear Enable Register  */
        uint32_t RESERVED1[24U];
  __IOM uint32_t ISPR[8U];   /* Interrupt Set Pending Register   */
        uint32_t RESERVED2[24U];
  __IOM uint32_t ICPR[8U];   /* Interrupt Clear Pending Register */
        uint32_t RESERVED3[24U];
  __IOM uint32_t IABR[8U];   /* Interrupt Active bit Register    */
        uint32_t RESERVED4[56U];
          /*  Note here: 8 bits */
  __IOM uint8_t  IP[240U];   /* Interrupt Priority Register      */

        uint32_t RESERVED5[644U];
  __OM  uint32_t STIR;       /* Software Trigger Interrupt Register */
} NVIC_Type;
```

Code 5.1. *NVIC structure declarations*

It is important to note in this declaration that the NVIC resembles a Swiss cheese, as many intermediate addresses (796 reserved int places, or a total of 3,184 addresses) are "reserved".

4 In the Keil IDE, these two files are core_cm3.h and stm32f10x.h.

The first five tables (NVIC_ISPR, NVIC_ICPR, NVIC_ISER, NVIC_ICER and NVIC_IABR) each contain eight elements. However, on the STM32, only three of these elements are actually used in each table. This is because the largest STM32 devices support up to 81 possible interrupts. Figure 5.3 illustrates each of these tables. Finally, since the STM32F10x family is limited to 59 interrupt lines, only two elements are actually relevant, as shown in Figure 5.3. The IP pseudo-registers will be explained and illustrated in section 5.3.3.

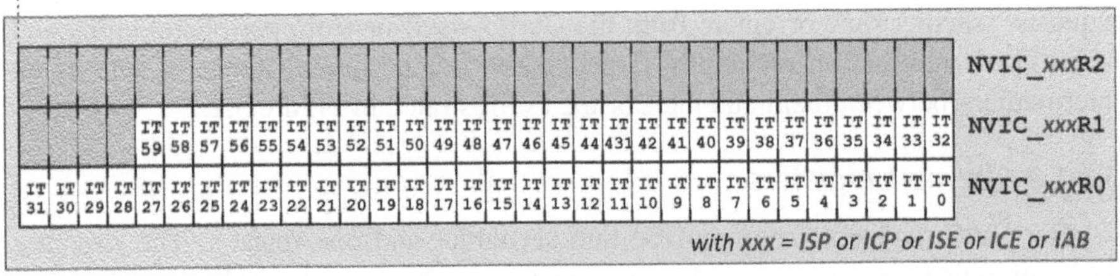

Figure 5.3. *Composition of the Cortex NVIC register groups. SFM32F10X case (excluding the connectivity line series)*

An additional register (STIR) allows the software-triggering (by writing the desired interrupt number into it) of a specific interrupt. As this triggering mode is quite unusual, we will not elaborate on it here.

5.3.2. *Conditions for an interrupt to be accepted*

Let us revisit Figure 5.2 to understand the "path" that an interrupt request follows. On the far left of the figure, we find the peripherals. The following chapters will detail the events that trigger these requests, but from a computing perspective, this is represented by setting a bit to 1 in a register. For all peripherals, there are always multiple possible causes. Here, Periph A is illustrated with triggers AxIF[5] and AyIF, while Periph B has triggers BxIF and ByIF.

Each of these causes can be disabled locally (on the peripheral side), which is the default state. For this purpose, an *Enable* bit is used, which, when combined with the request bit via an AND gate, either blocks or allows the request. In the figure, these are represented by the bits AxIE[6], AyIE, BxIE and ByIE. There are many scenarios where an event (e.g. AxIF) might occur but does not require any specific handling.

---

5 In most cases, the names of the existing bits will include the letters IF which stand for *Interrupt Flag*.

6 Here, IE stands for *Interrupt Enable*.

If a request is made and local validation is successful (as is the case for the ByIF and ByIE pair in the figure), the request – or more precisely, the number assigned to the request for each peripheral – is transmitted to the NVIC. Depending on the configuration, peripherals may have a single assigned number (as with Periph B, which is the most common case) or multiple numbers (as with Periph A).

Caution, it is necessary to add 16 to the transmitted number to find the index of the interrupt in the IVT[7]. For example, Timer 2 has an interrupt request number of 28, which corresponds to the 44th entry in the IVT. This distinction is important because, depending on the context, the offset of 16 between the table index and the interrupt number must be taken into account (see Figure 5.1).

If multiple causes generate the same interrupt vector, it will be the responsibility of the *handler* to determine in software by checking the *status register* of the relevant peripheral, which source triggered the request by testing the various trigger bits.

When the request reaches the NVIC, a bit is set in the NVIC_ISPR registers, known as the *Pending* register. Importantly, the disappearance of the cause does not clear the corresponding bit in the NVIC_ISPR register, which functions as a set-only register. The bit will only be cleared if the interrupt transitions to the *Active* state or if the corresponding bit in the NVIC_ICPR reset register is set to 1. However – this point is critical – *it is the responsibility of the handler to clear the cause of the interrupt*[8], which generally involves resetting the xxIF bit to 0, otherwise the cause is still active and the request will be re-triggered as soon as the previous request has been processed.

Finally, note that the NVIC_ISPR registers are writable; therefore, it is possible to trigger an interrupt in software by writing to the appropriate bit in an NVIC_ISPR register. While this is not a common practice, it can be very useful during debugging or testing phases.

A second level of validation is ensured by the NVIC. Similarly to the validation of triggers at the peripheral level, each interrupt line must be validated through its corresponding bit in one of the NVIC_ISER registers. These registers, along with their counterparts NVIC_ICER, function similarly to the *Pending* registers. Validation is performed by setting the corresponding bit in the NVIC_ISER register, while invalidation is done by writing a 1 to the corresponding bit in the NVIC_ICER register.

In the example shown in Figure 5.2, units numbered i, j and k issue requests. On the NVIC side, validation has been granted for lines 0, i, j and N. Line k, however,

7 This offset of 16 entries corresponds to various exceptions, as shown in Figure 5.1.

8 If the *handler* has been called, it means that the interrupt has entered the *Active* state, and therefore the *Pending* bit has been cleared to 0.

is blocked, and its request cannot proceed as long as the corresponding validation bit remains 0. Thus, two requests, no. i and no. j, are transmitted.

At this point, the priority level comes into play. Priority management will be explained in the next section, but the basic principle is that the highest priority prevails, setting the corresponding bit in the NVIC_IABR register to 1. This action triggers the redirection procedure. It is worth noting that multiple bits across the NVIC_IABR registers can be set to 1 simultaneously, indicating that an interrupt currently being handled was itself interrupted by a higher priority interrupt request.

Table 5.1 summarizes all possible actions using the various NVIC registers.

<table>
<tr><th>Register</th><th>Role</th><th>Writing the bit to 1</th><th>Writing the bit to 0</th><th>Reading a bit set to 1</th><th>Reading a bit set to 0</th></tr>
<tr><td>NVIC_ISPR</td><td>Set Pending</td><td>Pending state</td><td rowspan="4">No effect</td><td rowspan="2">IT is pending</td><td rowspan="2">IT is not pending</td></tr>
<tr><td>NVIC_ICPR</td><td>Clear Pending</td><td>Clear pending state</td></tr>
<tr><td>NVIC_ISER</td><td>Set Enable</td><td>IT validation</td><td rowspan="2">IT request will be accepted</td><td rowspan="2">IT request will not be accepted</td></tr>
<tr><td>NVIC_ICER</td><td>Clear Enable</td><td>IT invalidation</td></tr>
<tr><td>NVIC_IABR</td><td>Active Bit</td><td colspan="2">Impossible</td><td>Active IT</td><td>Inactive IT</td></tr>
</table>

Table 5.1. *Summary of interrupt registers*

5.3.3. *Priority management*

The Cortex-M3 architecture provides an advanced priority management system with the concept of groups and subgroups. It also allows chip manufacturers to use this core design to choose the number of priority levels they wish to implement. ARM specifies that each vector has a priority level, which can be encoded using up to 8 bits. Each of these priority level values is stored in one of the bytes of the 32-bit NVIC_IPR registers (see section 5.4).

Two extremely important points must be considered to correctly assign a priority level to an interrupt line:

– *The highest priority level is assigned the lowest value*, which is not the immediate logic.

– If the processor does not utilize the full capacity of the Cortex (i.e. only a portion of the 8 bits is used), *the most significant bits are only taken into account.*

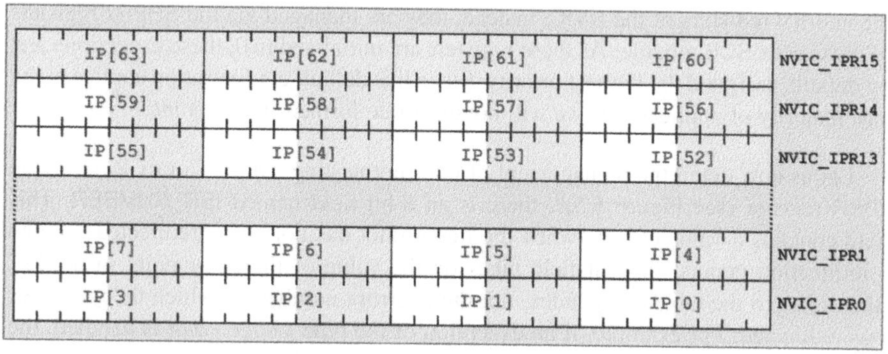

Figure 5.4. *IPR priority registers of the NVIC for the STM32F10x*

For the design of its STM32, STmicro© chose to consider only 81 vectors. Similarly, it opted for a priority encoding with only 16 levels (so represented using 4 bits). In this case, the significant bits for the priority level are those in positions 4–7.

Figure 5.4 illustrates the 32-bit NVIC_IPR registers and their division into 8-bit pseudo-registers, NVIC_IP. Only these NVIC_IP registers are declared in code example 5.1. In this figure, interrupts with numbers higher than 59 are grayed out because, although they exist in the Cortex architecture, they are not implemented on the STM32F10x. Similarly, the lower 4 bits of each byte are grayed out, as the μcontroller under consideration here supports only 16 priority levels.

Let us revisit code example 5.1, line 14: the primary interest of dividing the registers into bytes (more specifically uint8_t) instead of into int (uint32_t) for accessing the priority registers is that it provides a direct correlation between the interrupt number and the corresponding IP sub-register. Setting the priority level k (where $0 \leq k \leq 16$) for the interrupt number N (where $N < 60$) can be coded simply as:

```
/* A 4-bit shift to assign the most significant bits */
NVIC->IP[N] = k << 4;
```

Code 5.2. *Assigning the priority level*

Regarding priority levels, three exceptions have fixed priority levels that cannot be modified: the Reset vector with a priority level of -3, the NMI with a priority level of -2 and the Hard_fault vector with a priority level of -1. Since these levels are negative, they will always have higher priority than all other interrupts. The priority levels of the six other exceptions (see section 5.2.2) are configurable, but not through the internal registers of the NVIC. Instead, they are managed via the SHPRx registers of the Cortex SCB module. As these registers are initialized to 0, these exceptions are, by default, assigned the highest priority. Since this default configuration applies to the vast majority of applications, we will not elaborate further on this point.

Let us now detail the management of interrupt nesting. At the Cortex level, in the xPSR register (see Figure 5.5)[9], there is an 8-bit field named ISR_NUMBER. This field contains a value of zero when the μcontroller has not been "redirected". When a redirection occurs, this bit field takes on the value of the entry point in the IVT (this refers to the table entry index, not the interrupt number) to which the processor was redirected. For example, if an exception of the type *Usage Fault* is handled, the ISR_NUMBER field will take the value 6, as this exception corresponds to the sixth entry (i.e. the index in Figure 5.1) of the table.

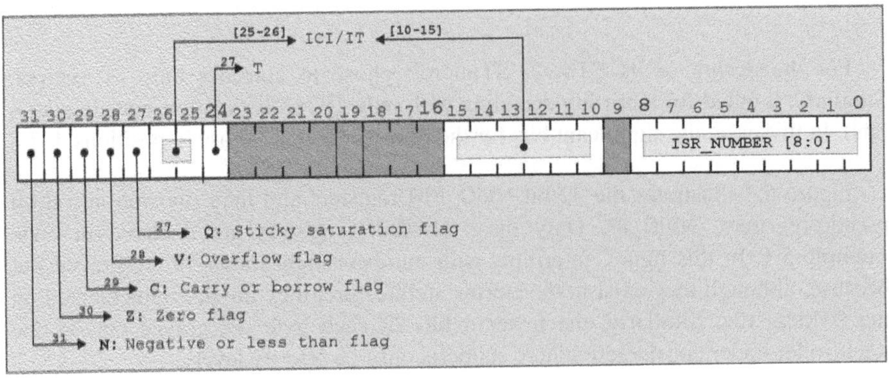

Figure 5.5. *xPSR register of the Cortex-M3*

When an interrupt request arrives, it is set to the *Pending* state. If the ISR field is zero (indicating no current redirection), the request transitions directly to the *Active* state. If this is not the case, the NVIC compares its priority level with the currently active one. If the new request has a higher priority (i.e. a lower numerical value), the NVIC triggers a new redirection, thereby interrupting the currently executing *handler*. The interrupted handler will resume once the new interrupt has been fully processed. This cascading of interruptions reflects the *Nested* nature of the interrupt manager.

9 This register notably contains the classic flags (N, C, V, Z), which are updated to provide a status report on the execution of an instruction.

Figure 5.6 illustrates the principle of nested calls. In this diagram, time progresses vertically from top to bottom. Four units are involved: the Cortex and the NVIC, as well as, for the sake of the example, two Timer units. Initially, Timer 2 (interrupt no. 28, corresponding to index 44 in the IVT), which has been programmed with a priority level of 4, triggers its event (here represented by the UIF bit being set to 1, indicating a counter overflow). The Cortex redirects to the *handler* for this Timer, and the ISR bit field is set to 44. Processing is completed before any other requests arrive, and the Cortex returns to its previous normal state afterward. In a second scenario, another request from the Timer causes a new redirection. However, this time, during the execution of the *handler*, a request from Timer 3 arrives. Since Timer 3 has been programmed in this example with a priority level of 2, which is higher than level 4, another redirection occurs, with the ISR field changing to 45. The end of the Timer 3 *handler* allows the sequence of the Timer 2 *handler* to resume, which itself concludes with a return to the normal state.

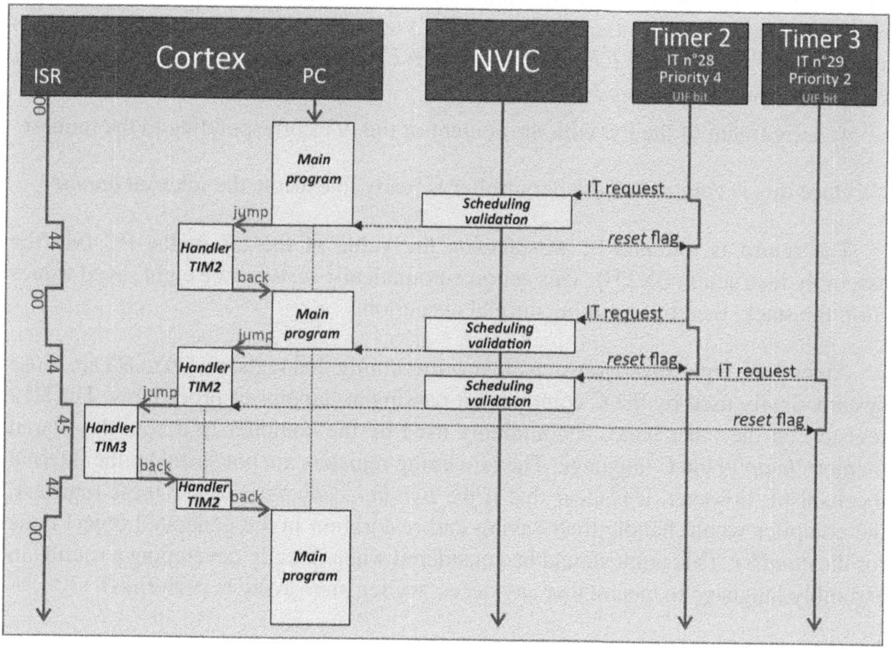

Figure 5.6. *Priority management*

An interrupt request at the same level as the current level does not trigger a new redirection. However, in the event that two interrupts of the same level occur simultaneously, the interrupt with the lower index will take priority.

5.3.4. *Redirection process steps*

Let us conclude the description of the redirection mechanism by detailing the steps involved. When the redirection order reaches the Cortex, it performs the following actions:

1) completion of the current instruction in assembly language;

2) saving eight specific registers to the stack, in the stacking order: *xPSR, PC, LR, R12, R3, R2, R1, R0* and *LR*. At this point, the original stack is in the state depicted in Figure 5.7 when the interrupt service routine starts;

3) assignment of the LR with a return code that allows the processor to correctly return from the exception. Unlike many other architectures, this processor does not have a dedicated instruction for exception return. Instead, the standard assembly instruction BX LR is used. This instruction loads the instruction pointer PC with the value contained in the LR. Special values are therefore defined to enable the interrupt return mechanism when assigned to the PC via the LR. Only three specific values are allowed[10]: $0{\times}FFFFFFF1$, $0{\times}FFFFFFF9$ or $0{\times}FFFFFFFD$; any other value will result in a *Usage Fault*;

4) assignment of the PC with the content of the IVT corresponding to the request.

Once this is completed, the μcontroller is ready to execute the relevant *handler*.

The return is initiated by transferring the value of the LR in the PC (via the assembly instruction BX LR). This action automatically restores the eight saved values from the stack, thereby resuming normal execution.

Among the eight saved registers, it is worth noting that registers R0 to R3 are those systematically used by the C compiler for passing arguments to procedures. The R12 register, on the other hand, is commonly used by the compiler to access the shared memory *heap* in the C language. The remaining registers are not saved by the internal mechanism; however, it is clear that if the *handler* code were to use these registers, the compiler would handle their saving and restoration in the generated object code for the *handler*. This point should be considered when directly developing a routine in assembly language to ensure that any necessary register saving is performed.

5.4. Case of external interrupt inputs

In many applications, it is necessary to use binary input signals to trigger a direct response from the processor. For instance, consider the case of an emergency stop switch, which must initiate a shutdown procedure.

---

10 This code depends on the execution *mode* of the Cortex, a point that is not detailed here.

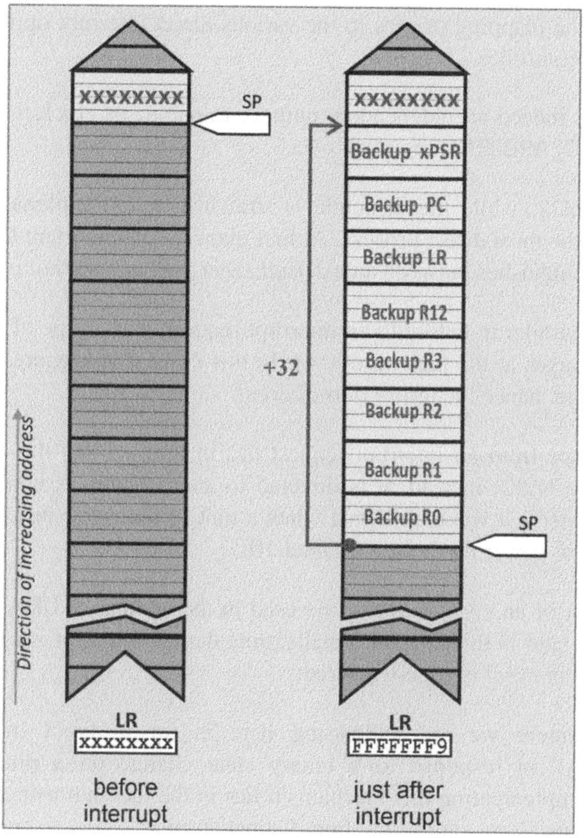

Figure 5.7. *State of the system stack immediately after a redirection*

Depending on the architecture on which the application will run, there are many possible configurations, but the principle remains the same: an edge (rising, falling or both) of an external signal connected to a μcontroller pin must trigger an interrupt. This mechanism is critical to ensure that an event is not missed while avoiding the need to continuously monitor the pin through polling.

5.4.1. *AFIO and EXTI peripherals*

The GPIO peripherals (Chapter 4) are complemented by the AFIO unit, which provides the following functionalities:

– to provide some options for I/O *remapping*, allowing the modification of the default assignments of pins to their alternate functions;

– to define the mapping of pins to the various direct interrupt options, known as *EXTI* for this μcontroller.

The AFIO is indeed an independent unit so, to use it, its clock must be enabled (bit 0 of the RCC_APB2ENR register).

For the STM32, while the principle is straightforward, implementing such an interrupt is not the most direct process. At first glance, it is important to note that this architecture distinguishes between an *external event* and an *external interrupt*.

An *event* is similar in nature to an interrupt request. It is a type of internal signal whose state changes at the hardware level. In this case, it is triggered by a pin that generates an edge, hence the term *external event*.

The difference from an interrupt request lies in the fact that the event does not propagate to the NVIC; instead, it is directed to another unit. A common use case for *external events* is a wake-up signal when a unit or the entire processor has been switched to a low-power mode (see Chapter 10).

This concept of an *event* will also be used in the context of DMA access, which we will discuss later in this chapter. Finally, note that an interrupt is a level-triggered signal, whereas an *event* is edge-triggered.

The requirement we are addressing here is for a direct interrupt to act "instantaneously" in response to a binary state change on a pin. The relative complexity of implementing this mechanism lies in the fact that using these external EXTI interrupts involves configuring four distinct entities:

– the GPIO, as the port must be configured as an input;

– the AFIO, the dedicated unit that maps the ports to the various interrupt lines;

– the EXTI, the component that handles the signals and forwards the interrupt requests;

– the NVIC, as it is necessary to set permissions and priorities.

The interaction between these four elements is illustrated in Figure 5.9.

5.4.2. *NVIC level*

Starting with the Cortex IVT, we can analyze the cascade of operations that allows a pin to trigger the execution of a specific *handler*. The table contains seven distinct entries (Table 5.2).

There are also four other vectors in this EXTI category that correspond to very specific uses, which we will not detail here:

– EXTI16 (index 1 in the IVT) connected to the *Programmable Voltage Detector* to monitor the supply voltage;

– EXTI17 (index 41 in the IVT) connected to the *Real Time Clock* alarm, primarily for handling wake-ups;

– EXTI18 (index 42 in the IVT) connected to the *USB Wakeup*, for managing USB wake-up events;

– EXTI19 (index 62 in the IVT) connected to the *Ethernet Wakeup*, for managing the wake-up of the Ethernet link.

Vector name	IVT index	IT number
EXTI0	22	6
EXTI1	23	7
EXTI2	24	8
EXTI3	25	9
EXTI4	26	10
EXTI9_5	49	23
EXTI15_10	56	40

Table 5.2. *Distribution of the EXTI in the IVT*

The configuration of the NVIC does not include any specifics for the EXTI. Permissions and priority levels are set exactly as described in the previous sections.

5.4.3. *GPIO and AFIO levels*

Whenever a pin is to be used, its electronic configuration must be considered. For EXTI, the pins must obviously be set to *input* mode, aligned with the implemented wiring.

For the 16 *true* external interrupts, the assignment of μcontroller pins to the different EXTI lines is initially handled by a multiplexer, which groups together the same bit positions of various ports. As the STM32 can include up to seven GPIO ports, the multiplexers are represented as shown in Figure 5.8.

The routing of a specific line among the seven possible GPIO ports is configured via the AFIO unit. The registers used for this configuration are the AFIO_EXTICRy registers (with y $= 0, \dots, 3$). These 16-bit registers each contain four 4-bit fields, where the value of each field configures the multiplexer as follows: 0×00 for the GPIOA port, 0×01 for the GPIOB port, ..., 0×06 for the GPIOG port. The first half-byte of AFIO_EXTICR0 configures the multiplexer for the GPIOX.0 lines, the second half-byte for GPIOX.1 and so on, up to the fourth half-byte of AFIO_EXTICR3, which configures the GPIOX.15 lines.

As the GPIOs are 16-line I/O ports, there are 16 possible EXTI lines, which are then distributed across the (sole) seven dedicated IVT vectors as follows:

– The first four lines (EXTI0 to EXTI4) are directly connected to their corresponding interrupt vector in the table.

– Lines 5–9 are combined using a five-input OR gate to form the EXTI9_5 vector.

– Lines 10–15 are combined using a six-input OR gate to form the EXTI15_10 vector.

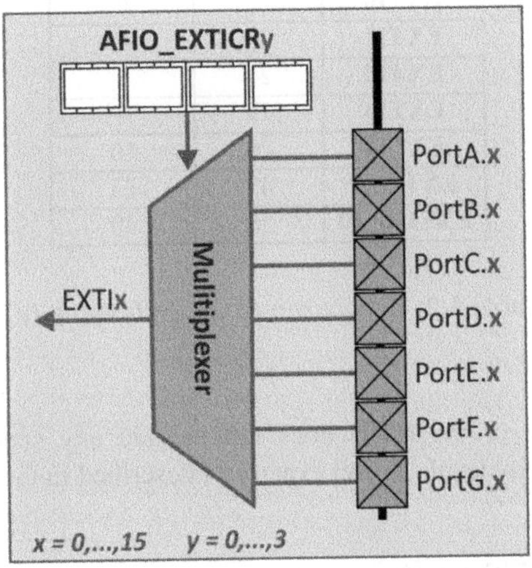

Figure 5.8. *Multiplexing of pins to generate the 16 possible EXTI lines*

Figure 5.9 illustrates these two points for a specific case: the configuration of pin PortB.10 as an EXTI.

On the right side of this figure, the multiplexing system for this particular case is shown. Since this involves input line 10, the 4 bits in positions 8–11 (the third half-byte) of the AFIO_EXTICR2 register are relevant. These bits are set to the value 0×01 to select the GPIOB port.

On the left side of the figure are the paths of the interrupt requests sent to the NVIC. The EXTI_10 signal originating from GPIOB.10 is one of the six signals that can trigger the EXTI10_15 vector.

The five registers shown in the figure complete the illustration of the EXTI-specific unit.

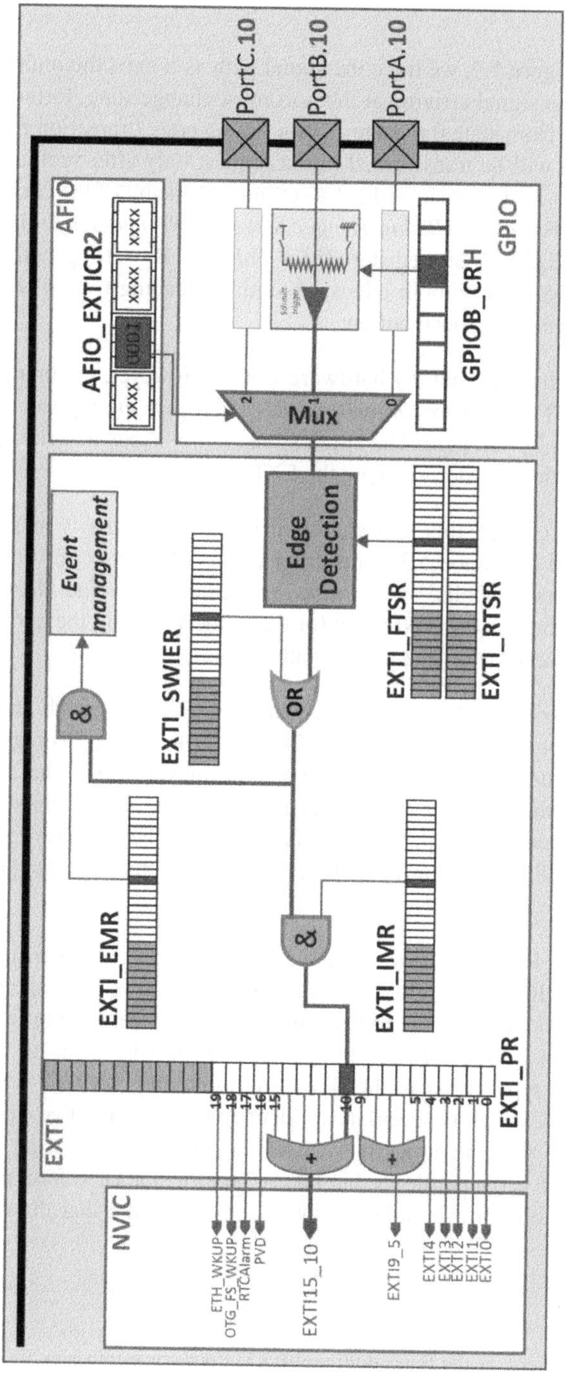

Figure 5.9. *Configuration of pin no. 10 of the GPIOB as the EXTI on the STM32F103. For a color version of this figure, see www.iste.co.uk/mahout/programming.zip*

5.4.4. *EXTI level*

Continuing with Figure 5.9, we trace the signal path as it exits the multiplexer. To recognize a request, the signal arriving at the port must change state, forming either a rising edge (transition from state 0 to state 1) or a falling edge (transition from state 1 to state 0). The signal will be transformed into a request only after such a detection. The user can choose to detect a rising edge by setting to 1 the bit of the corresponding rank in the EXTI_RTSR register (*Rising Trigger Selection Register*), a falling edge by setting the bit in the EXTI_FTSR register (F for *Falling*). By setting both bits to 1, the request will be triggered on both edges, potentially leading to two requests if a momentary press is made on a push button.

The request so far has been purely hardware-driven. However, the unit provides a specific EXTI_SWIER (*Software Interrupt Event Register*) register to allow generating this request by software. The application simply needs to write 1 to the bit corresponding to x in this register to create the EXTI_x request.

The final stage to convert this into an actual interrupt request is masking. This concept was discussed in section 5.3.2, referring to bits of type xx_IE. For the EXTI configuration, all 20 masking bits[11] are grouped in the IMR (*Interrupt Mask Register*) register. Each bit functions as an AND gate for the request: setting the corresponding bit to 1 allows the request to "proceed on its path".

The request then arrives at the final register which, in a sense, records and forwards it to the NVIC. Like the other registers in the EXTI unit, this EXTI_PR register (P for *Pending*) contains 20 usable bits. Setting a bit to 1 notifies the NVIC that the request is pending for processing. Despite the similar name, this local pending state should not be confused with its counterpart in the NVIC (one of the *Pending* registers). If we compare this to the description in section 5.3.2, these bits are equivalent to the *flag*-type bits xx_IF.

Caution, the EXTI_PR bits represent the cause that triggers the interrupt (when it is accepted by the NVIC and its priority level is sufficient). It is the responsibility of the interrupt routine to clear this bit to prevent the *handler* from being immediately executed again after it finishes. To clear the bit, care must be taken to understand that this register is of type rc_w1 in the STM32 terminology. The "r" indicates that the register is readable, which is necessary to identify which of the five (respectively, six) lines caused the EXTI9_5 (respectively, EXTI15_10) vector to trigger. The "w1" indicates that writing a 1 to a bit clears that bit ("c" for *clear*). Therefore, the *handler* must write a 1 to the bit corresponding to the request to signal that the request has been processed.

11 We are indeed at 20 here, as the four additional EXTI lines come into play from this point onward.

5.5. Guiding thread example: treating an EXTI exception

5.5.1. *Problem to solve*

On the central unit of the system, the user will navigate through the menus via push buttons. In this example, we will illustrate the use of interrupts triggered by pressing one of the push buttons. Figure 5.10 shows the very simple electronic schematic of the push button.

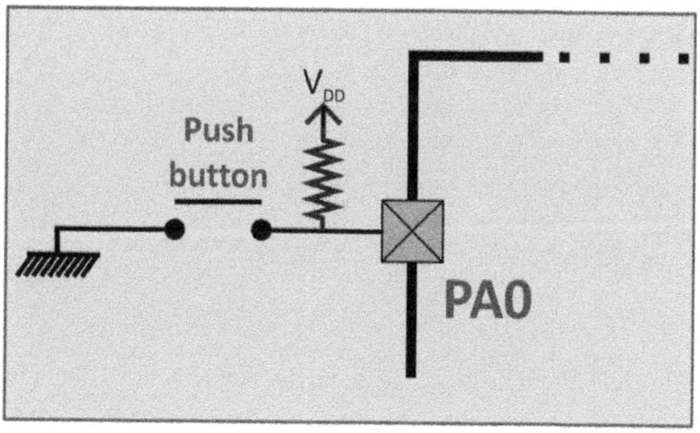

Figure 5.10. *Wiring diagram of the push button triggering an EXTI*

Regarding the configuration of the input, it should be noted:

– that the button is active at level 0, so the external interrupt must be configured to trigger on a falling edge;

– that the two voltage levels are defined, making it possible to configure the input as a *floating input*.

5.5.2. *Proposed solution*

Code example 5.3 implements the functionality.

```
#include "stm32f10x.h"
/******************************************************/
/* Guiding thread example                             */
/******************************************************/

int main(void)
{
/*********************************************/
/*      ==== IO CONFIGURATION ====           */
/* BP as input on PA.0, floating input       */
/*********************************************/
```

```
  RCC->APB2ENR|=RCC_APB2ENR_IOPAEN;      /* Ck GPIOA validation */

  GPIOA->CRL& =~ 0xF; /* Set the CNF:MOD field to 0, pin 0   */
  GPIOA->CRL |= 0x4;   /* PA0: floating input                */

/********************************/
/*     ==== AFIO mapping ====     */
/* EXTI0 connected to port A     */
/********************************/
    RCC->APB2ENR |= RCC_APB2ENR_AFIOEN; /*  Ck AFIO validation */
    AFIO->EXTICR[0] &= ~0xF;     /* EXTI0 connected to port A      */

/************************************/
/*     ==== EXTI CONFIGURATION ====     */
/************************************/
    EXTI->FTSR |= (1<<0); /* Falling edge            */
    EXTI->IMR |= (1<<0);  /* Enable local interrupt */

/*********************************************/
/*    ==== NVIC CONFIGURATION ====            */
/*    EXTI0 set to priority 2                 */
/* EXTI0 is the interrupt number 6 in the IVT */
/*********************************************/
  NVIC->IP[6] = 2<<4;          /* Most significant half-byte is
                                  assigned the value 2          */
  NVIC->ISER[0] |= 1<<6;       /* Enable EXTI0 at the NVIC level */


/*********************************/
/*     ====    While loop    ===     */
/*********************************/
  while(1);
}

/**********************************/
/*     ==== Interrupt handling ====     */
/*  Handler EXTI0                    */
/**********************************/
void EXTI0_IRQHandler(void)
{
  /* Trigger as soon as a falling edge occurs on PA.0 */
  EXTI->PR |= 0x1<<0;     /* Set the pending but (or flag) to 0
                             that triggered the interrupt
                                 locally */
  /* Here, the process to be executed... */
}
```

Code 5.3. *Proposed solution for IT handling*

5.6. Direct memory access

DMA is an important technique for reducing CPU load, as it enables direct data transfer between a peripheral and a memory region.

A typical example of DMA usage is the acquisition of N samples from an analog signal. An ADC unit has only one register that holds the result of the ADC. To sample a signal with a period T_e, assuming the processor does not have DMA channels, it would be necessary to program a Timer to trigger the conversion to the frequency $\frac{1}{T_e}$. At the end of a conversion, the ADC unit signals (via an interrupt request) that its task is complete and the processor core must then halt the current program (including performing all the intrinsic saves required during the interrupt redirection), read the register containing the result and write this result to the designated memory space (including managing the pointer). Finally, the processor must resume the program that was suspended and restore its previous state. This mechanism will be executed N times, thereby increasing the workload of the processor accordingly.

5.6.1. *Generalities*

If the processor includes a DMA unit, all transfers can be performed directly without intervention from the core. In the example described earlier, the Timer triggers the conversion requests via *event*-type signals rather than interrupt requests. Once the conversion is complete, the DMA unit handles storing the result in memory, managing any necessary pointer incrementation within the dedicated memory region. The processor will only receive an interrupt request after all N samples have been transferred, notifying it that the processing of the sampled signal can begin.

This technique requires an appropriate internal architecture. Since the processor core, during its standard operation, makes repeated accesses to RAM (in addition to program memory accesses to fetch instructions), the DMA unit must use a parallel pathway to read or write to memory without disrupting (or interrupting) the core. In the case of the STM32, this management is handled by the Bus Matrix, as shown in Figure 3.2. In addition to serving as a powerful routing mechanism for organizing these various transfers, it also performs arbitration in case of conflicts. It plays a crucial role in monitoring the execution of internal operations via a debugging module (JTAG probe). This component is part of the expertise of ARM©.

In addition to the acquisition of an analog signal over multiple samples, as mentioned earlier, the typical uses of a DMA primarily apply to two major application families: data reception and data transmission.

– For reception, the use of DMA corresponds to writing data into memory. A significant example of this usage is storing data received via a serial interface (USART, SPI bus, I²C bus, etc.): when data arrive in a continuous stream from an external process, it is unnecessary to burden the CPU with processing until all the data has been received. However, a notable challenge in such cases is that this type of transmission often has a variable length, with the message ending in a specific termination character. Thus, the end of the transmission must coincide with this expected character. With DMA, the operating principle is based on a predetermined number of transfers. Consequently, a strategy to monitor the received data must be implemented.

– For data transmission, the DMA will perform memory reads corresponding to the data to be transmitted. Symmetrically to the example with the ADC, consider the generation of an analog-like sinusoidal signal on an output pin. Under certain conditions (see Chapter 7), this type of signal can be generated using a PWM unit. To achieve this, a Timer x and the corresponding DMA channel can be configured so that they periodically trigger a transfer from memory to the TIMy_CCRz register of Timer y, which is used to generate the PWM on channel z . If the read address corresponds to a memory location containing the values (properly formatted) of the sinusoidal signal and a circular mode of operation is chosen for the DMA, the signal generation on the output will occur without any intervention from the core.

To perform read or write operations at regular and constant intervals without requiring the services of the ALU, it is necessary to define six elements:

– a trigger or *event*: this is an internal signal, where each rising edge will initiate the memory/peripheral transfer;

– a read address: a pointer to the memory in the case of transmission, or the address of the peripheral register in the case of reception;

– a write address, symmetrical to the previous item: the address of the peripheral register in the case of transmission, or a pointer to memory in the case of reception;

– the size of each transfer (1, 2, or 4 bytes for 32-bit processors);

– the management of pointers on the memory side and the peripheral side;

– the number of transfers to be performed.

5.6.2. DMA on the STM32F10x

The STM32F10x features up to two DMA units, respectively, named DMA1 and DMA2, with the second unit only available on processors from the *high-density* and *connectivity* lines. Since the operation of these units is identical, we will only detail the first one here. The only differences are the number and origin of the requests associated with each unit, with DMA2 handling fewer requests (21 requests distributed over five channels compared to 36 requests distributed over seven channels). The only additional information to note is that, in the event of a conflict between the two units (simultaneous access to the same address), the first unit takes priority.

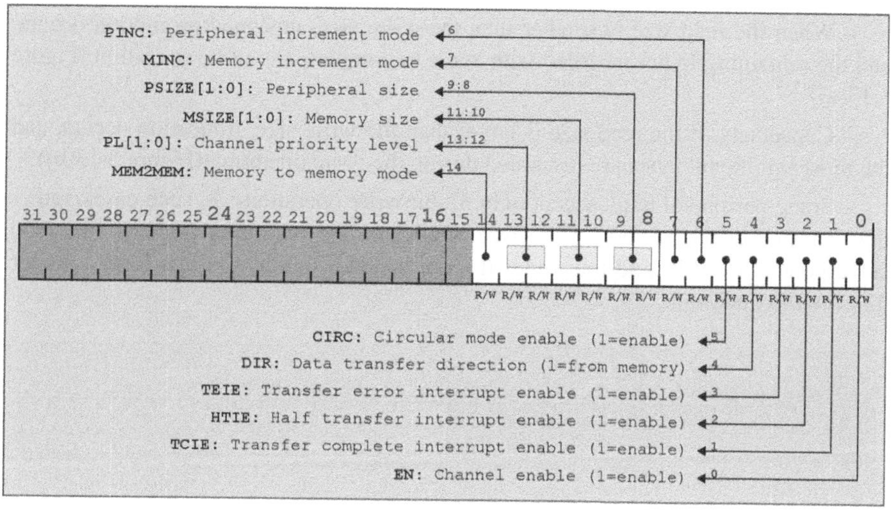

Figure 5.11. *The CCRx registers of the DMA unit ($x = 1, ..., 7$)*

As previously mentioned, performing a DMA transfer requires defining the source and destination addresses. These two addresses (represented as 32-bit values and called MA for memory access and PA for peripheral address) are stored in the DMA_CPARx and DMA_CMARx registers. The x in this notation (and the following ones) corresponds to the number of the channel involved, which for DMA1 ranges from 1 to 7. The P stands for peripheral, and the M stands for memory. Each of these addresses can serve as either the source or destination, depending on the setting of the DIR bit in the DMA_CCRx register (Figure 5.11); a value of 0 implies a read operation from the PA address.

Since the architecture supports memory-to-memory transfers (by setting the MEM2MEM bit in the DMA_CCRx register to 1), the PA address can potentially correspond to a memory address.

Next, it is necessary to define the number of transfers. This value (NDT) is encoded in the 16 least significant bits of DMA_CNDTRx (Figure 5.12).

The final essential parameters for fully configuring the transfer are the sizes of the data being read and written. The size of the accesses is configured in the DMA_CCRx register using 2×2 bits ($(00)_2$ for a byte, $(01)_2$ for a half-word, and $(10)_2$ for a word) in the PSIZE field for peripheral access and the MSIZE field for memory access. Since these two sizes can differ, three scenarios must be considered:

– When the read size is smaller than the write size, unsigned promotion occurs, and the remaining bytes are filled with zeros to complete the write operation (Figure 5.13(a)).

– Conversely, if the read size is larger than the write size, truncation occurs, and the most significant bytes are discarded during the write operation (Figure 5.13(b)).

– Some peripheral units accept only 32-bit write operations. In such cases, rather than causing an error, the architecture duplicates the read data (twice if the read corresponds to 16 bits and four times if it corresponds to a byte) to perform a proper 32-bit write operation.

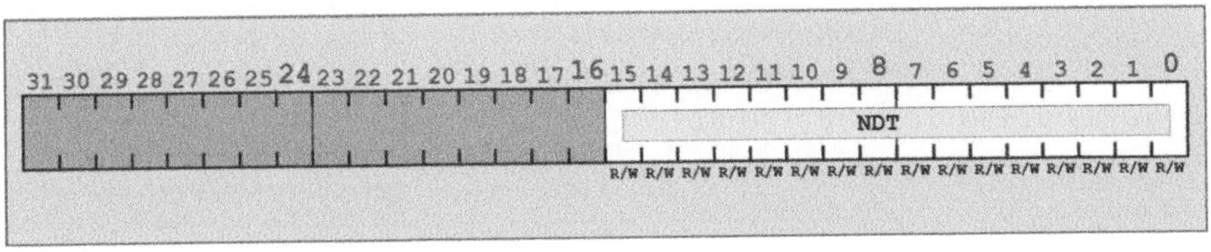

Figure 5.12. *The CNDTRx registers of the DMA unit (x* $= 1, ..., 7$*)*

Regarding write access, the least significant bit of the destination address will be ignored if the write is a half-word (16 bits) to ensure the parity and memory alignment required by the architecture. In the case of a word write (32 bits), and for the same reasons, the two least significant bits of the address will be ignored.

Now that the transfer is defined, the next step is to configure the mechanisms that trigger the transfers (referred to as triggers or *events*) and understand how they sequence. All this information is contained in the DMA_CCRx registers (Figure 5.11). For DMA1, the seven channels can be associated with 36 different triggers. The distribution of these triggers across the seven channels is illustrated in Figure 5.14. This means that on the triggering unit side, a validation bit must be set to authorize the sending of these requests. On the DMA unit side, for these requests to be accepted, the EN bit (DMA_CCRx) must be set to 1. In the specific case of memory-to-memory transfers, simply setting the validation bit to 1 (when the MEM2MEM bit is set to 1) is sufficient to initiate the transfer. In this case, the circular mode must be avoided, as it would result in continuous copying of the data.

Access conflicts between multiple DMA channels are managed by a priority encoded in the two PL bits (DMA_CCRx) (with 00 representing the lowest priority and 11 the highest). In the case of equality (same priority level), the channel number ultimately determines the priority (the lower the channel number, the higher its relative priority).

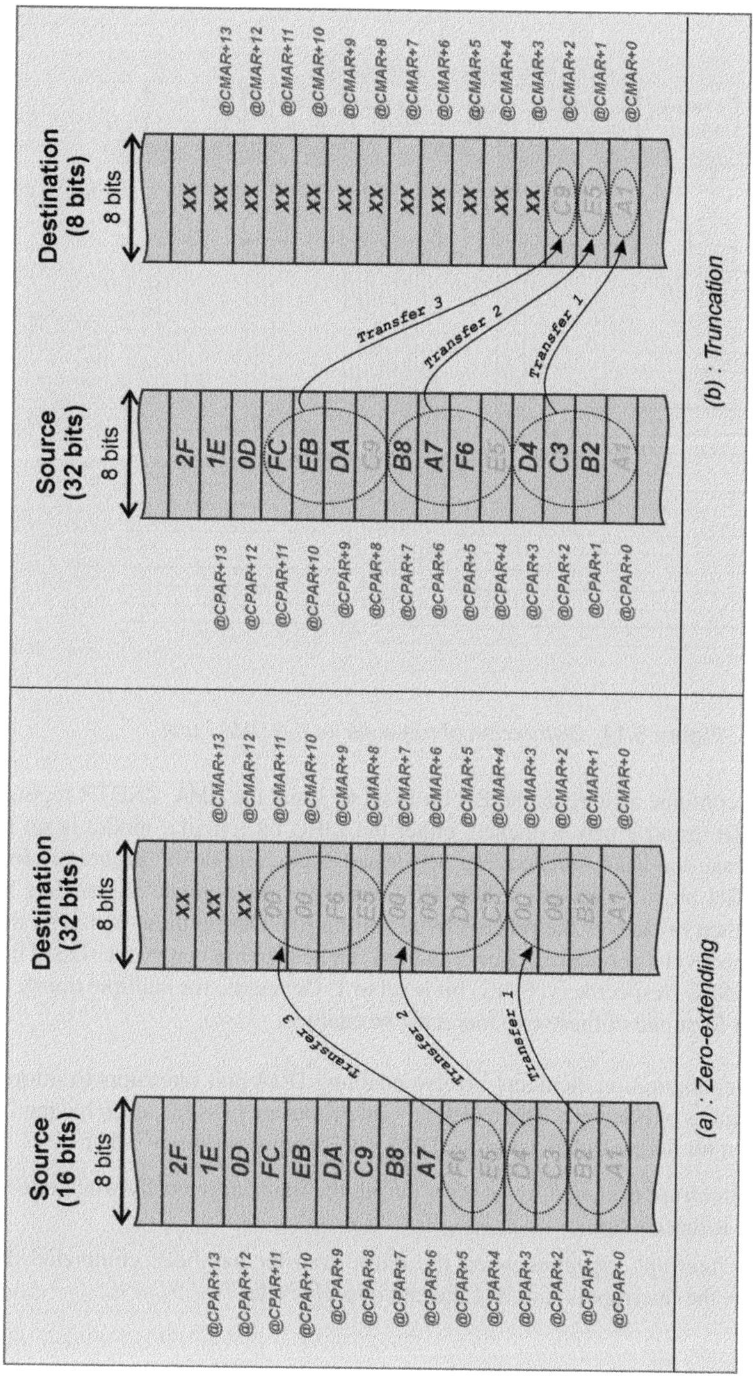

Figure 5.13. *DMA transfer with incrementation and different read and write sizes*

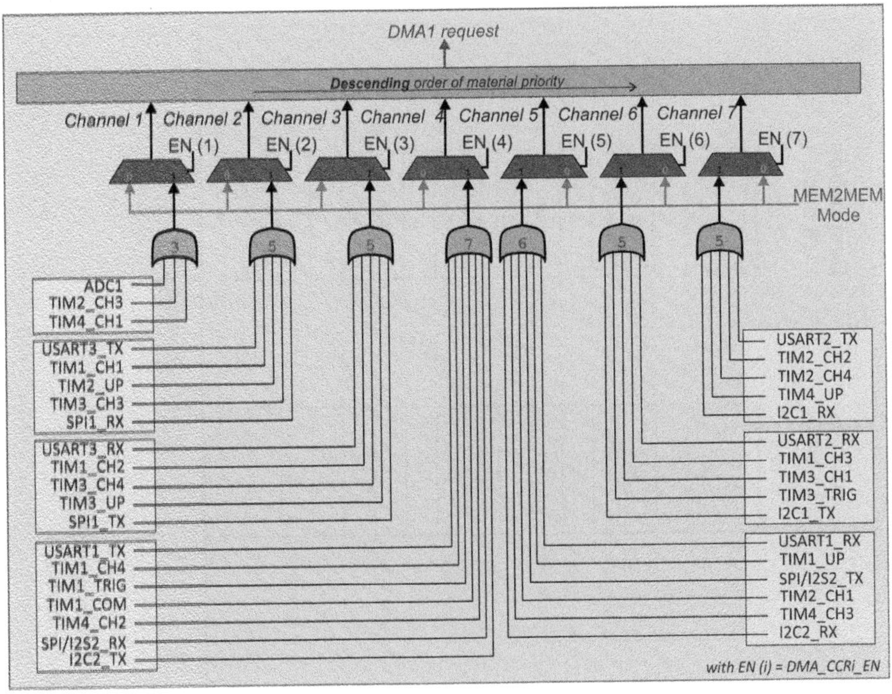

Figure 5.14. *Distribution of requests for the DMA1 unit*

Transfers continue as long as the EN bit is set to 1 and the DMA_CNDTR register is non-zero. To restart a new sequence, either the CIRC bit (circular mode) is set to 1, in which case the NDT transfers are performed cyclically, or the program, after clearing the EN bit to 0, reloads a new NDT value for the number of transfers to perform and then re-enables the process by re-setting EN. During these transfers, the memory (respectively, peripheral) access address can be incremented by the size of the access if the MINC (respectively, PINC) bit is set to 1. Generally, for multiple transfers (NDT > 1), at least one of these two bits must be enabled.

The final configuration elements involve enabling DMA unit interrupts to inform about the progress of transfers. Three different interrupts are possible, each having its own validation bit for each channel in the DMA_CCRx register (Figure 5.11):

– TEIEx: interrupt triggered by an error during the transfer, typically when one of the addresses is inaccessible.

– TCIEx: interrupt triggered when the entire transfer has been completed. In circular mode, the interrupt is raised at the end of each cycle.

– HTIEx: interrupt triggered when half of the transfers have been completed. If this bit is set to 1, each decrement of NDT that results in a value below half of the initial value will generate a new interrupt request.

– GIEx: global interrupt that corresponds to a logical OR of the three previous bits.

Each of these validations corresponds to a *flag* in the DMA_ISR register (Figure 5.15): TEIFx, TCIFx, HTIFx and GIFx.

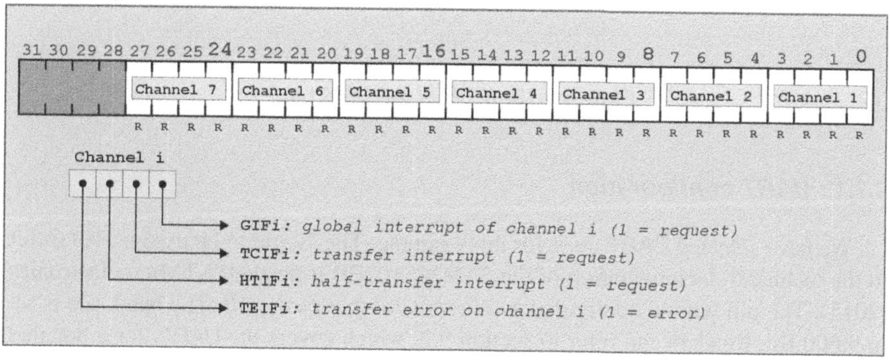

Figure 5.15. *ISR of the DMA unit*

When an interrupt is triggered, it is necessary to clear the corresponding *flag*. This clearing is done using the four bits of the DMA_IFCR register (Figure 5.16), in a manner perfectly symmetrical to the validation process:

– CTEIFx clears the interrupt caused by an error;

– CTCIFx clears the complete transfer interrupt;

– CHTIFx clears the half-transfer interrupt. Note that if the validation bit is not also cleared to 0, the next decrement of NDT will trigger the interrupt again;

– CGIFx clears all interrupt *flags*, including the global interrupt flag.

5.7. Guiding thread example: case of DMA programming

In the central unit presented in Chapter 1, a wireless transmission/reception HF feature is included. A dedicated module manages the transmission, interfaced with the STM32F103RB via an asynchronous communication link. Here, we illustrate an HF transmission, specifically sending a character string using the UART. This transmission will be carried out with the help of the DMA.

We will also provide an example of using DMA coupled with the ADC in Chapter 8 and a second example in conjunction with the I^{2}C module in Chapter 9 on communication buses.

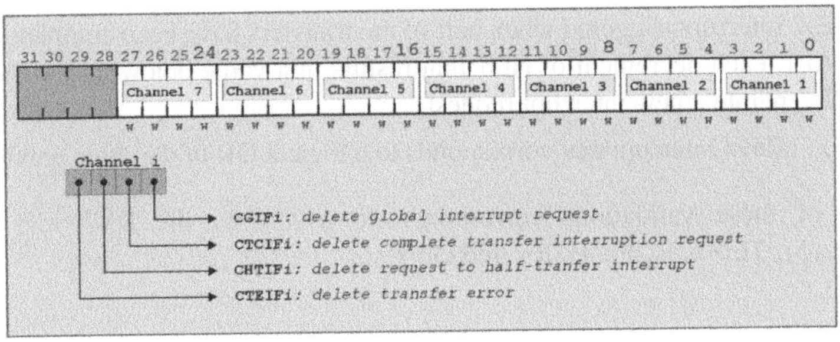

Figure 5.16. *IFCR of the DMA unit*

5.7.1. *UART configuration*

We have selected UART no. 1 for this example. The Tx pin to be used is PA9 (refer to the technical documentation of the STM32F103RB if needed) STMicroelectronics (2015). The pin will be configured as *alternate output push-pull*. The baud rate is set to 9,600 Bd. Readers can refer to section 9.2, which covers the UART, for a detailed understanding of the configuration.

5.7.2. *DMA configuration*

The Tx line of UART no.1 is connected to channel 4 of DMA1 (see Figure 5.14). The length of the DMA block (CNDTR) will depend on the length of the string to be transmitted.

5.7.3. *Program structure*

The main function is divided into two parts:

– in the first part, the code for configuring the UART and the DMA;

– in the second part, calls to the UART_Print function, which will trigger the actual transmission.

Caution, when the UART_Print function is called, it will start the DMA after adjusting the CNDTR register. However, if the function is called again immediately afterward, the message will be overwritten. Therefore, it is necessary to poll the DMA completion *flag* after the function is called. While an interrupt-based solution could have been considered, we opted for a polling-based version for the sake of simplicity and compactness.

Regarding access to DMA registers, in the reference manual STMicroelectronics (2011), STmicro© adopts a naming convention that differs from the one used in the stm32f10x.h *header* file for register definitions, which can be confusing for programmers. In this chapter, we have adhered to the naming convention used in the reference manual. One might have expected a structure of type DMA_Typedef containing all the registers mentioned in this chapter: ISR, IFCR, CCR1, CNDTR1, CPAR1, CMAR1, CCR2, CNDTR2, CPAR2, CMAR2, etc.

However, in the stm32f10x.h *header* file, there are not one but two types: DMA_Typedef and DMA_Channel_TypeDef. This approach results in less cumbersome structures. The previously mentioned registers are distributed across eight structures:

– DMA1 (ISR and IFCR registers);

– DMA_Channel1 (CCR, CNDTR, CPAR, CMAR registers), that is, CCR1, CNDTR1, CPAR1 and CMAR1;

– ...;

– DMA_Channel7 (CCR, CNDTR, CPAR, CMAR registers), that is, CCR7, CNDTR7, CPAR7 and CMAR7.

Code example 5.4 implements the required functionality.

```
#include "stm32f10x.h"

/************************************/
/* Guiding thread example          */
/************************************/

void UART_Print(char* MyString, int Len)
{
  /* Temporary disabling of the DMA                    */
  DMA1_Channel4->CCR &= ~DMA_CCR1_EN;
  /* Assignment of the DMA memory address              */
  DMA1_Channel4->CMAR = (uint32_t)MyString;
  /* Assignment of the DMA length                      */
  DMA1_Channel4->CNDTR = Len;
  /* Starting the DMA                                  */
  DMA1_Channel4->CCR |= DMA_CCR1_EN;

  /* Wait for the DMA transmission to complete         */
  while ((DMA1->ISR&DMA_ISR_TCIF4) == 0);
  /* Clear the Transfer Complete flag for channel 4    */
  DMA1->IFCR |= DMA_IFCR_CTCIF4;
}

int main(void)
{
/****************************************/
/*    ==== IO CONFIGURATION====         */
/* Tx, PA9, as alternate Output PushPull */
```

```
/****************************************************/
  RCC->APB2ENR |= RCC_APB2ENR_IOPAEN;   /* Enable Ck GPIOA */
  GPIOA->CRH &= ~(0xF<<4); /* set the CNF:MOD fields to 0  */
  GPIOA->CRH |= (0xA<<4) ; /* PA9 : alt. Output PushPull   */

/*******************************/
/*   ==== Basic UART ===        */
/*        9600Bds Tx            */
/*******************************/
  RCC->APB2ENR |= RCC_APB2ENR_USART1EN;   /* Enable Ck UART1 */
  USART1->CR1 |= USART_CR1_UE;     /* Enable  UART1           */
  USART1->CR1 &= ~USART_CR1_M;     /* 8 bits                  */
  USART1->CR2 &= ~(0x3<<12);       /* 1 bit stop              */
  USART1->BRR = 72000000/9600;     /* 9600 Bd               */
  USART1->CR1 |= USART_CR1_TE;     /* enable transmission     */

/****************************************/
/*   ==== UART config with DMA ====    */
/****************************************/

  RCC->AHBENR |= RCC_AHBENR_DMA1EN;     /* Enable DMA1                */
  USART1->CR3 |= USART_CR3_DMAT;   /* UART1 operation with DMA */
  /* Peripheral address assignment                                   */
  /* NB: a cast to int32 is necessary as DR is of type int16        */
  DMA1_Channel4->CPAR = (uint32_t)&USART1->DR;

  /* The CMAR address will be specified UART_Print()                 */
  DMA1_Channel4->CCR &= ~(0x3<<10);     /* MSIZE 8bits              */
  DMA1_Channel4->CCR &= ~(0x3<<8);     /* PSIZE 8bits               */
  /* PMINC = 0 (no incrementation on the peripheral side)           */
  DMA1_Channel4->CCR &= ~DMA_CCR1_PINC;
  /* MMINC = 1 (incrementation on the memory side)                  */
  DMA1_Channel4->CCR |= DMA_CCR1_MINC;
  /* no circular mode                                                */
  DMA1_Channel4->CCR &= ~DMA_CCR1_CIRC;
  /* Direction: memory to peripheral                                 */
  DMA1_Channel4->CCR |= DMA_CCR1_DIR;

/*******************************/
/*    ===== While loop====     */
/*******************************/

  UART_Print("Hello Word !\n\r", 14);
  UART_Print("Here uCSTM32...\n\r", 17);

  while(1);
}
```

Code 5.4. *Proposed solution for UART transmission using DMA*

6

Timers

6.1. General information on counters or Timers

Timers are probably the most important peripherals after GPIOs. Manufacturers may adopt several strategies when designing a Timer unit:

– create multiple types of Timers, each with a specific role;

– create a general multi-purpose Timer that can handle a variety of situations.

The first option results in simple but distinct Timers. The second option leads to a single multi-purpose Timer type that can be very complex to configure. STmicro© has chosen the second option, which can sometimes make the configuration more difficult.

These complex peripheral units offer a wide variety of operating modes. This variety necessitates configurations to enable the desired functionality. From a programming perspective, there is no additional difficulty, as every configuration ultimately involves assigning values to registers or parts of registers. However, the multiplicity of modes generates a large amount of documentation and functional diagrams that is sometimes confusing.

A semantic clarification is needed here: *counter* or *timer*? Fundamentally, there is no difference. These units *count* the transitions (rising edges, falling edges or both) of an input signal. Obviously, if this signal is periodic (such as a clock signal) and its frequency is known, the counter holds a value that can be easily converted into time, effectively acting as a Timer.

In the advanced modes of a Timer, such as Capture-Compare and PWM, the electrical activity of the pins will be linked to the unit.

For a color version of all the Codes in this chapter, see www.iste.co.uk/mahout/programming.zip

6.1.1. *Basic principle*

A Timer unit is based on three components:

– a counter itself, which increments or decrements with each detected edge;

– a reload value (also called the overflow value), which serves as a limit for counting;

– a prescaler that allows for the input clock of the counter that is acting as a timer to be slowed down, or to count only one edge out of *N* for the counter that acts in this way.

Figure 6.1 illustrates the dependence on these three components.

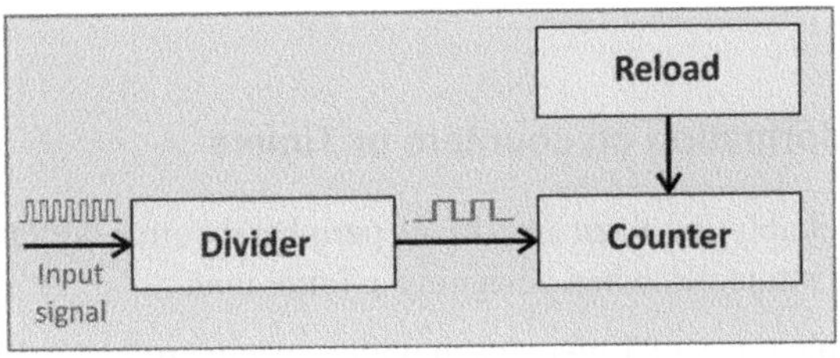

Figure 6.1. *Three basic components of a counter/Timer*

In the most standard operation, the counting unit increments from 0 to the overflow value and then returns to 0, repeating this cycle continuously. Figure 6.2 illustrates the temporal evolution of the counting register. An important aspect highlighted in this figure is the *overflow period*, which is often the primary value of interest in most applications.

This standard operation can be extended into numerous variations, which may or may not be available depending on the design choices of the manufacturer and which may be more convenient to implement. Let us cite, for example:

– counting down from the overflow value to 0;

– counting up from the overflow value to the maximum value;

– counting down from the maximum value to the overflow value;

– stopping the count when the overflow value (or 0) is reached.

Regardless of the variation used, the basic principle will remain the same.

6.1.2. *Timer units in the STM32F10x*

Timer units in the STM32F10x are diverse and sometimes offer specific functionalities. Generally, these units allow for precise time base generation such as regular execution of interrupts, PWM signal generation, duration measurement or triggering another Timer, ADC or other peripherals without CPU intervention.

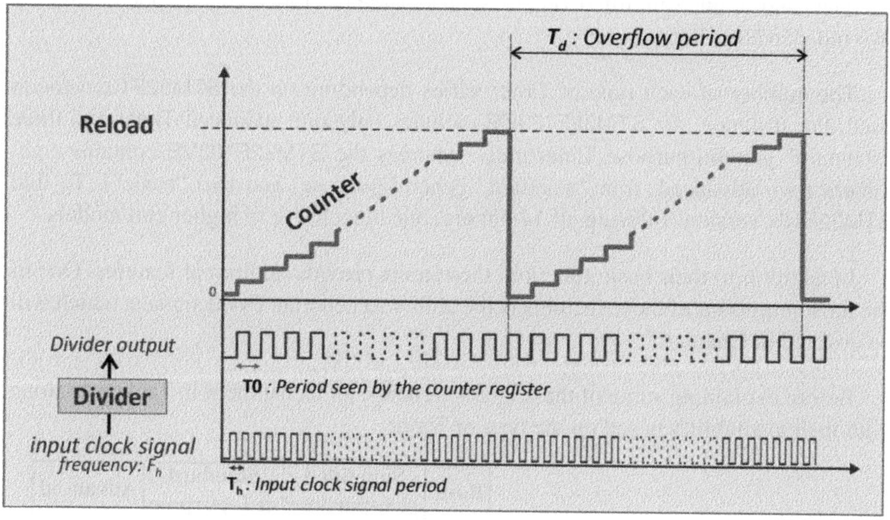

Figure 6.2. *Basic function of a counter/Timer*

Before detailing the "generic" operation of a Timer in the STM32F10x, let us start by listing the different families of Timers.

6.1.3. *Different types of Timers*

The STM32F10x μcontrollers feature up to 14 different Timers. These Timers are categorized into four subsets:

– *advanced* Timers: TIM1 and TIM8;

– *standard general-purpose* Timers: TIM2 to TIM5;

– *simplified general-purpose* Timers: TIM9 to TIM14[1];

– *basic* Timers: TIM6 and TIM7.

Of course, these four families share the same fundamental operation explained previously. In any case, three basic registers (prescaler, counter and overflow) are always included to generate an overflow event. The differences lie in the additional functionalities these units can offer, which will be detailed later. For example, basic

1 Timers 9 and 12 have minor differences compared to the other four units of this type, particularly in terms of interrupt handling.

Timers only include the core functionality, while the standard general-purpose units provide four independent input/output channels to manage PWM signals, incremental encoders and so on. Simplified Timers, such as TIM9 to TIM14, are equipped with only two independent channels.

The number of each type of Timer varies depending on the STM32F10x version used. For instance, the STM32F103RB includes only one advanced Timer and three "standard" general-purpose Timer units, whereas the STM32F103VE contains eight Timers (two advanced, four "standard" general-purpose, and two "basic"). To find STM32F10x versions offering all 14 Timers, one must move to higher end models.

In addition to their basic function, these units provide additional features. One of the most important of these features is the ability to generate PWM signals, which will be covered in Chapter 7.

Before explaining some of these characteristics, let us list them in Table 6.1, along with their availability based on the type of Timer.

	Basic	Simplified gen.-purpose	Standard gen.-purpose	Advanced
Number of External I/Os (Channels)	0	1 or 2[2]	4	6
Number of Different I/Os	1	2	6	8
Number of Inputs in the IVT	1	1	1	6
Timer using Internal Clock	√	√	√	√
Up/Down Count	∅	√	√	√
Slave Mode	∅	√[1]	√	√
One Pulse Mode	√	√[1]	√	√
Capture/Compare Function	∅	√	√	√
PWM	∅	√	√	√
PWM Input	∅	√	√	√
Incremental Encoders	∅	∅	√	√
DMA	∅	√	√	√

Table 6.1. *Characteristics of the different Timers*

6.2. Operating modes

It would be very difficult to detail all of these families and the full range of possibilities they offer. We will therefore continue by describing the most generic aspects of these Timers, which, in most cases, correspond to the Standard General Purpose family.

2 Uniquely for TIM9 and TIM12.

6.2.1. *General structure of a Timer*

An initial system-level approach, as shown in Figure 6.3, involves examining the various signals that such a Timer can receive or emit.

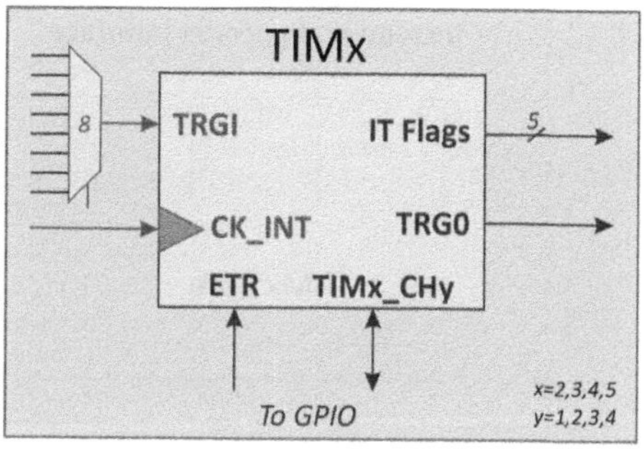

Figure 6.3. *Inputs and outputs of a Standard General Purpose Timer*

Let us detail the roles of these signals:

– *CK_INT* : this is the main clock of the Timer unit (connected to TIMxCLK from the RCC). Typically, its frequency is 72 MHz.

– *IT_Flags*: these are signals indicating and interrupt. There are five of them:

- UI (*Update Interrupt Flag*) triggered by an *Update* event, typically the Timer overflow;

- CC1I to CC4I (*Capture Compare Interrupt Flag*) triggered by a capture or compare event corresponding to one of the four Timer channels.

– Signals that interact with the outside world (via GPIOs):

- *ETR* (*External Trigger Input*): an input that allows, among other things, counting edges from an external source;

- *TIMx_CHy*: an input or output (depending on the mode of use), for example, the measurement of a time interval between two edges on a pin or the generation of a PWM signal.

– Internal signals used as triggers:

- *TRGO* (*Trigger Output*): it allows generating a signal to trigger an action on another peripheral;

- *TRGI* (*Trigger Input*): an input designed to receive a trigger signal. Multiple sources are possible (predefined). There are eight different sources.

From a functional perspective, it is possible to distinguish the various blocks shown in Figure 6.4.

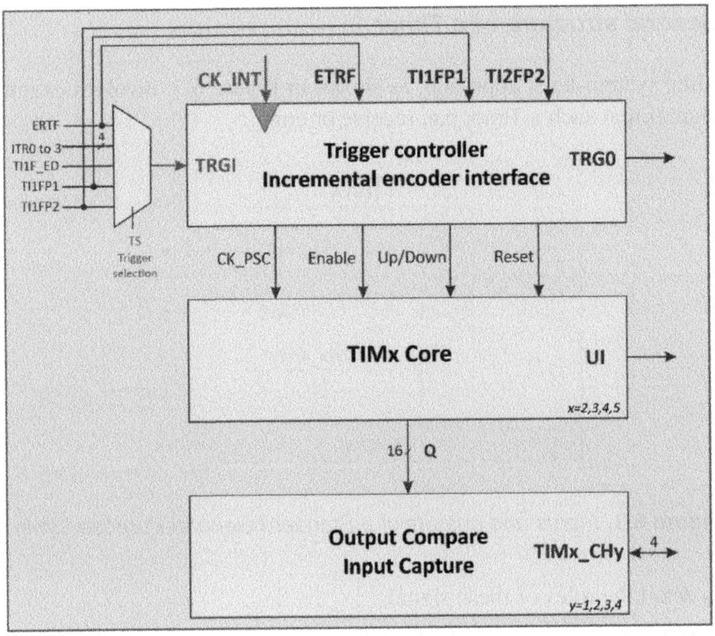

Figure 6.4. *Functional decomposition of a Standard General Purpose Timer. For a color version of this figure, see www.iste.co.uk/mahout/programming.zip*

6.2.2. Core *block: overflow, events and frequency*

For an STM32F10x, the three (16-bit) registers used to realize basic operations (Figure 6.2) are as follows:

– *TIMx_CNT*: the counter itself, which counts edges at the output of the PSC;

– *TIMx_ARR*: the overflow value;

– *TIMx_PSC*: the prescaler for the input signal *CK_PSC* (0 = division by 1, 1 = division by 2, etc.).

6.2.2.1. *Overflow*

In this central block, overflow is therefore a key event in the progression of the counting value.

This event can trigger actions such as:

– reloading the counter with the reload value;

– synchronous updating of certain registers;

– triggering conversions by an ADC unit;

– generating an interrupt request.

Mastering the overflow period is consequently a critical aspect of configuring these units. In general, the calculation of this period naturally depends on how the unit is implemented on the μcontroller. For STM32 devices, the overflow frequency F_d is given by the following formula[3], assuming the clock frequency driving the unit is F_h:

$$F_d = \frac{F_h}{(PSC + 1) * (ARR + 1)}$$

hence, the period is:

$$T_d = \frac{(PSC + 1) * (ARR + 1)}{F_h}$$

It is important not to forget the "+1" terms in the formula. The "+1" for the prescaler (PSC) accounts for the initial offset (0 corresponds to a division by 1), and the "+1" for ARR is due to the fact that returning to zero takes one cycle. For example, with three values, the sequence 0, 1, 2, 3, 0 takes four cycles, even though the maximum value is only 3.

One question lies in choosing the best pair (ARR-PSC) in order to achieve the desired overflow period. Although the formula used for the calculation is very simple, finding the optimal values is not so trivial: the registers can only hold integer values. Many combinations exist leading to a desired overflow frequency, but determining which combination provides the closest approximation is not obvious. A simple (but not necessarily exact) approach is to use the smallest possible prescaler value. This ensures that the input signal period of the counting register is as small as possible. If the chosen combination does not exactly match the desired value, the resulting error will be at most one counted time unit: the smaller the period, the smaller the error.

In practice, the technique involves selecting the largest possible reload value, which allows calculating the smallest feasible prescaler (a smaller prescaler value would require an overflow value larger than the maximum capacity of the register). This actual prescaler value is then rounded up to the next highest integer. The final step is to recalculate the integer overflow value corresponding to the rounded-up prescaler value.

Code example 6.1 provides an implementation of this technique. This implementation does not take into account potential overflows in the PSC and ARR registers.

3 This calculation is slightly different when counting is performed in *Center-Aligned* mode.

```
void Find_Combi(float Fdes, uint16_t *maxARR, uint16_t *maxPSC
    )
/* Fdes: desired frequency */
{
    uint16_t TempoARR, TempoPSC;

    TempoARR = 0xFFFF;
    TempoPSC = (uint16_t)(72e6/(Fdes*(float)(TempoARR+1))-1)+1;
    TempoARR = (uint16_t)(72e6/(Fdes*(float)(TempoPSC+1))-1);

    *maxARR = TempoARR;
    *maxPSC = TempoPSC;
}
```

Code 6.1. *Function for finding a PSC-ARR combination*

6.2.2.2. *Counting and downcounting*

In the default operation, the CNT register is incremented at each edge of the input signal. However, it is also possible to opt for decrementation. In this case, when the register reaches 0, the next decrement triggers an *update* event and the register reloads with the value stored in ARR. A third option is the so-called *Center-Aligned* mode. In this mode, the register increments from 0 to ARR; once this value is reached, it switches to decrementation on the next edge and triggers an *update* event. When it reaches 0, the mechanism changes again: on the next edge, it switches to incrementation and generates another *update* event. When calculating the duration between two events, there is a slight difference between the *Up* or *Down* modes and the *Center-Aligned* mode. In the latter case, the period is calculated as:

$$T_d = \frac{(PSC + 1) * (ARR)}{F_h}$$

Figure 6.5 illustrates the evolution of the CNT register and the difference in overflow periods for these three modes.

In typical use cases, the existence of these three different operating modes offers no advantage in particular. However, they become useful when the unit directly drives an I/O (in particular, PWM). This explains why these modes are not available in the basic and simplified versions of the Timers.

6.2.2.3. Update *event (UEV)*

This event has been mentioned previously but requires further detail. Its exact name is *UEV* for *Update EVent*. The various sources that trigger the UEV are:

– Timer *overflow* or *underflow*: this is the most common trigger and occurs automatically.

– Software: the user can manually trigger a UEV by setting the UG (*Update Generation*) bit. This bit is part of the special register called the EGR (*Event Generation Register*).

– Trigger controller block (depending on the selected *Slave* mode chosen).

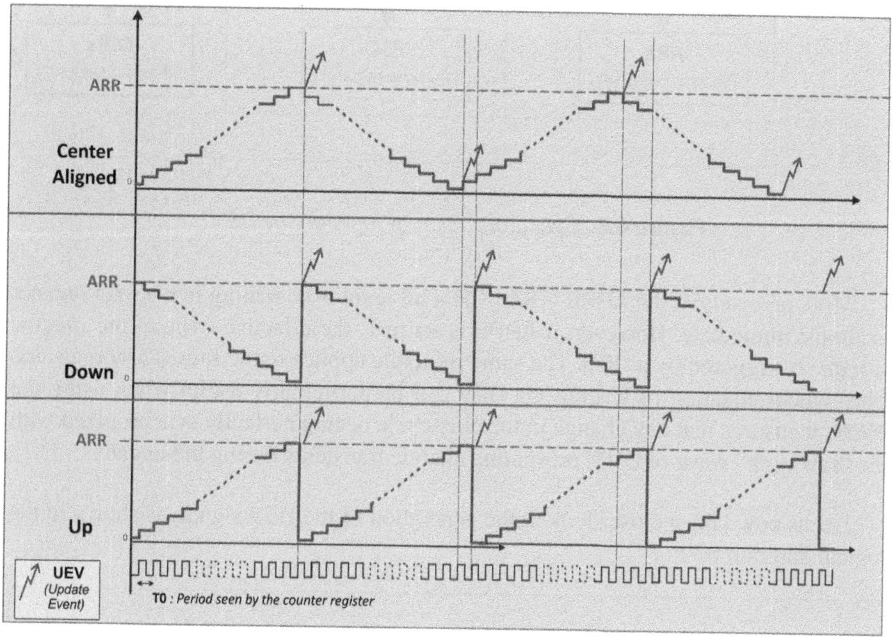

Figure 6.5. *Differences between the Up, Down and Center-Aligned modes*

This event is already known as the source of the UIF interrupt. However, it has another important role: synchronizing the writing of certain core Timer registers. Figure 6.6 illustrates this functionality.

Figure 6.6 illustrates how the ARR, PSC and the four CCRy registers (only one is shown in the figure) are written. Writing to one of these registers results in an immediate write to intermediate registers known as "preload registers", which are not the target registers themselves. For instance, writing to ARR first updates its *preload register* and is then effectively written to the final register (the *shadow register*) only on the rising edge of CK_INT or triggered by the UEV event.

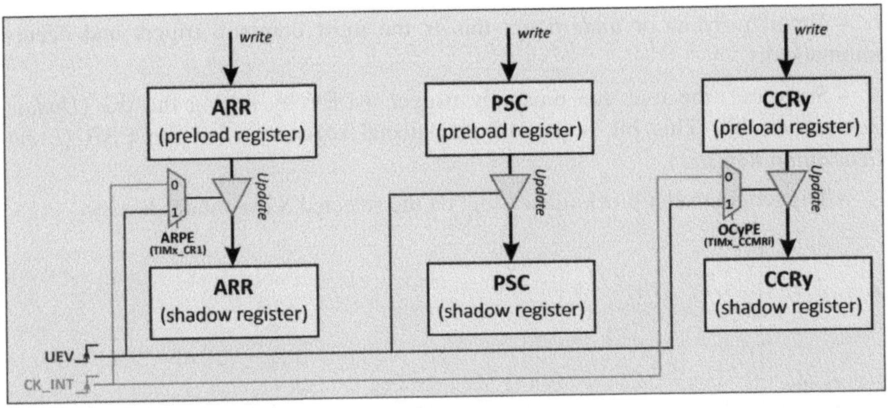

Figure 6.6. *Synchronization of registers by UEV*

More precisely, if the ARPE (TIMx_CR1) bit is set to 0, writing to the final register is almost immediate. However, if ARPE is set to 1, the effective write to the *shadow register* is triggered by a UEV. The same principle applies to the four CCRy registers. This synchronization of writing via UEV can be particularly useful when using the PWM: it ensures that any change in the duty cycle occurs perfectly synchronized with the "sawtooth" wave of CNT, preventing chaotic transients during the update.

Let us now take a closer look at the generation of the UEV signal, as shown in the logical diagram 6.7.

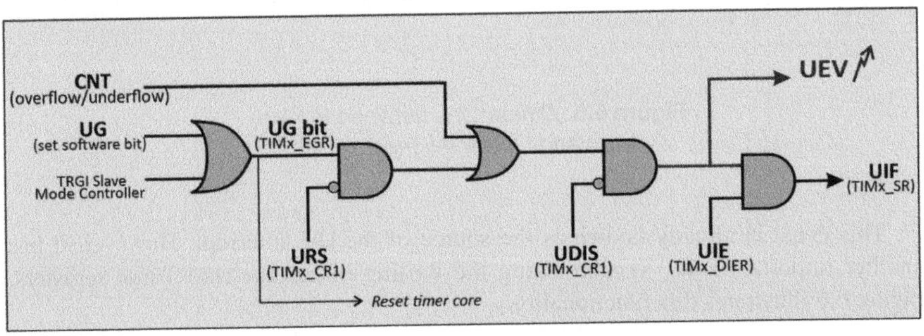

Figure 6.7. *Generation of the UEV event*

In this figure, the three sources triggering the UEV event are shown on the left. Along the signal path, two bits have the ability to block the triggering of the event:

– The URS (*Update Request Source*) bit. By default, it is set to 0. If it is set to 1, it disables all sources other than the *overflow* and *underflow* of the CNT.

– The UDIS (*Update Disable*) bit acts further downstream. By default, it is also set to 0, allowing stimuli to pass through. If the programmer sets it to 1, then the UEV is completely inhibited.

It is important to note the effect of setting the UG (*Update Generation*) bit to 1: whether it is triggered manually via software or automatically (depending on the *Slave* mode), its effect results in a reset of the Timer core, meaning that CNT is reset to 0.

6.2.3. Capture/Compare *block*

Unlike the central block, this block interacts with the external environment (it is therefore connected to GPIO units). If the signals are inputs, the block operates in *Capture* mode. Conversely, if the block drives output signals, it operates in *Compare* mode.

6.2.3.1. Capture *mode*

This mode, as its name suggests, is used to "capture" the content of the CNT register into one of the subordinate registers TIMx_CCRy. With such a capture, it becomes possible to timestamp one or more events relative to a reference point corresponding to the start of the Timer (modulo any overflows that occur before the capture). The capture is triggered by an external signal, similar to what we will see in section 6.2.4.2 for *Slave* mode. In advanced versions of Timer units, there are four input channels, providing four distinct capture possibilities. The range of possible connections is illustrated in Figure 6.8.

Immediately, note the "XOR" gate that combines the first three channels to feed into the first edge detector. This path can be selected using the TI1S bit in the TIMx_CR2 register (Figure 6.9) instead of the direct TI1 input. This particular configuration addresses a specific application: Hall effect sensors used for controlling *brushless* electric motors. We will not detail the principles of this application here.

Setting aside the previously mentioned point and, as shown in Figure 6.8, the four input channels are grouped into pairs. The first pair (TI1, TI2) has a cross-connection with the first two capture registers, while the second pair (TI3, TI4) is connected to the next two registers. For each input, it is possible to detect a rising or falling edge depending on the value of the corresponding polarity bit CCyP in the TIMx_CCER register (Figure 6.11). By adjusting the value of the CCyS bit field in the TIMx_CCMR$_{1,2}$ registers (Figure 6.10), each capture can be triggered by one of three events:

- the *n*th rising or falling edge of the first input in the pair;
- the *n*th rising or falling edge of the second input in the pair;
- the *n*th rising edge of the TRC signal.

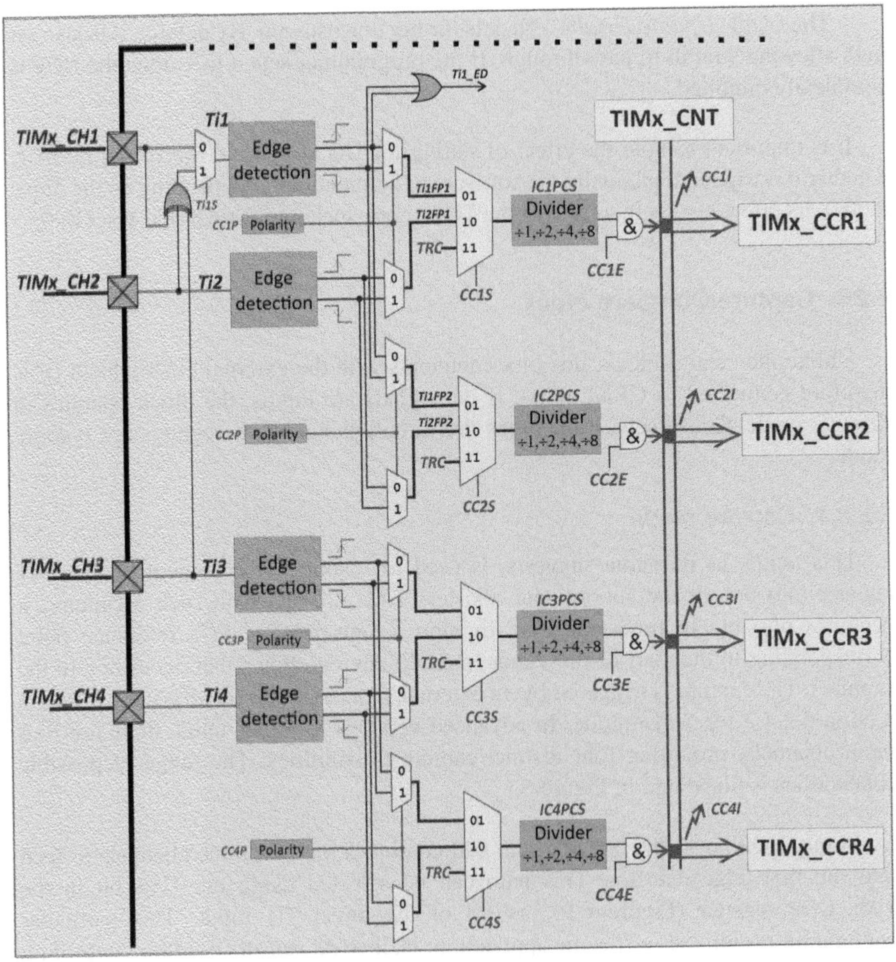

Figure 6.8. *Capture mode*

Before validating the capture, the request is filtered by a prescaler configured using the 2 bits of the IC1PSC field in the TIMx_CCMR$_{1,2}$ register. Therefore, the capture will only occur after detecting n edges.

At the output of this prescaler, there is a final validation stage controlled by the CCiE bits in the TIMx_CCER register.

The CCyI event is simultaneously triggered with the capture event. This is indicated by setting the CCyIF bit in the TIMx_SR register to 1. If the corresponding enable bit CCyIE in the TIMx_DIER register (Figure 6.12) has been previously set to

1, an interrupt request will be sent to the NVIC. For advanced Timers, this interrupt request can correspond to the specific TIMx_CC interrupt vector shared among the four channels. For other Timers (standard or simplified), the vector is shared with the overflow interrupt; the *handler* must determine the cause of the interrupt by reading the status of the xIF bits in the TIMx_SR register (Figure 6.13).

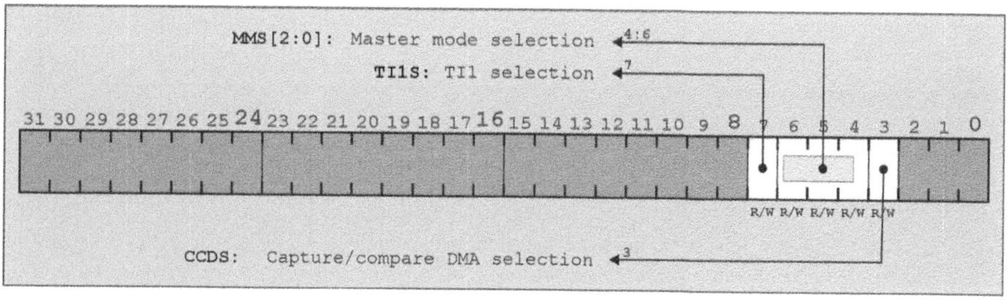

Figure 6.9. *TIM_CR2 configuration register*

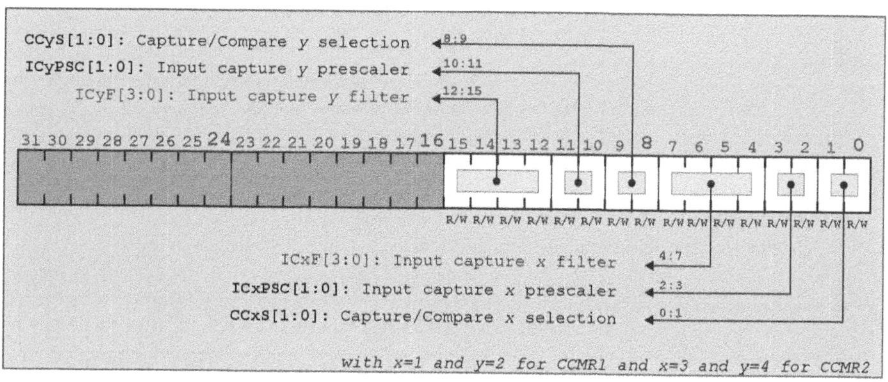

Figure 6.10. *TIM_CCMR$_{1,2}$ registers in capture mode*

6.2.3.2. Compare *mode*

The *Compare* mode is, in a way, the dual of the *Capture* mode. It operates by acting on an associated GPIO channel of the Timer in response to the counting progression. This mode is selected by setting the CCiS bit field to $(00)_2$ (with $i = 1, 2, 3,$ or 4).

First, there is what the documentation refers to as *forced output* mode, which bypasses the comparison logic to directly force the output channel to a high or low active state. This is done by setting the bit field OCyM to $(101)_2$ or to $(100)_2$, with the polarity bit CCyP determining whether the high and low states are inverted. This option is similar to the one that directly uses GPIO for output, but retains the interrupt-handling aspects of the *Compare* mode, even if it does not explicitly act on the output.

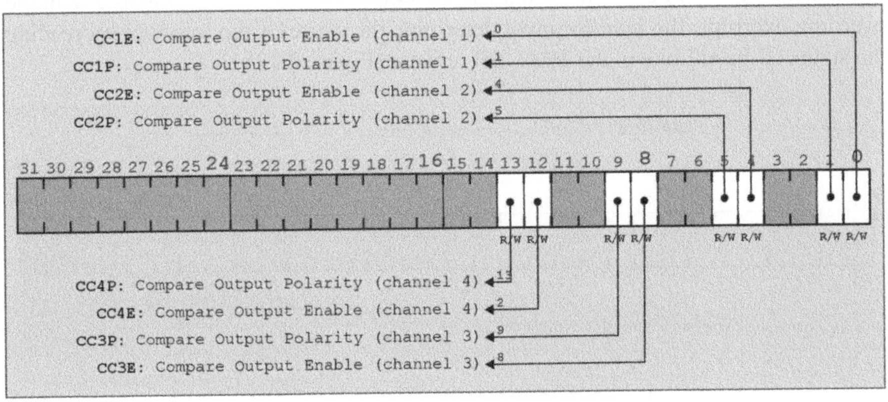

Figure 6.11. *Configuration register of the TIM_CCER Capture/Compare mode*

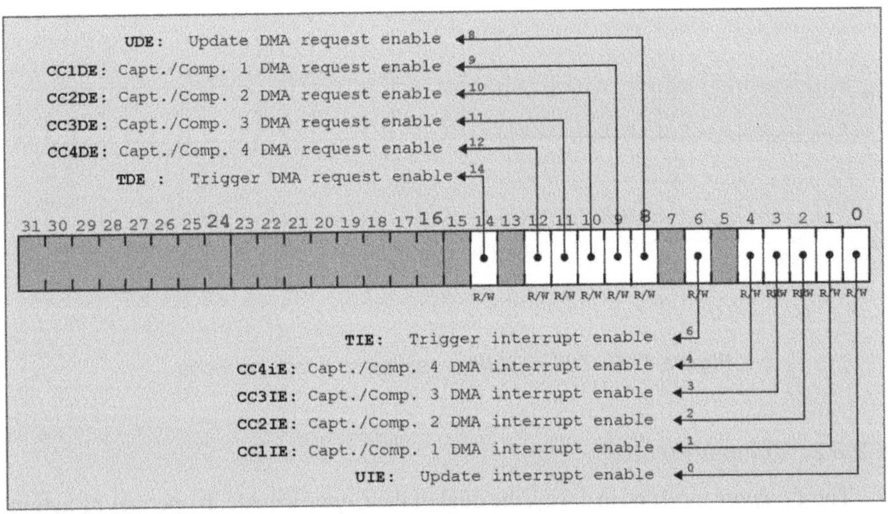

Figure 6.12. *IT enable and DMA TIM_DIER register*

The basic version of the *Compare* mode (see Figure 6.14) involves comparing the contents of the CNT register with one or more TIMx_CCRy registers. When these two values are equal, in addition to setting CCyIF to 1, four possible actions can occur on the output channel, depending on the value of the OCyM bit field (TIMx_CCMR$_{1,2}$ register) (see Figure 6.15):

– the associated output maintains its current level (OCyM $= (000)_2$);

– the associated output is set to active (OCyM $= (001)_2$);

– the associated output is set to inactive (OCyM $= (010)_2$);

– the associated output is toggled (inverted) relative to its current value (OCyM $= (011)_2$).

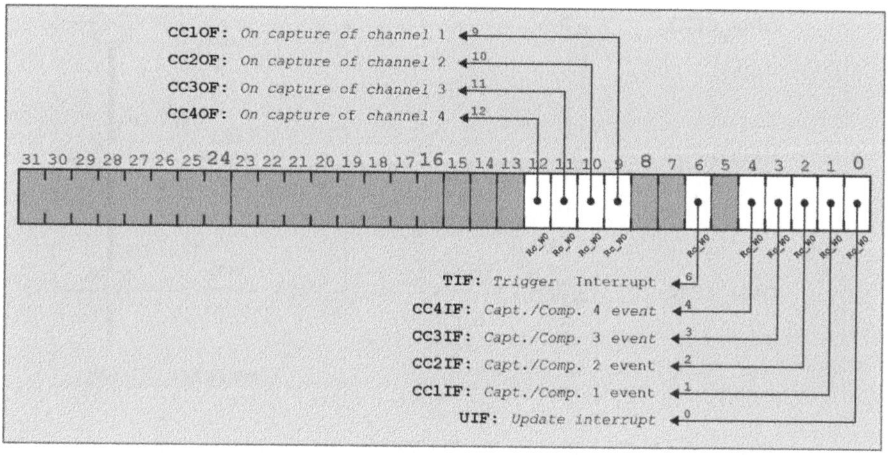

Figure 6.13. *TIM_SR status register*

The output pin will be set to 1 or 0 depending on the selected action and the imposed polarity (CCyP).

It is important to ensure that the enable bit for each of these output channels (CCyE bit in TIMx_CCER$_{1,2}$) is set to 1, as well as configuring the corresponding GPIO in *Alternate Output* mode.

It is also worth noting, as shown in Figure 6.14, that for advanced Timers (TIM1, TIM8), there is a global enable bit for the four outputs of these units (MOE bit in TIMx_BDTR).

6.2.4. Trigger *controller block and encoder interface*

This block is probably the most complex part of the Timer. It provides functionalities such as:

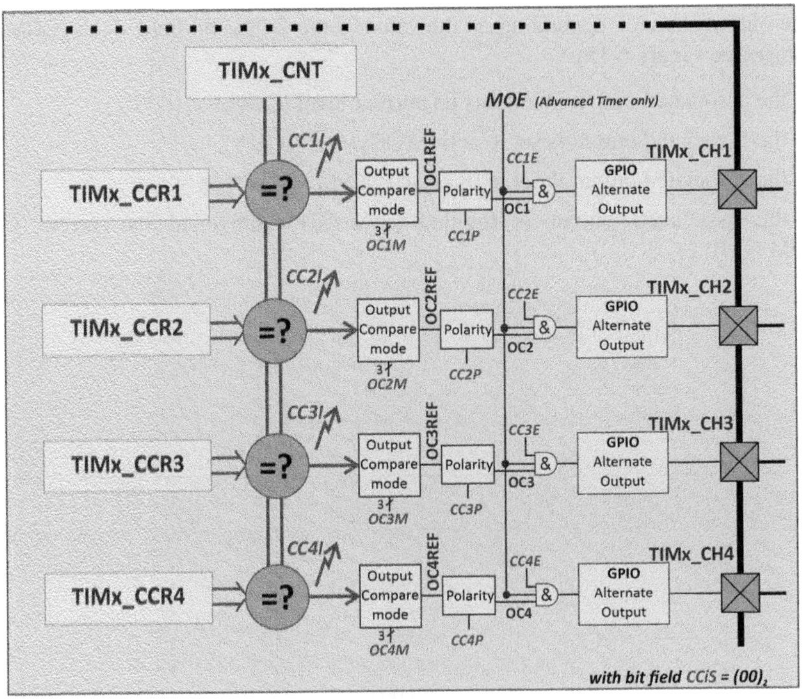

Figure 6.14. *Compare mode. For a color version of this figure, see www.iste.co.uk/mahout/programming.zip*

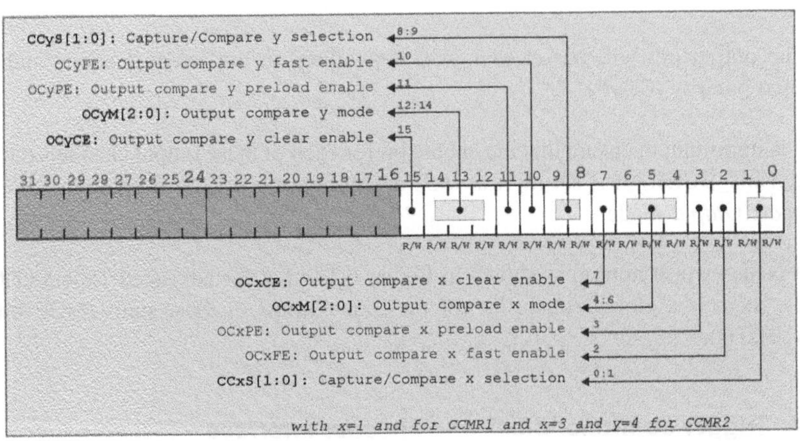

Figure 6.15. *Configuration registers TIM_CCMR$_{1,2}$ in Compare mode*

– selecting the clock source for the Timer core (i.e. CK_INT);

– managing *Master/Slave* modes, that is, triggering another Timer, ADC or DAC (*Slave*) from a Timer acting as a *Master*;

– managing the incremental encoder interface.

To enable all these actions, this block has the capability to override certain functionalities governed by configuration fields we have discussed so far. For example, *up/down* control or the enabling of the counter can be automatically managed by this block instead of being directly controlled through the DIR or CEN bits.

Note that everything discussed so far works correctly only if the *SMS* field in the TIMx_SMCR register (*Slave Mode Control Register*) is set to $(000)_2$ (Figure 6.16). In other words, if the user only wishes to use the functionalities described in the previous sections, this field must be set to 0, or rather, it must "remain at 0", as this is its default state after a reset. The standard usage modes (simple counting, *Input Capture*, *Output Compare*) are therefore one of the *Slave* modes: the *Slave Mode Disabled*.

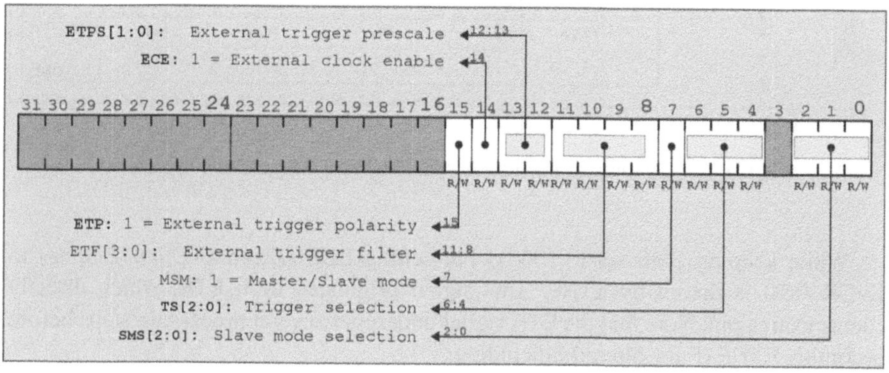

Figure 6.16. *TIM_SMCR configuration register in slave mode*

6.2.4.1. *Selecting the Timer core clock*

This section is relevant only in the context of *Slave Mode Disabled* (SMS $= (000)_2$) or *External Clock Mode 1* (SMS $= (111)_2$). These two modes are straightforward and do not strictly correspond to true *Slave* modes, even though the SMS field plays a role in their configuration. These two specific values are used to manage the clock of the Timer. Here, we will see how to simply select the clock for the prescaler, CK_PSC, from three possible inputs:

– CK_Int (the default source), also known as the *Internal Clock*;

– ETR (the external source for counting edges), also referred to as *External Mode 2*;

– TRGI, an input normally used to trigger specific *Slave* modes. In this context, it can be used as a clock source.

Figure 6.17 illustrates how the various bits in the register influence the construction of the CK_PSC signal (the input to the Timer core block). In the figure, the default configuration is shown with bold lines: both ECE bit and SMS field are set to 0. The Timer core is clocked by CK_INT (typically running at 72 MHz).

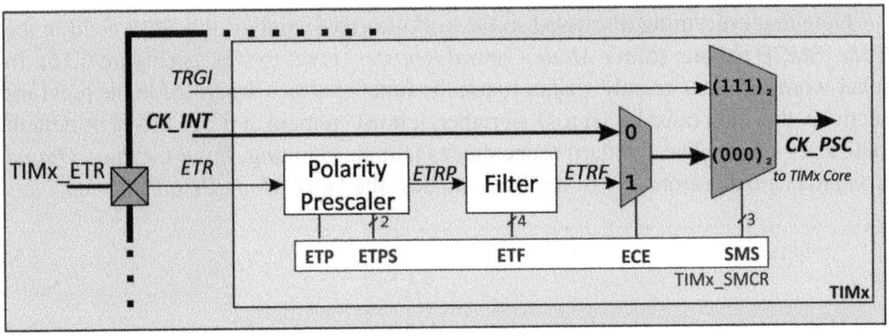

Figure 6.17. *Roles of the various bits in the TIMx_SCMR register*

While keeping SMS set to $(000)_2$ but setting ECE (*External Clock Enable*) to 1, CK_PSC is driven by ETRF. This signal originates from ETR, which directly comes from a pin. Note that the ETR signal undergoes several processing steps before becoming ETRF (F for filtered), including:

– the choice of the active edge: determined by the ETP bit. By default (bit set to 0), the rising edge is active;

– the option for frequency prescaling (controlled by the ETPS field) which generates the internal signal ETRP;

– the option for filtering to eliminate spurious pulses to finally produce the filtered signal ETRF.

By default, all these fields are set to 0, meaning that the ETR input (and the associated I/O) directly correspond to ETRF.

Finally, the last possibility involves the TRGI input. This input serves as the source for CK_PSC if the SMS field is set to $(111)_2$. Figure 6.18 illustrates all the possibilities for generating the TRGI.

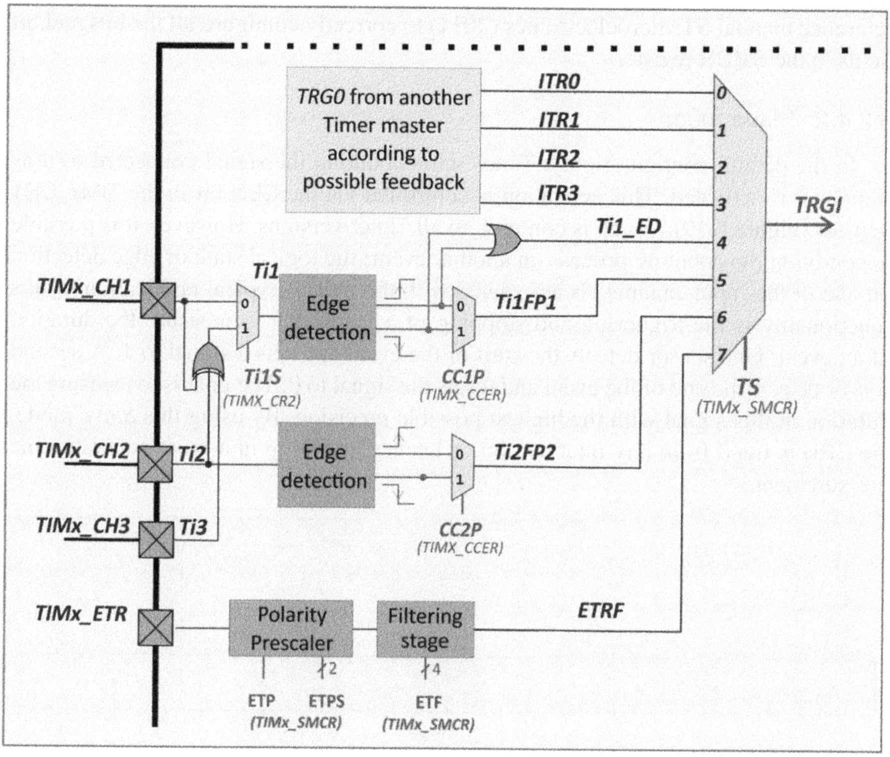

Figure 6.18. *Trigger signal generation*

This figure shows that there are three types of inputs for generating the TRGI signal:

– ITR0 to ITR3: signals originating from other Timers. These will be revisited in the next section dedication to the *Slave* mode.

– TI1ED, TI1FP1 and TI2FP2: these three inputs were analyzed in detail in section 6.2.3.1 regarding the Capture mode.

– ETRF: at a first glance, it might seem redundant to include this option, given that ETRF is already one of the three possible clock sources. However, this design choice allows ETRF to not only generate the clock CK_PSC (as previously discussed) but also to participate in the *Slave* modes of the Timer (similar to ITR0 to ITR3).

The SMCR register (Figure 6.16) plays a central role in configuring this part of the Trigger block controller and encoder interface, and we have only covered the main elements. Readers who wish to use these specific clock modes should refer to the reference manual STMicroelectronics (2011) to correctly configure all the bits and bit fields in the SMCR register.

6.2.4.2. Slave *mode*

In the default configuration, a Timer starts counting the signal connected to it as soon as it is activated. This activation is controlled via the CEN bit in the TIMx_CR1 register (Figure 6.19), which is common to all Timer versions. However, it is possible to condition the counting process on another event: the logical state or edge detection on one of the input channels is associated with the unit. A typical application of this functionality is the triggering and stopping of a stopwatch to measure the duration of an event. One sensor detects the start of the event and sets a signal to 1. A second sensor detects the end of the event and resets the signal to 0. The goal is to measure the duration of this signal with the highest possible precision. By using this *Slave* mode, the CPU is freed from any intervention or latency, resulting in a more accurate time measurement.

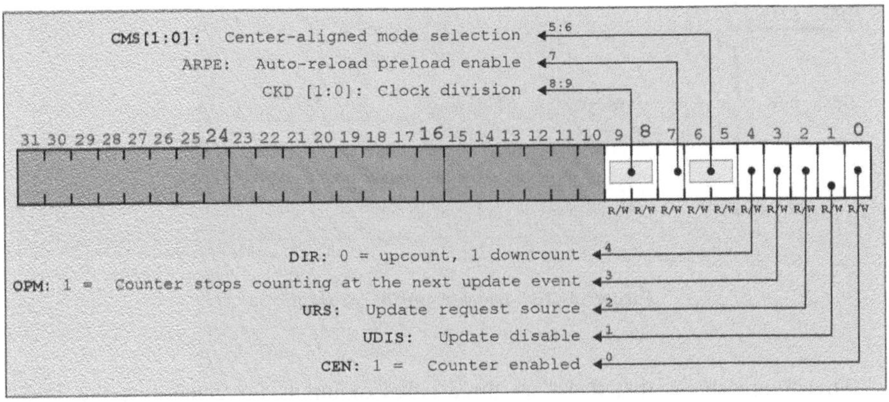

Figure 6.19. *CR1 register details*

Two elements fully define this *Slave* mode: the external signal that controls the mode, in addition to the behavior of the unit in response to this signal.

The external signal in question is none other than the TRGI input, as discussed in section 6.2.4.1. Although previously introduced in its role of generating the Timer core clock, the primary purpose of the TRGI is to enable the *Slave* mode. The various external sources that generate the TRGI were shown in Figure 6.18. It is worth noting that for many of the possible TRGI inputs, the polarity can be adjusted.

Before delving further into *Slave* modes, a question arises: How is the CK_PSC clock signal generated? Indeed, in this case, the SMS field is neither $(000)_2$ nor

$(111)_2$, so according to Figure 6.17, no clock source would be selected. In reality, this diagram is intentionally simplified. Configurations where SMS = $(1000)_2$ (*Reset Mode*) or SMS = $(101)_2$ (*Gated Mode*), or even SMS = $(110)_2$ (*Trigger Mode*), have the same effect on CK_PSC as SMS = $(000)_2$: the internal clock will be generated by CK_INT or by ETR, depending on the state of the ECE bit.

Let us now examine in detail the three possible behaviors in *Slave* mode:

– *Reset mode*, SMS = $(100)_2$: in this case, upon the rising edge of the TRGI signal, the CNT register is reset to 0 before resuming its count. Additionally, the *update* event UEV may be triggered, with its associated effects (refer to section 6.2.2.3 for details on this specific event). As in the standard use of the Timer, the CEN bit must be set to 1 to enable the Timer to start.

– *Gated mode*, SMS = $(101)_2$: counting (or downcounting) occurs only when the TRGI signal is at 1. Thus, TRGI acts on the level, not on the edge. When the signal returns to 0, the counter stops. Note, this behavior may seem counterintuitive: the CEN validation bit must be set to 1; otherwise, the counter will never start, even if TRGI is at 1.

– *Trigger mode*, SMS = $(110)_2$: this case corresponds to starting the Timer upon detecting a rising edge on the TRGI. In this mode, the CEN bit must initially be set to 0, as it is controlled by the TRGI input. Its transition to 1 is performed automatically by the hardware following the detection of the edge. It is important to note, however, that no further changes to the input signal can stop the unit: the CEN bit will not revert to 0 unless it is explicitly reset by software.

Figure 6.20 summarizes each of these three *Slave* modes.

6.2.4.3. One Pulse *mode*

The idea of this mode is to generate a pulse with a calibrated duration, triggered after a programmable delay by an external stimulus (typically an edge on a TIMx_CHy channel). This mode corresponds to a monostable function commonly used in electronics.

This functionality is active when the OPM bit in the TIMx_CR1 register is set to 1. It allows the unit to stop (and consequently reset the CEN bit to 0) as soon as an overflow occurs.

The *One Pulse* mode is primarily justified for output control. It can be considered a simplified use of the PWM functionalities, which will be explored in detail in Chapter 7. In this mode, a signal of duration T_{pulse} is generated after a delay T_{delay} following the start of the Timer, as illustrated in Figure 6.21. It is started by the *Trigger* signal, as previously discussed in the context of the *Slave* mode.

The Timer will be configured such that the time between its start and the overflow is equal to $T_d = T_{delay} + T_{pulse}$. To determine these durations, the additional registers

TIMx_CCRy are used, where x is the Timer number and y is the output channel number (ranging from 1 to 4 for advanced and standard Timers, and between 1 and 2 for Timers 9 and 12). In the default operation, when the CNT register increments, it is necessary to satisfy the condition $0 <$ TIMx_CCRy $\leqslant$ TIMx_ARR.

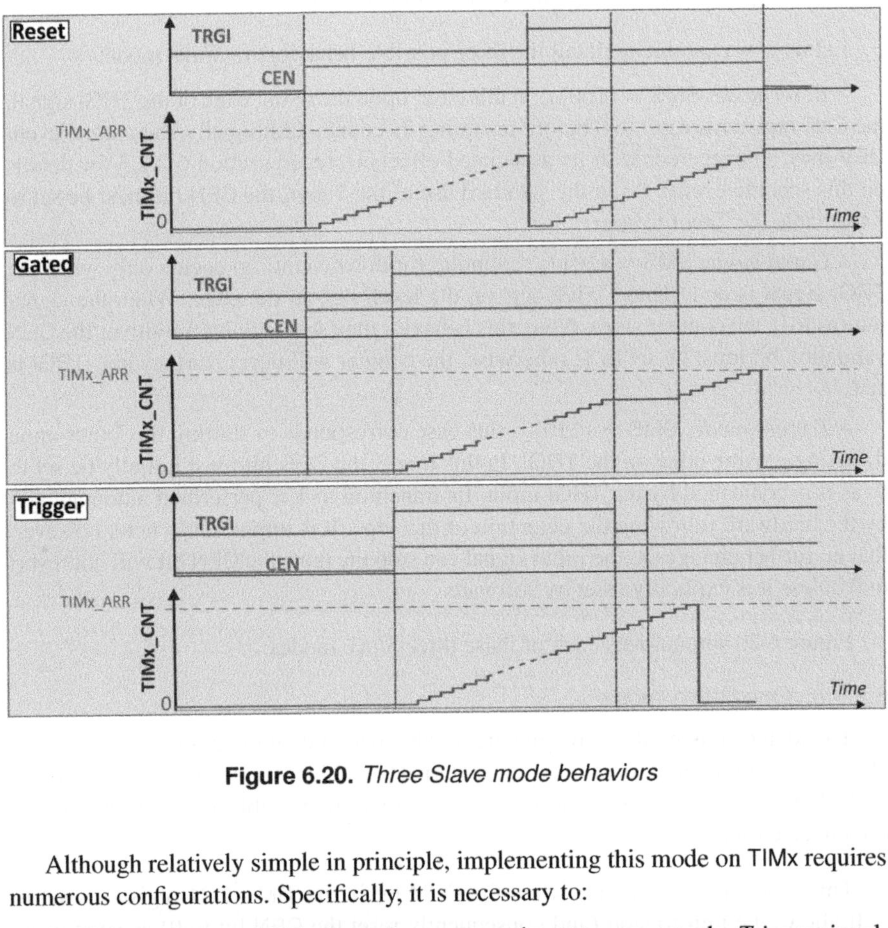

Figure 6.20. *Three Slave mode behaviors*

Although relatively simple in principle, implementing this mode on TIMx requires numerous configurations. Specifically, it is necessary to:

– configure the two GPIO channels: one as an input to generate the *Trigger* signal, and the other as an output for the delayed signal activation;

– select Timer triggering in *Slave/Trigger* mode (via the SMS field in TIMx_SMCR);

– choose the triggering edge (via the TIMx_CCMR1 register and the TS field in TIMx_SMCR);

– enable the output activation (via the TIMx_CCMR1 and TIMx_CCER registers, selecting *PWM mode* 2 for the OCzM field);

– set the TIMx_PSC and TIMx_ARR registers to achieve the desired duration $T_d = T_{delay} + T_{pulse}$;

– set the TIMx_CCRy register to achieve the desired pulse duration T_{pulse};

– set the OPM bit to 1 to enable the *One Pulse* mode.

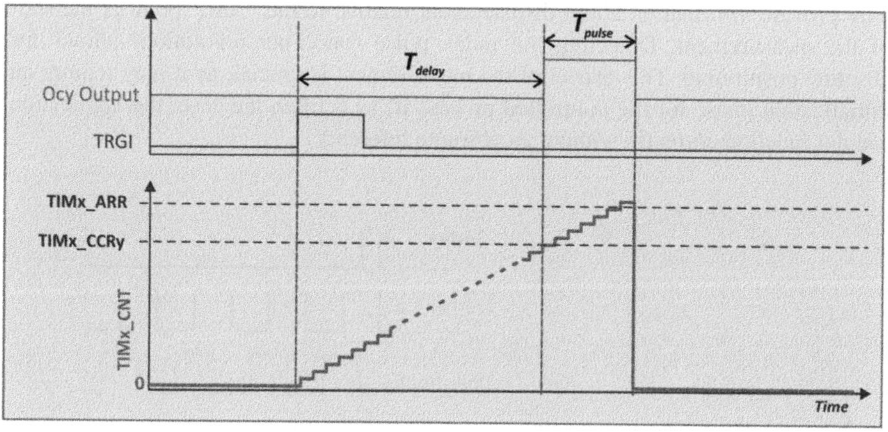

Figure 6.21. *One Pulse mode*

6.2.4.4. *Incremental encoder mode*

This mode is a specific case of the *Slave* mode. An incremental encoder is a device used to measure angular position digitally with high precision. It typically consists of a disk with two rows of n equally spaced slots (Figure 6.22). An LED combined with an optical sensor, positioned on either side of the disk, generates two square wave signals, channel A and channel B, with a period T_c as the disk rotates[4]. The n slots per track of the disk produce an angular displacement measurement of $\frac{2\pi}{n}$ radians between two rising edges of each channel. Since the two tracks are offset by a quarter of the period T_c, detecting all edges (both rising and falling) on both channels allows counting up to $4n$ edges per revolution, resulting in a resolution of $\frac{2\pi}{4n}$ radians. Naturally, the larger the value of n, the more precise the measurement. Additionally, measuring the frequency of these signals provides a way to determine the rotational speed of the axis. Note that the ARR register will be set to the maximum achievable count value minus 1 (depending on n, and on the edges considered in channels A and B).

4 There are other devices based on a single row of n slots but equipped with two optical sensors offset by half a step.

The offset between the two tracks is also necessary to determine the direction of rotation, allowing the system to decide whether to increment or decrement the stored value to calculate the relative position of the axis since startup[5].

Finally, an index provides an absolute reference for the entire system. The signals only provide information about displacement relative to the "zero" point at the start of the measurement. Detecting the index pulse (once per revolution) allows for absolute positioning. This aspect of the measurement is crucial, as it may require an initialization phase for the controlled process if, as is often the case, the application can not function correctly without an absolute reference.

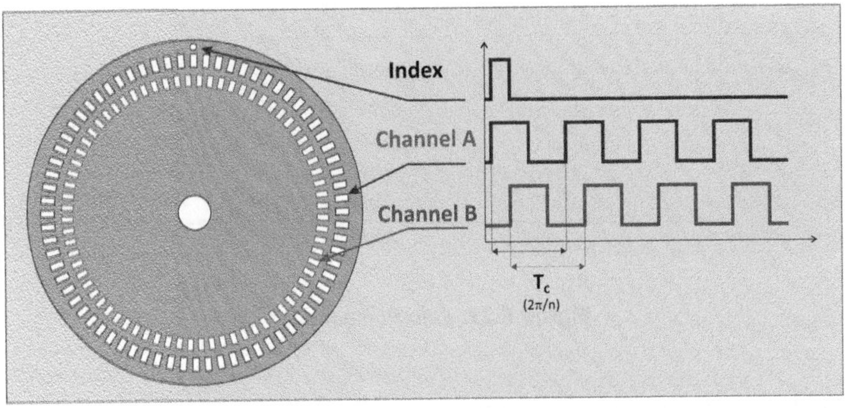

Figure 6.22. *Principle of an incremental encoder operating at a constant speed*

It is possible, using external interrupts for example (see section 5.4), to count angular displacement by detecting both rising and falling edges. While not entirely straightforward, it is certainly feasible. However, there is a much better option: using the *Encoder Interface* mode.

In this mode, simply connect the channel A and channel B signals to the TIMx_CH1 and TIMx_CH2 inputs, respectively, and configure the Timer accordingly so that the TIMx_CNT register directly contains the relative angular measurement value, modulo any overflow. However, note that the unit does not account for the index, meaning it can only provide relative positioning. It is the designer's responsibility to connect the "index" input to an independent GPIO pin and handle the detection of the reference position, preferably through an interrupt, though

5 There are also single-channel encoders that can be used if the axis of rotation moves in only one direction or for frequency measurement purposes.

polling is also an option. This detection allows for adjusting the measurement to make it absolute. In principle, this adjustment is only necessary once, provided there is no mechanical play and the Timer is never stopped. However, unless there are very stringent timing constraints, it is generally preferable to perform the adjustment upon each index detection.

In this specific mode, which actually consists of three sub-modes, the TRGI signal is no longer involved. Instead, the TI1FP1 and TI2FP2 signals take over. These inputs correspond to the channels A and B of the incremental encoder (refer to section 6.2.3.1 for details on connecting TI1FP1 and TI2FP2 to the Timer channels). The CNT count register is then fully managed by the incremental encoder interface block (Figure 6.4), which controls the input signal and determines the counting direction.

The three submodes in question are as follows:

– SMS = $(001)_2$: the system counts and downcounts the edges of TI1FP1. The resolution is therefore a half-period of the square wave signal arriving at this input, as counting is performed on both the rising and falling edges.

– SMS = $(010)_2$: the system counts and downcounts the edges of TI2FP2. Similarly, the resolution is a half-period of the signal arriving at this input, with counting also performed on both the rising and falling edges.

– SMS = $(011)_2$: the system counts and downcounts the edges of both TI1FP1 and TI2FP2. In this case, the resolution is a quarter-period of the input signals, therefore providing the highest resolution.

To conclude this section, referring to Figure 6.8, we aim to connect channel A to channel 1 and channel B to channel 2. The configuration should therefore be as follows:

– T1IS = 0 (TIMx_CR2);

– CC1P = CC2P = 0 (TIMx_CCER);

– CC1S = CC2S = $(01)_2$ (TIMx_CCMR1).

The PSC register must be set to 0 to avoid introducing any division in the counting/downcounting of edges.

6.2.5. Master *mode*

In this mode, a Timer referred to as the *Master* will control the operation of another unit. Figure 6.23 illustrates the association between two Timers, while 6.24 depicts the connection between a Timer and an ADC.

From Figure 6.18, we can observe that among the eight inputs of the multiplexer generating the TRGI signal, four are of I/O type (such as ETRF). The other four, labeled ITR0 to ITR3, originate from another Timer, depending on the interconnection possibilities shown in Figure 6.25.

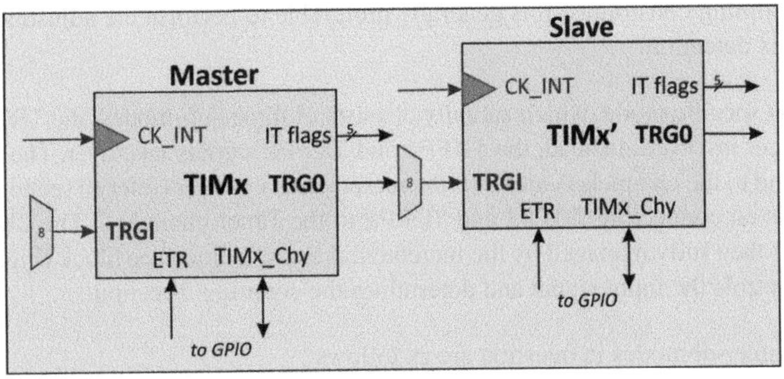

Figure 6.23. *Master/Slave relation between two Timers*

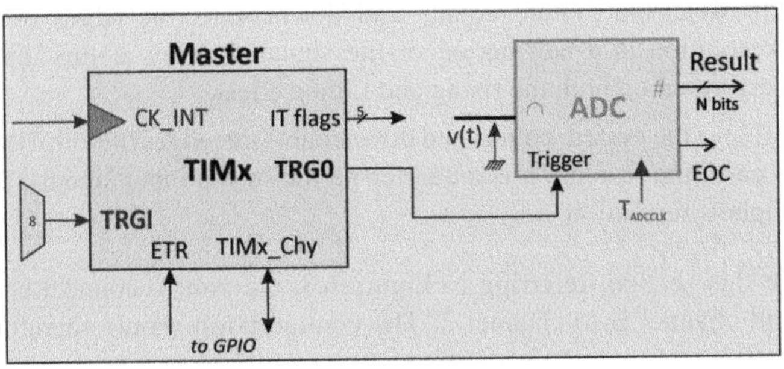

Figure 6.24. *Master Timer controlling an ADC*

Regardless of the *Slave* (Timer, ADC or DAC), it is the TRGO output of the *Master* Timer that triggers the event. This signal (Figure 6.26) can be generated by eight different causes within the operation of the *Master* Timer:

– *Reset*: the setting of the UG bit to 1, which causes a reset of the Timer;

– *Enable*: the start (enable) of the *Master* Timer;

– *Update*: the UEV event (see section 6.2.2.3) of the Timer;

– *CC1IF*: an interrupt request during a capture on channel 1;

– *OC1REF* to *OC4REF*: a comparison on one of the four channels of the *Master* Timer configured in *output compare* mode.

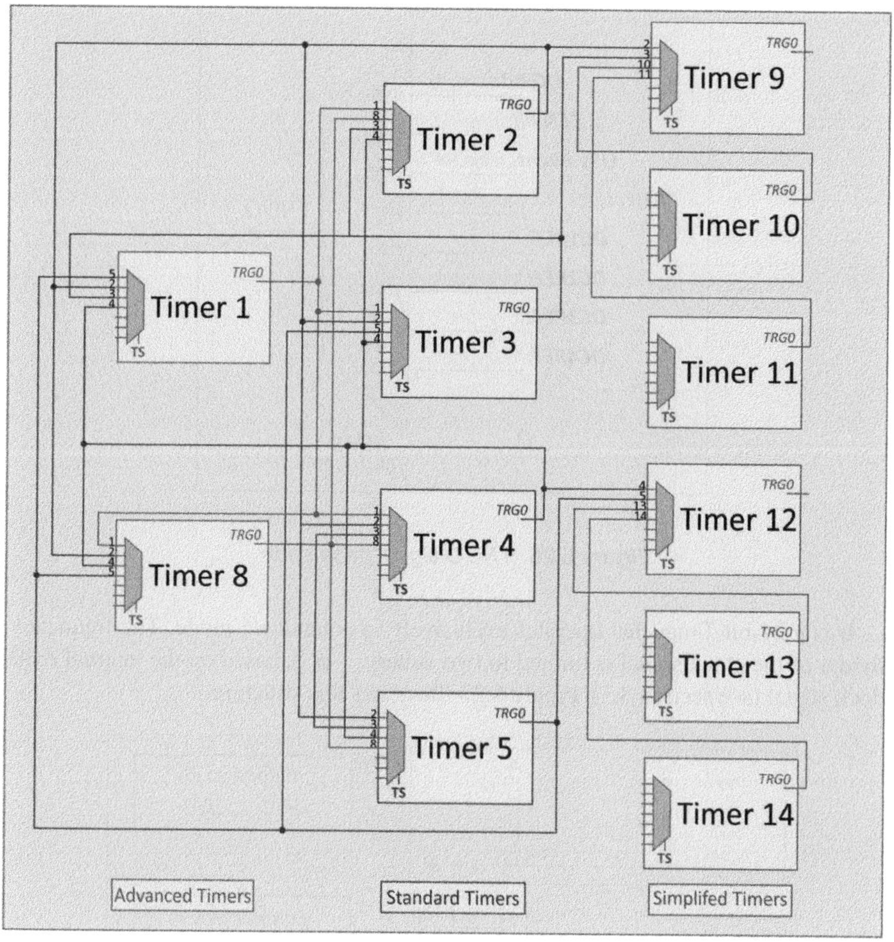

Figure 6.25. *Possible connections between Timers. For a color version of this figure, see www.iste.co.uk/mahout/programming.zip*

6.3. An additional Timer: the SysTick

The Cortex-M3 integrates an internal Timer within the core. It was designed by ARM© to facilitate the development of operating systems that are consistent across all implementations of this μcontroller core. In the context of *Bare Metal* usage (as considered in this book), it serves as an auxiliary Timer that can be particularly useful. While it is quite different from what has been presented so far, its extremely basic design ensures that its implementation is straightforward.

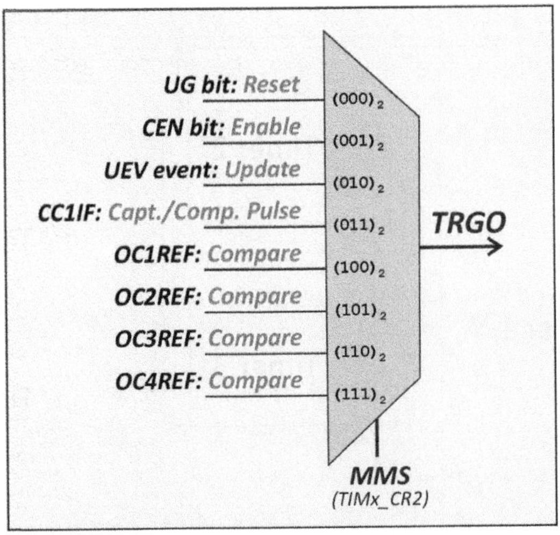

Figure 6.26. *TRGO signal generation*

It is a 24-bit Timer that operates exclusively in countdown mode. The frequency divider of the clock signal is limited to two values: 1 or 8, based on the internal AHB clock signal (see section 3.3). Figure 6.27 illustrates this structure.

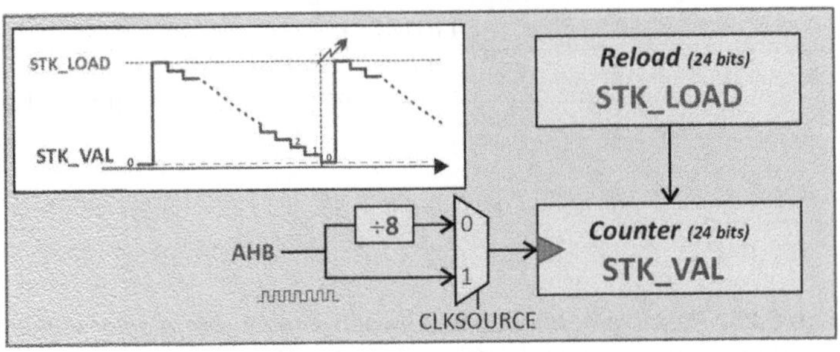

Figure 6.27. *Timer SysTick organization*

The SysTick Timer is organized around three registers:

– *STK_VAL*: a 24-bit counting register. Any write access to this register, regardless of the value provided, will reset it to zero;

– *STK_LOAD*: a 24-bit reload value register;

– *STK_CRTL*: a control register with only four useful bits:

- ENABLE, bit 0: enables (1)/disables (0) the countdown,

- TICKINT, bit 1: enables (1) the interrupt request,

- CLKSOURCE, bit 2: selects the AHB clock frequency divider, with 0 for $\frac{F_{\text{AHB}}}{8}$, and 1 for F_{AHB},

- COUNTFLAG, bit 16: reading it returns 1 if an overflow has occurred (i.e. if STK_VAL transitioned from 1 to 0) since the last read of the register.

The interrupt is generated when the countdown transitions from 1 to 0. This interrupt has its own specific interrupt vector in the NVIC, corresponding to entry no. 15 in the vector table (see Chapter 5).

The overflow period in cyclic operation, with an initial reload value set to $(N-1)$, is $N \times T_{in}$, where $T_{in} = \frac{1}{F_{\text{AHB}}}$ or $T_{in} = \frac{8}{F_{\text{AHB}}}$ depending on the value of the CLKSOURCE bit.

6.4. Guiding thread example

At the end of this chapter, we present only a relatively simple example of using a Timer. It demonstrates how to implement the incremental encoder mode. However, other examples in the upcoming chapters, particularly those on the ADC or PWM, will also make use of Timers. These additional applications will further illustrate some of the capabilities of these units.

6.4.1. *Case study: a control knob*

At the central unit level, there are one or more push buttons that allow the user to interact with the system. However, it may be more advantageous to use an encoder wheel (knob), especially for menu navigation. The counter capacity is arbitrarily set to 16 values associated with the encoder wheel. We propose a solution using Timer no. 4 in incremental encoder mode. This code focuses solely on initialization. It can be written directly into the main procedure or included in a dedicated driver.

This is an incremental encoder, so once this initialization code has been executed, the CNT register will update in response to pulses arriving on channels A (GPIOB.6) and B (GPIOB.7). To determine the relative movement of the knob since initialization, the application simply needs to read the CNT register.

6.4.2. *Code extract*

```
RCC->APB1ENR |= RCC_APB1ENR_TIM4EN;
RCC->APB2ENR |= RCC_APB2ENR_IOPBEN;

/* GPIOB 6..0 and GPIOB 7..0 as floating input */
GPIOB->CRL &= ~(0xF<<(7*4)) | (0xF<<(6*4));
```

```
GPIOB->CRL |= (0x4<<(7*4)) | (0x4<<(6*4));

/* Trigger Control Block: Slave mode = encoder mode 3 */
TIM4->SMCR &= ~TIM_SMCR_SMS;
TIM4->SMCR |= 0x3<<0;

/* Input Capture Output Compare Block */
/* Config. inputs Channel1 - TI1FP1 and Channel2 - TI2FP2 */
/* TI1 on Channel 1 */
TIM4->CR2 &= ~TIM_CR2_TI1S;
/* TI1FP1 on TI1, and TI2FP2 on TI2 */
/* Channel1 and Channel2 are inputs (CC1S = CC2S = 1) */
TIM4->CCMR1 &= ~(TIM_CCMR1_CC1S | TIM_CCMR1_CC2S);
TIM4->CCMR1 |= (1<<8 | 1<<0);
/* positive polarity */
TIM4->CCER &= ~(TIM_CCER_CC1P | TIM_CCER_CC2P);

/* TIMx Core Block: Modulo 16 */
TIM4->PSC = 0;
TIM4->ARR = 16-1;          /* N.b. max equals 15 */
TIM4->CR1 |= TIM_CR1_CEN;
```

Code 6.2. *Proposed solution for using a Timer in incremental encoder mode*

7

Pulse-Width Modulation (PWM)

REMARK.– This chapter introduces a specific mode offered by Timers. This mode allows output pins to be driven. One of its main applications is to serve as a substitute for a digital-to-analog conversion unit.

7.1. Generalities on PWM-type signals

Signals referred to as "pulse-width modulation", more commonly known under the acronym PWM, are relatively simple signals, as they are inherently binary signals.

7.1.1. *Definition*

A PWM signal is a *binary* digital signal consisting of a series of pulses with a fixed period T_{PWM}. Each pulse has its own duration, denoted here by T_h (for the duration associated with the high state). The duration of each pulse thus carries information that can range from 0 to T_{PWM}. For such signals, the *duty cycle* or *ratio*, often denoted by α, is commonly used and defined by $\alpha = \frac{T_h}{T_{\text{PWM}}}$. This ratio can vary from 0% to 100%.

For a given process, the period T_{PWM} is not intended to change over time in general. However, the duration T_h will vary to create the desired modulation.

Figure 7.1 illustrates such a signal, assuming that the high state corresponds to a voltage V_{max}. In this example, the duty cycle was reprogrammed after three periods.

The most common uses of these signals include information transmission, digital-to-analog conversion and motor control.

For a color version of all the Codes in this chapter, see www.iste.co.uk/mahout/programming.zip

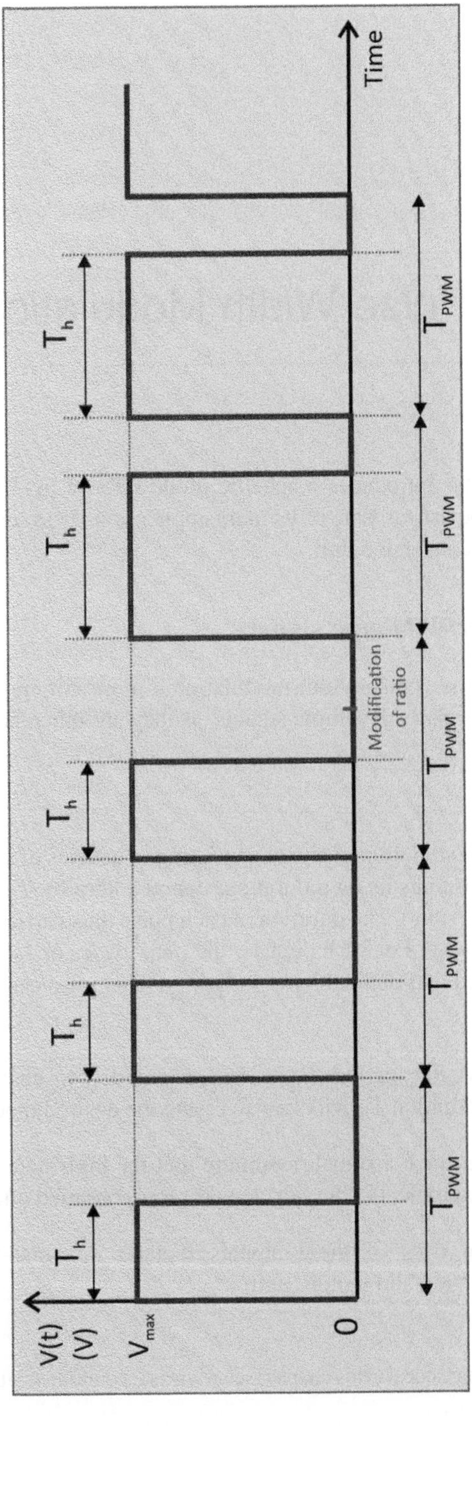

Figure 7.1. *PWM signal with a varying* T_h

7.1.2. *Use in information transmission*

Transmission of coded information via a PWM signal is possible, as is amplitude modulation (AM) or frequency modulation (FM). The main idea is that each new pulse, and therefore each new duration T_h, corresponds to a coded symbol. The receiver simply needs to measure the duration of the high states to decode the information for processing.

This technique is used, particularly in modeling, for transmitting "commands" between a control panel and a remote-controlled device. The actuator used is a servomotor (Figure 7.2), which is an electrically powered motor controlled to maintain a specific position.

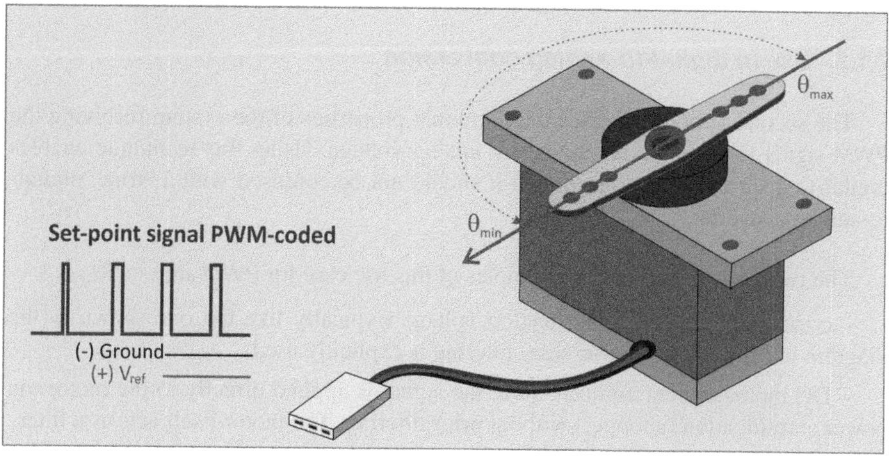

Figure 7.2. *"Classic" servomotor with a 180-degree range of motion*

The PWM signal, with its variable duration T_h, corresponds in this case to the angular position desired for the servometer. Typically (see Figure 7.3), the signal has a period of $T_{\text{PWM}} = 20$ ms and the duration T_h varies between 1 and 2 ms to represent the full range of servometer movement.

As illustrated on the right-hand side of this figure, for this type of servomotor, the position encoding over the range $[\theta_{min}, \theta_{max}]$ is confined to a narrow interval (only 5% of the duty cycle is utilized). Outside of this range, saturation occurs, and the motor is set to one of its extreme positions. On the timing diagram shown on the left-hand side of the figure, the angular movement of the motor axis is visible as T_h transitions from 1 to 2 ms, corresponding to the maximum range of motion.

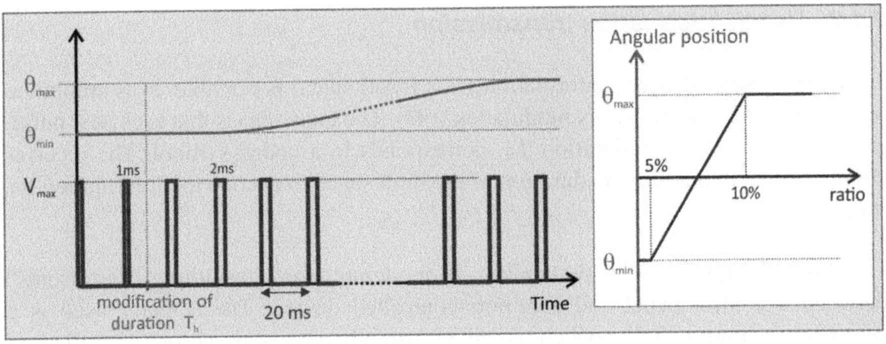

Figure 7.3. *PWM command encoding for a typical servometer*

7.1.3. *Use in digital-to-analog conversion*

The second application uses the harmonic properties of the system receiving the PWM signal to generate an equivalent analog voltage. Using this technique enables digital-to-analog conversion, though it should not be confused with a "true" digital-to-analog converter.

The two typical application examples of this use case for PWM are:

– creation of an equivalent analog voltage (typically like the one shown in the diagram in Figure 7.4). In this case, filtering is explicitly used;

– DC motor current control: here, the signal is applied directly to the motor via power amplification (chopper) without prior filtering. The motor itself acts as a filter.

7.1.3.1. *Application: creating an equivalent analog voltage*

The principle is to create an analog signal, denoted by $y(t)$, that varies over time (Figure 7.4). To achieve this using a PWM, it is common to place a low-pass filter at the output of the μcontroller that generates the PWM signal. The simplest filter is an RC circuit connected ahead of a buffer amplifier to avoid impedance issues.

The PWM signal is always characterized by its pulse duration but, in this case, the parameter of interest is no longer directly the duration T_h but instead the ratio (or duty cycle) $\alpha = \frac{T_h}{T_{\text{PWM}}}$. By setting the ratio in this example to 40%, the equivalent analog voltage then represents 40% of the maximum signal voltage. This effectively achieves the desired function, namely, digital-to-analog conversion. However, it is crucial to respect the frequency characteristics of the RC filter for proper operation. To understand this point, let us analyze the dynamics of this filter. Without delving into the details of the modeling, and assuming the buffer amplifier to be ideal and without gain, the filter is governed by the following differential equation, where $u(t)$

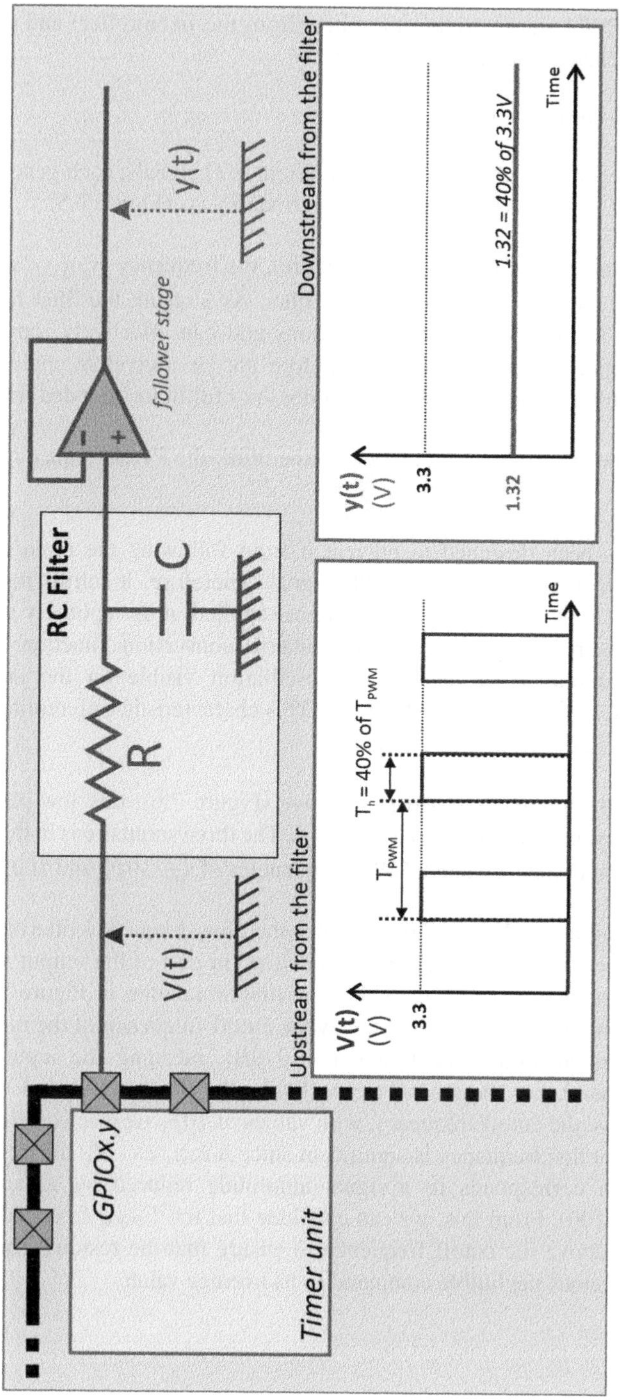

Figure 7.4. *Filtered PWM signal*

is the temporal PWM signal driving the filter (from the μcontroller) and $y(t)$ is the analog voltage generated at the filter output:

$$RC\dot{y}(t) + y(t) = u(t)$$

Observe the evolution of $y(t)$ for three different $u(t)$ signals, each generated with a duty cycle of 40%, but with three different periods T_{PWM} (Figure 7.5).

In the first simulation (at the top of the figure), the frequency $F_{PWM} = \frac{1}{T_{\text{PWM}}}$ is low compared to the cutoff frequency of the filter. As a result, the filter has enough time to respond to the sequence of alternations and can effectively reproduce the binary input signal. The output $y(t)$ is therefore not an equivalent analog voltage. In this case, the filter is ineffective because it does not fulfill its intended role.

For the second simulation, and especially the third, the PWM frequency has been increased.

The filter has been designed to prevent it from following the rapid successive alternations (high frequency) of the PWM signal. Therefore, it fulfills its role as it effectively only "sees" the average of the signal applied at its input. By selecting a sufficiently high frequency, the digital-to-analog conversion function is largely achieved. The amplitude of the residual oscillation visible on the output $y(t)$ decreases as F_{PWM} increases but will persist. This characteristic differentiates it from the use of a true digital-to-analog converter.

From a strictly frequency-based perspective (Figure 7.6), this low-pass filter is characterized by a cutoff frequency $Fc = \frac{1}{2\pi RC}$. The three simulations in this example were performed with the respective PWM frequencies of $\frac{F_c}{10}$, $10F_c$ and $100F_c$.

The Bode diagram in Figure 7.6 illustrates the "low-frequency filtering" aspects of the signal. This curve represents the attenuation (in dB) of the output signal as a function of the input signal frequency. For the first simulation in Figure 7.5, it was performed with an input frequency $\frac{F_c}{10}$ below the cutoff frequency of the filter. At this frequency, the attenuation is negligible ($\simeq$ 0 dB), meaning the input signal is accurately replicated. For the second (respectively, the third) simulation, the F_{PWM} frequency is above the cutoff frequency, with values of $10F_c$ (respectively, of $100F_c$). The attenuation at this frequency is significant since it reaches -20 dB (respectively, -40 dB), which corresponds to a signal amplitude reduced by a factor of 10 (respectively, of 100). From this, we can conclude that the F_{PWM} frequency must be configured well above the cutoff frequency to ensure that the residual ripple in the output signal becomes negligible compared to its average value.

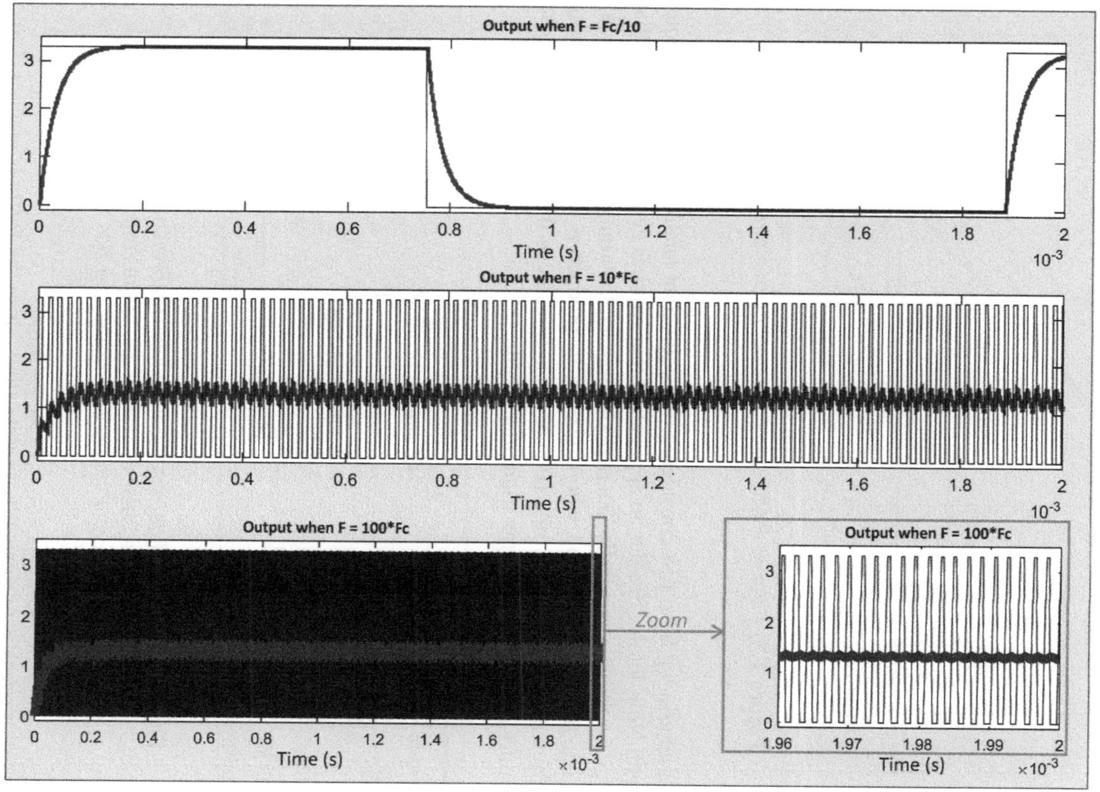

Figure 7.5. *RC filter simulation using different PWM frequencies. For a color version of this figure, see www.iste.co.uk/mahout/programming.zip*

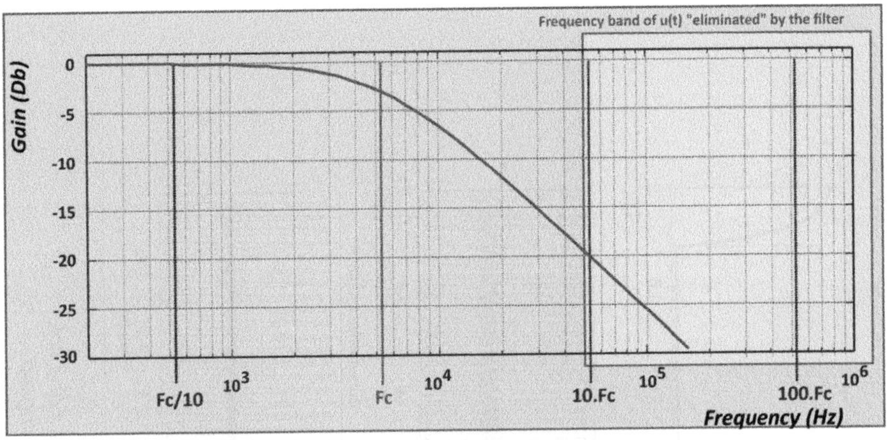

Figure 7.6. *Filtered PWM signal: frequency domain aspect*

In the scenario we have just considered, the equivalent analog signal was unique and constant. Now, let us consider an application that requires generating a signal that also evolves over time, potentially in a periodic manner. Continuing with the previous example, imagine an application whose goal is to produce a voltage $y(t)$ varying periodically with a triangular profile (Figure 7.7). To achieve this, it is necessary to adjust the duty cycle with the same triangular profile.

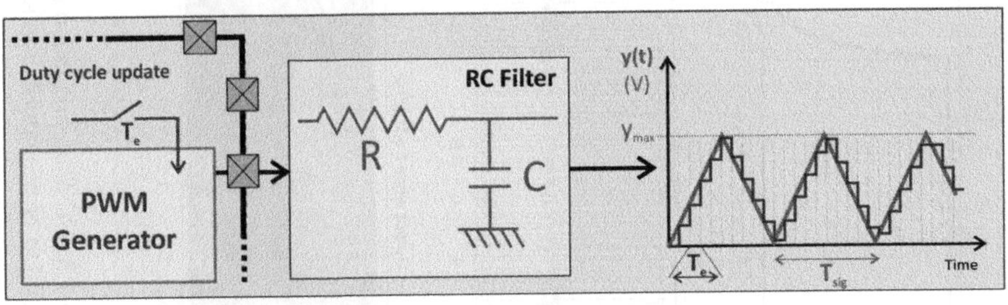

Figure 7.7. *Case of generating a periodic equivalent analog signal. For a color version of this figure, see www.iste.co.uk/mahout/programming.zip*

The entire process is intrinsically discrete-time, since the PWM is generated by a μcontroller. At best, the signal $y(t)$ can only approximate a stepped signal, entirely neglecting the inherent dynamics of the filter. Specifically, to generate this type of output signal, the duty cycle must be updated at a fixed periodicity T_e, referred to as the sampling period.

Three distinct frequencies must therefore be considered in this scenario:

– the frequency $F_{sig} = \frac{1}{T_{sig}}$ of the signal intended to be created at the output of the filter;

– the sampling frequency $F_e = \frac{1}{T_e}$, which determines how often the duty cycle is refreshed;

– the frequency $F_{PWM} = \frac{1}{T_{\mathrm{PWM}}}$ of the PWM signal upstream of the filter.

To ensure the frequency coherence of the system, it will be necessary to verify that $T_s \gg T_e \gg T_{\mathrm{PWM}}$.

The values of R and C of the filter must therefore be dimensioned so that its cutoff frequency satisfies $F_{sig} < F_c \ll F_{PWM}$.

7.1.3.2. *Application: motor control*

The use of PWM when controlling an electric motor (whether it is a DC motor, synchronous motor, asynchronous motor, or *brushless* motor) is fundamentally different from its use with a servomotor, even though both involve motors.

For this type of application, which involves power conversion, there is no longer a need to place an RC filter between the μcontroller output and the motor. However, an intermediate stage is required: a chopper circuit that acts as a power amplifier. This is necessary because a μcontroller cannot supply sufficient current levels to power the motor directly.

Let us leave aside the frequency characteristics of the power stage and focus solely on those specific to a DC motor. These characteristics are identical to those of a filter. As a first approximation, the "slow" mechanical dynamics of the motor correspond to the same first-order ordinary differential equation:

$$\tau\dot{\Omega}(t) + \Omega(t) = K_m u(t)$$

with $\Omega(t)$ representing the rotational speed of the motor, τ is referred to as the time constant of the motor and K_m is its static gain.

Therefore, the use of direct control via a PWM signal is feasible. The frequency considerations to be respected are exactly similar to those stated for the RC filter[1], specifically $F_{PWM} \gg \frac{1}{2\pi\tau}$.

1 Here, we are discussing the voltage control for small-power motors only. For larger motors, it will also be necessary to control the current, which will involve another time constant, the electrical one.

In practice, however, a very high frequency F_{PWM} is not used because the chopper could experience significant power losses. A common guideline is to set the frequency F_{PWM} between 20 and 50 kHz to avoid hearing the mechanical vibrations of the windings[2].

7.2. Implementation of PWM in an STM32F10x μcontroller

7.2.1. *Basic operation*

In a μcontroller, the function that enables the generation of such a signal is systematically associated with a Timer module. For certain μcontrollers, there are Timer units specifically dedicated to this purpose. In the case of the STM32, the *advanced, standard* and *simplified* Timer units (see Chapter 6) can be used to implement the generation of such a signal.

The PWM function in these μcontrollers is essentially a subset of the *Compare* mode (see section 6.2.3.2). Figure 6.14 can be complemented upon with the simplified Figure 7.8, which provides details on how the PWM signal is constructed.

In this figure, the relevant registers are shown:

– the three basic registers of a Timer: the counter CNT, the auto-reload register ARR and the prescaler register PSC, which adjusts the frequency division. As explained in Chapter 6, this trio enables the Timer to count and overflows at the desired period. Therefore, it is solely the configuration of the PSC/ARR pair that determines the PWM period T_{PWM};

– the fourth register, CCRx, is the one that allows for the PWM pulse duration T_h to be adjusted.

The generation of the signal primarily relies on two comparators and logic for managing the output signal. Let us consider the most standard case first, with possible variations discussed later. The management logic corresponds to the operation of an R/S flip-flop. In this setup, the first comparator resets the CNT counter to zero, thereby controlling the overflow period. It also sets the output signal to a high state, functioning as the *set* input of the flip-flop. The second comparator, which compares CNT with CCRx, acts on the *reset* input of the flip-flop: when the two registers are equal, the PWM signal transitions back into the low state.

---

2 The frequency F_{PWM} can exceed 50 kHz, but in such cases, a detailed analysis of the chopper becomes necessary.

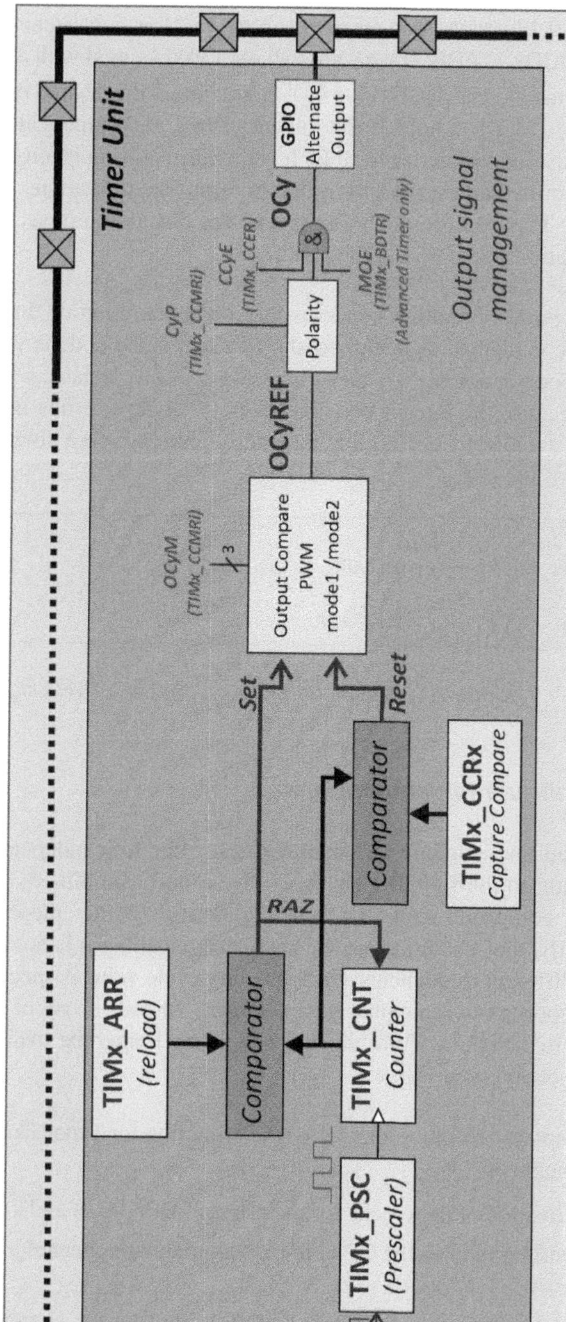

Figure 7.8. *Simplified architecture of the PWM functionality within a Timer unit*

Figure 7.9 illustrates this standard operation. For consistency, it is necessary to ensure that CCRx $<$ ARR. If we want to have a PWM signal with a duty cycle of $x\%$, it is necessary to calculate CCRx $= \frac{x.\text{ARR}}{100}$ to maintain the desired ratio. However, again note that these registers hold 16-bit integer values, and numerical quantization means that not all resolutions are achievable. It is therefore advantageous (or even necessary) to set ARR to the highest possible value to minimize limitations arising from integer calculations. This consideration aligns with the discussion in section 6.2.2 regarding the configuration of the PSC-ARR pair.

Another point of caution concerns the implementation of this calculation. If the ratio variable is defined as unsigned short int and if the code is written as in the first version of code example 7.1, then the TIMx->CCRy register will be zero after the operation because the integer division ratio/100 always results in 0. In practice, this issue can be avoided by performing the multiplication before division, as shown in the second line of the code.

```
/*  Incorrect syntax! */
    TIMx->CCRy = TIMx->ARR * (ratio/100)
/*  Correct syntax! */
    TIMx->CCRy = (TIMx->ARR * ratio)/100
```

Code 7.1. *Updating the duty signal of a PWM signal*

7.2.2. *Configuration and options*

Advanced and standard Timer units each offer four independent PWM outputs, corresponding to the four I/O channels of the unit. Simplified Timers, on the other hand, are equipped with two such outputs. While these channels operate independently, they share the same Timer base, meaning it is not possible to program them with different frequencies. Only the duty cycle value is specific to each channel. It is also important to remember the exclusivity of use: if one of the four channels is configured to handle a PWM signal, it will no longer be available for any other function (such as *capture*).

The complete configuration of the PWM function for Timer x on channel y requires the following steps:

– the activation of the clocks for the relevant GPIO port and Timer x;

– the configuration of the GPIO pin associated with channel y in *Alternate Output* mode;

– the configuration of the TIMx_CCMR1 register for channels 1 and 2 or the TIMx_CCMR2 register for channels 3 and 4 (see Figure 6.15) with:

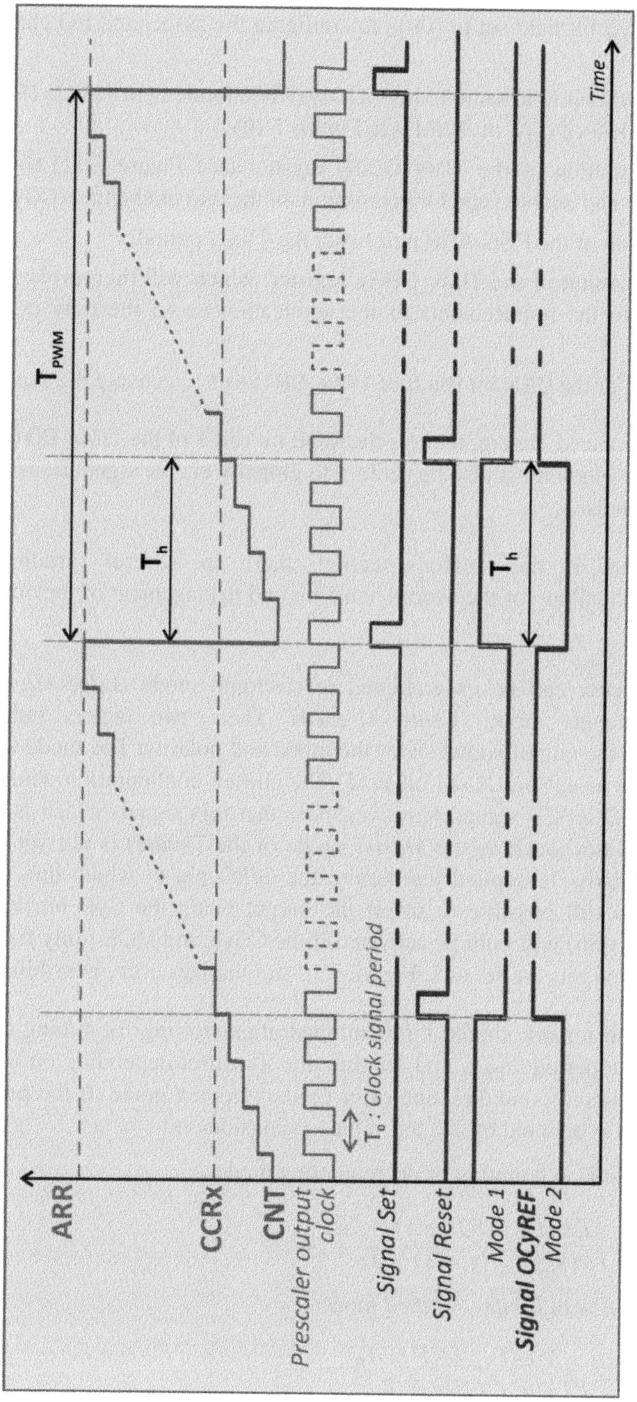

Figure 7.9. *Generation of the PWM signal in a Timer unit*

- the CCyS bit field set to $(00)_2$ to configure the associated I/O channel as an output,

- the OCyM bit field set to either $(110)_2$ (PWM mode 1) or $(111)_2$ (PWM mode 2) to select the desired type of PWM (see Figure 7.10);

– the configuration of the TIMx_CCER register (see Figure 6.11) to select the polarity (CCyP) and enable signal transmission on the output channel (CCyE);

– the selection of the PSC-ARR pair to set the T_{PWM} period;

– the initialization of the TIMx_CRRy register, which will then evolve over time and according to the requirements of the application to set the duty cycle (or T_h duration);

– the setting of the CEN bit (bit 0 of TIMx_CR1) to 1 to activate the function.

Note, for advanced Timers, there is the MOE bit (bit 1 of the TIMx_BDTR register, see Figure 7.8), which must also be set to 1 to globally enable signal transmission on the output channels.

As mentioned in the previous section, there are several variations in the configuration that allow for the overall behavior and management of the output signal to be modified.

First, the Timer can be programmed in sawtooth mode (*Edge-Aligned*) or in symmetrical triangle mode (*Center-Aligned*). Then, two factors influence the management of the output signal state: the mode and polarity. The mode (either 1 or 2) is configured using the OCyM bit field. The chosen configuration determines the shaping of the OCyREF signal. However, note that this signal, which is useful for other functionalities (such as the *Master* mode of the Timers) is not yet the output signal OCy. Polarity is applied just before the GPIO pin to which this function is connected. It is still possible to invert the output using the CyP bit. Finally, the physical output (pin) will only be activated if the CCyE and MOE (only for advanced Timers) validation bits are set to 1. Figure 7.10 summarizes every possibility.

An important remark should be mentioned after viewing the timing diagram in Figure 7.10. The period T_{PWM} and the duration T_h differ depending on whether the Timer operates in only one direction or in *Center-Aligned* mode. If the period at the prescaler output is denoted by T_0, the values to consider are:

– If the Timer is in counting or decrementing mode:

$$T_{\text{PWM}} = (TIM\text{x\_}ARR + 1) \times T_0$$
$$T_h = (TIM\text{x\_}CCR\text{y} + 1) \times T_0$$

– If the Timer is in *Center-Aligned* mode:

$$T_{\text{PWM}} = 2 \times TIM\text{x\_}ARR \times T_0$$
$$T_h = 2 \times TIM\text{x\_}CCR\text{y} \times T_0$$

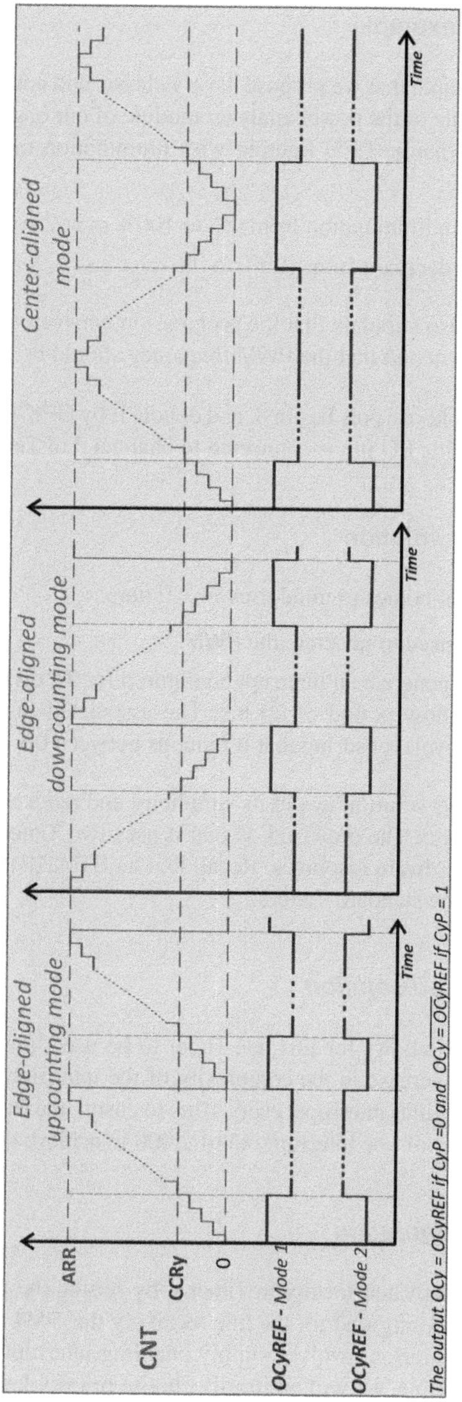

Figure 7.10. *PWM signal as a function of the counting direction, the PWM mode and the polarity*

7.3. Guiding thread example

The application example that we propose is very classic and could be implemented on the central unit module or the power analyzer module of our ongoing example. The idea is to implement dynamic LED lighting with illumination modulated in a two-phase breathing pattern:

1) a linear increase in illumination from 0% to 100% over 2 s;

2) a similarly linear decrease from 100% to 0% over 2 s.

The specifications also stipulate that the progression between each step should be 1% at each new increment and that the PWM frequency should be 100 kHz.

Arbitrarily, we will choose port B, pin 8, and denote it by GPIOB.8. In the *mapping* of the STM32F103RB, this I/O pin is connected to channel 3 of Timer 4 by default.

7.3.1. *First possible solution*

The first solution that comes to mind uses two Timers:

– Timer 4 is clearly used to generate the PWM.

– Timer 3 is used to generate an interrupt configured for 2 s divided by 100, which results in a Timer overflow period of 20 ms. The associated interrupt routine will calculate the new duty cycle, ensuring that it remains between 0% and 99%.

The advantage of this solution lies in its simplicity and reduced CPU load, which does not have much to do. The drawback is that it uses two Timers, which is a little excessive in terms of hardware resources. Recall that an STM32F103RB has only one advanced Timer and three standard Timers.

7.3.2. *Second adopted solution*

This second solution allows for just one Timer to be used, the one for the PWM. This results in a slight increase in the complexity of the interrupt routine. The Timer will be configured for regular interrupts every 10μs to ensure the PWM. The duty cycle will be modified at a rate of one interrupt out of 2,000 to achieve the required 20 ms.

7.3.3. *Interrupt configuration*

Interrupts must be activated locally in Timer 4 by setting the UIE (TIMx_SR) bit. The NVIC must also be configured for the line receiving the TIM4 interrupts, which is line no. 30. This configuration involves simply enabling interrupt no. 30 and setting its priority (for this example, we will arbitrarily choose priority level 2).

7.3.4. *The PWM configuration itself*

The PWM will correspond to the output of channel no. 3 of Timer 4. Therefore, it is necessary:

– to configure channel no. 4 as an output. For this, the 2-bit field CC3S (TIM4_CCMR2) must be set to $(00)_2$;

– to select the desired *Compare* mode, either PWM mode 1 or PWM mode 2. Here, we will opt for mode 1 by setting the OCM3 (TIM4_CCMR2) field to the value $(110)_2$;

– to set the possible configurations for the evolution of the CNT register: we opt for the *Edge-Aligned* mode, which is perfectly suited for our use. To do this, the CMS (TIMx_CR1) field must be set to $(00)_2$ to avoid one of the *Center-Aligned* modes and remain in the default *Edge-Aligned* configuration;

– to adjust the polarity of the OC3 signal relative to the OC3REF signal we just configured: we choose not to change the polarity, so the OC3P (TIMx_CCER) bit will be set to 0;

– to enable the OC3 output, as it is not active by default, the OC3E (TIMx_CCER) bit must be set to 1. Note that if we had chosen TIM1, for example, which is an Advanced Timer, it would also have been necessary to set the MOE (TIM1_BDTR) bit to enable the OCy output.

7.3.5. *The GPIO configuration*

The GPIOB.8 pin carries the output signal. This pin must therefore be preempted by the PWM unit rather than being managed by the ODR, which handles it in the default binary I/O configuration. The pin will thus be configured as *Alternate Output*. Since the LED requires both high and low levels to function, let us choose the *Push-Pull* technology instead of *Open Drain*. Therefore, the pin configuration is *Alternate Output Push-Pull*.

7.3.6. *Code excerpt*

The code example 7.2 demonstrates the expected functionality. Notably, in this example, unused pins 9–15 are configured as *Input Pull-Down* (rather than *Floating Input*) to prevent these lines from changing states erratically (capacitive coupling) due to the influence of our PWM output.

```
int DutyValue;  /* duty cycle evolution between 0 and 99              */
int Up_down;    /* signed increment of the duty cycle (+1 or -1)      */
int Cpt_TPWM;   /* Period counter PWM.T_PWM=10µs, Te=20ms.            */
                /* Cpt_TPWM incremented at each T_PWM (IT)            */
                /* Modification of the ratio every 20ms               */

```

```
/**********************************/
/* Update duty cycle Cy PB8      */
/**********************************/
void TIM4_IRQHandler(void)
{
    /* Set IT source flat to 0 */
  TIM4->SR &= ~TIM_SR_UIF;
    /* Management modulo 2000 (to update every 20ms)*/
  Cpt_TPWM++;
  if (Cpt_TPWM == 2000)
  {
    Cpt_TPWM = 0;
  /* Update duty cycle   */
    TIM4->CCR3 = ((DutyValue*(TIM4->ARR))/100);
  /* Ramp management */
    DutyValue += Up_down;
    if (DutyValue == 99) Up_down = -1;
    else if (DutyValue == 0) Up_down = +1;
  }
}
/**********************************/
/*    == Main procedure ==       */
/**********************************/
int main(void)
{
  DutyValue = 0;
  Up_down = 1;
  Cpt_TPWM = 0;
/**********************************************/
/* GPIOB 8: Altenate Output push-pull        */
/* GPIOB 9 to 15 configured as input pull-down */
/*          to avoid capacitive coupling     */
/**********************************************/
  RCC->APB2ENR |= RCC_APB2ENR_IOPBEN;    /* Enable Ck GPIOB */
  GPIOB->CRH = 0x88888880;
  GPIOB->CRH |= 0xA;
  GPIOB->ODR = 0;
/**************************************/
/* TIMER UNDER TEST: TIM4            */
/* PWM + IT configuration            */
/**************************************/
  RCC->APB1ENR |= RCC_APB1ENR_TIM4EN;
/* Timer core configuration */
/* TIM4 configured for PWM at 100kHz */
/* TPWM = 10µs */
/* ARR*PSC = 10 * 72 = 720 */
/* ARR to maximize (systematically to achieve resolution) */
/* Best possible PWM */
  TIM4->PSC = 0;
  TIM4->ARR = 720-1;
```

```
/* PWM configuration (Capture / Compare section) */
/* Channel 3 as output (CC3S = 00b) */
  TIM4->CCMR2 &= ~0x3;
/* Mode 1 => Rcy=0 if CCRy=0 Rcy=100% if CCRy=ARR (OC3M=110b) */
  TIM4->CCMR2 &= ~TIM_CCMR2_OC3M;
  TIM4->CCMR2 |= 0x6<<4;
/* Edge Aligned Mode, CMS = 00b */
  TIM4->CR1 &= ~TIM_CR1_CMS;
/* Adjustment of OC3 polarity */
  TIM4->CCER &= ~TIM_CCER_CC3P;
/* Enabling OC3 output */
  TIM4->CCER |= TIM_CCER_CC3E;
/* Initializing duty cycle to */
  TIM4->CCR3 = 0;
/* Configuring interrupt */
  TIM4->DIER |= TIM_DIER_UIE;
  NVIC->ISER[0] |= 1<<TIM4_IRQn; /*TIM4_IRQn = 30*/
  NVIC->IP[TIM4_IRQn] = 2<<4;
/* Enabling TIM4 */
  TIM4->CR1 |= TIM_CR1_CEN;
/**********************************************/

  while(1)
  {
  }
}
```

Code 7.2. *Proposed solution to manage an LED using PWM*

8

Analog to Digital Converter

An ADC (*analog to digital converter*) provides the quantified digital representation of an analog voltage that remains stable during the conversion time. Thus, any sensor converting a physical quantity into an analog voltage will be connected to the μcontroller via an ADC.

8.1. Generalities and operating principles

8.1.1. *Role and definitions*

The design of an ADC can be based on various technologies. However, regardless of the technology used, the following specific elements can always be distinguished (Figure 8.1):

– an analog input;

– a digital output;

– a clock to operate the internal sequential logic, typically a state machine. This will be referred to as ADCCLK;

– a trigger input to allow the conversion, which will be referred to as *Trigger*;

– an output signal indicating that the digital data has been successfully converted. This signal will be referred to as EOC *(End Of Conversion)*.

Figure 8.2 illustrates the sequence of events for a conversion. When the conversion command is issued, the converter operates for the conversion time T_{conv}. After this period, the converted data are provided, and the output EOC (the *flag*) is set to 1.

For a color version of all the Codes in this chapter, see www.iste.co.uk/mahout/programming.zip

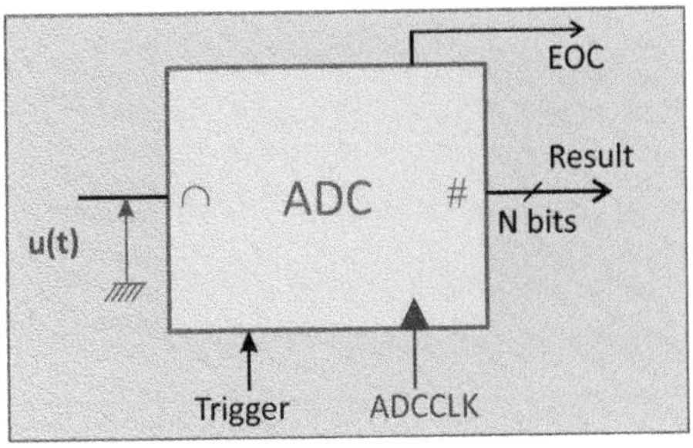

Figure 8.1. *ADC: single block*

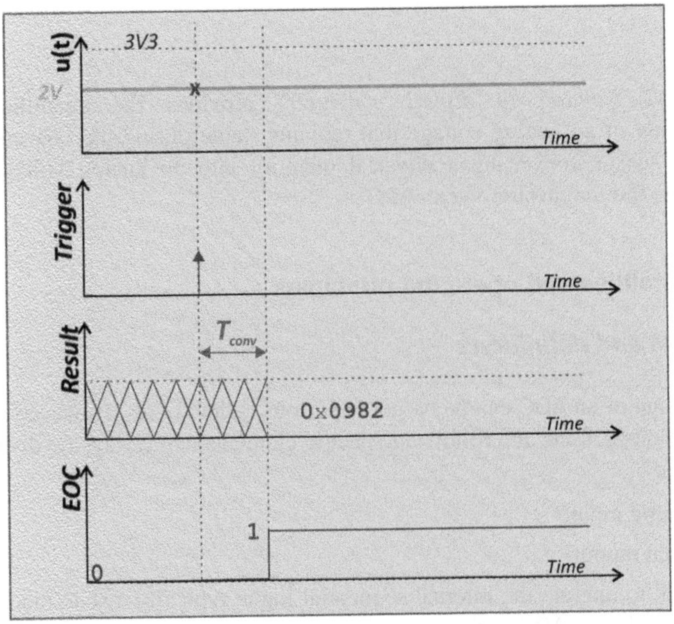

Figure 8.2. *Chronology describing the ADC operation*

Figure 8.3 illustrates the input–output characteristic of the ADC, with the analog input voltage U on the horizontal axis and the digitized output data (denoted as Result). Here, we consider the example of a 12-bit ADC operating within the range $[0V, 3.3V]$, which is widely used in μcontrollers. Thus, the maximum analog input value of 3.3V corresponds to the maximum digital output value of $0{\times}FFF$ (4095).

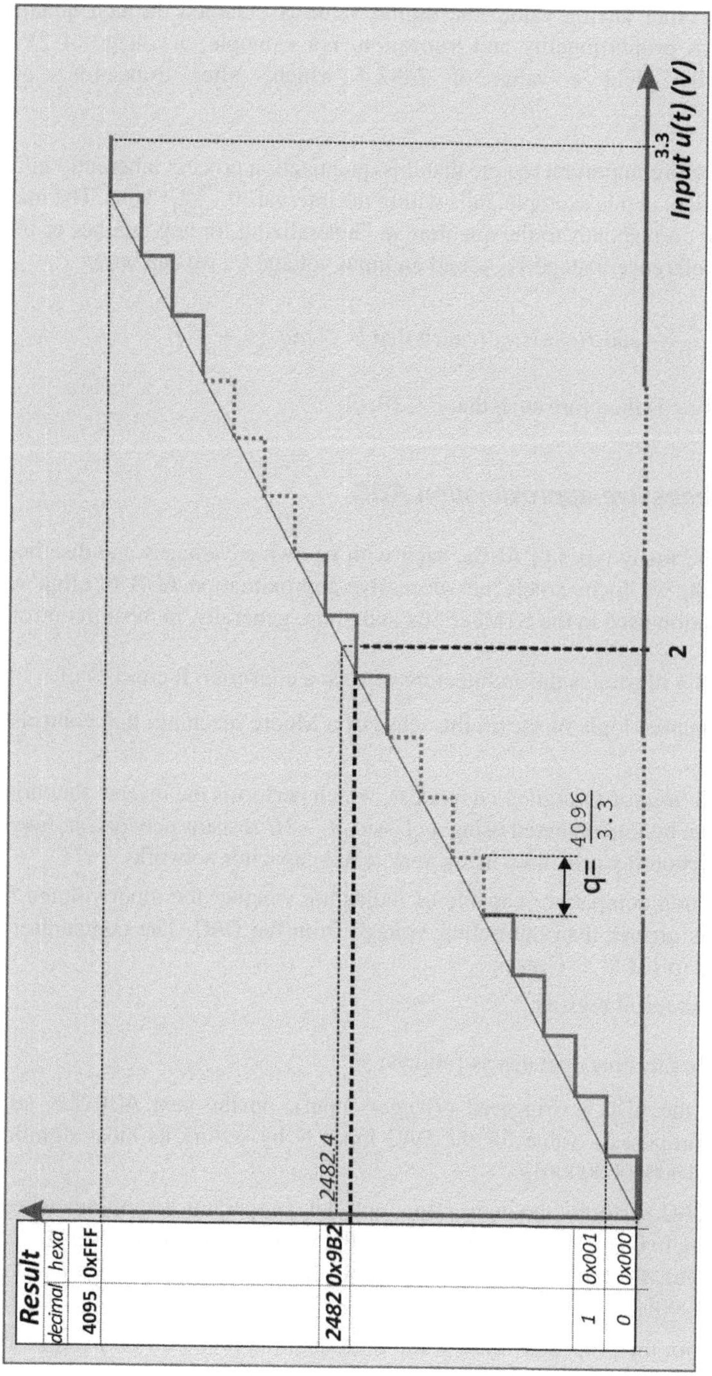

Figure 8.3. *I/O characteristic of a 12-bit/3V3 ADC*

For any other analog value, the digital value is obtained through quantization, which means proportionality and truncation. For example, a voltage of 2V would proportionally yield a value of 2482.4 which, after truncation, becomes $2482 = 0\times 982$.

It is therefore important to note that this quantization process inherently introduces an error, which, in this example, falls within the interval $\left[0, \frac{3.3}{4096}\right]$ volts. The maximum of this error corresponds to the quantum q. Generalizing for any number of bits N, a maximum reference voltage V_{ref}, and an input voltage U, we can write:

$$q = \frac{V_{ref}}{2^N} \text{ and } Result = n \text{ such that } U \in [nq, (n+1)q)\,.$$

The error ϵ is therefore such that $\epsilon \in (0, q)$.

8.1.2. *Successive-approximation ADC*

There are many types of ADCs, each with its own advantages and disadvantages. In this book, we focus solely on successive-approximation ADC to align with the implementation used in the STM32F10x and, more generally, in most μcontrollers.

Figure 8.4 illustrates the architecture of such a converter. It consists of:

– a sequential logic block (in the sense of a Moore machine) that controls all the components;

– a DAC (*digital-to-analog converter*), which performs the inverse function of the ADC and can be implemented using a classic $R - 2R$ resistor network or, based upon the same dichotomy principle, using a switched-capacitor network;

– an analog comparator capable of indicating whether the input voltage U to be converted is greater than the output voltage from the DAC. The comparator output Comp is set to 1 if $U > U_{DAC}$;

– a 12-bit result register.

The state machine operates as follows:

– After the ADC is triggered (*Trigger* input), on the next ADCCLK edge, the sequencer proposes a value for the DAC input Q by setting its most significant bit to 1, $Q = (100000000000)_2$.

– The DAC performs the conversion, and the comparator determines whether the input voltage to be measured is greater than the value proposed by the DAC:

- If yes, the proposed value is too low, though the bit set was a good choice: $Q = (100000000000)_2$.

- If no, the proposed value is too high, and the proposed bit must be cleared: $Q = (000000000000)_2$.

– The sequencer generates a new value for Q by setting the next bit to 1, which means: $Q = Q + (010000000000)_2$.

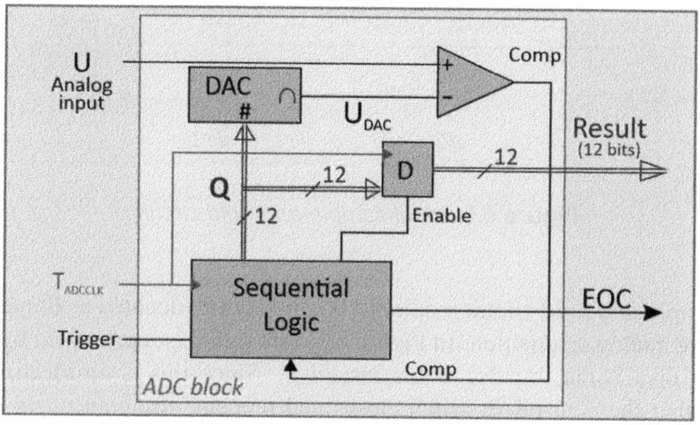

Figure 8.4. *Block diagram of a 12-bit successive-approximation ADC*

This process is repeated 12 times and, on the final iteration, the value of Q corresponds to the approximated result. The EOC signal is set to 1, and all output D flip-flops latch the result by setting the *Enable* input to 1.

For the ADC to produce its result, 12 clock edges are required. This duration is referred to as the intrinsic conversion time of the ADC (a term specific to this book), denoted as T_{ADC}.

8.1.3. *Variable voltage measurement*

8.1.3.1. *Idealized approach*

We have examined and understood the principle of an ADC, particularly the successive-approximation ADC. However, the description provided is strictly valid only for a continuous (constant) voltage U which, a priori, disqualifies the ADC from measuring variable voltages. In reality, the voltage only needs to remain "stable" during the conversion process, which lasts at least 12 clock edges (T_{ADC}).

To address this, a sample-and-hold circuit (Figure 8.5) is used. Its function is to measure the voltage at a given instant t_0 and then hold that voltage (essentially storing it) in a capacitor for the entire conversion time of the ADC, T_{ADC}.

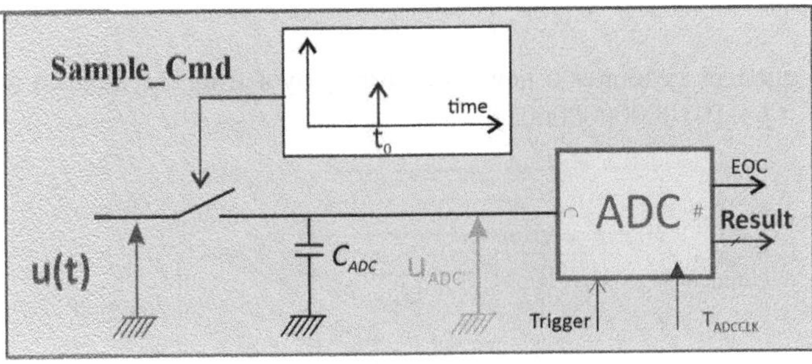

Figure 8.5. *Ideal sample-and-hold circuit*

This sample-and-hold circuit requires a control signal (denoted as Sample_Cmde) to trigger the analog acquisition. In Figure 8.5, this signal is represented by an arrow, reminiscent of a Dirac impulse at the instant t_0. Since this is an idealized model, it assumes that the controlled switch closes and reopens instantaneously during the impulse. The C_{ADC} capacitor (on the order of 10 pF) is therefore charged to the precise voltage value corresponding to sampling time t_0. Thus, the ADC can perform the conversion as long as the interval between two successive samples, denoted as T_e, is greater than the intrinsic conversion time of the ADC. Figure 8.6 illustrates the voltage waveforms $u(t)$ and U_{ADC} across the capacitor.

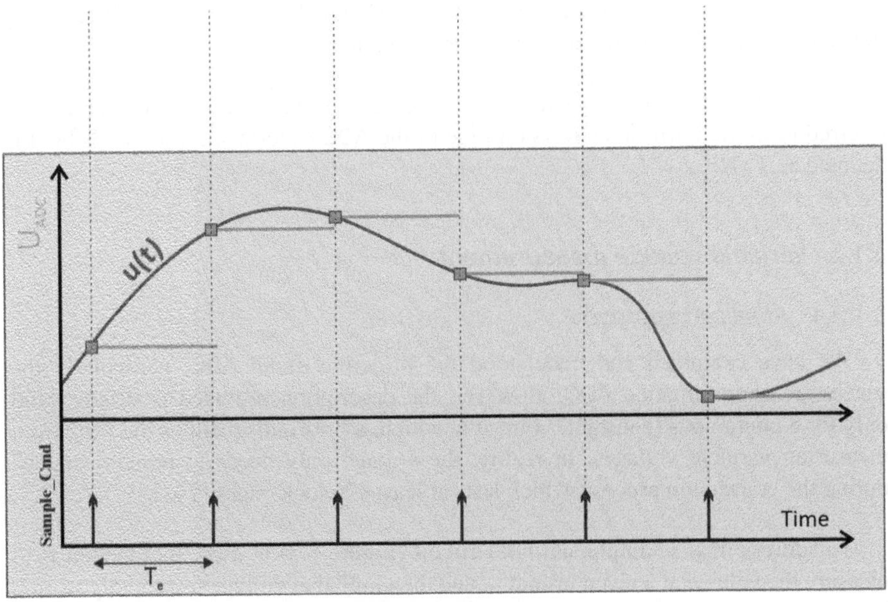

Figure 8.6. *Sampling, ideal case*

8.1.3.2. *Real-world approach*

The sampling process in the capacitor becomes slightly more complex in reality because the switch does not have zero resistance. Even if it did, the electronic device upstream of the μcontroller (such as a sensor) would likely have a non-zero equivalent series resistance (Thévenin resistance), denoted here as R_{AIN} (see Figure 8.7). Overlooking or underestimating what may seem like a minor detail can be disastrous and completely compromise the acquisition process. Figure 8.8 illustrates the actual behavior of U_{ADC}, showing the characteristic dynamics of a capacitor charging. It becomes evident that the Sample_Cmde signal must have a minimum duration to ensure that the capacitor is fully charged. This duration is called the *sampling time*[1] (or *Sample Time*), denoted T_s.

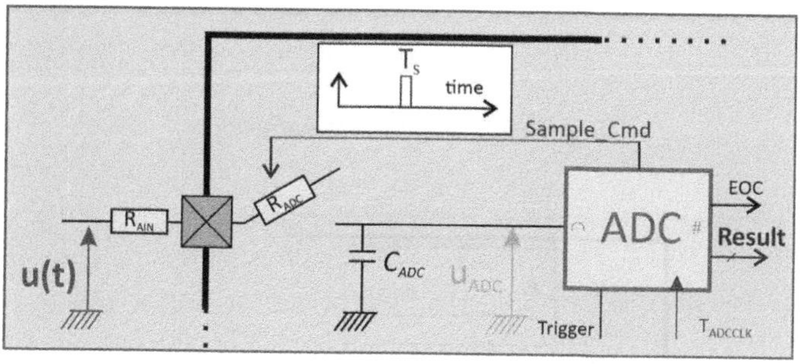

Figure 8.7. *Sample-and-hold circuit diagram*

This duration must allow the expected value to be reproduced within $\frac{1}{2}$ of the least significant bit. By expressing the exponential charge of the capacitor, we obtain the following relation:

$$T_s = (N + 1)\ln(2) \times (R_{AIN} + R_{ADC}) \times C_{ADC}$$

which, in the case of the STM32 and according to the manufacturer's documentation, has $R_{ADC} = 1\ k\Omega$ and $C_{ADC} = 8\ pF$.

This relation thus defines the minimum sampling time T_s required to achieve the maximum resolution of the ADC.

1 The term "sampling time" T_s may seem ambiguous, as it could be confused with the sampling period T_e. However, we have retained this notation consistent with the documentation STMicroelectronics (2011).

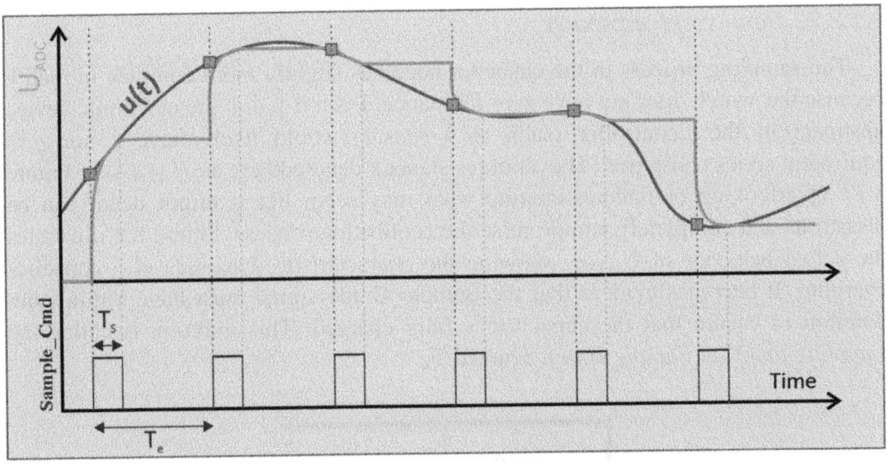

Figure 8.8. *Real-world sampling*

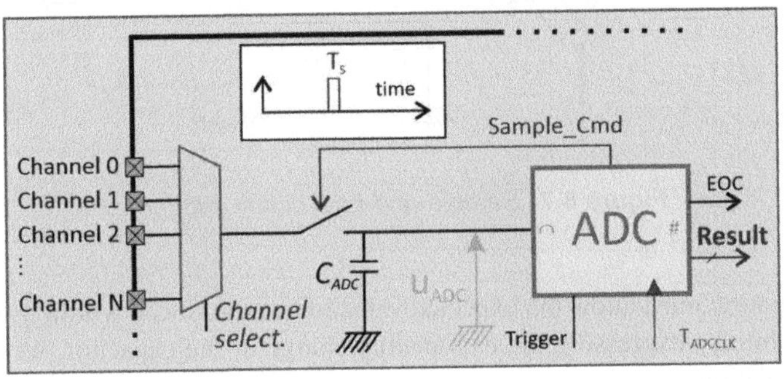

Figure 8.9. *Multiplexing ADC input channels*

8.1.4. *Multi-channel ADC*

It is very common to measure multiple analog channels in a system. However, manufacturers do not implement as many ADCs as there are possible input channels. Instead, they use a multiplexer upstream of a single ADC, which selects the analog channel to be measured. Naturally, since the ADC resource is shared, the maximum conversion speed per channel decreases proportionally to the number of channels to be processed. Figure 8.9 shows a simplified representation of an ADC unit with multiple analog inputs, while Figure 8.10 illustrates timing diagrams for processing three input signals, $u_0(t)$, $u_1(t)$ and $u_2(t)$.

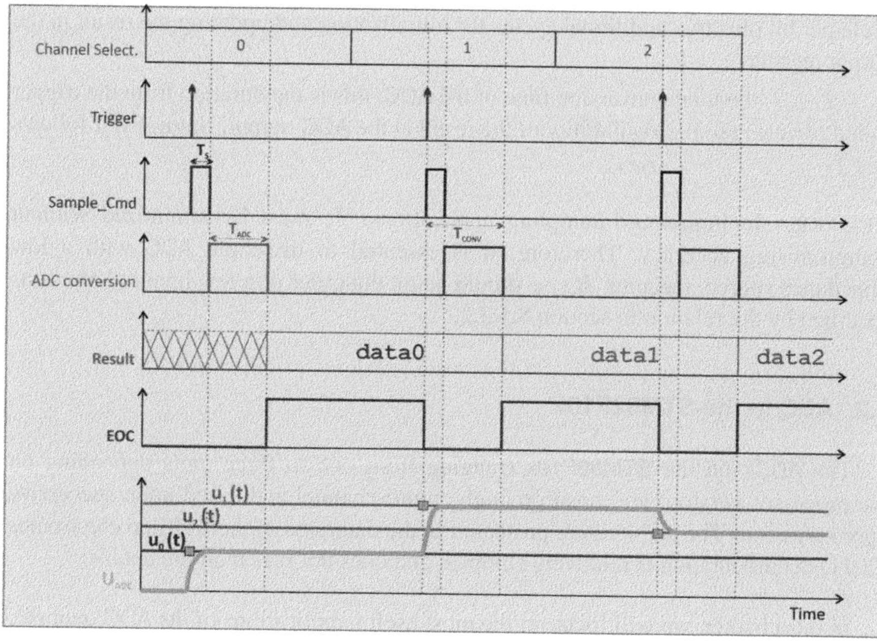

Figure 8.10. *ADC conversion timing diagram for three multiplexed channels*

REMARK.– In this representation of the multi-channel ADC, which also illustrates the reality of sampling, we observe that the *Trigger* input no longer directly activates the successive approximation ADC (Figure 8.10). Instead, it initiates the acquisition phase of the voltage in the capacitor, meaning it generates the *Sample_Cmde* signal that controls the sample-and-hold circuit. It is the end of the sampling phase (the falling edge of *Sample_Cmde*) that actually triggers the successive approximation ADC.

8.1.5. *Overview of the ADC timings*

As a summary, let us emphasize the key timing aspects inherent to the ADC by detailing the three specific durations involved in its operation:

– T_s, the sampling time (*Sampling Time*): it corresponds to the duration for which the sample-and-hold switch remains closed, that is, the time required to charge the internal capacitor C_{ADC} to the required precision ($\frac{1}{2}$ of its least significant bit).

– T_{ADC}, the intrinsic conversion time of the ADC: corresponds to the execution time of the state machine in the successive approximation ADC. It must be a multiple of T_{ADCCLK} since the sequencer is synchronous and driven by $ADCCLK$. Typically, for a 12-bit ADC, we have $T_{ADC} = 12 * T_{ADCCLK}$, meaning one clock cycle per bit plus two additional cycles for initialization and updating the result in the output register.

– T_{Conv}, the total conversion time of the ADC: this is the duration from the trigger signal (*Trigger*) to the availability of the result at the ADC output. Naturally, it follows that $T_{Conv} = T_s + T_{ADC}$.

REMARK.– In high-speed sampling applications, T_s must be minimized without compromising accuracy. Therefore, it is essential to drive the ADC with a low impedance source, meaning R_{AIN} should be on the order of a few hundred ohms, as specified by the relation in section 8.1.3.2.

8.2. ADC in the STM32F10x

The ADCs on the STM32F10x (ranging from one to three units depending on the processor version) are, unsurprisingly, multi-channel and based upon successive approximation. The architecture presented in the diagrams of the STMicroelectronics (2011) documentation is relatively complex and does not reveal all the details.

In this chapter, we will focus on the most useful applications of the ADC, namely:

– performing a conversion on a single channel;

– performing a conversion on multiple channels using DMA.

Additionally, we will discuss operation with interrupts as well as continuous and discontinuous modes. We will deliberately omit the interleaved mode and the injected channel mode, as these are of secondary importance, along with the *analog watchdog*. A reader who has understood the concepts presented in this chapter should have no difficulty referring to the documentation to grasp these additional features.

8.2.1. *Simplified architecture of the ADC*

The diagram in Figure 8.11 represents the architecture of the ADC, aiming to facilitate the understanding of its operating modes. This diagram is both simplified compared to the manufacturer's representation and slightly more detailed in certain aspects, such as input channel multiplexing. These additions are based on various textual descriptions, diagrams and timing charts provided in the reference manual.

8.2.1.1. *Multiplexing and sampling of channels*

This multiplexing has a unique feature compared to other architectures, as it is dual. Indeed, moving from left to right across Figure 8.11:

– *18 channels* named ADC12_In0 to ADC12_In17[2], where:

- the first 16 channels are routed to GPIO pins,
- one channel is connected to the internal temperature sensor,
- the last channel is used for measuring the internal reference voltage;

– *16 inputs* of the ADC named Analog_1 to Analog_16. This naming, Analog_i, is specific to this book and does not appear in the STM32F10x documentation. We propose it here to clearly differentiate between the two states of multiplexing.

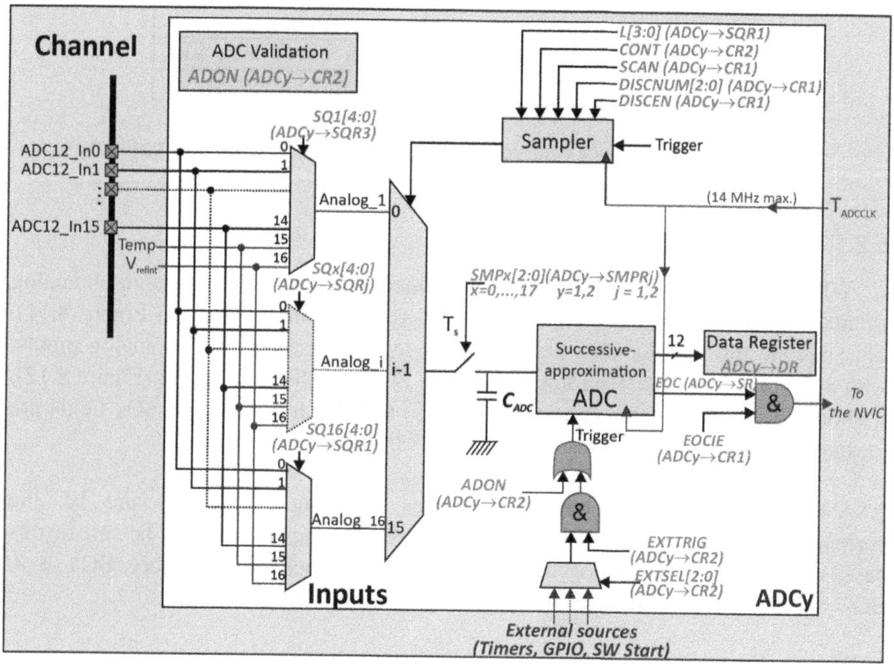

Figure 8.11. *Simplified architecture of the STM32 ADC*

Caution, channel numbering typically ranges from 0 to 17. However, the analog inputs are numbered from 1 to 16, so this numbering, chosen by STmicro©, may lead to some confusion.

8.2.1.1.1. Sixteen analog inputs

The ADC is natively designed to operate in *multi-channel* mode, even for a single conversion. The L[3:0] field of the SQR1 register (Figure 8.12) allows one to define

2 ADC12 refers to the fact that the pins are identical for both ADC no. 1 and ADC no. 2.

the number of desired analog inputs (up to a maximum of 16), following the sequence of analog inputs presented in Table 8.1.

In *Regular* mode, the only mode discussed here, the scanning of analog inputs Analog_i always proceeds in ascending order without skipping any input and starts from Analog_1. To go further, note that there is an *Injected* mode that allows breaking the monotony of this regular sequencing, though this is not detailed here.

L[3:0]	Processed input number	Processed analog inputs
0	1	Analog_1
i	i+1	Analog_1 to Analog_{i+1}
15	16	Analog_1 to Analog_16

Table 8.1. *Number of inputs to be processed as a function of length L*

8.2.1.1.2. Eighteen analog channels

When the number of analog inputs is defined, it is necessary to assign an analog channel to the desired input (the first set of 18-input multiplexers in Figure 8.11). This is done through the SQx fields (16 bits in total, as there are 16 analog inputs, with x ranging from 1 to 16) found across the SQR1, SQR2 and SQR3 (Figure 8.12). It should be noted (as this can lead to errors) that the lower weight SQx fields are located in the highest numbered register: SQR3.

EXAMPLE 8.1.– If the application requires sampling channels 3 and 10, the corresponding SQR1 and SQR2 fields (in the SQR3 register) should be set. In this case, only the first two analog inputs of the ADC are needed. Therefore, SQ1 = 3, SQ2 = 10. The L field in the SQR1 register will be set to 1.

8.2.1.1.3. Sampling durations

In this ADC, the sampling duration is individualized per channel (not per analog input). This means that the user can specify the sampling duration T_s for each of the 18 possible channels. The SMPR1 and SMPR2 registers (Figure 8.13) contain these 18 fields, SMP0 to SMP17. The user can select T_s from eight possible values. These eight durations are defined as non-integer multiples of the clock cycle T_{ADCCLK}, according to the values in Table 8.2. It is also worth noting that the lower weight SMPx fields are located in the SMPR2 register.

EXAMPLE 8.2.– As before, if the application samples channels 3 and 10, it is necessary to modify the respective SMP3 and SMP10 fields (in the SMPR2 and SMPR1 registers, respectively) to set the desired sampling duration for each channel (depending on T_{ADCCLK}).

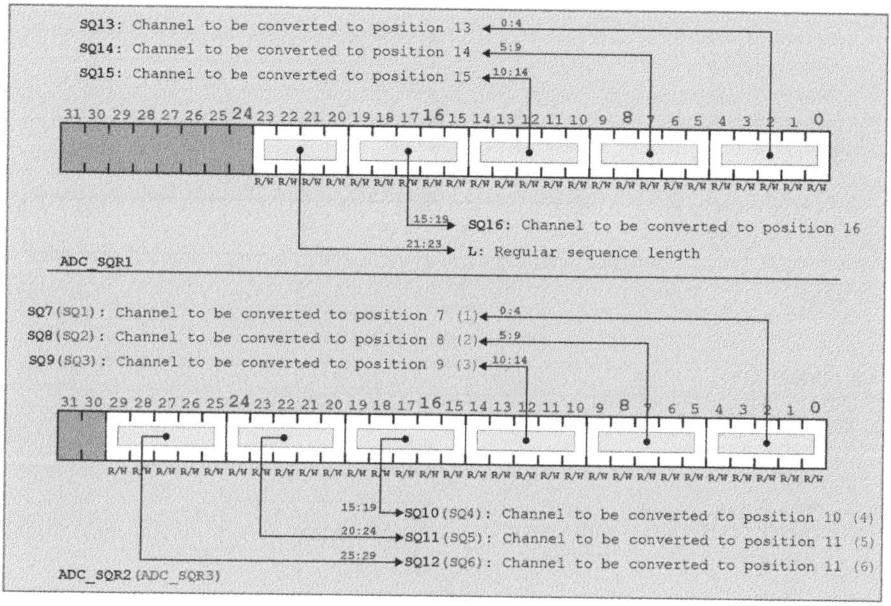

Figure 8.12. *SQRx registers of the ADC*

Binary value	Number of T_{ADCCLK} cycles	T_s in μs
$(000)_2$	1.5 cycles	0.13
$(001)_2$	7.5 cycles	0.63
$(010)_2$	13.5 cycles	1.13
$(011)_2$	28.5 cycles	2.38
$(100)_2$	41.5 cycles	3.46
$(101)_2$	55.5 cycles	4.63
$(110)_2$	71.5 cycles	5.96
$(111)_2$	239.5 cycles	19.96

Table 8.2. *Possible "Sample Time" values with $F_{ADCCLK} = 12$ MHz*

8.2.1.2. *Triggering the ADC*

Typically, and as shown at the bottom of Figure 8.11, there is a trigger input that can be activated by several external sources to the ADC. This feature is controlled through the ADCy_CR2 register (Figure 8.14), and is activated via the EXTTRIG bit.

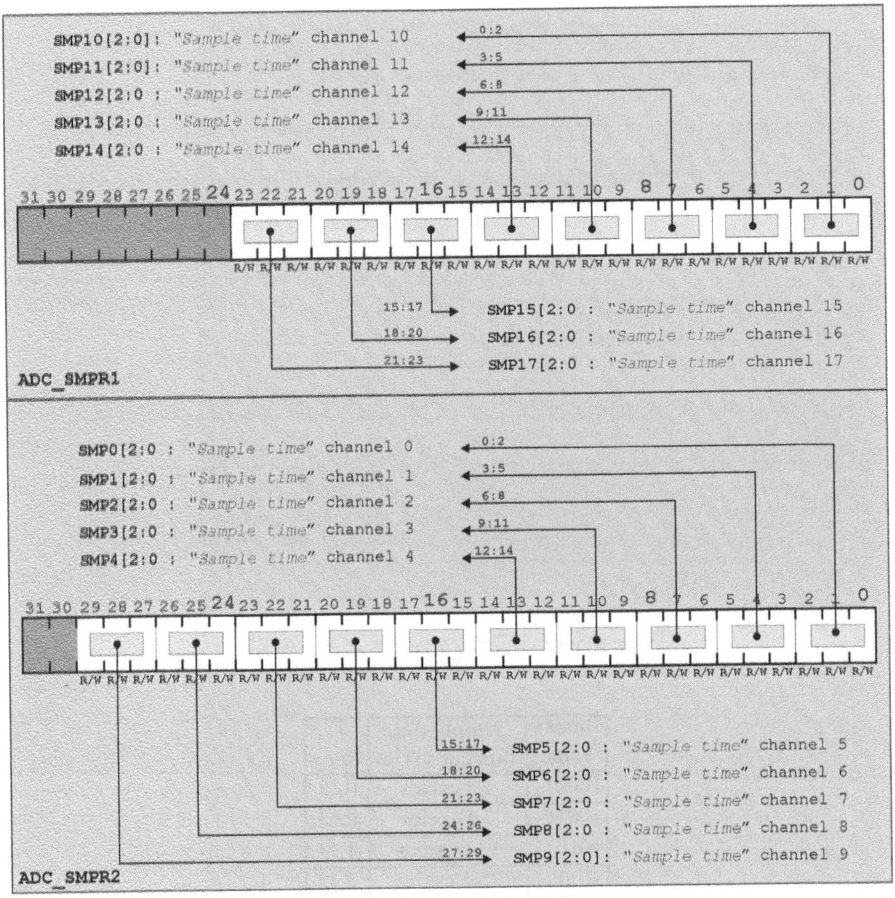

Figure 8.13. *SMPR registers of the ADC*

Table 8.3 lists the possible triggers for the EXTSEL bit field, grouped into three main categories:

– by software: the trigger is activated by setting the SWSTART bit to 1. This is not strictly an external trigger since the bit belongs to the ADC itself;

– by a Timer event, specifically a *Capture/Compare* or TRG0 event;

– by an external pin.

There is another way to trigger the ADC in simple mode, which is less intuitive but widely used: it involves using only the ADON bit (rank 0 of ADC_CR2).

EXTSEL value	Trigger
$(000)_2$	Timer 1 *CC1 event*
$(001)_2$	Timer 1 *CC2 event*
$(010)_2$	Timer 1 *CC3 event*
$(011)_2$	Timer 2 *CC2 event*
$(100)_2$	Timer 3 *TRGO event*
$(101)_2$	Timer 4 *CC4 event*
$(110)_2$	Exti Line 11
$(111)_2$	Software Start

Table 8.3. *Possible ADC triggers*

This bit is particular because it serves two roles:

– The first is setting it to 1, which is essential because it activates the ADC.

– Then, setting it again to 1, without resetting it to 0, triggers the *regular* sequence acquisition. However, it is important to note that even if external triggering is enabled (EXTTRIG bit = 1), it is possible to start the conversion by writing 1 to ADON, even though this may seem counterintuitive.

Finally, it is important to reset the ADON bit to 0 if we want to reduce the power consumption of the ADC.

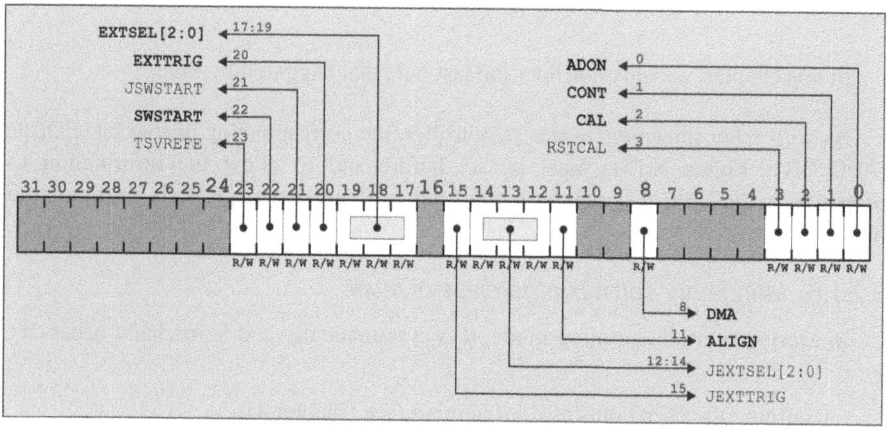

Figure 8.14. *CR2 configuration register of the ADC*

8.2.1.3. *Conversion results*

The result is read from the DR (*Data Result*) for regular conversions. The register contains 16 bits, while only 12 bits are used for the result. To align these 12 bits correctly, the ALIGN bit in the ADC_CR2 register is used. By default (when

ALIGN = 0), the result is right aligned. However, the result can be left aligned (fractional format context) by setting the ALIGN bit to 1. In both cases, the four remaining bits are set to 0 after a conversion.

8.2.1.4. *ADC calibration*

It is necessary to calibrate the ADC in order to avoid significant loss of precision, particularly for low converted values. The documentation recommends performing a calibration each time the ADC is awakened, meaning that after the first setting of the ADON bit to 1. This calibration is very simple to perform as it involves setting the CAL bit (ADC_CR2) and then waiting for it to return to 0, marking the end of the calibration process.

8.2.1.5. *ADC interrupts*

There are three interrupt sources:

– one from the *analog watchdog*;

– one triggered by the completion of an *injected* conversion (not covered here);

– one indicating the end of a *regular* conversion, called EOC.

These three sources correspond to bits in the *status register* ADC_SR. These bits are set to 1 when the event occurs and must be manually cleared to 0 in software if they triggered the interrupt. However, reading the DR automatically clears the EOC bit.

In this chapter, we only consider the last one, that triggered by EOC.

As with other interrupts in this μcontroller, the corresponding enable bit, EOCIE (ADC_CR1, Figure 8.15), must be set beforehand to allow the information to propagate to the NVIC. Chapter 5 on interrupts explains how to properly configure the NVIC.

8.2.1.6. *Mandatory settings regardless of mode*

In every proposed operating mode, it is systematically and beforehand necessary to:

– configure the GPIO pins as *Analog input* (see Chapter 4);

– set ADCCLK to a frequency below 14 MHz[3], typically by adjusting the ADCPRE field (RCC_CFGR register). For example, selecting a division by 6 if the APB2 clock is at its default frequency of 72 MHz;

– enable the ADC clock by setting the ADC1EN bit (RCC_APB2ENR) for ADC1;

3 Maximum value indicated for the ADC.

– configure the desired analog channel(s) (see Figure 8.11);

– set the desired sampling time(s) T_s (ADC_SMPR registers);

– configure the triggering mode (external or not). In the case of external triggering, it may be necessary to configure the triggering peripheral, typically a Timer;

– choose whether the data are left or right aligned (Align bit in ADC_CR2);

– wake up the ADC by setting the ADON bit in ADC_CR2;

– start the calibration (see section 8.2.1.4).

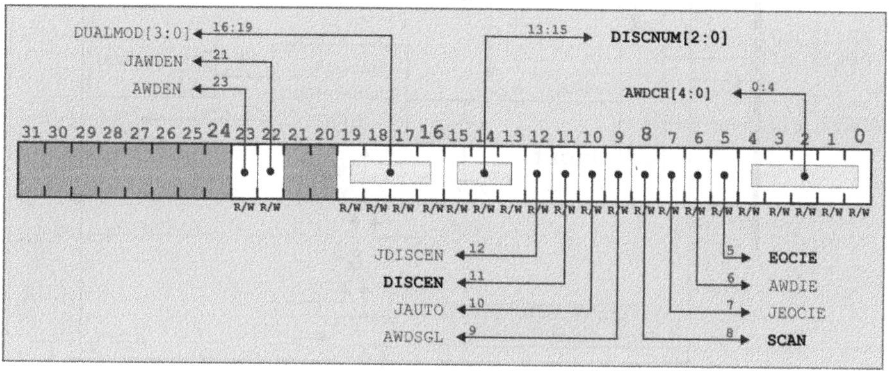

Figure 8.15. *CR1 configuration register of the ADC*

If an interrupt is also desired at the end of each conversion, it will be necessary to:

– activate the EOCIE bit in ADC_CR1;

– configure the NVIC (see Chapter 5), knowing that the NVIC number for both ADCs is unique and corresponds to 18.

8.2.2. *ADC functional modes*

STM32 μcontrollers feature a complex and versatile ADC, designed to accommodate various use cases, from simple to advanced. Below is a list of the most relevant functional modes, which are commonly used in practical applications and will be detailed further in the following sections:

– *Single-channel mode*: a trigger initiates a single conversion, and the result is stored in the DR, after which the ADC stops converting.

– *Continuous single-channel mode*: after a conversion request, the ADC continuously starts a new conversion as soon as the previous one is completed, without stopping.

– *Scan mode*: a conversion request triggers the sequential conversion of all $(L+1)$ programmed channels as quickly as possible, after which the ADC stops.

– *Continuous scan mode*: the same sequence as the previous mode, except that after a single conversion request, the scan restarts from the beginning of the sequence as soon as it is completed.

– *Discontinuous scan mode*: this is a specific *Scan* mode in which a conversion request triggers the conversion of a subgroup of channels. In this mode, the continuous option cannot be enabled.

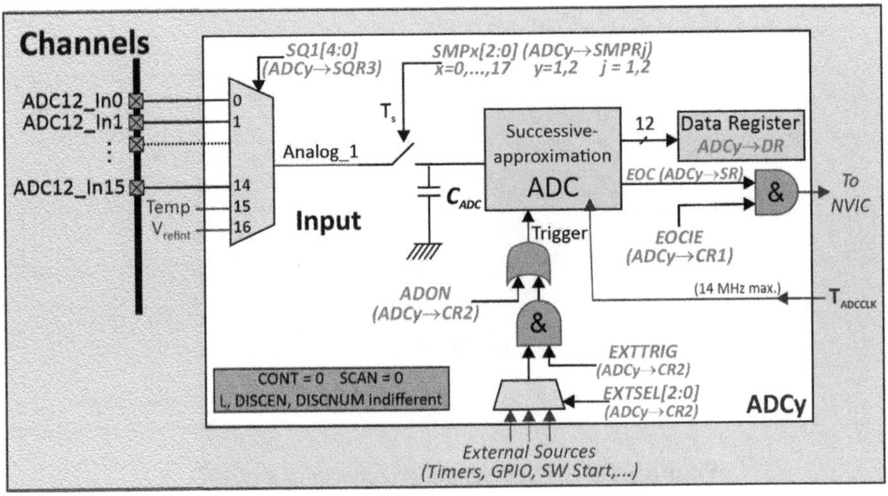

Figure 8.16. *Reduced architecture of the ADC in single conversion mode on the STM3210x*

Figures 8.17 and 8.18 provide timing diagrams for these different modes, specifying the triggering time as well as the handling of the end of conversion EOC *flag*. Table 8.4 summarizes the specific configurations for these five modes.

8.2.2.1. *Single-channel conversion modes, single or continuous*

This use case can be summarized via Figure 8.16, which is a simplified version of Figure 8.11.

In this configuration, the multiplexing section is greatly simplified since only a single analog channel is processed. Furthermore, the SCAN bit (ADC_CR2, Figure 8.14) is set to 0 and, as a result, the L field of ADC_SQR1 (Figure 8.12) is ignored.

If the CONT bit (ADC_CR2) is set to 0, then the operation is very simple: each trigger initiates a conversion and produces a result. Conversely, if this bit is set to 1, a single trigger of the ADC causes it to perform conversions continuously with a periodicity equal to T_{Conv} between each result. At the end of each conversion, the EOC bit is set (see Figure 8.17).

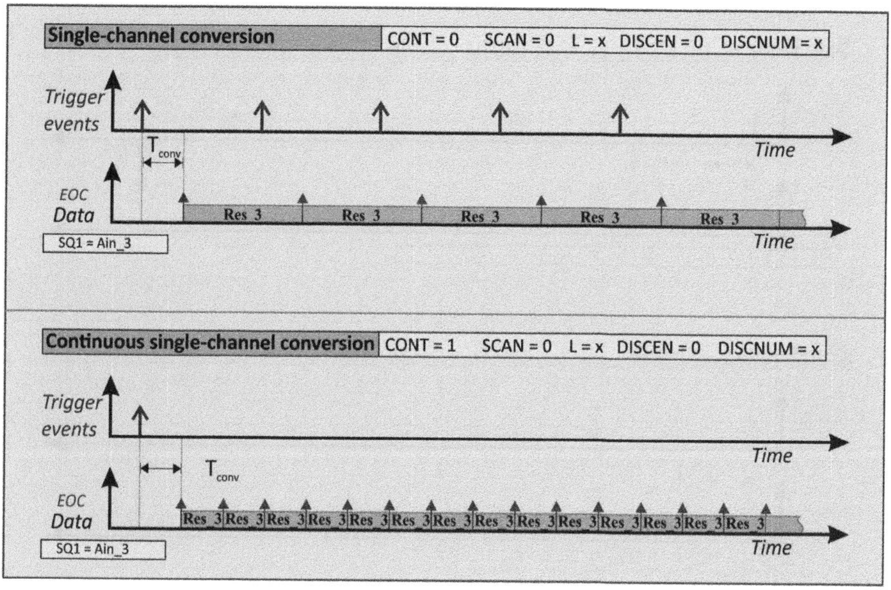

Figure 8.17. *Timing diagrams of the ADC "single-channel" conversion modes. For a color version of this figure, see www.iste.co.uk/mahout/programming.zip*

8.2.2.2. *Multi-channel scan modes, single or continuous*

In this use case, the scan mode is required by setting the SCAN bit (ADC_CR2) to 1. Referring to Figure 8.11, we can understand how the sequencer performs a scan across multiple channels. On each conversion request, the sequencer moves the input multiplexer across each programmed channel sequentially. Each time a conversion is completed, the conversion on the next channel starts immediately, without delay. In other words, with each ADC trigger, N channels are processed.

It should be noted in Figure 8.18 that the EOC bit is set to 1 only when the last of the N conversion values is available in the DR. This means that the first $N-1$ conversions cannot be retrieved except by using DMA (as discussed later).

As with single-channel conversion, the conversion can be continuous (CONT bit $=1$). In this case, once a scan is completed, another one starts without waiting. Figure 8.18 gives an overview of the operation.

8.2.2.3. *Discontinuous mode*

This discontinuous mode is reserved exclusively for scan modes, meaning it only applies to multi-channel conversions. It is somewhat particular and deserves closer attention.

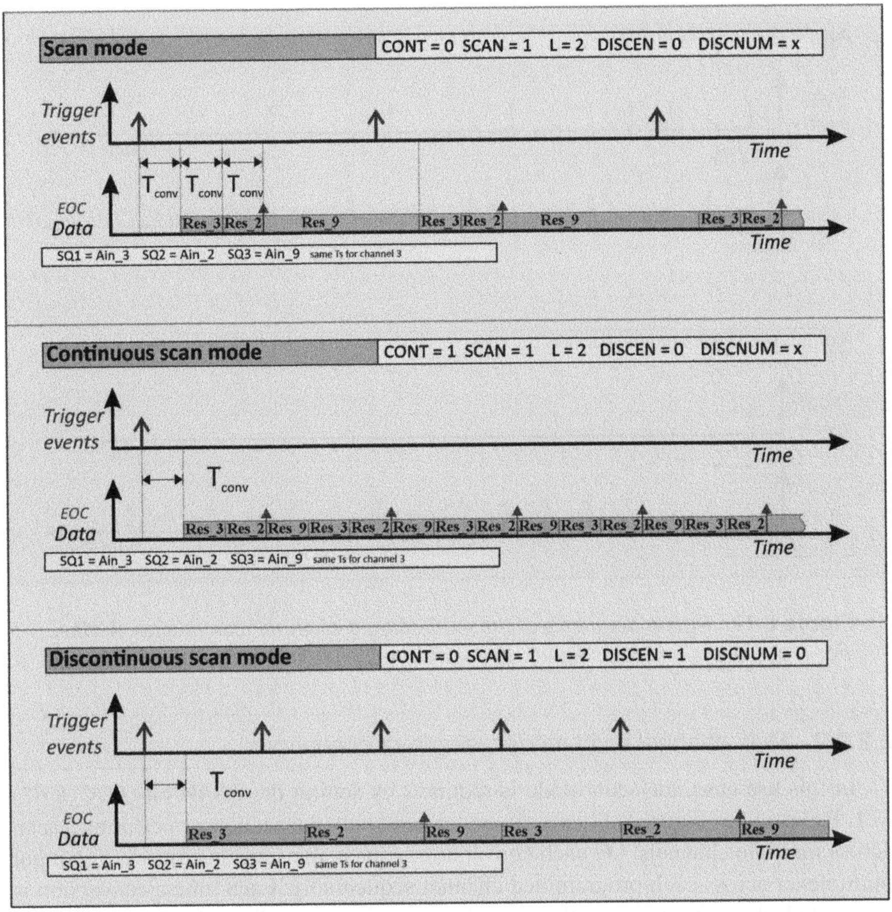

Figure 8.18. *Timing diagrams of the ADC "scan" conversion modes. For a color version of this figure, see www.iste.co.uk/mahout/programming.zip*

In particular, discontinuous mode excludes continuous mode (the two modes cannot coexist). It is activated by setting the DISCEN bit in ADC_CR2 to 1.

In this mode, each trigger does not initiate all N conversions corresponding to the N channels, but rather a subset consisting of k channels, where the choice of k is specified by writing the value $k - 1$ in the DISCNUM[2:0] field (ADC_CR2). However, note that k is not necessarily a multiple of N, meaning the number of conversions in the last sequence may not be the same as in the previous ones.

Mode	CONT	SCAN	L[3:0]	DISC-EN	DISC-NUM [2:0]	EOC activation
Single-channel	0	0	X	0	X	After each conversion
Continuous single-channel	1	0	X	0	X	After each conversion
Scan	0	1	$N-1$	0	X	After the conversion of a group of N channels
Continuous scan	1	1	$N-1$	0	X	After the conversion of a group of N channels
Discontinuous scan	0	1	$N-1$	1	$k-1$	After the conversion of a group of N channels

Table 8.4. *Summary of the various ADC functional mode configurations*

EXAMPLE 8.3.– If $N = 8$, $k = 3$, and assuming for simplicity that the eight channels range from channel 0 to channel 7, then each trigger event will result in:

– first *Trigger* edge: conversion of channels 0, 1, 2;

– second *Trigger* edge: conversion of channels 3, 4, 5;

– third *Trigger* edge: conversion of channels 6, 7, EOC is set;

– fourth *Trigger* edge: conversion of channels 0, 1, 2;

– fifth *Trigger* edge: conversion of channels 3, 4, 5;

– six *Trigger* edge: conversion of channels 6, 7, EOC is set;

– etc.

In the last timing diagram of Figure 8.18, an example is illustrated with $k = 1$. In this case, each trigger event processes only one channel at a time. Such a configuration can be useful for sampling N channels, each at a regular interval. Here again, as in the case of scan mode, using DMA is mandatory. The ADC interrupt cannot be used to retrieve individual samples because the EOC *flag* is not set after each conversion, but instead only after each group of N conversions.

8.2.3. *DMA with ADC*

Using DMA provides a key advantage by reducing the CPU load, as the processor does not need to intervene to retrieve analog input samples. Its use is:

– possible in single-channel conversion mode to sample a block of data (e.g. when performing frequency analysis of a signal);

– required in scan mode.

For this, the DMA bit (ADC_CR2) must be set to 1. The DMA obviously receives the conversion data contained in the DR (which changes over time). More importantly, it also receives an "event" signal that activates after each conversion (unlike EOC, which activates only after N conversions, except in single-channel mode). It is through this signal, which is not explicitly described in the reference manual, that the DMA is able to write data to memory as it is converted.

To understand and configure how to implement DMA, we refer the reader to the end of Chapter 5.

8.3. Application: the power analyzer

For this equipment, it is necessary to measure three analog quantities representing the phase voltage, phase current and inverter current.

This functionality will be handled by ADC1, which will be configured in *Scan* mode across three channels, with a DMA configuration.

As explained in the overall presentation of the application, the μcontroller used for the power analyzer is an STM32F103.

Without going into the details of the electronics, Table 8.5 provides information on the R_{AIN} resistances of the analog sections for each channel, as well as the IO pins where each signal arrives.

Signal to measure	R_{AIN}	IO pin
U_{Phase}	$10\ k\Omega$	PA0: GPIO A bit 0
I_{Phase}	$2.2\ k\Omega$	PC0: GPIO C bit 0
$I_{Inverter}$	$2.2\ k\Omega$	PA4: GPIO A bit 4

Table 8.5. *Description of the ADC analog inputs within the power analyzer context*

The correspondence between the IO pin and the analog channel is referenced from the STM32F103x *datasheet* STMicroelectronics (2015). This documentation provides a pin description table that establishes the correspondence between the analog input ADC12_in0 and pin 0 of the GPIOA port. This first channel is therefore connected to both ADC1 and ADC2. In our case, we are only using ADC1.

8.3.1. *Determining the sampling duration T_s*

The general relation from section 8.1.3.2 with $R_{ADC} = 1\ \text{k}\Omega$, $C_{ADC} = 8\ \text{pF}$ allows for the minimum sampling time for each channel to be determined.

For example, for the second input (channel ADC12_in10) with $R_{AIN} = 2.2\ k\Omega$, the relation gives:

$$T_s = (N+1)\ln(2)\times(R_{AIN}+R_{ADC})\times C_{ADC} = 230.9\ ns$$

We now need to assign the required value in the SMP10 field (Figure 8.13). Table 8.2 provides the time in cycles. Typically, the ADC is configured with a 12 MHz clock, so we calculate the number of cycles required as $Nb_{Cy} = \frac{T_s}{T_{Cy}} = T_s \times F_{\text{ADCCLK}} = 230.9.10^{-9} \times 12.10^6 = 2.77$. The closest larger value in Table 8.2 gives us 7.5 cycles.

A similar calculation allows us to determine 13.5 cycles is needed for the in0 channel (since the R_{AIN} resistance is higher).

Table 8.6 summarizes the different properties of each channel.

Signal to measure	IO pin	IO conf.	ADC channel	T_s
U_{Phase}	PA0	*Analog input*	ADC12_in0	SMP0 = $(010)_2$
I_{Phase}	PC0	*Analog input*	ADC12_in10	SMP10 = $(001)_2$
$I_{Inverter}$	PA4	*Analog input*	ADC12_in4	SMP4 = $(001)_2$

Table 8.6. *Descriptions of the ADC analog inputs in the power analyzer context*

8.3.2. *Code excerpt for configuration*

The mode selected for the ADC is a *Scan Mode* over three channels. Each burst of measurements is initiated with a periodicity of 10 μs. This periodic trigger is ensured by Timer TIM3. An interrupt is triggered at the end of each burst (DMA *Transfer Complete*), so that the user can process the measurements.

```
/* zone of 3 3-bit integers , conversion results of 3 channels */
uint16_t BufferDMA[3];

int main(void)
{
/*****************************************/
/*     GPIO analog input PA0/PC0/PA4     */
/*****************************************/
   RCC->APB2ENR |= RCC_APB2ENR_IOPAEN; /* Validation Clk GPIOA */
   RCC->APB2ENR |= RCC_APB2ENR_IOPCEN; /* Validation Clk GPIOC */
   GPIOA->CRL &= ~(0xF<<0);            /* PA0 in Analog input  */
   GPIOC->CRL &= ~(0xF<<0);            /* PC0 in Analog input  */
   GPIOA->CRL &= ~(0xF<<4*4);          /* PA4 in Analog input  */

/**************************************************************/
/* Setting ADC (12 MHz, ADCCk En, ADOn, Cal                   */
/* sequencing of the 3 channels , SMPx (Ts),                  */
```

```
/* SCAN 3 channels , Ext Trig TIM3 TRGO, DMA activation */
/*******************************************************/
   RCC->CFGR &= ~RCC_CFGR_ADCPRE;
   RCC->CFGR |= RCC_CFGR_ADCPRE_DIV6;   /* ADCCKLK = 12 MHz  */
   RCC->APB2ENR |= RCC_APB2ENR_ADC1EN;  /* ADC Ck validation */
   ADC1->CR2 |= ADC_CR2_ADON;           /* ADC Wake up       */
   ADC1->CR2 |= ADC_CR2_CAL;            /* Start calibration */

/* Wait for calibration end */
   while ((ADC1->CR2 & ADC_CR2_CAL) == 1);

   ADC1->SQR3 = 0 | 10<<5 | 4<<10; /* ain0/ain10/ain4          */
   ADC1->SMPR2 = 2 | 1<<12; /* SMP0="13.5" and SMP4 ="7.5"    */

   ADC1->SMPR1 = 1;    /* SMP10 = 1 (7.5 cy); */
/*  NB: here, we did not use masks because we assume   */
/*  that the ADC is not shared with other applications */

   ADC1->SQR1 &= ~ADC_SQR1_L;        /* set the L field to 0 */
   ADC1->SQR1 |= (3-1)<<20; /* L = 2, i.e., 3 conversions */

   ADC1->CR1 |= ADC_CR1_SCAN;                     /* SCAN mode */
   ADC1->CR2 |= ADC_CR2_EXTTRIG; /* config. in ext. trig. */
   ADC1->CR2 &= ~ADC_CR2_EXTSEL;
   ADC1->CR2 |= 0x4<<17; /* Trigger Sel = TIM3 TRGO event */
   ADC1->CR2 |= ADC_CR2_DMA;   /* DMA validation          */

/***********************************************************/
/* DMA1 channel 1 conf. (for ADC) - transfer of 3 data     */
/***********************************************************/
   RCC->AHBENR |= RCC_AHBENR_DMA1EN;       /* DMA1 clk validation */
   DMA1_Channel1->CPAR = (uint32_t)&(ADC1->DR);      /* @ periph.*/
   DMA1_Channel1->CMAR = (uint32_t)&BufferDMA[0]; /* @RAM buffer*/
/* Msize=Psize=16bits, Minc=1, Circ, Valid. IT Trf complete */
   DMA1_Channel1->CCR = DMA_CCR1_MSIZE_0 | DMA_CCR1_PSIZE_0 |
   DMA_CCR1_MINC |DMA_CCR1_CIRC | DMA_CCR1_TCIE;
   DMA1_Channel1->CNDTR = 3;                /* 3 data to transmit */
   DMA1_Channel1->CCR |= DMA_CCR1_EN; /* DMA1 channel 1 valid. */
   NVIC->IP[11] = 1<<4;       /* Priority 1 on line 11 (DMA ch1) */
   NVIC->ISER[0] |= NVIC_ISER_SETENA_11;       /* Line 11 valid. */

/****************************************/
/*    TIM3 10e-6s configuration         */
/****************************************/
   RCC->APB1ENR |= RCC_APB1ENR_TIM3EN; /* TIM3 ck validation */
   TIM3->ARR = (10*72-1);                 /* 10e-6s periodicity */
   TIM3->PSC = 0;
   TIM3->CR2 &= ~TIM_CR2_MMS;
   TIM3->CR2 |= 2<<4;         /* TRG0 switches to update timer */
   TIM3->CR1 |= TIM_CR1_CEN;                      /* Timer start */
```

```
/* General wait loop */
  while(1);
}
/*****************************************/
/*      1 DMA1 Channel1 handler          */
/*****************************************/
void DMA1_Channel1_IRQHandler (void)
{
  DMA1->IFCR|=DMA_IFCR_CTCIF1;     /* clear IT flag */
  /* ... actions to be taken... */
}
```

Code 8.1. *Proposed DMA configuration to convert three ADC channels*

9

Some Communication Buses

This chapter covers three communication buses commonly found in embedded computing: UART (*Universal Asynchronous Receiver Transmitter*), SPI (*Serial Peripheral Interface*) and I^{2}C (*Inter-Integrated Circuit*). The interest in these buses is to facilitate wired digital communication between components by standardizing exchange parameters such as data transfer speed, data format, additional data for communication reliability, data delimitation and address definition. Notably, all three involve serial communication (as opposed to parallel communication). Typically, these buses use an 8-bit data format.

9.1. Introduction

Transmissions over these three buses are baseband transmissions that occur in the form of voltage signals. In these transmissions, time is divided into regular intervals called T_s (symbol time). Thus, a symbol is a specific voltage shape with a fixed duration T_s. For example, in a UART transmission, there are two possible symbols: high level or low level.

The symbol rate R can then be defined as the reciprocal of the symbol duration T_s, that is, $R = \frac{1}{T_s}$. This symbol rate is specific in bauds (Bd). For example, a transmission at 9,600 Bd corresponds to symbols with a duration of $\frac{1}{9{,}600} = 104\ \mu s$. If we consider there to be only two symbols, each is associated with one bit, that is to say, one symbol represents 0 and the other 1. In this case, the bit rate, denoted by D, is given by $R * 1$ bit $= 9,600$ bit/s[1].

For a color version of all the Codes in this chapter, see www.iste.co.uk/mahout/programming.zip

1 Note that there is sometimes confusion between *bauds* and *bit/s* because most transmissions (such as I^{2}C, UART and SPI) are binary (only two symbols are possible), so that the bit rate

Transmission buses are distinguished according to whether the transmission or reception of data requires a clock signal. In the absence of a clock, the transmission is referred to as asynchronous; if a clock is present, the transmission is said to be synchronous. In synchronous communication, each symbol (in the buses of interest, each bit) is transmitted at each clock edge. The UART is an asynchronous bus, whereas both SPI and I^2C are synchronous. Note that a synchronous version of the UART exists (not detailed here due to its limited prevalence), known as the USART (*Universal Synchronous/Asynchronous Receiver Transmitter*).

From an electronic perspective, the difference between synchronous and asynchronous transmission lies in the presence of a clock that indicates the stable state of each bit. Consequently, sampling each bit becomes trivial. In asynchronous transmission, however, the sampling instants must be anticipated by precisely knowing the transmission speed (the *baud rate* R), as in the case with a transmission using a UART unit.

From a system perspective, the concept of a clock is of little significance. The key question is: "Is the arrival time of a message controlled?" If so, the transmission is considered synchronous. This is the case for SPI in *Master* mode. In *Slave* mode, however, the arrival time is not known, and it depends on when the *Master* sends the message. This situation places us in an asynchronous mode from a system standpoint. The distinction from the system perspective is important. Indeed, if the transmission is asynchronous, reception interrupts are virtually unavoidable. In contrast (SPI *Master* mode), interrupts can be used, but they are not strictly necessary.

Another distinction among these three buses is based on their capacity to connect only two devices or multiple devices. The UART is exclusively designed for communication between two devices. The SPI bus is based on a *Master–Slave* relationship. A master-type device can be connected to multiple slave-type devices[2]. The I^2C bus supports communication among multiple masters and multiple slaves.

To conclude this introduction, note that the UART and SPI buses are among the most basic communication peripherals. There is no communication protocol beyond the definition of the data frame format, nor is there any concept of addressing. From the standpoint of data transmission reliability, the UART incorporates a parity bit into each frame, which can be verified by the receiver to discard corrupted data. In contrast, the SPI offers a slightly more advanced and reliable mechanism based on a CRC (*Cyclic Redundancy Check*) calculation. In the case of the I^2C bus, a rudimentary

---

and symbol rate are identical. There are transmissions in which a single symbol carries several bits (QAM, ADSL, etc.). In such cases, the bit rate is significantly larger than the symbol rate.

2 The SPI units of the STM32 can also handle multi-master communications; however, this type of communication is very uncommon.

communication protocol exists. This bus uses 7-bit addresses[3] to identify each device in communication.

Even on *mainstream* μcontrollers (see section 1.4.2), such as the STM32F103, more advanced data transmission technologies exist, such as the CAN bus and the Ethernet protocol, both defined by the *Open Systems Interconnection* (OSI) standards. However, programming these communication technologies is considerably more complex. We do not address them in this book.

9.2. UART units

9.2.1. *Generalities*

UART units allow data to be transmitted and received asynchronously at the same time (this is known as *Full-Duplex* communication).

We can consider a few examples of exchanges between two devices that involve UART: between a μcontroller and a PC, between a Raspberry Pi and a μcontroller, between two μcontrollers, between a μcontroller and a communication modem.

Two devices communicating via UART must have matching configurations. Among the configurable parameters, the UART standard defines:

– the *baud rate*, which is a multiple of submultiple of 9,600 Bd. The following baud rates are generally supported: 1,200, 2,400, 4,800, 9,600, 19,200, 38,400, 57,600 and 115,200 Bd;

– the data *length*, which can range between 7 and 9 bits, with 8 bits of data being the most common;

– the *number of stop bits*, which can be 0.5, 1, 1.5 or 2 bits; typically, only one stop bit is used;

– the *parity*, which is an optional bit. In the case of even parity, this bit is added to the frame so that the total number of 1 bits in the data plus the parity bit is even. In the case of odd parity, the same principle applies, except that the total number of 1 bits must be odd;

– the *flow control*, which is often disabled, employs additional control lines to manage situations where the receive *buffer* is full.

Note that a *start* bit is always present at the beginning of each communication.

Table 9.1 lists the composition of the various commonly used frames.

3 An extension to 10-bit address encoding exists, but is rarely used.

Length	*Start* bit	Number of useful data bits	Parity bit	*Stop* bit
10 bits	1	8	0	1
10 bits	1	7	1	1
11 bits	1	9	0	1
11 bits	1	8	1	1

Table 9.1. *Summary of standard UART frames*

In the absence of flow control signals, which is the case in the vast majority of applications, a UART transmits data via a line called Tx and receives data via a line called Rx (see Figure 9.1). To indicate the start of a transmission, the UART inserts a specific bit, known as the start bit, which is recognized by the received UART. Each bit is then transmitted sequentially at the predetermined transmission rate. The LSB (*Least Significant Bit*) is transmitted first. The final bit is immediately followed by one (or more, depending on the configuration) stop bit(s). When the hardware flow control mechanisms are enabled, two additional lines are required, named RTS (*Ready To Send*) and CTS (*Clear To Send*).

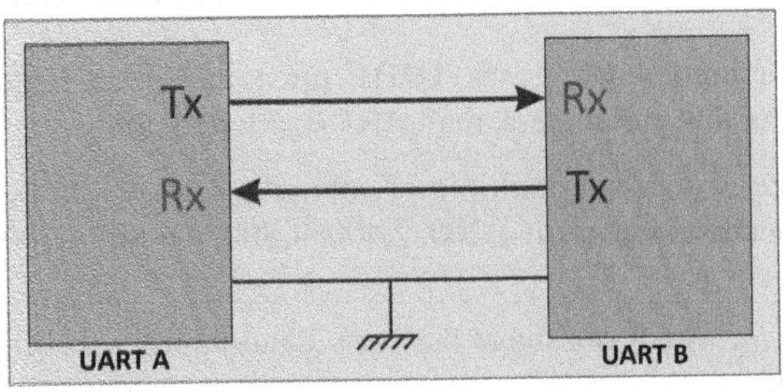

Figure 9.1. *Interconnection between two UARTs*

Figure 9.2 shows an asynchronous transmission of the character "]", whose hexadecimal code in the ASCII table is 0x5D, that is, in binary $(01011101)_2$.

Note that the signal rests at level 1. Thus, the start bit is 0 while the stop bit is 1. If this frame is transmitted by UART A, UART B, which is listening on the line, will detect the falling edge of the start bit. Knowing the transmission rate, UART B can then determine the sampling instants required to sample each bit and reconstruct the byte. After the stop bit, UART B resumes waiting for the next start bit.

Figure 9.1 shows an interconnection between two UARTs operating at typical digital circuit voltage levels (5V or 3.3V). These levels can sometimes be insufficient, for example, when transmitting over long distances or in noisy environments.

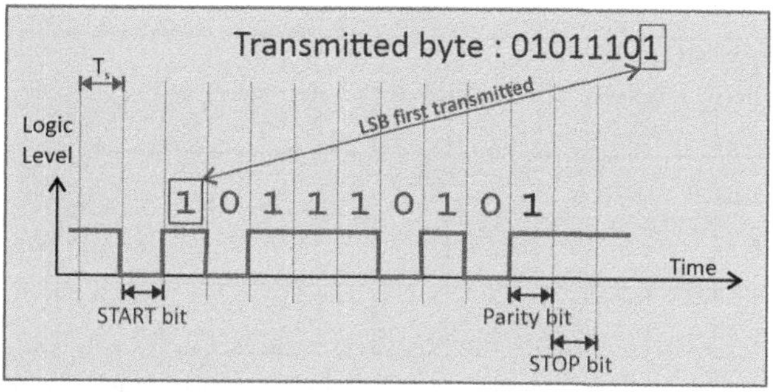

Figure 9.2. *Example of an asynchronous frame with even parity*

To facilitate the implementation of UART serial communication over distances of the order of a meter, standards exist to regulate, among other aspects, the electrical levels. The RS-232 standard is the most commonly used.

This standard provides voltage levels significantly higher than a μcontroller's output level to ensure greater robustness. Figure 9.3a illustrates the correspondence between the controller's output voltage and the voltage on the line. Logical inversion is also observed. Finally, the standard specifies a voltage between $+3$V and $+25$V for a 0 level and between -3V and -25V for a 1 level.

Specialized circuits exist for voltage level adaption, such as the widely used MAX232, originally offered by Maxim Integrated Products and also available under various part numbers from other manufacturers (Figure 9.3b). With only a few capacitors connected to the component, the MAX232 is capable of generating voltages on the order of ± 12V.

There are also RS-422 and RS-485 standards. With RS-422, the Rx and Tx lines become differential (TD+, TD- and RD+, RD-), which enhances noise immunity. As a result, both the transmission distances and data rates are increased, while still operating in *Full-Duplex* mode. The RS-485 standard also employs differential signaling but uses only two wires, Data+ and Data-. This is the *Half-Duplex* mode and supports multi-master operation.

9.2.2. *Reading/writing techniques*

There are several approaches to managing data transmission and reception, ranging from the most efficient in terms of CPU load, which employ DMA mechanisms, to the least efficient, which rely solely on *flag* polling. We propose an intermediate method: using interrupt mechanisms for handling data reception and a polling mechanism for data transmission.

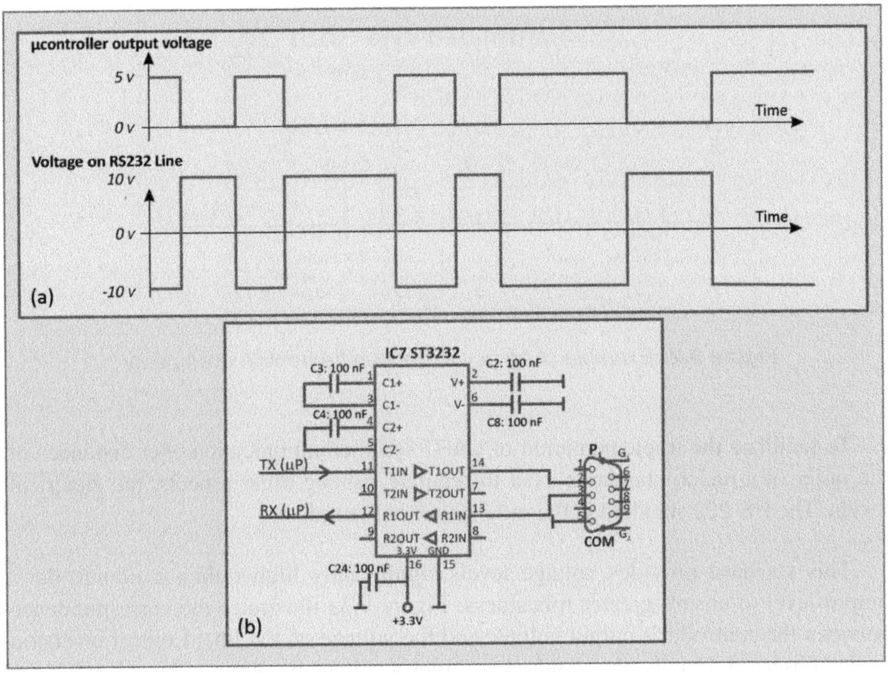

Figure 9.3. *Timing diagrams and circuitry related to the RS-232 standard*

9.2.2.1. *UART transmission*

Transmission is entirely managed by the user, as they initiate the transmission request. We will not use interrupts (although this is feasible) for data transmission; instead, we will simply wait after transmitting each byte until the data has been effectively sent. Thus, there are two steps to follow:

1) write a data byte into the transmit register;

2) wait (by polling) for the *flag* to be set, indicating that the data has been transferred.

One might think that the second polling step is optional, but checking the *flag* is essential as it prevents a new byte from overwriting the previous one that has not yet been transmitted.

As soon as one wishes to transmit not just a single byte (which often corresponds to a character) but strings of characters, it is very common to initiate the transmission with a call to a function of the form `void putString(char *chain)`. This function is based on another function of the form `void putchar(char car)`, which adheres to the aforementioned procedure to send each character of the string one by one.

9.2.2.2. *UART reception*

In practice, data reception is asynchronous in that the application programmer cannot predict when one or more data bytes will arrive in the receive *buffer*. In such situations, foregoing interrupt mechanisms is virtually impossible. Indeed, it is rarely acceptable to block the processor and all other activities until a *flag* indicates that data are present in the receive *buffer*. Unlike data transmission, polling the *flag* is therefore not advisable.

In the case of reception, it is almost indispensable to use an interrupt triggered by the activation of the reception *flag* at the peripheral level. When multiple characters are expected, a common solution is to store each incoming character in an array at every reception interrupt until an end-of-string character or predetermined length is detected. This way, a string of characters can be progressively constructed automatically without monopolizing the processor in a polling loop.

9.2.3. *UART configuration on the STM32F10x*

The STM32F10x integrates up to five peripheral UART units. When reviewing the STM32F10x reference manual, we notice that there are, in fact, few registers dedicated to the UART units. They appear in the *Register Map* in the following order:

– a standard status register (SR) that facilitates the management of various flags for interrupt requests;

– a data register (DR);

– a dedicated register (BRR) for controlling the bit transmission rate;

– three configuration registers (CR1, CR2, CR3) for transmission;

– a dedicated register for configuring the UART in specific modes related to the *Smartcard* or *IrDA* protocols, which will not be addressed in this book.

Let us now detail the most common registers.

9.2.3.1. *Data register*

A UART peripheral on an STM32F10x features a data register (DR) in which the user can read or write. In reality, this is a logical register accessible to the user but composed of two internal pseudo-registers: the TDR (*Transmit Data Register*) for transmitting data and the RDR (*Receive Data Register*) for receiving data (see Figure 9.4). These two internal registers are not directly accessible to the programmer.

The DR is a register in which only the nine least significant bits are accessible for reading and writing to facilitate data reception or transmission. Several data formats (see Table 9.1) are possible in the STM32F10x: from 7 to 9 data bits depending on whether parity is used. When parity control is enabled, the MSB of the data is overwritten by the parity control bit on the transmitter side, and reading this bit during reception does not yield a data bit but the parity bit.

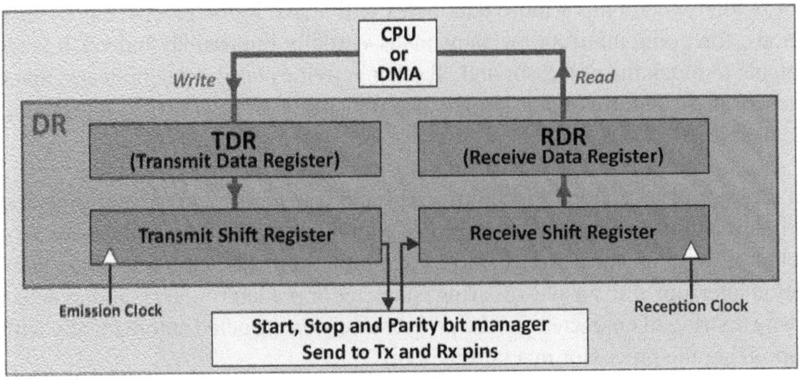

Figure 9.4. *Detailed overview of the UART DR*

Figure 9.5. *UART DR*

9.2.3.2. *Various useful flags in the SR*

The SR Register (see Figure 9.6) provides access to various flags that are useful for managing transmissions. Some of these flags are used to indicate a problem that may have occurred during transmission:

– PE (*Parity Error*), which is set when a PE occurs during the parity check of the received data bits. For example, in Figure 9.2, the number of bits is even. If the user has selected even parity, the PE flag will not be set;

– FE (*Frame Error*) and NE (*Noise Error*), both of which are associated with the detection of degraded transmission conditions due to factors such as noise or desynchronization. They are not tied to a potential interrupt request since their activation occurs simultaneously with the data reception flag, as will be discussed later in this section;

– ORE (*OverRun Error*), which is raised if data are overwritten before they can be read or written. It may be associated with an interrupt request (provided that the EIE bit in the CR3 register is set). This interrupt is triggered when new data arrive while the previous data have not yet been read.

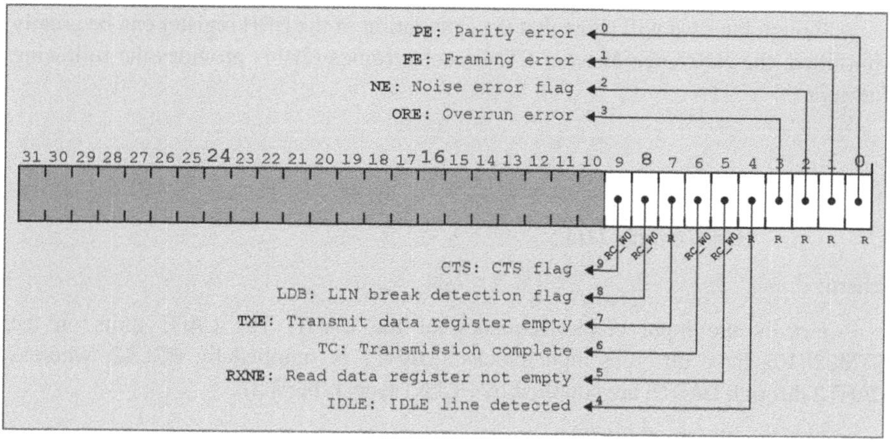

Figure 9.6. *SR register of a USART*

In reception, the flag in the SR register that indicates whether data are present in the RDR is the RxNE (*Read Data Register Not Empty*) bit. The UART can handle interrupt mechanisms for data reception.

During transmission, the flag indicating that the UART is capable of transmitting data, that is, that the DR register (actually the TDR) is empty, is the TxE (*Transmit Data Register Empty*). As with data reception, an interrupt can also be associated with the flag.

9.2.3.3. *Transmission speed control in the BRR*

To exchange data between a transmitter and a receiver, the UART requires both to agree on the bit transmission rate, thereby eliminating the need for a synchronization clock signal. This configuration is carried out via the BRR (*Baud Rate Register*), as shown in Figure 9.7.

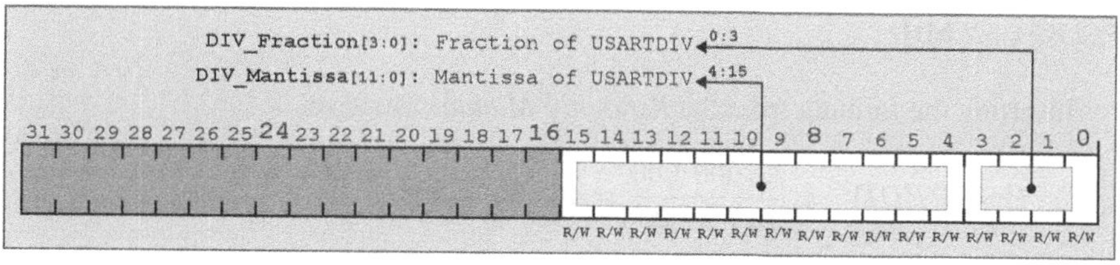

Figure 9.7. *BRR register of a USART*

Let us detail the calculation of the integer part and the fractional part.

Although later we will show that the calculation of the BRR register can be greatly simplified, the *Reference Manual* STMicroelectronics (2011) provides the following formula:

$$D = \frac{Fck}{16 * USARTDIV}$$

where:

– Fck is the input clock frequency of the UART. The UART units on the STM32F10x have different input clocks: UART1 is supplied by PCLK2, whereas UART2 through UART5 are supplied by PCLK1 (see Table 3.2);

– D is the bit rate in bits/s;

– $USARTDIV$ is a fractional number (more precisely in the 12.4 format). This means that 12 bits are allocated to the integer part and 4 bits to the fractional part. Consequently, the weight of each bit differs from that of standard binary representation, so that $USARTDIV$ must be interpreted using these new weights: $\left[2^{11}\, 2^{10}\, 2^{9}\, 2^{8}\, 2^{7}\, 2^{6}\, 2^{5}\, 2^{4}\, 2^{3}\, 2^{2}\, 2^{1}\, 2^{0}\, 2^{-1}\, 2^{-2}\, 2^{-3}\, 2^{-4}\right]$. Since the least significant weight in this representation is 2^{-4} rather than $1(= 2^0)$, the value of $USARTDIV$ is that of BRR multiplied not by 2^0, but by 2^{-4}, that is: $USARTDIV =$ BRR $\times 2^{-4}$, or equivalently, BRR $= 16 * USARTDIV$.

The value of the BRR will then be determined simply by calculating:

$$BRR = \left(\frac{Fck}{D}\right)$$

Let us consider two examples of calculation.

EXAMPLE 9.1.–

1) We desire a baud rate of 9,600 Bd and assume that UART1 operates with PCLK2 = 72 MHz.

Inverting the formula from the *Reference Manual*, we have:

$$USARTDIV = \frac{72,000,000}{16 * 9,600} = 468.75 = 468 + \frac{12}{16}$$

hence:

– DIV_Mantissa $= 468$;

– DIV_Fraction $= 12$;

– $\Rightarrow$ BRR $= 468 << 4 + 12$.

By calculating the BRR directly using the proposed formula, we directly obtain:

$$BRR = \left(\frac{72,000,000}{9,600}\right) = 7,500$$

The previous result is confirmed since $7,500 = 468 \ll 4 + 12$.

2) Now, let us consider a baud rate of 115,200 Bd with PCLK1 running at 36 MHz. We have:

$$BRR = E\left(\frac{36,000,000}{115,200}\right) = (312.5) = 312$$

An error will occur due to truncation since the BRR is defined as an integer. Consequently, the effective baud rate will be approximately 115,384 Bd. Note that an error would also arise when using the formula from the *Reference Manual* STMicroelectronics (2011). Indeed, this error is unavoidable as long as the decimal portion cannot be expressed as a fraction with a denominator of 16.

9.2.3.4. *Configuration registers CR1, CR2 and CR3*

The standard configuration for UART serial communication, the only one covered in this book, is as follows:

– 8 data bits;

– 1 start bit;

– 1 stop bit;

– no parity control;

– no hardware slow control.

All UART units in the STM32F10x features three configuration registers, CR1, CR2 and CR3 registers, as shown in Figures 9.8, 9.9 and 9.10.

It will be necessary to examine the first two configuration registers, although in most cases it is not necessary to modify the default settings. If we outline the configuration steps, we find:

– In the CR1 register, the essential parameters are as follows:

- The UE bit (*USART Enable*) enables the peripheral or disables it to conserve energy (not that the peripheral must still receive its clock signal).

- The M bit specifies the size of the data payload, either 8 or 9 bits, keeping in mind that there is always a start bit and that the number of stop bits is defined in another register. By default, this bit is set to 0, corresponding to 8 data bits.

- The PCE, PS and PEIE (*Parity Control Enable*, *Parity Selection* and *Parity Error Enable Interrupt*) bits manage parity control. If PCE is set to 1 (default is 0), the transmitter calculates the value of the eighth bit (or the ninth for 9-bit transfers), which is inserted as the MSB of the data (immediately preceding the stop bit(s)) and is checked by the receiver. When parity control is enabled, the receiver sets the PE *flag* in the SR register if it detects corrupted data. An exception may also be raised if the PEIE bit is set to 1.

- The TE and RE (*Transmission Enable* and *Reception Enable*) bits allow the transmission and reception functions to be enabled or disabled.

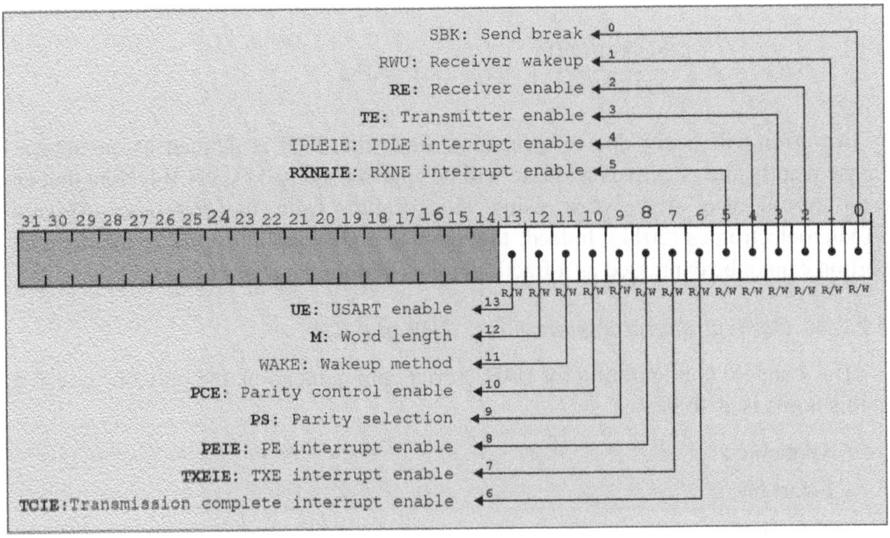

Figure 9.8. *CR1 register of a UART*

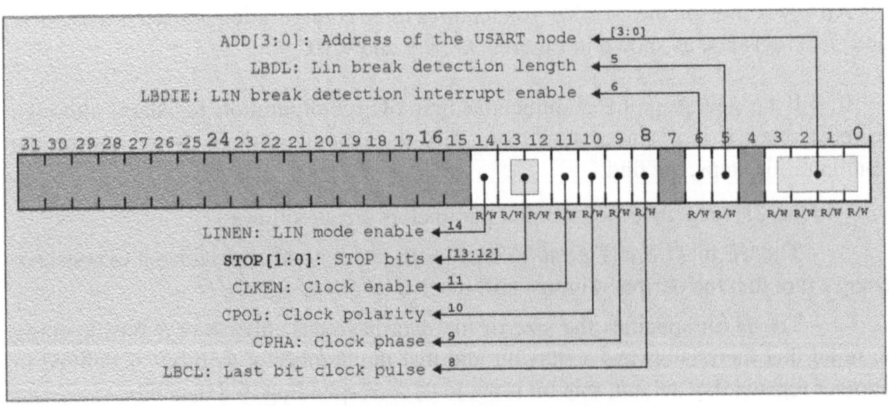

Figure 9.9. *CR2 register of a UART*

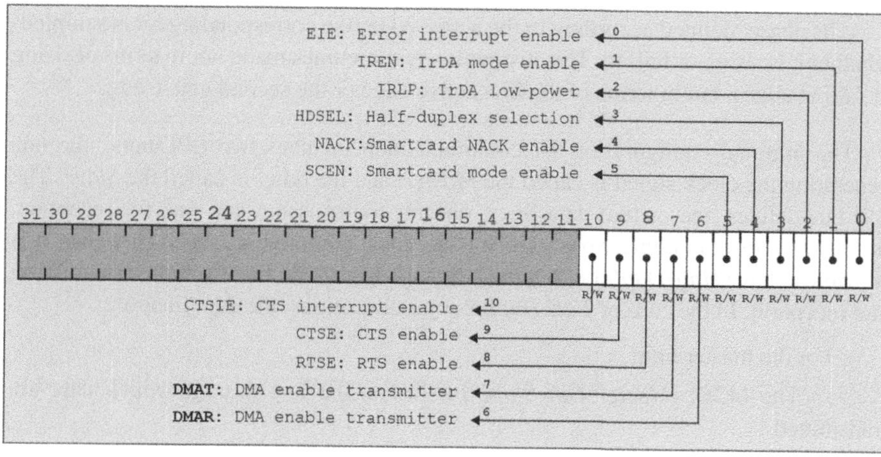

Figure 9.10. *CR3 register of a UART*

– In the CR2 register, the only useful bit field in a standard configuration is that of the configuration bits for the number of stop bits. By default, the value $(00)_2$ indicates a single stop bit at the end of the transmission.

In the CR1 register, we can also choose which interrupts to manage. In our approach, which involves handling interrupts only during data reception, this is the RxNEIE bit.

In the CR3 register, the UART can be configured to use DMA mechanisms, which are:

– the DMAT bit, to enable DMA for transmission;

– the DMAR bit, to enable DMA for reception.

Regarding DMA configuration, please refer to Chapter 5. Although we have only discussed the polling strategy for transmission, we invite the reader to consult the chapter on DMA to explore the transmission approach using this technique, which includes sample code.

9.3. SPI units

9.3.1. *Generalities*

The SPI bus is the simplest of the synchronous buses based on a synchronization clock line. There are four types of clock configurations, depending on:

– its polarity, defined by the idle state of the clock (0 or 1);

– its phase, defined according to the active edge (the corresponding bit is sampled) whether it is rising or falling. This distinction is sometimes made not in terms of rising or falling edges, but in terms of the first active edge or the second active edge.

The minimal configuration for communication involves two SPI units: the one generating the clock signal is called the *Master*, and the other is called the *Slave*. The SPI bus defines one or two data lines, one for transmission and one for reception, in *Full-Duplex* communications, which is the most common scenario. However, it is possible to have *Half-Duplex* communication using a single line for both transmission and reception. In the case of *Full-Duplex* communications, the data lines are:

– For the master unit:

- The MOSI (*Master Out Slave In*) line is the line through which data are transmitted.

- The MISO (*Master In Slave Out*) line is the line through which data are received.

– Conversely, for the slave unit:

- The MOSI line is the line through which data is received.

- The MISO line is the line through which data is transmitted.

The master uses one or more lines to enable communication with one or more slaves. These lines are designated under various names depending on the manufacturer, commonly SS or CS, for *Slave Select* or *Chip Select*. They are sometimes also labeled as *nCS* or *nSS* to emphasize the active low-logic used in slave selection, where a low-level voltage is applied. For the same reason, they are occasionally represented as ($\overline{CS}$, $\overline{SS}$).

In Figure 9.11(b), the MISO lines of *Slave 1* and *Slave 2* are connected. However, since both units are capable of transmitting data, a conflict may arise if one drives a 1 while the other drives a 0. Therefore, the role of the $\overline{CS}$ lines is to:

– disconnect (using an internally controlled switch implemented in the *Slave*) the MISO line when $\overline{CS} = 1$ (which is equivalent to having the *Slave* unselected);

– connect the MISO line when $\overline{CS} = 0$ (which selects the *Slave*).

In this way, only one *Slave* is connected to the *Master*, resulting in the configuration shown in Figure 9.11(a).

During communication with a single slave, it may be tempting not to use the *Master*'s $\overline{CS}$ line connected to the *Slave*'s $\overline{CS}$ line. However, doing so would be a mistake. Without the $\overline{CS}$ information, the *Slave* can only decide when to sample the 8-bit data by counting clock edges. After the eighth edge, the byte is assumed to have been fully received and can therefore be processed. Thus, if a clock edge is missed, all subsequent characters will be erroneous. By employing the $\overline{CS}$, the *Slave* can adopt an alternative approach: on the falling edge of $\overline{CS}$, its clock edge counter is reset to zero. Consequently, if a clock edge is lost, only the current byte will be affected. Subsequent bytes will be properly realigned (with the counter reset to 0 on the next falling edge of $\overline{CS}$).

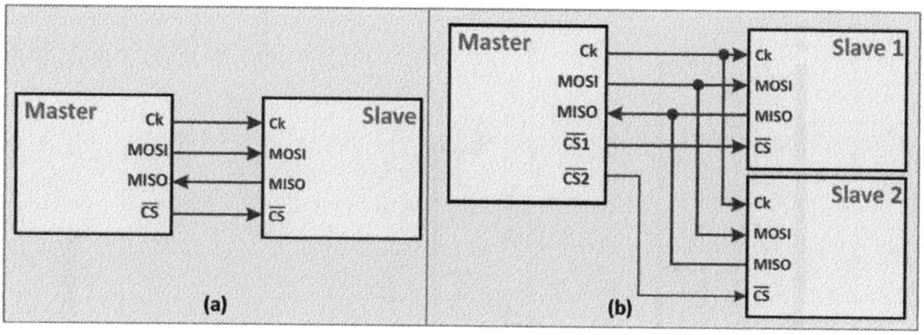

Figure 9.11. *SPI configuration with one or two Slaves*

9.3.2. *Shift register-based read/write techniques*

9.3.2.1. *Principle of a shift register*

On SPI devices, data exchanges are based on the implementation of shift exchanges (D flip-flops in series), as illustrated in Figure 9.12.

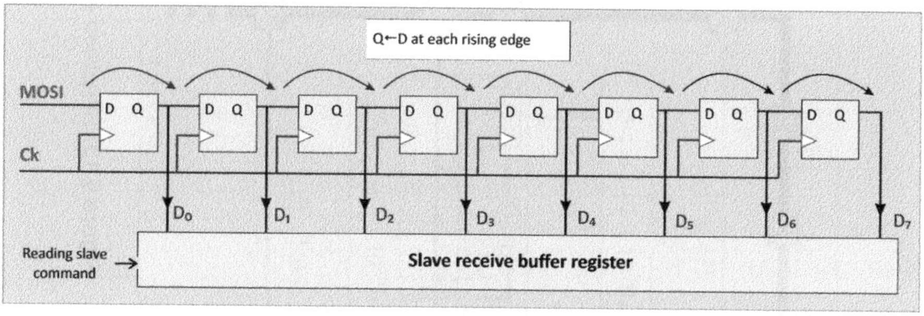

Figure 9.12. *Shift and read registers of an SPI*

To better understand this mechanism, which requires that the master and slave exchange one bit with each clock pulse, we will refer to Figure 9.13. This figure depicts the architecture of the STM32F10x in a greatly simplified form compared to that shown in the *Reference Manual* STMicroelectronics (2011). It is representative of the architecture of any SPI device using the four-wire mode, where the MOSI and MISO lines are on separate wires to support *Full-Duplex* transmissions. We find:

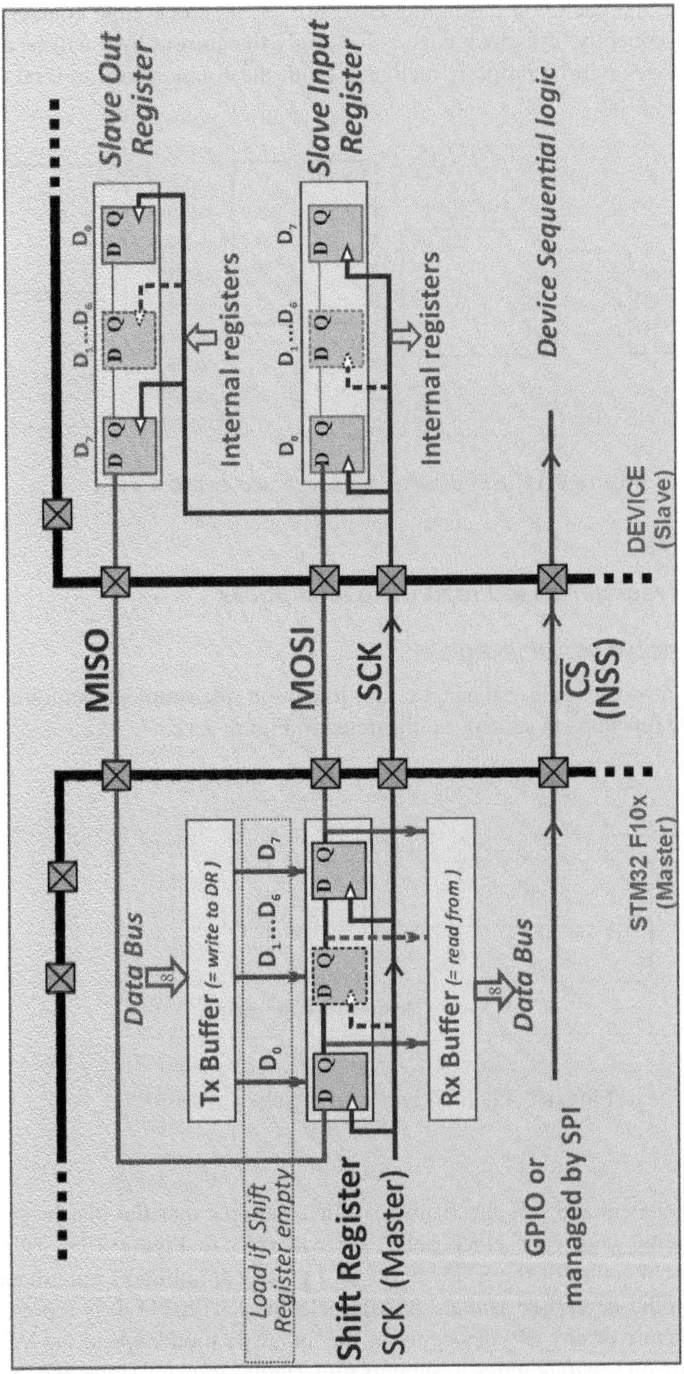

Figure 9.13. *Simplified architecture of a Master/Slave operation*

– the μcontroller in *Master* mode, connected to an SPI component, with an 8-bit data frame in MSB-first mode, meaning that the most significant bit is transmitted first;

– the MISO line for data reception;

– the MOSI line for data transfer;

– the clock signal generated by the STM32F103 in *Master* mode;

– the $\overline{CS}$ line, which enables the activation of the component in *Slave* mode;

– the essential registers related to the data of the SPI peripheral. The *Shift Register* consists of eight D flip-flops connected in series. It can be forced into parallel loading via the pseudo-register Tx Buffer and can be read through the pseudo-register Rx Buffer. The Shift Register is unique. It serves both for transmission and reception[4].

On the *Slave* side, for the sake of generality, we have represented only two registers: one for input (to receive data sent by the μcontroller) and one for output (to transmit data to the μcontroller), both clocked by the same SCK signal.

The synchronization clock SCK drives both the serial register on the STM32F10x side and the serial registers on the component side. When the CPU writes to DR, it writes into the Tx Buffer. At the next clock cycle, the content is transferred into the *Shift Register*. Automatically, eight clock edges are sent at the programmed frequency.

The 8 bits are then completely copied into the *Slave Input Register* of the *Slave*. Simultaneously, the *Shift Register* of the STM32F10x is filled with the data presented by the component on the MISO line (the output of the *Slave Out Register*). The sequence shown in Figure 9.14 outlines the operations at each edge of the synchronous clock.

The preceding time sequence precisely described the serial transfer at each clock edge. At the end of the process, the bits to be transmitted, T7...T0, are successfully copied into the input register of the *Slave*, while output bits of the *Slave*, O7...O0, are simultaneously copied into the *Shift Register* of the *Master*. Finally, note that the RxNE flag (*Rx Not Empty*) indicates that eight new bits have arrived in the *Shift Register* and can be read via the DR register. Conversely, the TxE flag (*Tx Empty*) indicates that the *Tx Buffer* is available to receive a new byte. The CPU can then write data into the DR register (if a serial transmission is in progress, the SPI peripheral will wait for the transfer to complete before copying data into the *Shift Register*).

4 We thus find, as with the UART peripheral discussed in section 9.2, the principle of providing the programmer with access to a single DR register even though, at the μcontroller level, two registers exist: the Tx Buffer and the Rx Buffer. Writing to DR places data into the Tx Buffer, whereas reading from it retrieves data from the Rx Buffer. Consequently, reading the DR register does not return what the program has just written to it. Instead, it provides the data received by the SPI.

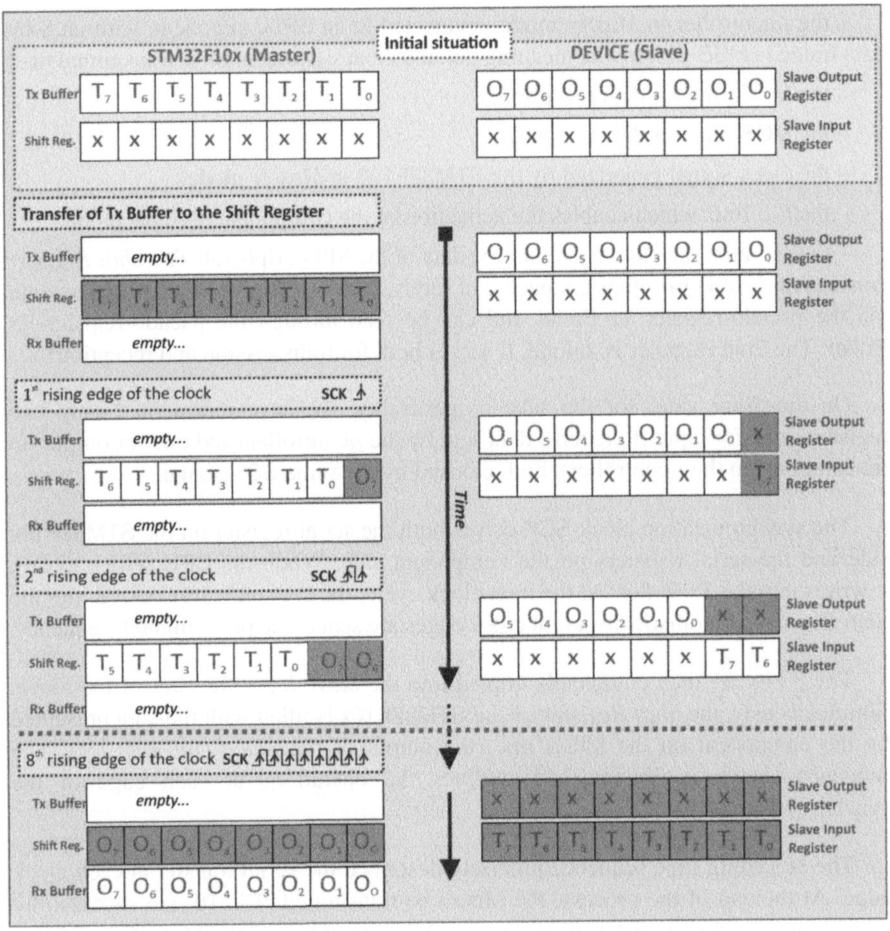

Figure 9.14. *Sequencing of a Master/Slave operation*

9.3.2.2. *Reading/writing techniques*

The principle of transmission synchronization, where each transmitted bit corresponds to one received bit, requires some discipline in managing data transmissions and receptions. If the *Master* is solely transmitting data to the component, this principle has no impact. However, the situation becomes more complex when there is an exchange involving alternating transmissions and receptions by the *Master*. Indeed, it is not simply a matter of chaining wrote operations and then reading from the DR register, as such a sequence would yield an inconsistent result. Consider a simplified case where the μcontroller (acting as *Master*) communicates with an accelerometer (acting as *Slave*) via a SPI link. To obtain the accelerometer's measured acceleration value encoded in one byte, the

μcontroller sends a command (also encoded in 1 byte) to the accelerometer through its MISO line. If, after writing the command into the DR register, the μcontroller immediately reads from the DR register, the read operation will not produce the measurement value from the accelerometer, since the register will have been filled as the command was transmitted. We propose the following algorithm for a write followed by a read.

The algorithm for receiving the acceleration measurement is as follows:

1) wait until the DR register is empty by polling the TxE flag;

2) place the command (1 byte) into the DR, which causes the command's bits to be transmitted on the MOSI line while meaningless bits are simultaneously received on the MISO line and stored in the DR register;

3) wait for the complete reception of the meaningless data by polling the RxNE flag;

4) clear the DR register by reading it;

5) place a meaningless byte into the DR register (e.g. 0×00);

6) wait for the complete reception of the data corresponding to the acceleration measurement by polling the RxNE flag;

7) retrieve the acceleration measurement by reading the DR register.

9.3.3. *SPI configuration on the STM32F10x*

The STM32F10x devices feature up to three SPI peripheral units (SPI1, SPI2 and SP3 registers). As with the UART, the reference manual informs us that there are ultimately few registers dedicated to the configuration of these units. In the *Register Map*, they appear in the following order:

– two registers (CR1 and CR2) for configuring transmission;

– a standard flag SR that manages various flags for interrupt requests;

– a DR, as previously presented;

– three registers related to the use of CRC computation for ensuring the reliability of data transmission (CRCPR, TXCRCR and RXCRCR).

Let us begin with the DR.

9.3.3.1. *Data register*

The DR register is the only data register accessible to the programmer. In section 9.3.2.1, we detailed the principle of using two sub-registers to allow simultaneous reading and writing. The DR register is 16 bits wide because two formats are supported during transmission: 8-bit or 16-bit data.

9.3.3.2. *CR1 and CR2 configuration registers*

As with the UART peripheral, the default configuration of the two registers will be satisfactory in most cases. Consider the following most common configuration:

– the STM32F10x will operate as the *Master*;

– the activation of the *Slave* device ($\overline{CS}$) is not managed by the SPI peripheral but will be handled by software using a GPIO pin;

– 8-bit data;

– two distinct lines for MOSI and MISO;

– transmission with the most significant bit transmitted first.

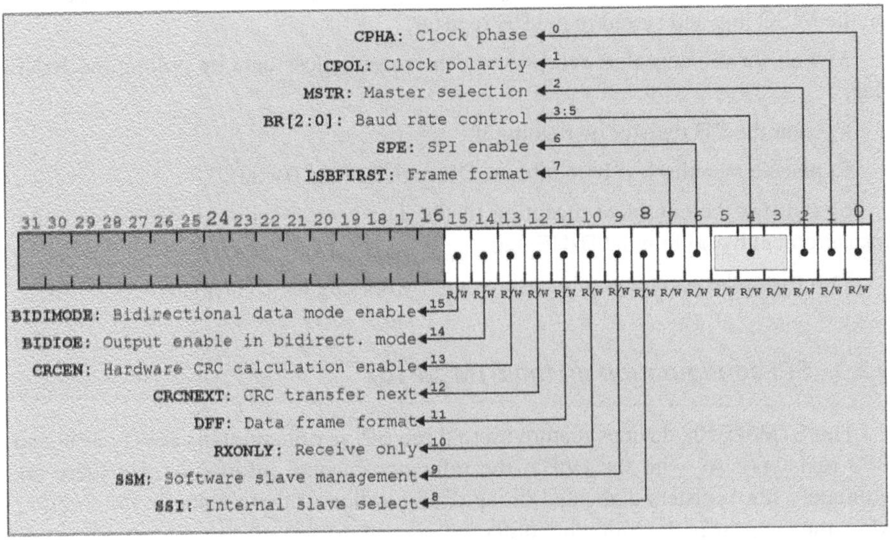

Figure 9.15. *CR1 register of an SPI*

If we follow the configuration steps, we find the CR1 register (Figure 9.15)

– two bits, CPOL and CPHA, to configure the phase and polarity of the SCK clock signal, as illustrated in Figures 9.16 and 9.17;

– three bits, BIDIMODE, BIDIOE and RXONLY, to choose between one- or two-line modes for the MOSI/MISO signals as well as *Full-Duplex* mode. By default, the configuration uses two distinct lines and *Full-Duplex* mode;

– the DFF bit, which allows selecting between 8- or 16-bit data frames; by default, SPI handles 8-bit frames;

– the LSBFIRST bit, for selecting either MSB-first (most significant bit first) or LSB-first (least significant bit first) mode; by default, MSB-first mode is selected;

– the peripheral enable bit, SPE. Note that by default this bit is 0, meaning the peripheral is disabled;

– a three-bit field, BRR, for controlling the data transmission speed by setting the divider for the peripheral's input clock frequency. The divider value is given by 2^{BRR+1}. SPI1 is connected to the PCLK2 clock, while SPI2 and SPI3 are connected to the PCLK1 clock. By default, the divider is 2;

– the MSTR bit for configuring the peripheral in *Slave* or *Master* mode; by default, *Slave* mode is selected.

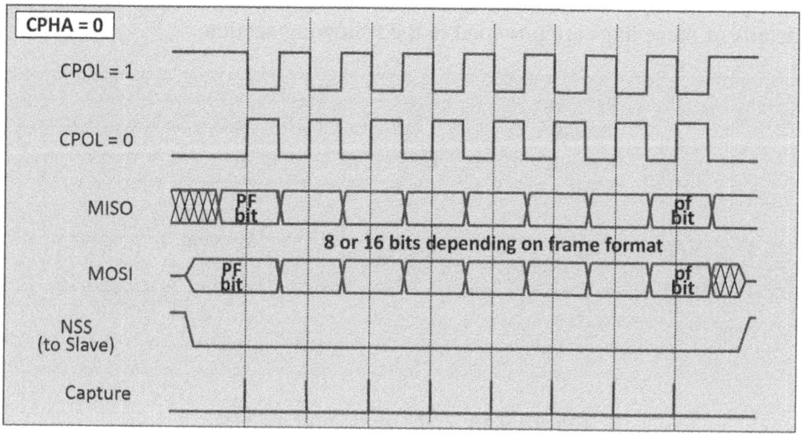

Figure 9.16. *SPI with first-edge latching*

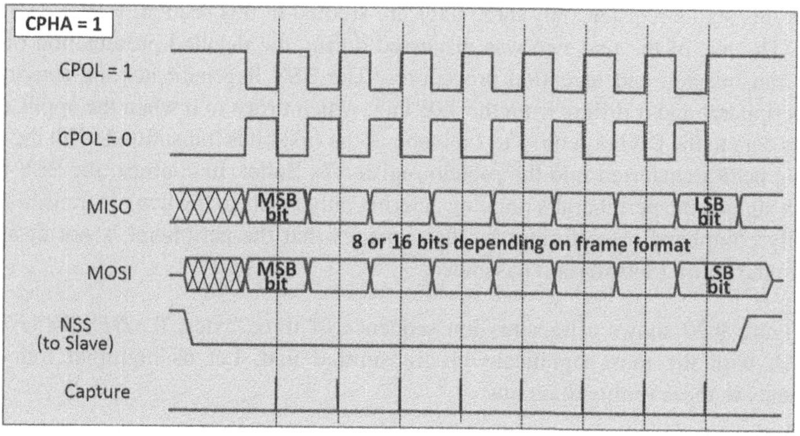

Figure 9.17. *SPI with second-edge latching*

Other bits are available to configure the enabling the frame reliability via CRC calculation. By default, this function is disabled. There are also two bits, SSM and SSI, which can be used by an STM32F10x configured in *Slave* mode. These two bits allow for the software emulation of the *Slave* activation line. To enable this emulation, SSM must be set to 1, which will then be ignored.

Regarding SPI transmissions, the CR2 register (Figure 9.18) essentially contains the configuration bits for the interrupt requests that manage the data buffer. Since we are considering the STM32F10x configured in *Master* mode, the use of interrupts is not mandatory. A polling-based approach to monitoring the flags is entirely acceptable. The details of these flags are provided in the following section.

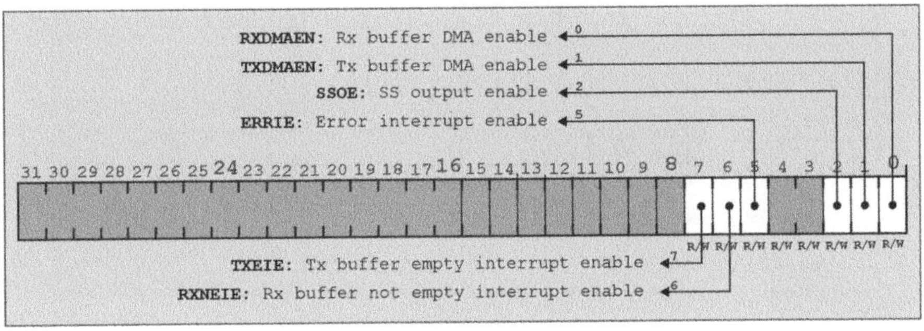

Figure 9.18. *CR2 register of an SPI*

9.3.3.3. *Various useful flags of the SR register*

In this status register, only three flags are studied in this section, RxNE, TxE and BSY. The use of the first two was discussed during the detailed presentation of the data transmission and reception procedures. The BSY flag indicates the activity of the peripheral and it differs from the TxE flag, which drops to 0 when the application writes data to the DR but returns to 1 as soon as the first bit is transmitted, with the data having been transferred into the pseudo-register Tx Buffer. In contrast, the BSY flag, which signals the peripheral's ongoing activity, only resets to 0 when the transmission is fully completed. Monitoring this flag ensures that the peripheral is not disabled before the entire transmission has ended.

Figure 9.20 shows a transmission sequence of three bytes, $0{\times}BF$, $0{\times}4F$ and $0{\times}C3$, with the most significant bit transmitted first. Let us highlight four key moments in these timing diagrams:

1) The DR register receives the new value (here, $0{\times}BF$). Note that the TxE flag is then set to 1, indicating that the DR register can be written to.

2) The contents of DR are immediately transferred to the Tx Buffer. Consequently, the TxE flag drops to 0, indicating that a new write to DR should not be performed.

The Busy indicator is set to 1, signaling that a transmission is in progress. At this state, the shift register is also loaded, and serialization begins.

3) Since the shift register is loaded and actively serializing, the Tx Buffer becomes free to receive a new value: TxE returns to 1.

4) The last bit, bit 0, has just been transmitted along with its corresponding clock edge: the entire byte has been transferred, and the Busy flag can revert to 0.

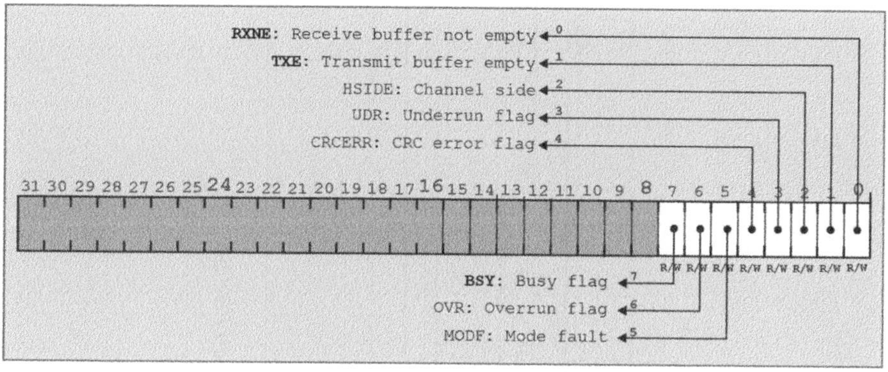

Figure 9.19. *SR register of an SPI*

9.4. I²C bus

Like the SPI bus, the I²C bus is widely used to interface sensors or actuators. In the vast majority of cases, a μcontroller's I²C is employed in *Master* mode. Although manufacturers systematically provide the option to operate in *Slave* mode, we have chosen to present only the *Master* mode in detail.

9.4.1. *Generalities*

The I²C bus is a synchronous communication bus designed by Philips in the 1990s (with its latest update dating from 2014). Unlike the other two protocols discussed in the previous sections, it uses addresses to enable communication between various components. Although it employs only a single data line, the bus remains bidirectional but operates in *Half-Duplex* mode, which prevents simultaneous transmission and reception. From a physical standpoint, this bus is very simple, requiring only three lines:

– the ground line;

– the SDA line (*Serial Data Line*), which carries the data bits;

– the SCL line (*Serial Clock Line*), which carries the synchronization clock.

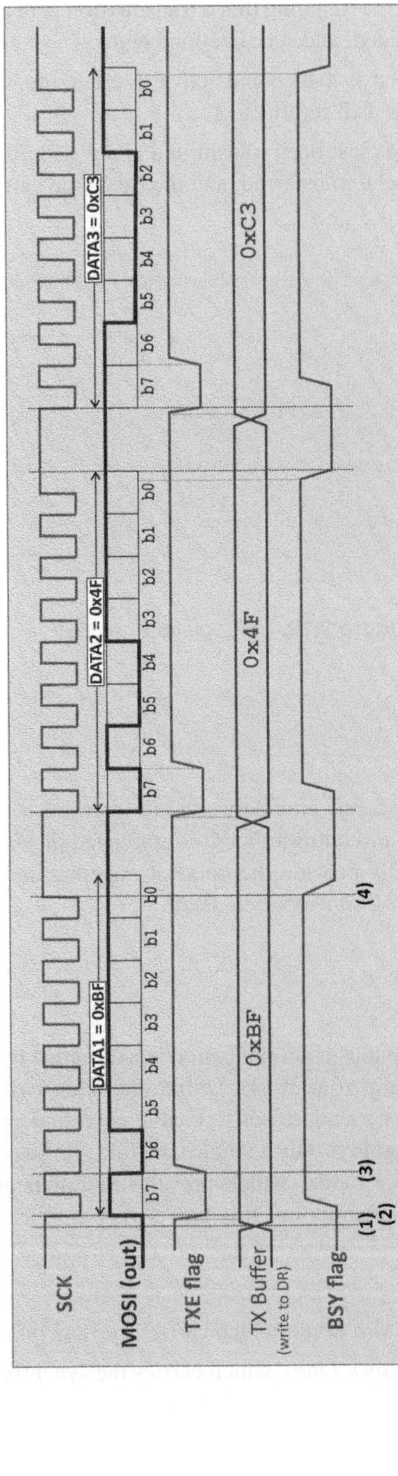

Figure 9.20. *Activation of the SPI BSY bit*

On these three lines, as many I²C devices as desired can be connected, up to a limit of 128 addresses, as defined by the address space specified in the standard[5].

As with the SPI, I²C components can assume two roles when active on the bus:

– The *Master* role: this is the device that directs the communication. It generates the SCL clock line and may both transmit and receive bytes.

– The *Slave* role: this is the device that undergoes the data transfer, either transmitting or receiving.

The bus enables the design of a multi-master system, meaning that several devices operating as *Masters* can concurrently access the bus to communicate with units in the *Slave* role. This use case, which requires *Masters* to ensure that the bus is available before using it, is not very common.

Figure 9.21 shows an example of the wiring for a network consisting of five devices, including two *Masters*.

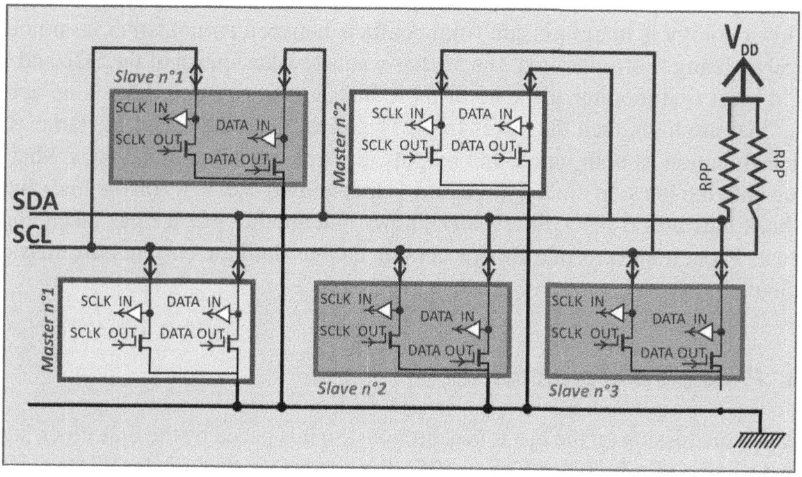

Figure 9.21. *Example of an I^2C network with two Masters and three Slaves*

9.4.2. *Electrical topology of the I^2C bus*

We observe in Figure 9.21 that the two lines, SCL and SDA, are connected to the V_{DD} tension via *pull-up* registers (with a typical value ranging from 5 to 10 kΩ).

5 A 10-bit address extension, providing up to 1,024 addresses, exists but will not be considered in this book.

These values are provided as guidelines. The more I^2C devices that are connected together, the larger the equivalent capacitance between a line (SCL and SDA) and the 0V reference becomes important. The designer must therefore conduct a thorough electronic analysis to determine the appropriate *pull-up* resistor value based on this capacitance and the desired transmission speed. This means that, without any action from the components, the lines remain high, but this high state is considered weak (or recessive). The components have the ability to force the line low (to 0V) in a strong (or dominant) manner.

For the network to operate without short-circuiting, each unit connected to the bus must have its SDA and SDL lines configured as outputs in an *Open Drain* configuration. Thus, when the output MOSFET is off, the high state (V_{DD}) is imposed on the line via the *pull-up* resistor. Conversely, if the MOSFET is on, the line is pulled low (0V). The strong/weak (or dominant/recessive) concept means that if one element forcefully drives the line to 0V by turning on its MOSFET, the line is forced to 0V even if other circuits are attempting to drive it to V_{DD}.

This topology is therefore safe from conflicts between two *Masters*, as no output can end up being short-circuited. If a *Master* wants to take control of the SCL and SDA lines, it must first monitor the state of these lines and verify that there is no activity (if the lines are high, then the bus is free). The *Master* can then send its frame. Since the lines function as both inputs and outputs, the transmitter can read back what it is driving onto the lines. In this way, if a bit 1 is transmitted (i.e. V_{DD} on the line) and the read-back indicates 0 (0V), the *Master* knows that another *Master* has taken control before it. Then, it must refrain from accessing the bus until the current transmission is complete.

9.4.3. *Principle and protocol*

Data transmission on the bus is synchronous, so it is paced by the SCL clock signal. When the bus is idle, both the SDA and SCL lines remain at the high level (1, i.e. V_{DD}).

9.4.3.1. *Bit transmission*

The bit to be transmitted is placed on the SDA signal, but the receiver will only recognize the bit if it remains stable. That is to say, constant throughout the entire duration of the clock pulse's high state. In other words, the SCL signal must return to a low state (0V) before any change occurs on the SDA line.

The example shown in Figure 9.22 (in the central part of the timing diagram) depicts a transmission that begins with three bits: 0, 1 and 1, across the first three clock pulses. During the fourth clock pulse, the SDA signal is not stable, rendering the data invalid.

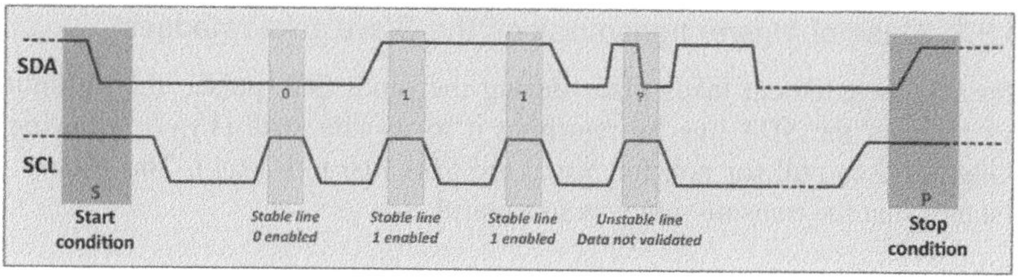

Figure 9.22. *Transmission of bits and start/stop conditions*

9.4.3.2. *Frame delimitation*

An I^2C frame (Figure 9.22) begins with a start condition (denoted *S*) and ends with a stop condition (denoted *P*):

– The start condition is characterized by the SDA line passing to 0 before the *SCL* line passes to 0.

– The stop condition is identified by both lines returning to their idle state (V_{DD}), with SCL rising first, followed by *SDA*.

9.4.3.3. *Acknowledgment*

9.4.3.3.1. Principle

The I^2C bus is distinguished from SPI by a systematic acknowledgment (*Acknowledge*, denoted as Ack) for each byte (Figure 9.23). Every transmitted byte must therefore be acknowledged by the receiver, thus ensuring a basic level of reliability.

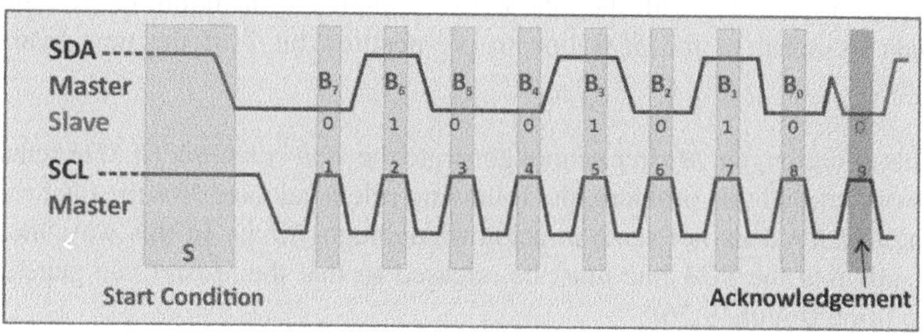

Figure 9.23. *Example of acknowledgment after sending the byte* $0{\times}4A = (01001010)_2$. *For a color version of this figure, see www.iste.co.uk/mahout/programming.zip*

If this is not the case, then either it is normal operation (later we will see that a non-acknowledgment "Nack" is entirely normal), or it indicates a detectable transmission error. Consequently, the physical transmission of a byte comprises 9 bits: the 8 data bits provided by the transmitter, accompanied by the Ack bit provided by the receiver.

9.4.3.3.2. Case of *Master* transmission, "the *Slave* acknowledges"

The acknowledgment takes place during the ninth SCL pulse: the transmitting *Master* releases the *SDA* line by returning it to its idle state (V_{DD}), allowing the receiving *Slave* to pull (or not, for *Nack*) the *SDA* line to 0 (*Ack*). The *Master* then understands that the transmission was successful.

Once the acknowledgment bit (*Ack* or *Nack*) has been transmitted, the *Slave* sets the *SDA* line back to 1 to release control, allowing the *Master* to either send more bytes, generate a stop condition, or, as we will see later, generate a *repeated start*.

It is also possible that the *Slave* is too slow to respond to the clock rate imposed by the *Master*. There is no minimum clock speed, and any device unable to keep up is allowed to signal this by holding the SCL clock line low. Since the device generating the clock monitors the state of the SCL line, it "knows" immediately when there is a problem and waits for the release of the SCL line. Once this occurs, it can resume transmission or issue a *stop condition*. Figure 9.24 illustrates this case.

9.4.3.3.3. Case of *Master* reception, "the *Master* acknowledges"

In this case, by definition, the *Master* always drives *SCL*, while the *Slave* drives the 8 data bits on SDA. To enable acknowledgment from the *Master*, the *Slave* releases the *SDA* line during the ninth bit (*Ack*) by setting it to V_{DD}.

Note that even when the *Master* is in reception mode, it is responsible for generating the sequence of nine *SCL* pulses. The *Slave* must therefore have set *SDA* (the seventh bit of the byte) before the first *SCL* pulse arrives. In other words, once a byte has been received (with the nine pulses completed, including the *Ack* bit), the *Slave* takes control of the *SDA* line to pre-position bit 7 of the next byte to be transmitted.

In this situation, the *Master* cannot generate the *stop condition* (if *SDA* remains at 0). To work around this problem, the following rule is adopted: for the final required byte, the *Master* does not send an acknowledgment (*Nack*). In this way, the *Slave* understands that the *SDA* line must be released so that the *Master* can generate the stop condition (Figure 9.26).

9.4.3.4. *I²C addressing*

The main advantage of the I²C bus, aside from its ability to support multi-master operation, is its capacity to address multiple devices. Often, I²C topologies consist of one *Master* and several *Slaves*.

Thus, the first step in an exchange of bytes between a *Master* and a *Slave* is to transmit the *Slave's* address. This transmission is accompanied with information that indicates the direction (transmission or reception) of the subsequent data transfers.

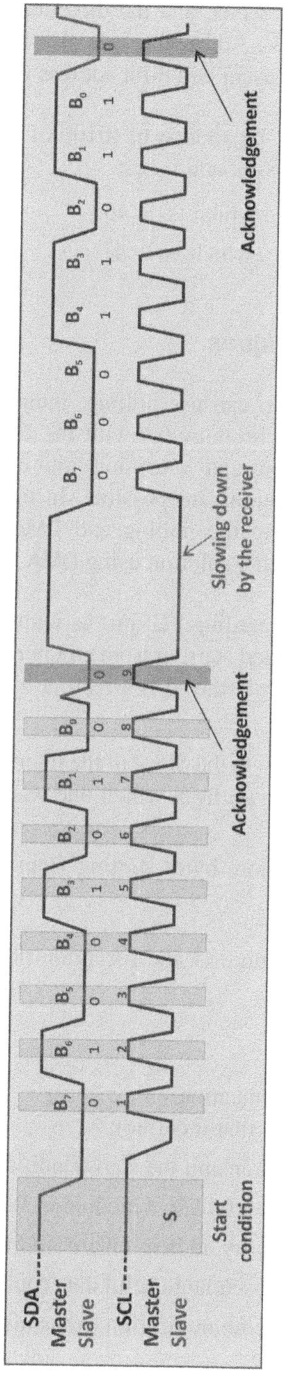

Figure 9.24. *Example of receiver-imposed slowdown between the transmission of the byte* $0\times4A$ *and the byte* $0\times1B$

The address is encoded using 7 bits, and the direction of the upcoming transfer is indicated by an eighth bit, $R/\overline{W}$. Addressing can also be viewed as a paired 8-bit address for writing ($R/\overline{W} = 0$) or as an odd 8-bit address for reading ($R/\overline{W} = 1$).

For example, if a *Slave* has a 7-bit address of $(0100\ 011)_2$, that is, 0×23, then this device can be seen as having two 8-bit addresses:

– @ for writing: $(0100\ 0110)_2$, which is 0×46;

– @ for reading: $(0100\ 0111)_2$, which is 0×47.

9.4.4. *Reading/writing techniques*

For these communications, we can use polling, interrupt or DMA mechanisms. Since the communication is synchronous (as with the SPI) and we are limited to *Master* mode, both transmission and reception are entirely controlled by the μcontroller. Consequently, all options are possible. In the section dedicated to the STM32F10x, we will only present the polling and DMA methods. In the guiding thread example, we will detail such a solution using DMA.

One final point to highlight regarding I^{2}C: just as with SPI, every exchange (read or write) is systematically performed starting from an internal memory address within the *Slave* component. Therefore, whether it is a read or a write, the process must be carried out in two steps:

– transmission from the *Master* to the *Slave* of the internal memory address, which we will refer to as the *Word Address*, from which one wishes to write or read one or more bytes;

– writing or reading one or more bytes starting from the previously transmitted internal address.

The main principles of transmission and reception described below are divided into distinct phases.

9.4.4.1. *I^{2}C transmission*

– Phase 1: starting the communication:
  - access the I^{2}C bus (verify that it is free);
  - initiate communication (transmit the start condition);
  - transmit the I^{2}C address of the *Slave* module in *Write* mode ($R/\overline{W}$ bit $= 0$);
  - transmit the internal memory address (*Word Address*).

– Phase 2: transmitting the subsequent useful data (polling/IT/DMA).

– Phase 3: termination of the communication (transmission of a stop bit).

Figure 9.25 illustrates the typical appearance of a transmission frame. In this configuration, the *Slave* module acknowledges systematically.

9.4.4.2. *I²C reception*

Reception is somewhat more complicated. Indeed, writing the address pointer (which is necessary for the following read) requires an initial access to the device in write mode. Once the pointer has been set, a second address is made, this time in read mode.

– Phase 1: start the communication:

- access the I²C bus (after verifying that it is free);

- initiate communication (transmit the start condition);

- transmit the I²C address of the *Slave* module in *Write* mode (last $R/\overline{W}$ bit = 0);

- transmit the internal memory address (*Word Address*, as shown in Figure 9.26).

– Phase 2: re-accessing the device in read mode:

- restart the communication (transmit the repeated start condition);

- transmit the I²C address of the *Slave* module in *Read* mode (last $R/\overline{W}$ bit = 1).

– Phase 3: receiving the requested $N - 1$ bytes with acknowledgment, *Ack* (these can be stored using polling, interrupts or a DMA).

– Phase 4: receive the final byte and with a non-acknowledgment, *Nack*.

– Phase 5: terminate the communication (transmit the stop bit).

Figure 9.26 illustrates the typical structure of a transmission frame.

Whether in read or write mode, errors can occur (e.g. during bus access, when an I²C address is not acknowledged, when a byte is not acknowledged, etc.). Additionally, communication may take too long. Therefore, mechanisms must be in place to handle interruptions in read and write processes to prevent the μcontroller from being stalled. To address this, the I²C module includes an essential error interrupt system. The programmer must implement these error-handling interrupts to secure the read and write procedures. Finally, note that some μcontrollers provide a dedicated reset bit (in the case of the STM32F10x, this is the SWRST in the I2C_CR1 register). This bit allows resetting the I²C module, enabling recovery from a stalled read or write sequence.

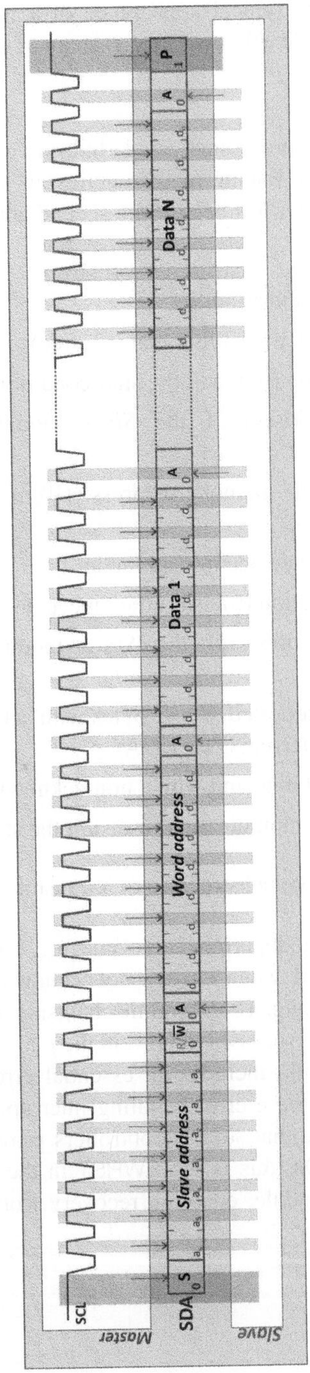

Figure 9.25. *Typical write frame: transmission of N bits of data*

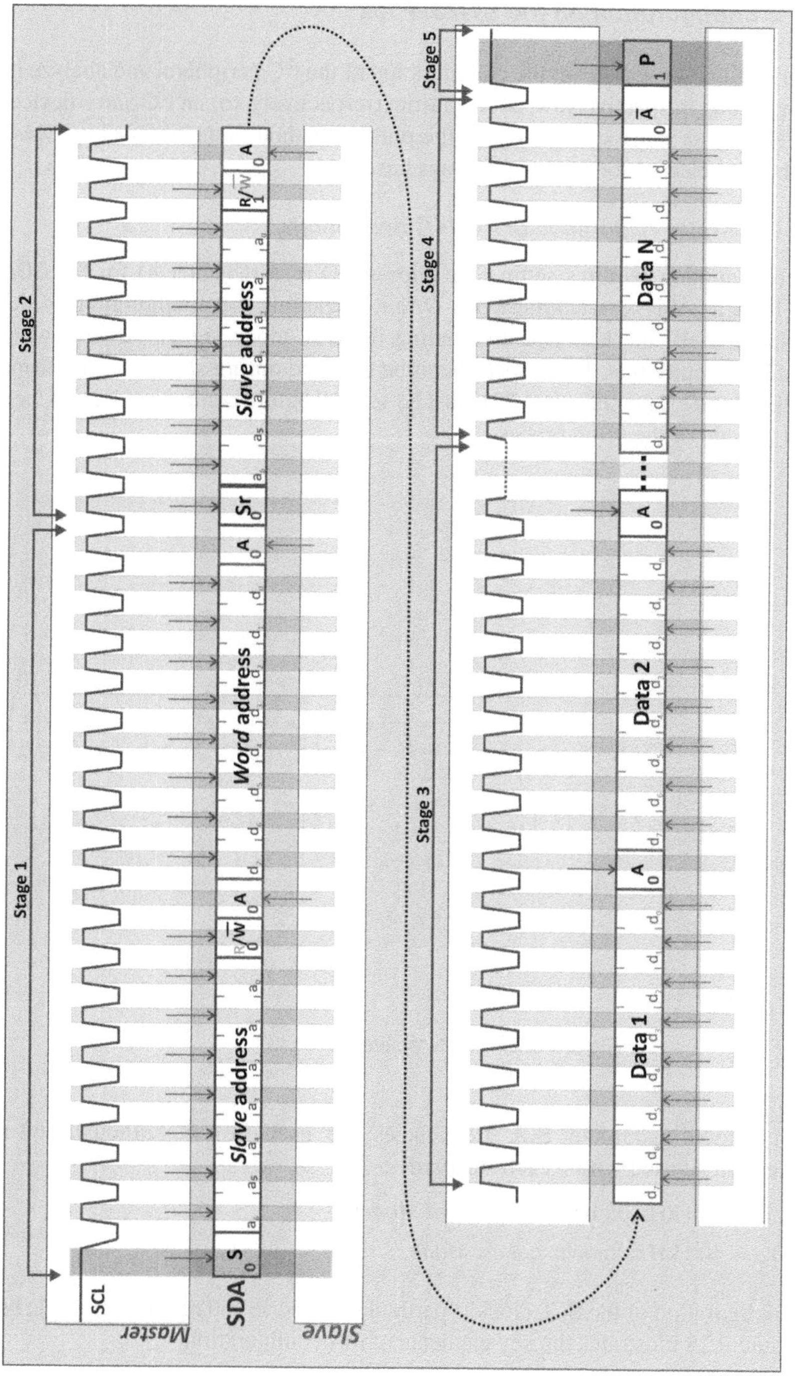

Figure 9.26. *Typical read frame: reception of N bytes of data. For a color version of this figure, see www.iste.co.uk/mahout/programming.zip*

9.4.5. I^2C configuration on the STM32F10x

In this section, we will detail the configuration of the I²C peripheral and analyze in depth how to read (respectively, write) data from (respectively, to) an I²C *Slave* device. We have chosen to focus specifically on the polling method first, followed by DMA, which is highly relevant for this synchronous bus.

9.4.5.1. *General configuration of the I^2C peripheral*

The configuration requires setting the chosen I/O pins (Chapter 4) for the SDA and SCL lines as *Alternate Output Open Drain*. Regarding the configuration of the I²C peripheral itself, the key aspect is setting the SCL clock signal. All following configurations require that the I²C peripheral be disabled during setup, which means that the PE bit (I2C_CR1, Figure 9.27) must be set to 0 before configuration, and then set to 1 at the end of the setup process.

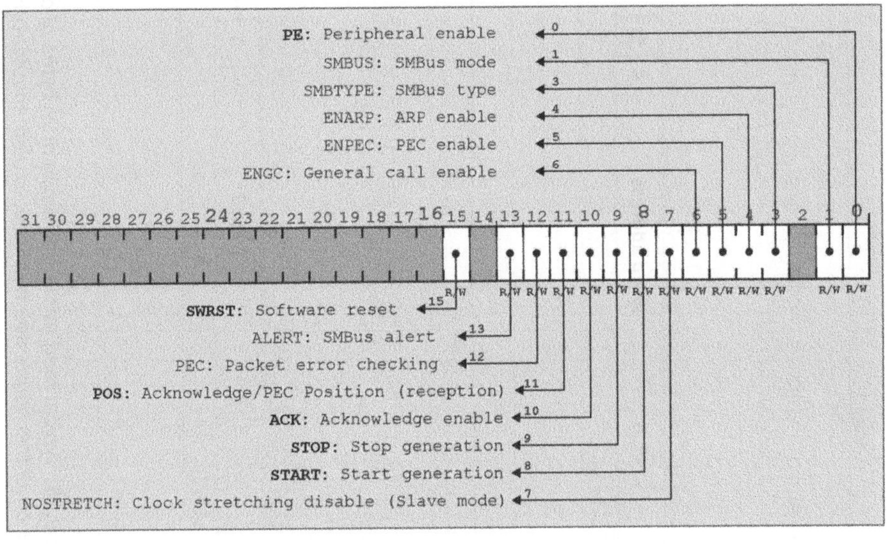

Figure 9.27. *CR1 register of an I²C*

Two common maximum SCL frequencies are used in I²C (although lower frequencies can be used within each standard):

– FSCL = 100 kHz, known as *Standard Mode*;

– FSCL = 400 kHz, known as *Fast Mode*.

The configuration of the SCL clock is particularly precise and requires multiple bit fields. Figure 9.28 illustrates the key elements of this configuration.

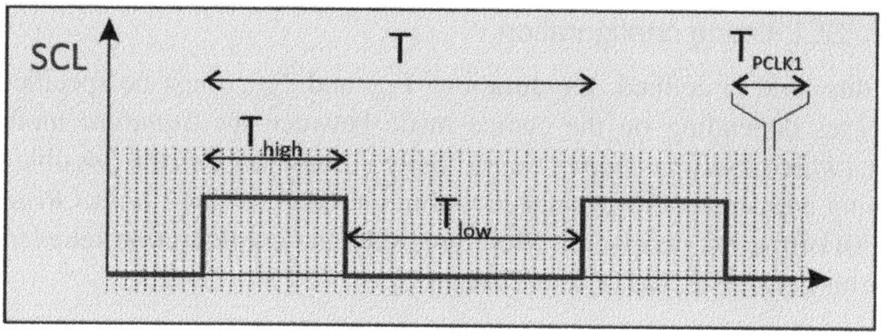

Figure 9.28. *SCL clock configuration using a time quantum*

9.4.5.1.1. Time quantum configuration

Everything in this configuration is adjustable: the low-state duration (T_{low}), the high-state duration (T_{high}) and ultimately the clock period T. To enable fine-tuned adjustments, the I²C module relies on a time quantum, which serves as the reference duration. This quantum is simply the period of the input clock signal to the I²C unit, T_{PCLK1}, which varies depending on the chosen RCC configuration.

To achieve this, the input clock to the peripheral (F_{PCLK1}) must meet the following conditions:

– $F_{PCLK1} \in [2$ MHz; 50 MHz$]$ in steps of 1 MHz for *Standard* mode (100 kHz);

– $F_{PCLK1} \in [4$ MHz; 50 MHz$]$ in steps of 1 MHz for *Fast* mode (400 kHz).

It is essential to ensure that these frequency ranges are respected, potentially by adjusting the RCC unit settings. The FREQ[5:0] bit field (I2C_CR2, see Figure 9.29) allows specifying the input frequency provided to the peripheral. To configure this, write the applied input F_{PCLK1} frequency in MHz. For example, if $F_{PCLK1} = 36$ MHz then, quite simply, FREQ[5:0] = 36.

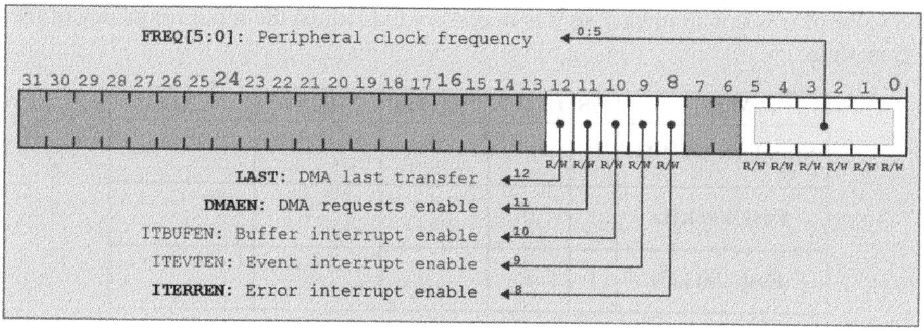

Figure 9.29. *CR2 register of an I²C*

9.4.5.1.2. SCL timing configuration

Once this field is defined, the durations T_{low} and T_{high} must be specified. There are two cases depending on the choice made between the *Standard* mode or the *Fast* mode (which itself has two options). Table 9.2 summarizes the possible settings. These timing adjustments are managed within the CCR (*Clock Control Register*, see Figure 9.30) of the I²C peripheral. More precisely, the configuration relies on setting the bits or bit fields, F/S, DUTY and CCR[11:0].

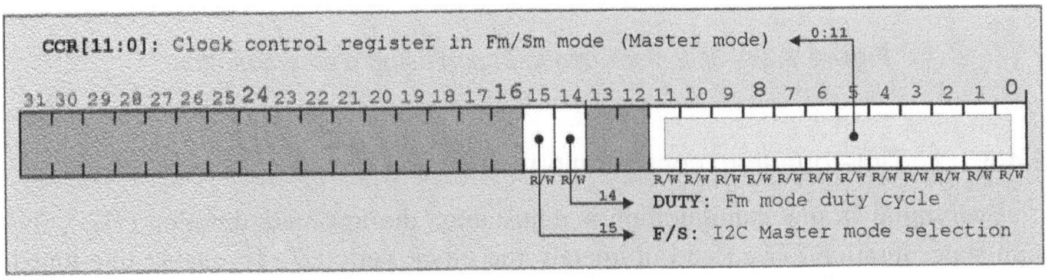

Figure 9.30. *CCR register of an I²C*

EXAMPLE 9.2.– The clock is to be configured at 400 kHz and with $\frac{T_{high}}{T_{low}} = \frac{1}{2}$. The DUTY bit must be set to 0. The period is $T = T_{high} + T_{low} = \frac{1}{400.10^3}$, that is, 2.5 μs.

From Table 9.2, we can write:

$$T = n * T_{PCLK1} + 2n * T_{PCLK1} = 3n * T_{PCLK1}$$

From this, with $F_{PCLK1} = 36$ MHz, we deduce:

$$n = \frac{T \times F_{PCLK1}}{3} = \frac{2.5.10^{-6} \times 36.10^6}{3} = 30$$

In Table 9.2, it should be noted that, in the last mode ($T_{high} = 9$ and $T_{low} = 16$), the value of n is not an integer so it is necessary to readjust the input frequency of the I²C module.

Mode	F/S	DUTY	CR[11:0]	T_{high}	T_{low}
Standard 100 **kHz**	0	x	n (180)	n*T_{PCLK1} (5 μs)	n*T_{PCLK1} (5 μs)
Fast 400 **kHz**	1	0	n (30)	n*T_{PCLK1} (833 ns)	2*n*T_{PCLK1} (1,667 μs)
Fast 400 **kHz**	1	1	n (3,6)	9*n*T_{PCLK1} (900 ns)	16* n*T_{PCLK1} (1,6 μs)

Table 9.2. *Clock configuration via the CCR register of an I^2C. In blue: example with $F_{PCLK1} = 36$ MHz correct. In red: example with $F_{PCLK1} = 36$ MHz incorrect. For a color version of this table, see www.iste.co.uk/mahout/programming.zip*

9.4.5.1.3. Rise time configuration

I²C peripherals also allow for the adjustment of the SCL signal rise time. Once again, this timing is based on the T_{PCLK1} time quantum. The I²C standard specifies that:

– In *Standard* mode, the rise time t_F is a maximum of 1 μs.

– In *Fast* mode, the rise time t_F is a maximum of 300 ns.

The value should therefore be set on the lower 6 bits of the TRISE register as $\frac{t_F}{T_{PCLK1}}$. If the result is fractional, it should be rounded up to the next highest integer value.

For example, if F_{PCLK1} = 36 MHz, to operate in *Standard* mode, it is necessary to set: $TRISE = \frac{t_F}{T_{PCLK1}} = 1\ \mu s * F_{PCLK1} = 36$.

9.4.5.2. *Starting a communication (*start, I²C Slave @ *and* Word @*)*

Section 9.4.4 highlights common steps in the read or write procedures. This is phase 1, which involves:

– accessing the bus (check if it is free using the BUSY bit, as shown in Figure 9.31);

– start the communication (transmitting the start condition);

– transmitting the I²C address of the *Slave* module in *Write* mode (last bit $R/\overline{W} = 0$);

– transmitting the internal memory address (*Word Address* in Figure 9.26).

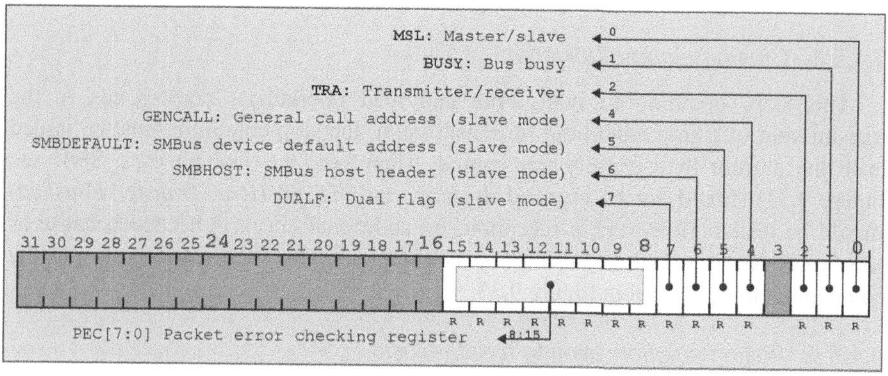

Figure 9.31. *SR2 register of an I²C*

This sequence is described in flowchart format in Figure 9.32.

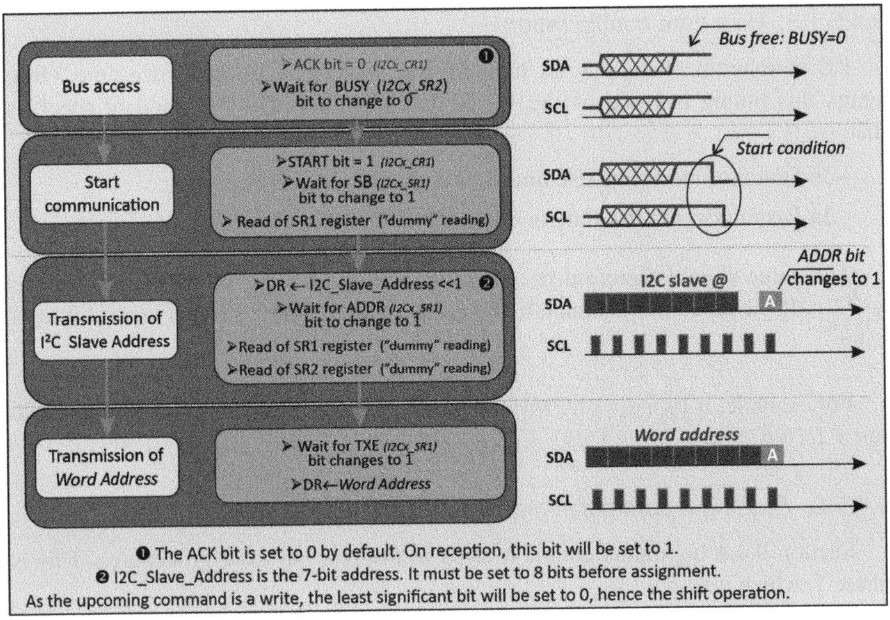

Figure 9.32. *Starting sequence of an I^2C communication*

Next, we will continue to describe I²C transactions as sequences. To simplify the description, the four previous steps from Figure 9.32 are combined into a single step, which we will call "start communication".

9.4.5.3. *Closing a communication*

This step, common to both write and read operations, corresponds to the transmission of a stop condition. In transmission, the stop condition must be issued once the current byte is fully transmitted. Therefore, the TxE bit (I2C_SR1, see Figure 9.34) should not be checked. Instead, the BTF bit (*Byte Transfer Finished*) should be tested. However, in reception, no additional check is needed because as soon as RxNE is set, the transmission is complete. The sequence for closing the communication is shown in Figure 9.33.

9.4.5.4. *Polling solution: writing a data block*

The aim here is to test the TxE flag and then write the next byte to be transmitted into the DR. In the following algorithm, we assume that:

– n is the number of bytes to send;

– Cpt is a counter initialized to 0 at the start;

– Tab[] is the array containing the n bytes to be processed.

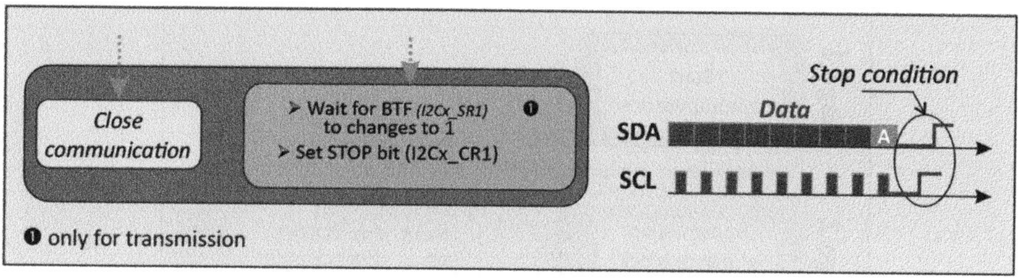

Figure 9.33. *Closing sequence of an I²C communication*

The sequence is illustrated in Figure 9.35.

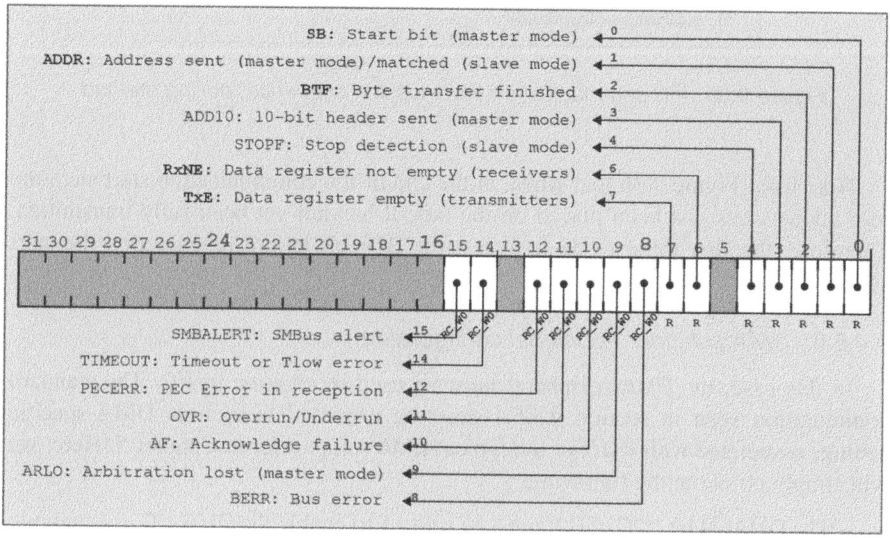

Figure 9.34. *SR1 register of an I²C*

9.4.5.5. *Polling solution: reading a data block*

In section 9.4.4, we saw that the process required a new start in order to switch the *Slave* module back to reception mode. In the I²C protocol, a "restart" is necessary (without needing to stopped) and will be followed again by the I²C address, but this time in read mode.

Another major difference lies in the fact that the *Master* must acknowledge. Therefore, the ACK bit (I2C_CR1) must be set to 1. However, for the last byte, acknowledgment should not occur. Therefore, the ACK bit must be set to 0 immediately after receiving the penultimate byte (or just before receiving the last byte).

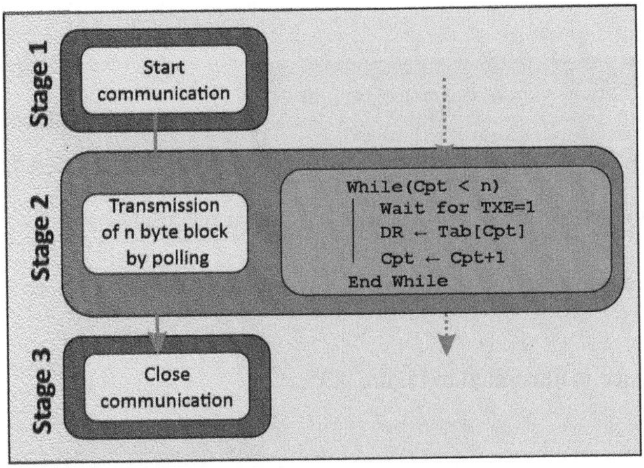

Figure 9.35. *I²C communication transmission sequence: polling method*

Note from Figure 9.36 that when, at the end of the communication start step, the read address has just been placed on the bus; it has not yet been fully transmitted. Therefore, the first thing to do is to test the BTF bit before regenerating the start condition.

9.4.5.6. *DMA solution: additional configuration*

In this case, the DMA peripheral must be used in addition to I²C. The standard configuration seen in section 9.4.5.1 must be extended to include DMA-specific settings associated with I²C. For the typical DMA setup, refer to Chapter 5. Here, we will simply point out the following:

– The DMAEN bit (I2C_CR2) must be set to 1 to enable the DMA-I²C association.

– The LAST bit (I2C_CR2) must be set to 1. This configuration is crucial because it automatically prevents the acknowledgment of the last byte during a reception, which eliminates the need for manual intervention (unlike in the polling method).

9.4.5.7. *DMA solution: writing a data block*

On the STM32F10x, if the DMA is enabled, it becomes active after the I²C addressing phase is completed. It is triggered automatically and paced by the TxE flag. The DMA counter determines the number of bytes to be transmitted. All that has to be done is prepare the DMA, that is to configure it, then simply validate it.

In our case, we will use polling for everything related to I²C addressing as well as for transmitting the internal write address. Only after this will the DMA be enabled, allowing for the transfer of the data block.

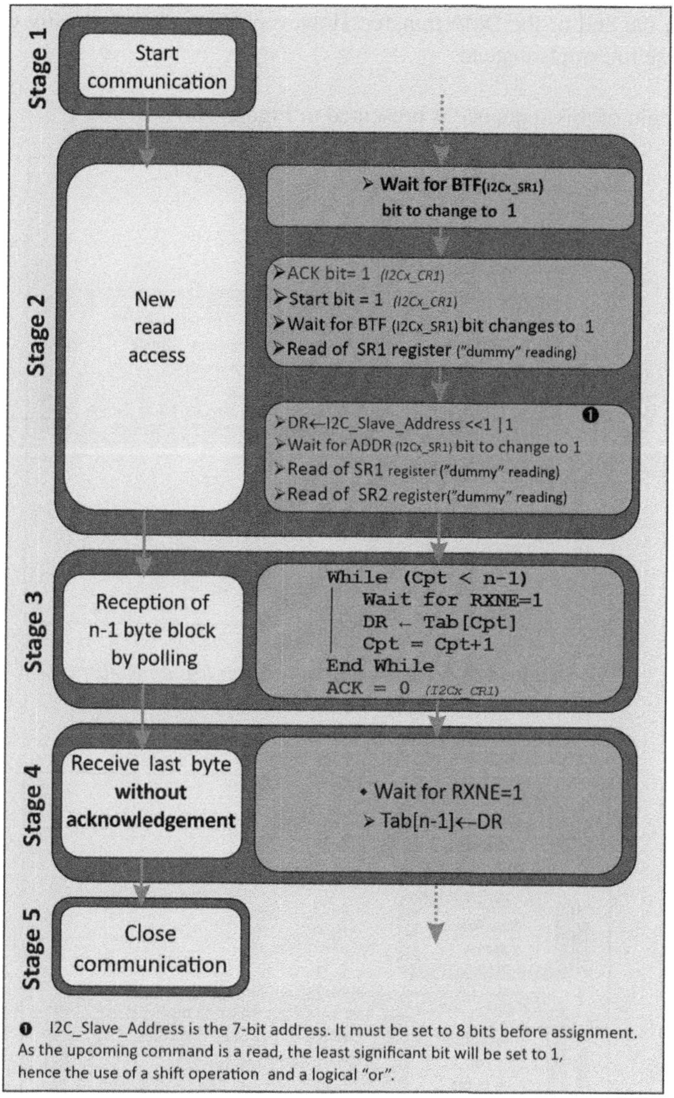

Figure 9.36. *I^2C communication reception sequence: polling method*

Finally, once the DMA transfer is complete, the write operation is finished. This detection can be performed through polling or by using an interrupt on the TCIFx flag (DMA1_ISR). Given the synchronous nature of the transmission, we will opt for polling at the end of the DMA transfer. However, the reader can easily configure the DMA to use interrupts instead.

The logic of this sequence is presented in Figure 9.37.

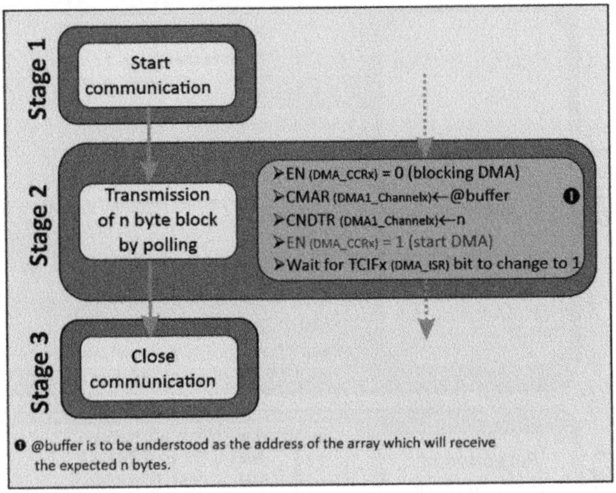

Figure 9.37. *I^2C communication transmission sequence: DMA method*

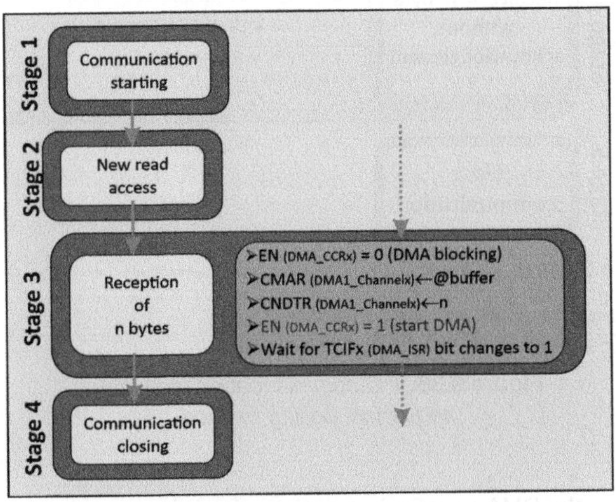

Figure 9.38. *I^2C communication reception sequence: DMA method*

9.4.5.8. *DMA solution: reading a data block*

The mechanism is quite symmetrical to that of transmission. After the restart for reading (*restart*), the bytes will be sampled in reception for acknowledgment, except for the last byte (thanks to the *LAST* bit, as described in the section on general configuration). Once the RxNE flag is set, the DMA will increment its memory pointer position until the total number of bytes programmed in DMA is reached. Phases 1 and 2 of the polling method remain unchanged. Phases 3 and 4 are merged, making the DMA reception process simpler.

9.5. Guiding thread example

To illustrate this chapter on communication buses, we propose the following:

– to cover the UART in interrupt mode (reception);

– to detail the I^{2}C in DMA mode.

It is worth noting that Chapter 5 on interrupts and the DMA provides a complete example regarding UART transmissions using DMA.

9.5.1. *UART reception in interrupt mode*

9.5.1.1. *Problem to solve*

The central unit and control devices communicate using a 433 MHz HF module via a UART. This type of transmitter/receiver is widely used (e.g. in remote controls for door openers, alarm systems and constructing machinery control). It is important to "harden" the communication by using, for example, a five-character preamble that allows us to "almost" certainly identify our communication network. The next byte will indicate the length of the following frame. In this case, the interrupt mode is well-suited: upon receiving each byte, the system tests if the preamble is correct; if not, the byte is discarded. Once the preamble is successfully passed, the length byte is received, enabling the construction of the subsequent data frame. Essentially, this forms a state machine, which we will not detail here.

9.5.1.2. *Proposed solution*

Just like the example described in Chapter 5, we will consider UART no. 1 of the STM32F103RB. The initial configuration (baud rate, number of bits, etc.) have already been covered in the suggested example. The additional points that need to be addressed during initialization are as follows:

– UART in reception: configure the UART module for reception, not just transmission, but setting the RE bit (USART_CR1) to 1;

– enable interrupts locally: set the RxNEIE bit (USART_CR1) to 1;

– enable interrupts at the NVIC level. For this, it is necessary to identify the interrupt number for UART no. 1. According to the reference manual (in the "Interrupts and Events" chapter), the interrupt number is 37. Then, simply set the fifth bit in the ISER1 register to 1 (since 37 is greater than 31, the corresponding register to modify is ISER1, not ISER0);

– set the interrupt priority (0 for maximum priority, 15 for minimum priority). Write the priority value to the IP[37] register, shifting it left by 4 bits to align it correctly within the register.

Now that the configuration is complete, it is necessary to implement the associated *handler*, which is named USART1_IRQHandler. The various steps of this routine are as follows:

– To clear the flag that triggered the interrupt: in this *handler*, the flag at the source of this interrupt must be cleared immediately (otherwise the interrupt with be restarted indefinitely). This flag is RxNE (USART_SR). There are two ways to do this:

- clear the RxNE flag directly using a mask;

- read the data from DR, which will automatically clear the RxNE flag (this is the most common method).

– To perform the appropriate software processing using the state machine mentioned earlier (or any other action): if we follow the layered programming logic presented in the book, a function containing the state machine will be called in the higher layer via a function pointer (Chapter 2).

With the main principles having been described, the next step is to proceed with some relatively simple C programming, which we will not detail here.

9.5.2. *Temperature measurement via the I^2C bus and DMA*

9.5.2.1. *Problem to solve*

The control unit, which is responsible for managing the air conditioning based on commands from a remote central unit, must measure the local temperature. The electronic architecture (see Chapter 1) indicates the use of an I^2C temperature sensor (reference ADT7410).

The following information is found in the *datasheet* of the component:

– The address of the I^2C component (encoded on 7 bits): the five most significant bits are fixed as $(10010)_2$. Two external pins (denoted A_1 and A_0) allow for the full address of the component to be selected (so up to four such sensors can be used on the same bus). We arbitrarily choose $(A_1\ A_0) = (00)_2$. The last I^2C address is $(1001000)_2 = 0{\times}48$.

– The internal address used for configuration (*Word Address*) is $0{\times}03$.

– The internal address used to retrieve the temperature value (*Word Address*) is 0×00. The temperature is provided using 16 bits, so it is necessary to read the byte at address 0×00, and then the byte at address 0×01.

The main program must therefore:

– configure the component, which means writing the configuration to the internal address 0×03;

– during a temperature request is made, the component must read from address 0×00.

9.5.2.2. *Proposed solution*

To illustrate this example, we propose to do so through two files: one containing the main program (principal.c), and the other being the I^{2}C (Driver_I2C.c). The function prototypes and parameters should be designed in accordance with the read/write logic we just presented.

9.5.2.3. *Driver_I2C.h file*

In the Driver_I2C.h *header*, we will define a structured type that contains all the necessary information for I^{2}C transmission/reception. This includes the I^{2}C address, the read/write address, a pointer initialized to the data array to be transferred/read and, finally, the number of bytes to be processed (code example 9.1).

```
typedef struct
{
    char SlaveAddress7bits; /* I2C component address */
    char WordAddress; /* Internal address of the component */
    char *Ptr_Data;   /* Address of the data array
                         to be transmitted or received */
    char Nb_Data;     /* Number of data
                         to be transmitted/received */
}
I2C_RecSendData_Typedef;
```

Code 9.1. *Structure declaration for I^{2}C access*

The initialization function only requires the name of the I^{2}C being used. We choose to set the SCL frequency to 100 kHz (code example 9.2).

```
void I2C_Init(I2C_TypeDef *I2Cx);
```

Code 9.2. *Prototyping the I^{2}C initialization function*

The write function therefore takes two parameters: the first is the I²C being used, and the second is the structured variable that holds the appropriate values (code example 9.3).

```
void I2C_PutString(I2C_TypeDef *I2Cx,  I2C_RecSendData_Typedef *
    DataToSend);
```

Code 9.3. *Prototyping the I²C read/write function*

The read function (code example 9.4) is very similar.

```
void I2C_GetString(I2C_TypeDef *I2Cx, I2C_RecSendData_Typedef *
    DataToReceive);
```

Code 9.4. *Prototyping the I²C read function*

9.5.2.4. *Principal.c file extract*

Code example 9.5 shows how to request the temperature from the ADT7410 component.

```
/* Declaration of the required structured variable */
I2C_RecSendData_Typedef    I2C_Temp;
/* Reception array for the two temperature bytes */
char AT7410_Temp[2];

/* 2 bytes to read to obtain the 16-bit temperature */
I2C_Temp.Nb_Data = 2;
/* Internal address of the temperature byte is 0x00 */
I2C_Temp.WordAddress = 0x0;
/* Assigning the reception buffer */
I2C_Temp.Ptr_Data = AT7410_Temp;
/* Assigning the 7-bit I2C component address */
I2C_Temp.SlaveAddress7bits = 0x48;
/* Initializing the I2C */
I2C_Init(I2C1);
/* Actual temperature reading */
I2C_GetString(I2C1,&I2C_Temp);
```

Code 9.5. *Using the I²C driver to read the temperature*

9.5.2.5. *Driver_I2C.c file*

Code example 9.6 presents the complete code that includes initialization, as well and the read and write functions in DMA mode. In this solution, it would have been advisable to choose an interrupt mode for DMA rather than simple polling. This choice was made for the sake of code simplicity. Readers who wish to implement an interrupt at the end of the DMA process can refer to the treatment of the guiding thread example in Chapter 8 on the ADC.

```
/*==============================================================*/
/*=========== I2C INITIALIZATION =============================*/
/*==============================================================*/
void I2C_Init(I2C_TypeDef * I2Cx)
{
  /* Configuration of PB6 and PB7 in Alternate OD */
   RCC->APB2ENR |= RCC_APB2ENR_IOPBEN; /* GPIOB Clk activation */
   GPIOB->CRL &= ~(0xF<<(6*4));
   GPIOB->CRL |= (0xE<<(6*4));
   GPIOB->CRL &= ~(0xF<<(7*4));
   GPIOB->CRL |= (0xE<<(7*4));

 /* Configuration of I2C1 */
   RCC->APB1ENR |= RCC_APB1ENR_I2C1EN; /* I2C1 Clk activation */
 /* Fine adjustment of SCL */
   I2Cx->CR2 &= ~I2C_CR2_FREQ;
   I2Cx->CR2 |= 36;   /* Set FREQ field to 36 as FPCKL1 is 36MHz */
   I2Cx->CCR = 180;   /* Thigh = Tlow = 5µs (180 = 5µ*36M),
                                meaning FSCL = 100kHz , 50% */
   I2Cx->TRISE = 36;     /* Rise time set to 1µs (36 = 1µ*36M) */
   I2Cx->CR1 |= I2C_CR1_PE; /* Enable I2C */

 /* Additional settings for DMA operation */
   I2Cx->CR2 |= I2C_CR2_DMAEN; /* Enable DMA for I2C*/
 /* Allows DMA to issue a Nack on the last received byte */
   I2Cx->CR2 |= I2C_CR2_LAST;

 /* DMA configuration */
 /* DMA1 channel 6 for transmission , channel 7 for reception */
   RCC->AHBENR |= RCC_AHBENR_DMA1EN; /* DMA1 Clk activation */
 /* @peripheral assignment: for the DR */DMA1_Channel6->CPAR = (
     uint32_t)&I2Cx->DR;
   DMA1_Channel7->CPAR = (uint32_t)&I2Cx->DR;
 /* Set data transfer: 8 bits   */
   DMA1_Channel6->CCR &= ~DMA_CCR6_PSIZE;
   DMA1_Channel6->CCR &= ~DMA_CCR6_MSIZE;
   DMA1_Channel7->CCR &= ~DMA_CCR7_PSIZE;
   DMA1_Channel7->CCR &= ~DMA_CCR7_MSIZE;
 /* Configure increment settings */
   DMA1_Channel6->CCR &= ~DMA_CCR6_PINC; /* I2C side: none */
   DMA1_Channel7->CCR &= ~DMA_CCR7_PINC;
   DMA1_Channel6->CCR |= DMA_CCR6_MINC; /* RAM buffer side: +1 */
   DMA1_Channel7->CCR |= DMA_CCR7_MINC;
 /* Configure circular mode */
```

```
  DMA1_Channel6->CCR &= ~DMA_CCR6_CIRC; /* non-circular */
  DMA1_Channel7->CCR &= ~DMA_CCR7_CIRC;
/* Set DMA transfer direction */
/* Buffer to I2C (write) */
  DMA1_Channel6->CCR |= DMA_CCR6_DIR;
/* I2C to Buffer (read) */
  DMA1_Channel7->CCR &= ~DMA_CCR7_DIR;
}

int Dummy_Read_Buffer;
/*==============================================================*/
/*======== I2C DMA TRANSMISSION: PutString ===================*/
/*==============================================================*/
void I2C_PutString(I2C_TypeDef * I2Cx, I2C_RecSendData_Typedef *
    DataToSend)
{
/*************************************************************/
/**    PHASE 1: STARTING COMMUNICATION                      **/
/*************************************************************/
/* ACCESS TO THE BUS */
  I2Cx->CR1 &= ~I2C_CR1_ACK ;   /* No acknowledgment */

 while((I2Cx->SR1&I2C_SR2_BUSY) == I2C_SR2_BUSY);    /* Wait */
/* START COMMUNICATION */
  I2Cx->CR1 |= I2C_CR1_START; /* Send Start Condition */

 while(!(I2Cx->SR1 & I2C_SR1_SB )){}; /* wait for SB */
  Dummy_Read_Buffer = I2Cx->SR1; /* dummy read */
/* SEND I2C Slave @ */
/* Send I2C @ with Write bit */
  I2Cx->DR=DataToSend->SlaveAddress7bits <<1;

 while (!(I2Cx->SR1 & I2C_SR1_ADDR)) {}; /* Wait for ADDR OK */
  Dummy_Read_Buffer = I2Cx->SR1; /* dummy read */
  Dummy_Read_Buffer = I2Cx->SR2; /* dummy read */
/* SEND internal word @ to the slave */

 while (!(I2Cx->SR1 & I2C_SR1_TXE)) {};    /* Wait until Tx empty
    */
  I2Cx->DR = DataToSend->WordAddress; /* Send Word @ */

/*************************************************************/
/**    PHASE 2: WRITING VIA DMA                             **/
/*************************************************************/
/* Disable DMA for configuration */
  DMA1_Channel6->CCR &= ~DMA_CCR6_EN;
/* Assign buffer address */
  DMA1_Channel6->CMAR = (uint32_t)DataToSend->Ptr_Data;
/* set number of bytes to read */
  DMA1_Channel6->CNDTR = DataToSend->Nb_Data;
```

```
/* Start DMA */
  DMA1_Channel6->CCR |= DMA_CCR6_EN;

  while ((DMA1->ISR&DMA_ISR_TCIF6)==0); /* Wait for full DMA */
  DMA1->IFCR |= DMA_IFCR_CTCIF6; /* Clear DMA full Flag */

/**************************************************/
/**   PHASE 3: Closing communication            **/
/**************************************************/
  while (!(I2Cx->SR1 & I2C_SR1_BTF)) {}; /* Wait */
  I2Cx->CR1 |= I2C_CR1_STOP;  /* Generate stop condition */
}

/*=========================================================*/
/*========  I2C DMA RECEPTION: GetString  ================*/
/*=========================================================*/
void I2C_GetString(I2C_TypeDef * I2Cx, I2C_RecSendData_Typedef *
    DataToReceive)
{
/**************************************************/
/**   PHASE 1: STARTING COMMUNICATION           **/
/**************************************************/
/* ACCESS TO THE BUS */
  I2Cx->CR1 &= ~I2C_CR1_ACK ; /* No acknowledgment */

 while((I2Cx->SR1&I2C_SR2_BUSY) == I2C_SR2_BUSY); /* Wait */
/* STARTING COMMUNICATION */
  I2Cx->CR1 |= I2C_CR1_START; /* Send Start Condition */

 while(!(I2Cx->SR1 & I2C_SR1_SB )){}; /* Wait for SB */
  Dummy_Read_Buffer = I2Cx->SR1; /* dummy read */
/* SEND I2C Slave @ */
  I2Cx->DR=DataToReceive->SlaveAddress7bits<<1; /* send I2C @
      with Write bit */

 while (!(I2Cx->SR1 & I2C_SR1_ADDR)) {}; /* Wait for ADDR OK */
  Dummy_Read_Buffer = I2Cx->SR1; /* dummy read */
  Dummy_Read_Buffer = I2Cx->SR2; /* dummy read */
/* SEND internal Word @ to the slave*/

 while (!(I2Cx->SR1 & I2C_SR1_TXE)) {}; /* Wait for Tx empty */
  I2Cx->DR = DataToReceive->WordAddress; /* Send Word @ */

/**************************************************/
/**   PHASE 2: New access in read mode (restart)  **/
/**************************************************/
/* WAIT FOR END OF TRANSACTION */

 while (!(I2Cx->SR1 & I2C_SR1_BTF)) {};/* Wait */
/* RESTART */
```

```
    I2Cx->CR1 |= I2C_CR1_ACK; /* Enable acknowledgments */
    I2Cx->CR1 |= I2C_CR1_START;    /* Send Start Condition */

  while(!(I2Cx->SR1 & I2C_SR1_SB )){}; /* Wait for SB */
    Dummy_Read_Buffer = I2Cx->SR1;    /* dummy read */
/* SEND I2C Slave @ in Read mode */
/* send I2C @ with Read bit = 1 */
    I2Cx->DR=((DataToReceive->SlaveAddress7bits <<1)|1);

  while (!(I2Cx->SR1 & I2C_SR1_ADDR)) {};  /* Wait for ADDR OK */
    Dummy_Read_Buffer = I2Cx->SR1;  /* dummy read */
    Dummy_Read_Buffer = I2Cx->SR2;  /* dummy read */

/***********************************************/
/**   PHASE 3: Reception of n bytes DMA READ   **/
/***********************************************/
/* Disable DMA for configuration */
    DMA1_Channel7->CCR &= ~DMA_CCR7_EN;
/* Assign buffer address */
      DMA1_Channel7->CMAR = (uint32_t)DataToReceive->Ptr_Data;
/* set number of bytes to read */
    DMA1_Channel7->CNDTR = DataToReceive->Nb_Data;
/* Start DMA */
    DMA1_Channel7->CCR |= DMA_CCR7_EN;

  while ((DMA1->ISR&DMA_ISR_TCIF7)==0); /* Wait for DMA full */
    DMA1->IFCR |= DMA_IFCR_CTCIF7; /* Clear DMA full Flag */
/***********************************************/
/**      PHASE 4: Closing communication       **/
/***********************************************/
    I2Cx->CR1 |= I2C_CR1_STOP;  /* Generate Stop condition */
}
```

Code 9.6. *Proposed solution for the I^2C driver*

10

STM32 Power Management

10.1. Introduction

A μcontroller has partial operating modes that allow it to consume less energy. This feature is extremely important for embedded applications. While the basic technique remains the same, namely, suspending the clock and/or the power supply of a subsystem of the μcontroller, its implementation is very specific to each manufacturer. Therefore, this chapter will exclusively address the approach proposed by STmicro© for its STM32F10x μcontrollers.

To fully understand the benefit of this practice, let us consider the application in the guiding thread example of remote control devices. These devices are used to update the temperature setting for an air conditioning system (heating mode) via an infrared link. To do this, each remote control communicates wirelessly with the central unit, which makes all the decisions. Once this action is completed, the device waits for approximately 30 min before reconsidering the setting by querying the central unit again. Each remote control device is powered by a battery. In this case, it is very relevant to put the μcontroller to sleep during these 30 min, leaving only a Timer running as the active peripheral during this sleep period, which can then wake up the system. The gain in autonomy is huge, as shown by the diagram in Figure 10.1.

We can therefore understand the importance of studying these specific modes. Before going into further detail, let us clarify a few terms:

– *Run Mode*: The "normal" operating mode. The CPU is running, and the peripherals are also active. In this mode, the only way to save energy is by powering down unnecessary peripherals and/or reducing the various operating frequencies (CPU, peripheral units) via the RCC and its multiple PLLs and adjustable dividers.

For a color version of all the Codes in this chapter, see www.iste.co.uk/mahout/programming.zip

– *Low-Power Mode*: This mode contrasts with the *Run* mode and is subdivided into three sub-modes (increasing order of energy efficiency):

- *Sleep Mode*;
- *Stop Mode*;
- *Standby Mode*.

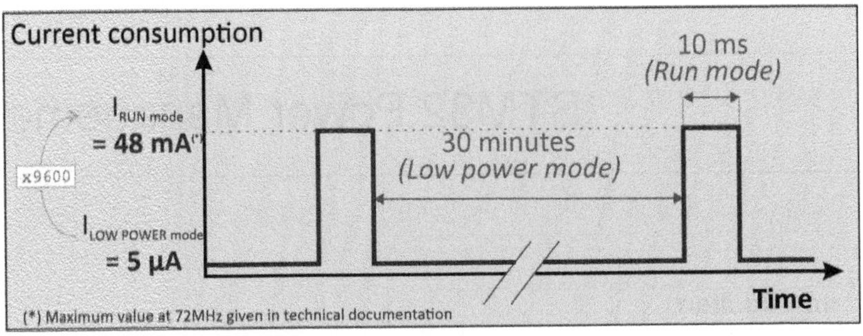

Figure 10.1. *Typical current consumed by an STM32F10x in Standby mode*

The aim of this chapter is to study the three *Low-Power* sub-modes: specifically, how to enter and exit them. However, before diving into that, we must first explore the subdivision of the μcontroller into several zones (called domains), followed by an examination of the types and sources of reset. Finally, a review of the RTC will be essential to fully understand the *Low-Power* modes, particularly for the *Standby* mode.

10.2. Domains of the μcontroller

The STM32F10x is composed of numerous peripherals that are distributed across various domains. Until this chapter, it was not necessary to understand this division. However, the very principle of *Low-Power* modes relies on this structure. Figure 10.2 illustrates this distribution of the μcontroller into different domains.

10.2.1. 1.8V Domain

As the name suggests, this part of the μcontroller is powered by $1.8V$, provided by a voltage regulator that converts the $3.3V$ supply (V_{DD}) to 1.8V. It mainly includes the components studied in this book, namely, the peripheral units as well as the Cortex-M3 processor. It also contains the RAM and Flash memory. The power to this entire domain can be cut off by the switch controlled by the V_{DD} Domain (see Figure 10.2), which corresponds to *Standby* mode, the mode with the lowest current consumption.

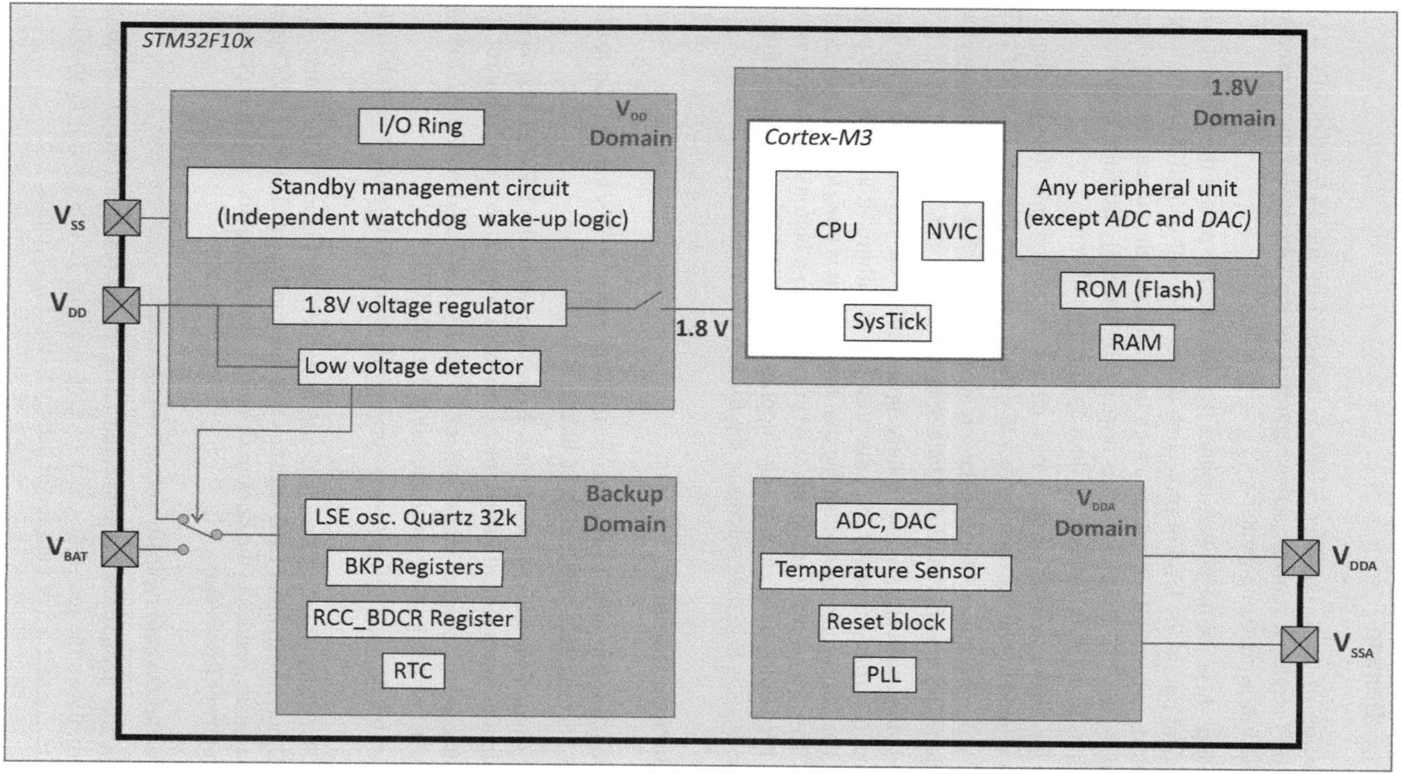

Figure 10.2. *Architecture of an STM10x μcontroller divided into several domains*

10.2.2. V_{DD} Domain

This region of the μcontroller is always powered by the V_{DD} (typically 3.3V) and V_{SS} (0V) inputs. It remains active regardless of the *Low-Power* mode used and includes the following components:

– I/O Ring: these are the power supplies that feed the I/O pins at their closest point to the physical pin (at the level of protection diodes and pull-up/pull-down resistors). In other words, when a GPIO outputs a high level on a pin, the current leaving the pin is supplied by the "I/O Ring", which is powered by the V_{DD} Domain. However, the GPIO belongs to the *1.8V Domain*, as does any peripheral unit.

– *Standby* management circuit; this circuit is responsible for handling all operations related to waking up from *Standby* mode (also see Figures 10.7 and 10.9).

– 1.8V voltage regulator: this regulator is crucial to *Low-Power* mode management since it determines whether the *1.8V Domain* is powered or not.

– *Low-Voltage* detector: if the voltage upstream of the regulator, that is, V_{DD}, drops below a certain threshold (e.g. due to a power failure), it activates the power switch for the *Backup Domain*, ensuring that this domain is powered not by V_{DD} but by V_{BAT}. This V_{BAT} pin is designed to be connected to a button-cell battery, which consumes very little power since it only supplies the *Backup Domain*. If no battery is present and V_{DD} is lost, the contents of the *Backup Domain* are erased.

10.2.3. Backup Domain

This domain continues to operate even if the entire *1.8V Domain* (Cortex-M3, peripherals) is no longer powered. It includes:

– RTC (*Real Time Clock*), which is a basic counter in the STM32F10x, lacking built-in calendar management (unlike more modern μcontrollers from STmicro©);

– low-frequency external clock system (typically associated with a 32,768 kHz quartz crystal), which provides a clock source for the RTC;

– ten 16-bit registers (42 registers for *high-density* μcontrollers) called *backup registers*;

– BDCR register (*Backup Domain Control Register*, see Figure 10.6), which is part of the RCC but, unlike other RCC registers that are implemented in the *1.8V Domain*, the BDCR register resides in the *Backup Domain* to ensure that its content is preserved even when power loss occurs.

The *Backup Domain* typically serves two use cases:

– When the μcontroller is unpowered (V_{DD} drops below a critical threshold): this domain allows the real-time clock to keep running. In this case, it is absolutely necessary to connect a 3-V button-cell battery to the V_{BAT} input.

– When the μcontroller has a valid V_{DD} but has been placed in *Standby Mode*. This domain becomes essential because the *1.8V Domain* is no longer powered. The RTC counter can still operate while the rest of the circuit (*1.8V Domain*) is completely shut down. This counter can, for example, wake up the μcontroller.

10.2.4. V_{DDA} Domain

This is a region of the μcontroller powered by a dedicated source (V_{DDA}, V_{SSA}) separate from (V_{DD}, V_{SS}). It is therefore possible, and even recommended, to place an LC filter between V_{DD} and V_{DDA} to eliminate noise that may be present on V_{DD}, preventing it from propagating to V_{DDA}. This domain includes, in particular, the ADC and the internal temperature sensor.

10.3. *Reset* on STM32

The reset process has already been discussed from the programmer's perspective in Chapter 5 on interrupts, specifically addressing the *System Reset*. For the STM32F10x μcontroller, there are three different types of resets.

10.3.1. System Reset

Such a reset restores all registers to their initial values, except for the registers in the *Backup Domain* and the RCC_CSR register. Naturally, it triggers a reset interrupt by setting PC to the default value stored at address 0×00000004. The registers that are not affected by a *System Reset* include all those belonging to the *Backup Domain*, as well as certain bits (reset flags) in the RCC_CSR register (which will be discussed in more detail later).

Figure 10.3 summarizes the possible sources that can trigger a *System Reset*.

The nRST pin is bidirectional. Typically, it is connected to a push button, with the second contact tied to ground (V_{SS}). Thus, as soon as any reset source connected to the OR gate input becomes 1, a reset pulse is generated and transmitted to the output MOSFET (on the right). This causes the nRST pin (normally at 1 *via* the R_{PU} resistor) to go to 0. This allows for a "synchronized" reset to be transmitted to all circuits external to the μcontroller that would have their own reset pin connected to this nRST pin.

Among the various sources of reset, we have:

– the nRST pin itself, viewed as an input: forcing it to 0 via a push button leads to a *System Reset*;

– the two Watchdogs, WWDG (*Window Watchdog*), and IWDG (*Independent Watchdog*) due to expire (see Chapter 3);

– a forced *Software Reset*. This is triggered by setting bit 2 (SYSRESETREQ) in the AIRCR register (*Application Interrupt and Reset Control Register*) of the SCB peripheral unit (*System Control Block*), which is part of the Cortex-M3. Note that the activation is secure: it must be accompanied by writing a key ($0\times5FA$) in the upper 16 bits of AIRCR (bit field named VECTKEY). In the C language, this is done as follows:

SCB->AIRCR = $0\times5FA$ << 16 | 1 << 2

– A *Power Reset*: this occurs when (Figure 10.4):

- the supply voltage V_{DD} or V_{DDA} rises above a threshold (approximately 2 volts). This is referred to as POR (*Power On Reset*), and represents the normal startup of the system;

- the supply voltage V_{DD} or V_{DDA} drops below a threshold (approximately 2 volts), which may indicate a power failure. This is referred to as PDR (*Power Down Reset*): the μcontroller can no longer operate reliably, so it protects itself from erratic behavior by triggering a *System Reset*. Note that it is possible to configure a different comparison threshold (*Programmable Voltage Detector*, PVD), for example $2.5V$ to trigger an interrupt (PVD connected to EXTI16) just before the *System Reset* occurs, which would allow emergency backups to be made (see the *Power* unit, in particular the CR register).

– A *Low-Power Management Reset*: this is a very specific mode. In fact, it is possible, during program downloading, to configure two specific bits in the *User Option Bytes* STMicroelectronics (2012) so that entering *Stop* or *Standby* mode actually results in a simple reset instead of effectively transitioning into one of these two *Low-Power* modes.

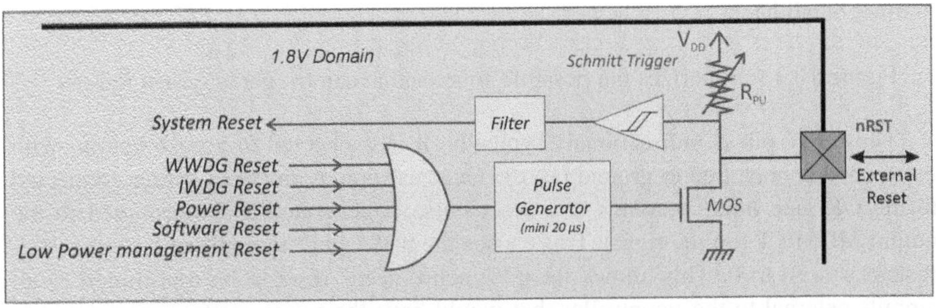

Figure 10.3. *Electronic architecture of System Reset management*

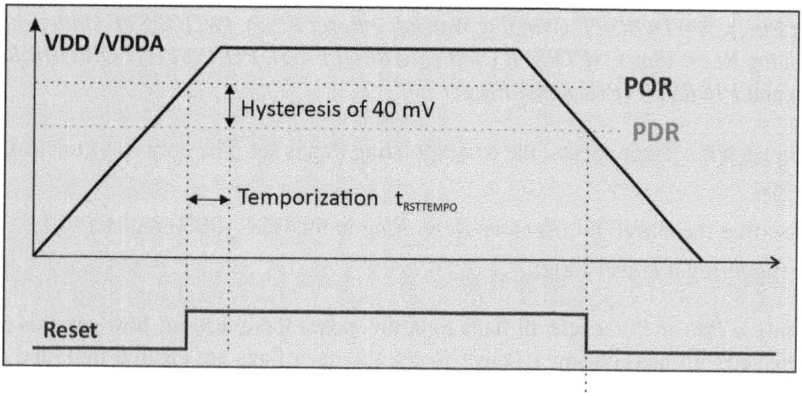

Figure 10.4. *Triggering of Power On Reset and Power Down Reset*

10.3.2. Power Reset

According to the diagram in Figure 10.3, a *Power Reset* triggers a *System Reset*. As a result, all registers are reset to their default state, except for those in the *Backup Domain*. Note that the reset flags in the RCC_CSR register are also cleared. The *Power Reset* has two possible sources:

– a POR or PDR;

– exiting from *Standby* mode.

10.3.3. Backup Domain Reset

This reset places all registers in the *Backup Domain* in their reset configuration. There are two possible sources for such a reset:

– one arising from software, by setting the BDRST bit to 1 in the RCC_BDCR register (Figure 10.6);

– the other arising from hardware, occurring when V_{DD} or V_{BAT} rises above the required threshold (approximately 2V), when both voltages were previously below this threshold.

10.3.4. Reset flags *(RCC_CSR) management*

Previously, we mentioned the CSR register of the RCC peripheral without going into any further details. This section will now focus on it. Figure 10.5 illustrates the contents of this register. The most significant bits store the history of various reset sources that have occurred. The names of these bits are descriptive enough to identify the cause of the reset and includes the bits: LPWRRSTF (*Low Power Management*

Reset Flag), *WWDGRSTF* (*Window Watchdog Reset Flag*), *IWDGRSTF* (*Independent Watchdog Reset Flag*), *SFTRSTF* (*Software Reset Flag*), *PORRSTF* (*POR/PDR Reset Flag*) and *PINRSTF* (*PIN Reset Flag*).

For each reset that occurs, the corresponding flag is set. The only ways to clear this flags are:

– setting the RMVF bit (*Remove Reset Flag* in the RCC_CSR) register to 1;

– triggering a *Power Reset*.

Since a *Power Reset* sets all flags to 0, this poses the question: how can this reset be detected? In fact, during a *Power Reset*, the reset flags are cleared first, and then the PORRSTF flag is set to 1.

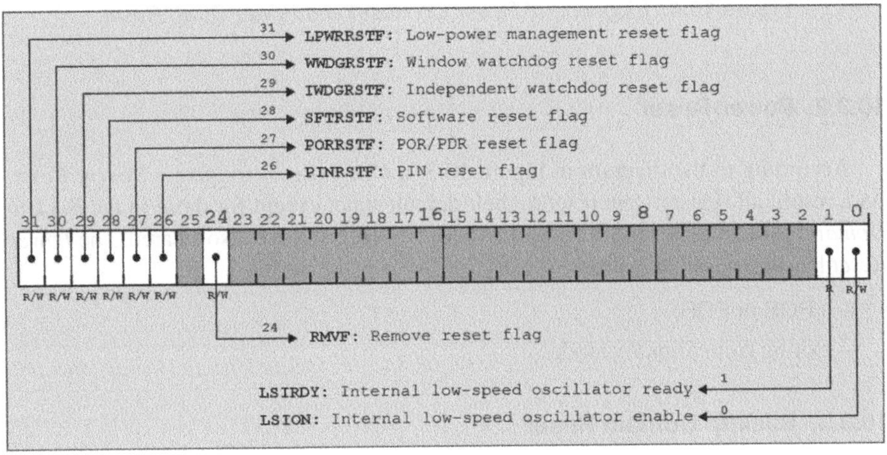

Figure 10.5. *CSR (Control/Status Register) of the RCC peripheral*

10.3.5. *STM32F10x* reset *summary*

Table 10.1 summarizes the various types of resets, their causes and their effects on the associated registers of the μcontroller.

From Table 10.1, several typical scenarios emerge, each with its own impact on how the reset occurs on the STM32F10x:

– Power-up while V_{BAT} is connected to V_{DD} and V_{DDA}: this results in the most complete reset.

– Power-up while V_{BAT} is connected to a button cell battery: the *Backup Domain* is the only part unaffected by the reset, with everything else being reset.

– Pressing the reset button (nRST is set to 0): the *Backup Domain* and reset flags in RCC_CSR remain unchanged, whereas everything else is reset.

– Exiting *Standby* mode: only the *Backup Domain* and the PWR_CSR register (Figure 10.11)[1] remain unaffected, whereas everything else is reset.

Reset cause	Reset type	Effects on the registers and domains		
		All except RCC_CSR and *Backup Domain*	RCC_CSR	*Backup Domain*
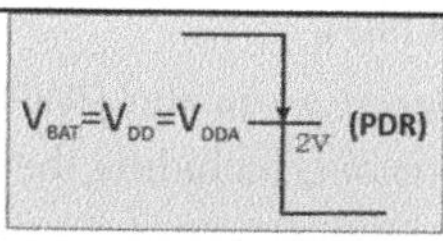 $V_{BAT}=V_{DD}=V_{DDA}$ 2V (PDR)	*Power Reset + Backup Domain Reset*	*Reset state*	*Reset state*	*Reset state*
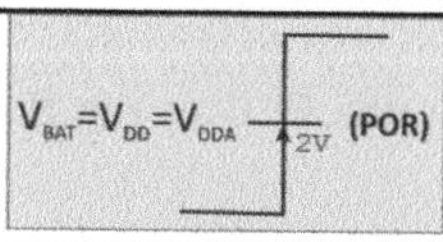 $V_{BAT}=V_{DD}=V_{DDA}$ 2V (POR)	*Power Reset + Backup Domain Reset*	*Reset state*	*Reset state*	*Reset state*
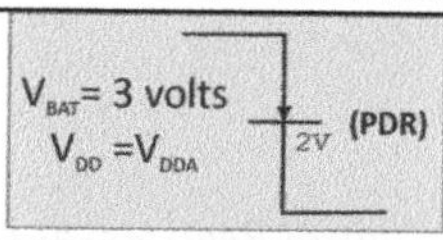 V_{BAT}= 3 volts $V_{DD}=V_{DDA}$ 2V (PDR)	*Power Reset*	*Reset state*	*Reset state*	Unchanged
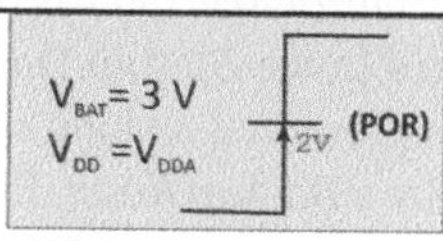 V_{BAT}= 3 V $V_{DD}=V_{DDA}$ 2V (POR)	*Power Reset*	*Reset state*	*Reset state*	Unchanged
Exit *Standby Mode*	*Power Reset*	*Reset state*	*Reset state*	Unchanged
BDRST bit = 1 (RCC_BDCR)	*Backup Domain Reset*	Unchanged	Unchanged	*Reset state*
nRST pin low state WWDG/IWDG raised SYSRESETREEQ bit = 1 *Low Power Manag. Reset*	*System Reset*	*Reset state*	*Unchanged*	Unchanged

Table 10.1. *Sources of resets and their effects on the four domains*

10.4. RTC registers

This is an essential peripheral for exiting *Standby* mode, although the unit can also be used to exit *Stop* mode or *Sleep* mode.

1 Be careful not to confuse PWR_CSR with RCC_CSR.

10.4.1. *Secure access to the* Backup Domain

As we have already seen, the RTC is part of the *Backup Domain*. The manufacturer has implemented a protection mechanism to prevent accidental writes to this domain, particularly after a reset.

Thus, after a *System Reset*, write access is locked. To unlock it, the following steps must be performed in order to:

– enable the clocks for the *Power* and *Backup Domain* peripherals by modifying the APB1ENR register in the RCC (the PWREN and BKPEN bits);

– set the DBP bit (*Disable Backup Domain Write Protection*) in the PWR_CR register. This allows access to any register in the *Backup Domain*, including the RTC which is of interest here.

This procedure must always be followed before writing the RTC or the *Backup Register*, if they are used.

10.4.2. *RCC_BDCR registers*

We have already mentioned the BDCR (*Backup Domain Control Register*) as being a special case, as it is managed by the RCC unit but is located in the *Backup Domain* (only partially, as we will see). Because of this, its value is preserved as long as the *Backup Domain* remains powered or has not been reset to 0 by a *Backup Reset*. Figure 10.6 provides a detailed breakdown of this register.

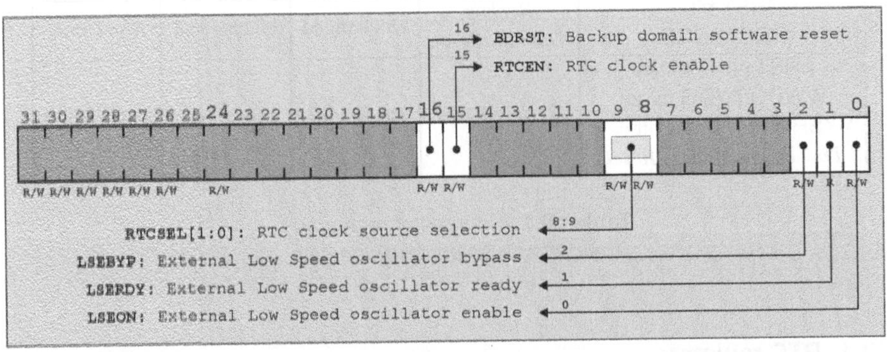

Figure 10.6. *BDCR (Backup Domain Control Register) of the RCC unit*

Only certain bits are actually implemented in the *Backup Domain*, specifically:

– LSEON: activates the external oscillator. A 32,768 kHz quartz crystal must be connected to the LSE inputs (PC14 and PC15).

– LSEBYP: when set to 1, it allows the oscillator to be driven by an external square wave signal (instead of a quartz crystal).

– RTCSEL[1:0]: selects the clock source for the RTC.

– RTCEN: enables the RTC internal counter.

Setting the BDSRT bit to 1 triggers a *Backup Domain* reset, resetting all the previously mentioned bits. However, BDSRT itself is not cleared automatically, which prevents any further writes to the *Backup Domain*. It can only be cleared to 0 explicitly by software or through a *POR reset*.

TIP.– To perform a software *Backup Domain Reset*, the BDRST bit must be set to 1 and then cleared to 0 (a simple pulse).

10.4.3. *RTC register structure*

It is essentially a 32-bit counter with a 20-bit prescaler. Figure 10.7 shows the internal architecture of the RTC, along with the main registers and bits that govern its configuration.

The white zone in the figure represents the *Backup Domain*, which remains powered on in *Standby* mode[2]. As shown in the figure, the RTC can be clocked by three different sources, LSE (external quartz clock, typically clocked at 32,768 kHz), HSE divided by 128 (high-frequency external quartz clock, typically at 8 MHz) and LSI (low-frequency internal clock, at 40 kHz). It is important to note that when the RTC is used for periodic wake-up from *Standby* mode, only the LSE and LSI can be used. To enable these clock sources, either the LSEON bit (RCC_BDCR) or the LSION bit (RCC_CSR) must be activated.

The RTC_Second, RTC_Alarm and RTC_Overflow signals are events. The first is generated by the prescaler, which is typically configured to trigger every one second. The second, RTC_Alarm, allows for longer time intervals since it is adjusted using a 32-bit counter. Finally, the last one corresponds to the overflow of the 32-bit counter.

These three signals can set the corresponding flags in the RTC_CRL register (except in *Standby* mode or when powered solely by VBAT, as the RCC_CRL register is not powered in these two cases). These flags can serve as potential interrupt sources sent to the NVIC. Additionally, the RTC_Alarm signal is routed to a multiplexer that also takes input from the external WKUP pin. When triggered, they generate the WUF (*Wake-Up Flag*), which indicates a wake-up from *Standby* mode.

---

2 Be careful, however, as the NVIC is not powered in *Standby* mode.

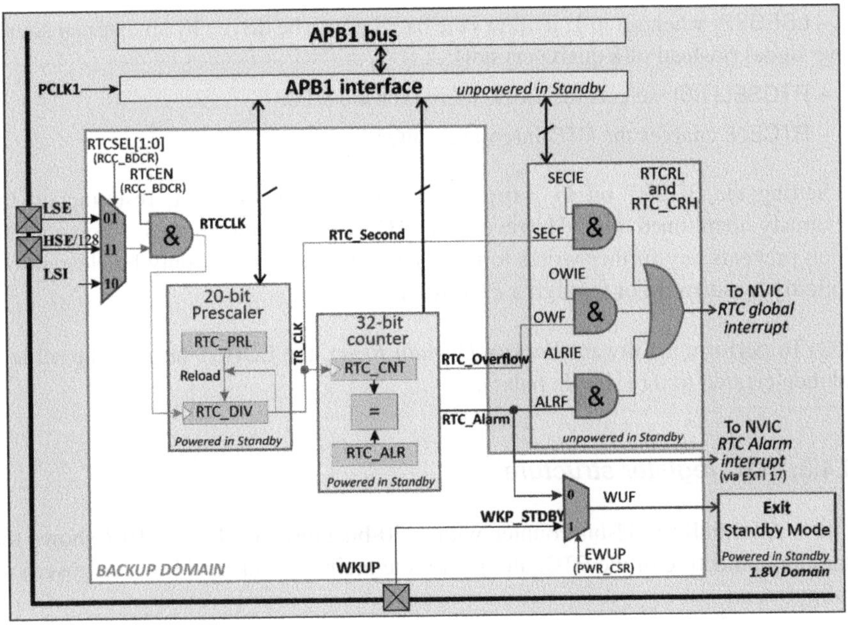

Figure 10.7. *Internal architecture of the RTC. For a color version of this figure, see www.iste.co.uk/mahout/programming.zip*

In summary, the RTC generates three types of signals (highlighted in red in Figure 10.7):

– the *RTC Global Interrupt* signal, typically routed to the NVIC;

– the *RTC Alarm* event, which passes through EXTI 17, meaning it can be used as an interrupt source or as an event capable of waking up the μcontroller from *Sleep* or *Stop* mode;

– the WUF event, which is a unique event that is one of the very few capable of waking up the μcontroller from *Standby* mode.

10.4.4. *Reading/writing RTC registers*

10.4.4.1. *Reading*

Reading the Prescaler, CNT and Alarm registers, as well as the RTC flags, is typically done via the APB1 bus (Figure 10.7). The problem when reading these registers arises when ABP1 has just been reactivated (clock enabled) while the entire RTC part has not yet been stopped thanks to the RTC clock. This situation occurs during a *System Reset*, a *Power Reset*, when waking-up from *Stop* mode, or when waking up from *Standby* mode: an early read operation returns a corrupted value (usually 0) because the APB1 interface and the RTC are not yet synchronized (transient state).

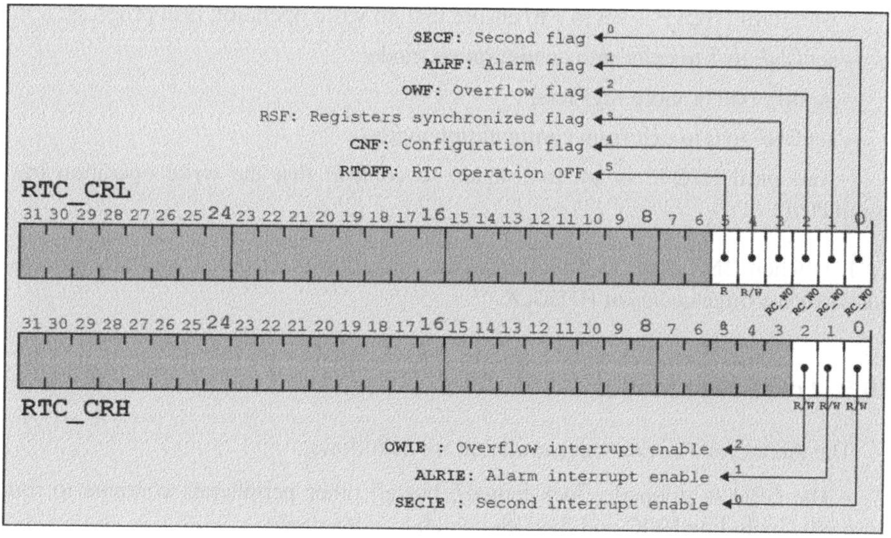

Figure 10.8. *CRL and CRH registers of the RTC unit*

To solve this issue, the RTC_CRL register contains a bit named RSF (*Register Synchronized Flag*), which indicates whether the RTC and the ABP1 bus are properly synchronized.

In terms of programming, the procedure before reading RTC registers is as follows:

– clear the RSF flag to 0;

– wait until RSF is set to 1;

– read the desired registers.

10.4.4.2. *Writing*

Similarly, when writing to RTC registers via the APB1 interface, the changes are not applied immediately. Since APB1 and the RTC operate on different clocks, there is a latency before the write operation actually takes effect. Here again, a mechanism is provided to ensure that the write is fully completed, which is done using the RTOFF and CNF bits of the RTC_CRL register:

– CNF (*Configuration Flag*): when set to 1, modifications to the CNT, PRL and ALR registers are allowed. When reset to 0, the write operations take effect.

– RTOFF (*RTC Operation Off*): a read-only bit that indicates whether a write operation is completed. A 1 indicates that no operation is in progress, whereas a 0 indicates that a write operation is currently being executed.

In terms of programming, the procedure for writing to the CNT, PRL and ALR registers is:

– wait until RTOFF is set to 1 to ensure that no write operation is in progress;

– set CNF to 1 to enter into configuration mode;

– modify one or more registers;

– set CNF to 0 to exit from configuration mode;

– wait until RTOFF is set to 1 again to confirm that the write operation has completed.

It is when CNF is set to 0 that the write operation is executed, and this process takes at least three cycles of RTCCLK.

10.5. *Low Power* modes

The three *Low Power* modes available are as follows:

– The CPU is stopped (clock halted), but all other peripherals continue to run normally, including NVIC and SysTick, which is *Sleep* mode.

– The entire *1.8V Domain* is halted (all clocks are stopped), which is *Stop* mode.

– The *1.8V Domain* is completely powered down, which is *Standby* mode.

These three modes contrast with the standard *Run* mode. In each of these cases, specific bits are necessary, spread across both ST's *Power* peripheral and ARM's core (*Cortex-M3*).

There are three different ways to enter *Low Power* mode:

– By the assembler instruction WFI (*Wait For Interrupt*). The system enters into *Low Power* mode and will exit upon any validated interrupt. In the C language, the function __WFI() is used.

– By the assembler instruction WFE (*Wait For Event*). In this case, the system enters into *Low Power* mode and will exit upon an event, which does not require NVIC configuration for an interrupt. In the C language, this corresponds to the __WFE() function.

– In an automatic manner, if the SLEEPONEXIT bit is set to 1. As soon as the lowest priority ongoing interrupt finishes, the system enters *Low Power* mode without requiring an explicit command (WFI or WFE).

10.5.1. *Event and interrupt*

To fully understand the difference between the ways of entering *Low Power* mode, it is essential to distinguish between an interrupt and an event.

An *interrupt* is the asynchronous arrival of a signal that reaches the NVIC, and then triggers the associated *handler* (interrupt routine). This signal is *level-sensitive* (which is why the flag causing the interrupt must be cleared in the *handler* code).

An *event* is the asynchronous arrival of a signal that propagates within the μcontroller and triggers a specific action (e.g. an *Update Event* in a Timer resets the CNT register to 0). Among these actions is the ability to wake up the μcontroller from a *Low Power* mode. Unlike an interrupt, an event does not require the NVIC to perform its function. This signal is *pulse based.*

Figure 10.9 illustrates the *hardware* architecture enabling wake-up from various *Low Power* modes. This diagram highlights the RTC, the entire interrupt handling system (including the NVIC and CPU), as well as specific peripherals like EXTI and AFIO.

Starting from the end of this diagram, the CPU has two key inputs[3], one being the NVIC (black circuit) and the other called the *External Event Input* (blue circuit). When entering sleep mode via the WFI, wake-up occurs through an interrupt (black circuit), handled by the NVIC, whereas when entering sleep mode via the WFE, wake-up occurs through an event (blue circuit), coming from the EXTI module. Finally, wake-up from *Standby* mode is exclusively handled as a reset (red circuit), which is the only powered section. The wake-up information is carried by the WUF flag (PWR_CSR).

10.5.2. *Key bits for* Low Power *modes*

10.5.2.1. *Bits inside the Cortex-M3*

Several bits are involved at the CPU level, which is understandable since the core itself is the first to enter sleep mode. These bits, located in the *System Control Block* of the Cortex-M3, are found in the SCB_SCR (*System Control*) register (Figure 10.10) and are as follows:

– SLEEPONEXIT: when set to 1, as soon as the μcontroller exits an interrupt, it enters *Sleep* or *Stop* mode (depending on the state of the SLEEPDEEP bits) and PDDS (described below). In the case of multiple nested interrupts, if an interrupt is interrupted by a second one, the system will enter sleep mode only after the first (lowest priority) interrupt has fully completed.

– SLEEPDEEP: when set to 1 during the execution of a WFI or WFE instruction, the *Low Power* mode entered will be *Stop* or *Standby* mode. From the perspective of the Cortex, both modes correspond to deep sleep states.

3 Chapter 5 provides further details on these points.

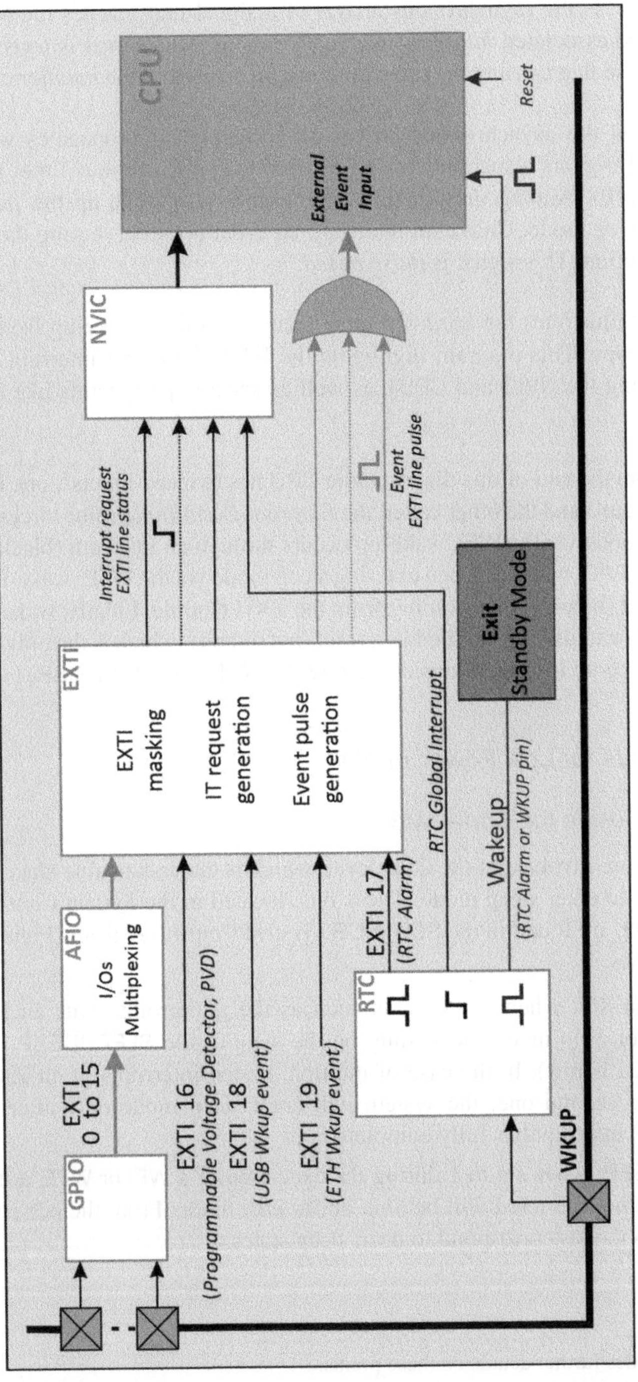

Figure 10.9. *Architecture to wake-up from Low Power mode*

– SEVONPEND (*Send Event ON Pending*): when set to 1, it allows the CPU, which was put to sleep by a WFE, to wake up due to a pending interrupt request, without actually triggering the interrupt handler. The pending interrupt request from a peripheral must not have been authorized at the NVIC level, and then this request is converted into a simple event. The user must manually clear the *pending* bit on the NVIC side using the NVIC_ICPR register, and also reset the flag in the peripheral that caused the request. The advantage of this is that any peripheral, not just the EXTI, will be able to wake up the CPU.

It seems to be simpler to use EXTI lines after a WFE (as it does not require manually clearing any flags). This mode (SEVONPEND) is specifically designed to wake up the CPU from an event coming from a peripheral other than the EXTI lines. This avoids the need to set up an interrupt system with an associated *handler*.

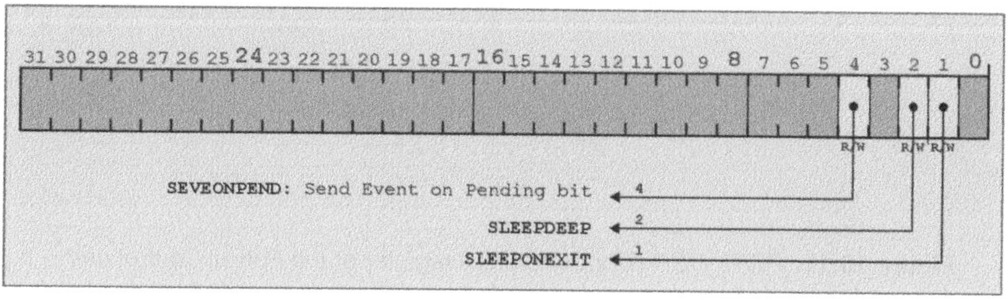

Figure 10.10. *SCR register of the SCB unit in the Cortex-M3*

10.5.2.2. *External bits outside the Cortex*

Low Power management is also handled by two registers in the dedicated *Power Control* peripheral unit, namely, the PWR_CSR and PWR_CR registers.

The PWR_CSR register[4] (Figure 10.11) contains three essential bits:

– EWUP (*Enable WKUP pin*): if this bit is set to 1, the WKUP pin is active. If the bit is 0, the RTC alarm is active. The two are mutually exclusive.

– SBF (*Standby Flag*): reading 1 in this bit indicates that a wake-up from *Standby* mode has occurred.

– WUF (*Wakeup flag*): it indicates that the WKUP pin or the Alarm RTC signal has been triggered.

The PWR_CR register (Figure 10.12) contains nine useful bits. Below are the most important bits for managing *Low Power* mode:

4 This register is not reset to 0 upon waking up from *Standby* mode.

– CSBF and CWUF are two bits that allow clearing the SBF and WUF flags in the PWR_CSR register, respectively.

– PDDS (*Power Down SleepDeep*): when the CPU enters *SleepDeep*, this bit differentiates between *Stop* mode (PDDS = 0) and *Standby* mode (PDDS = 1).

– LPDS (*Low Power SleepDeep*): in *Stop* mode, the 1.8V regulator remains operational but can be further optimized to reduce power consumption. When LPDS is set to 0, the regulator operates in normal mode. When set to 1, the regulator switches to *Low Power* mode. However, when the regulator is in *Low Power* mode, exiting *Stop* mode takes longer.

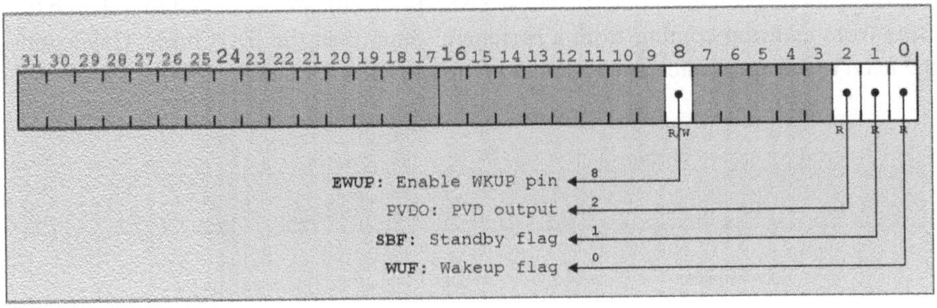

Figure 10.11. *PWR_CSR (Control/Status) register of the Power Control unit*

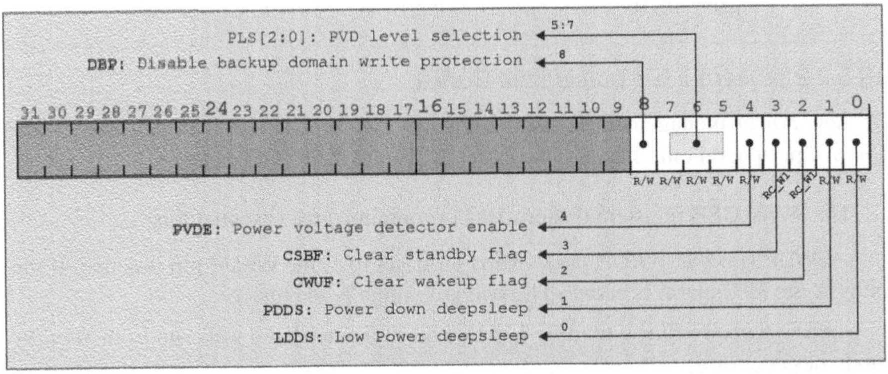

Figure 10.12. *PWR_CR (Control/Status Register) of the Power Control unit*

10.5.3. Sleep *mode*

The *Sleep* mode is an operation where the CPU is stopped (the main clock is frozen). It is the first of the three *Low Power* modes.

10.5.3.1. *Entering* Sleep *mode*

To enter this mode, the *SleepDeep* bit in the SCB unit of the Cortex must be set to 0. After this initial setting:

– If the SLEEPONEXIT bit is set to 0, entering *Sleep* mode is a software controlled by invoking either the WFI or WFE instruction.

– If the SLEEPONEXIT bit is 1, entering *Sleep* mode is hardware controlled and occurs at the end of the execution of the lowest priority interrupt *handler*.

In the first case, entering WFE will occur immediately only if no event has occurred. For example, if an event wakes up the CPU (*Low Power_Run*), then on the WFE, the central unit returns to *Sleep* mode. However, if an event wakes up the CPU (*Low Power_Run*) and another event arises, then the first WFE will not take effect. Figure 10.16 illustrates this (section 10.6.4).

10.5.3.2. *Exiting* Sleep *mode*

The exit from this mode depends on how the μcontroller entered it.

If entry into this mode was triggered by a WFI or SLEEPONEXIT, then any properly validated interrupt request that occurs wakes up the core by entering the corresponding *handler*.

If the entry was caused by a WFE, then any event reaching the CPU's *External Event Input* can bring it back to *Run* mode. Figure 10.9 shows that any event from an EXTI line is therefore capable of triggering the wake-up. Any interrupt request not configured at the NVIC level can also lead to wake-up, provided that the SEVONPEND (Figure 10.10) has been previously set to 1.

It should be noted that in *Sleep* mode, since the NVIC is still powered, an interrupt can also wake up the CPU that was put to sleep by a WFE. However, this is not recommended. Indeed, if WFE is used, it is precisely to allow wake-up without executing an interrupt *handler*.

The I/Os remain in the same state as in *Run* mode. For example, if an LED is wired and turned on, it will continue to shine (and consume power) when switching to *Sleep* mode.

10.5.4. Stop *mode*

In this mode, not only the CPU is halted, but all peripherals belonging to the *1.8V Domain* are also stopped. The *1.8V Domain* remains powered, but the regulator can operate in power-saving mode (LPDS bit, Figure 10.12). The ADC must be turned off (ADON $= 0$) as well as the DAC to prevent them from consuming power. Indeed, both the ADC and DAC are in the *VDDA Domain*, whose power supply remains active.

10.5.4.1. *Entering* Stop *mode*

Entering this mode is done exactly as in the previous mode (*Sleep*). The difference lies in the need to first:

– activate the SleepDeep bit in the SCB_SCR register of the Cortex;

– deactivate the PDDS bit of the *Power Control* register (PWR_CR register).

Be careful, in order to enter this mode (regardless of the method), all pending interrupt bits for all EXTI lines must be cleared (Figure 10.7), as well as the *RTC Alarm* flag.

10.5.4.2. *Exiting* Stop *mode*

Here too, there is a great similarity with exiting *Sleep* mode. However, it should be noted that upon returning to *Run* mode, the HSI clock takes over. Therefore, if the user wishes to use another clock source, they must reconfigure the desired clock upon exiting *Stop* mode.

The possible ways to exit this mode are (depending on the entry method via WFI, WFE, or SLEEPONEXIT):

– WFI or SLEEPONEXIT: by an interrupt, but only those related to EXTI. Indeed, the other peripherals are stopped and can no longer generate an interrupt;

– WFE: by an event triggered by an EXTI line.

So, typically, the wake-up will be triggered by an I/O or by the RTC through an interrupt or an event.

In this case as well, the I/Os retain the same state as in *Run* mode.

10.5.5. Standby *mode*

Now, we are in the situation where the *1.8V Domain* is no longer powered. This mode is therefore the most energy efficient but also inevitably the slowest to return to *Run* mode. It is important to be aware that, in this case, the contents of the RAM memory are lost.

10.5.5.1. *Entering* Standby *mode*

This mode is one of the two forms of the Cortex's SleepDeep. The SleepDeep bit must be set to 1. Additionally, this is what differentiates it from *Stop* mode, the PDDS (*Power Down Deep Sleep*) bit must be set to 1. Entry into *Standby* mode can be done using either WFI or WFE, which has no impact on the wake-up process. Furthermore, the WUF (PWR_CSR) bit must be forced to 0.

10.5.5.2. *Exiting* Standby *mode*

Waking up from *Standby* mode can only occur through a reset. Referring to Figure 10.9, the possible wake-up sources from this mode can be listed as:

– the nRST pin, which triggers a *System Reset*;

– the IWDG *watchdog*, which also triggers a *System Reset*;

– the WKUP pin, which, via the RTC, generates a WUF event if the EWUP bit is set to 1;

– an RTC alarm trigger, occurring when the RTC reaches the value stored in the ALRH and ALRL registers, provided the EWUP bit is set to 0.

In the last case, RCC configuration is required. Either LSI or LSE must be selected, as HSE is not available in *Standby* mode.

Finally, note that the SBF bit (PWR_CSR) will be very useful to determine whether the return to *Run* mode was triggered from *Standby* mode or standard reset.

Upon return, all I/Os are in high impedance (floating input), the Reset pin remains functional, as does the WKUP pin if it is enabled for wake-up.

10.6. Software architecture and using *Low Power* modes

The use of *Low Power* modes somewhat disrupts traditional programming habits, as it requires integrating periods of processor inactivity and thus the absence of a running program.

In this section, we provide some points for reflection and skeleton algorithms to implement the use of *Low Power* sequences.

To illustrate this implementation, we consider the following elements:

– the main program main(): we assume an initial configuration part, followed by the traditional infinite loop, while(1), which may be empty or not depending on the application's needs;

– two interrupt routines: handler_ITa and handler_ITb;

– two interrupt sources: *ITa* and *ITb*, or two events, *Evtx* and *Evty*.

In our configuration, *ITa* has a priority of 3 and is therefore higher priority than *ITb*, whose priority has been set to 7.

10.6.1. *Classical software architecture*

In this first case (Figure 10.13), without *Low Power* mode, the chronological sequence (vertically) described an *ITa* that is fully processed, followed by the processing of *ITb*. Finally, *ITb* is triggered again, and its processing is interrupted by an *ITa*. There is nothing new here compared to what was covered in Chapter 5.

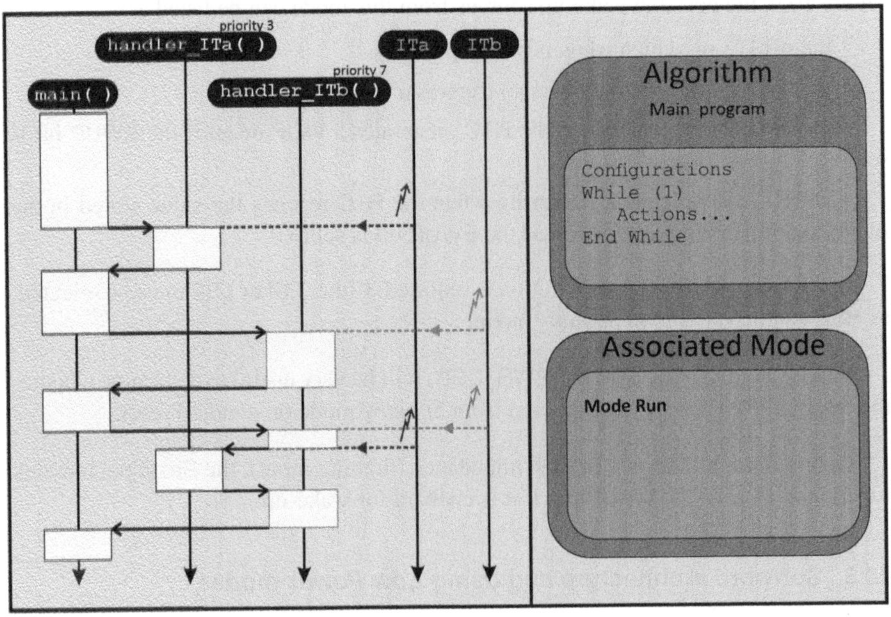

Figure 10.13. *Classic Low Power mode sequence. For a color version of this figure, see www.iste.co.uk/mahout/programming.zip*

The CPU is constantly active, with no periods of rest.

10.6.2. *Sleeping in main(), WFI instruction*

When the interrupt ends, the program resumes after the WFI instruction (Figure 10.14).

10.6.3. *Automatic sleep upon interrupt exit*

When the interrupt completes, the system automatically switches to *Sleep* or *Stop* mode without ever returning to main() (Figure 10.15).

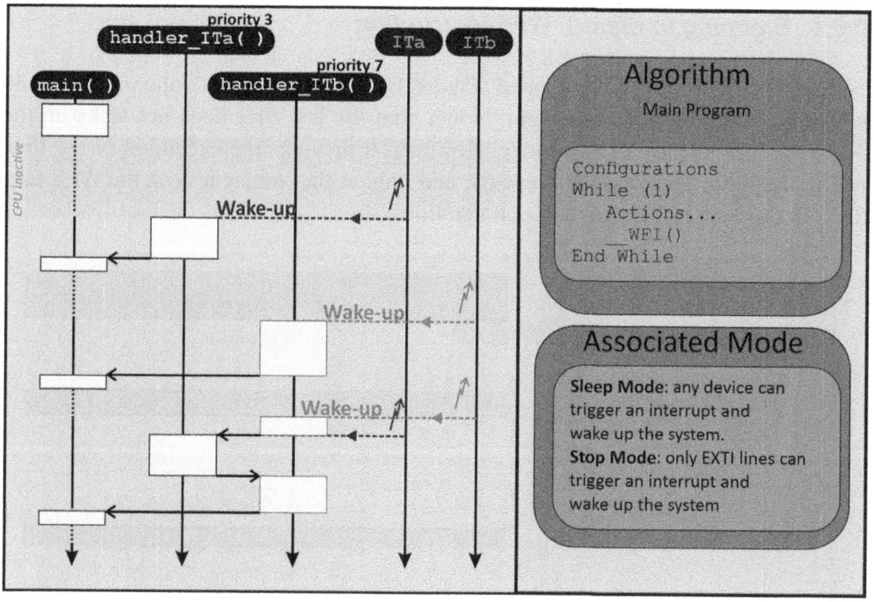

Figure 10.14. *Sleep sequence using WFI*

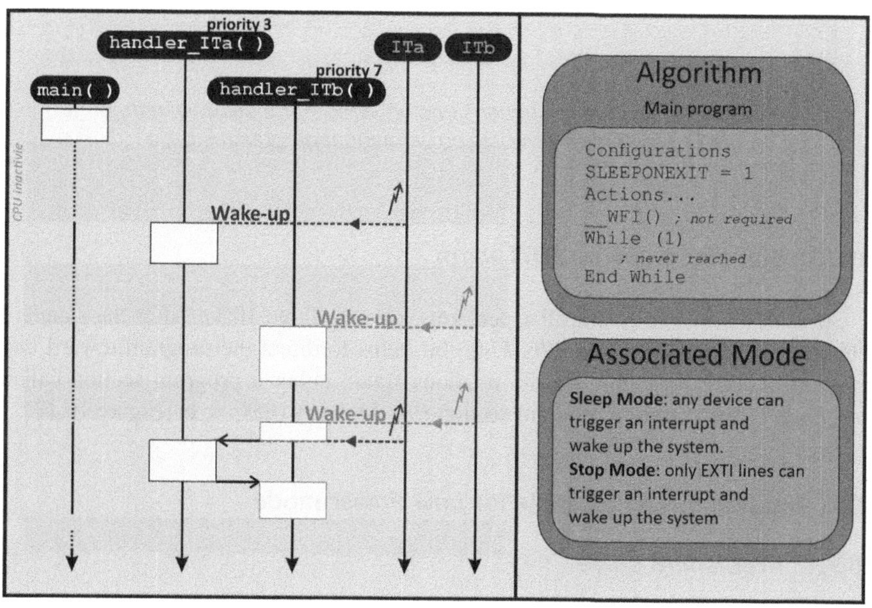

Figure 10.15. *Automatic sleep sequence*

10.6.4. *Sleeping in main(), WFE instruction*

Here, no interrupt is programmed (Figure 10.16). The work is done in main() and then stops, resuming upon an event. Notice that the last *Evty* does not wake up the CPU since it is already in *Run* mode. However, it prevents the execution of the final WFE in the loop. The loop then restarts, and only at that moment does the WFE take effect. In this case, there are two loop iterations.

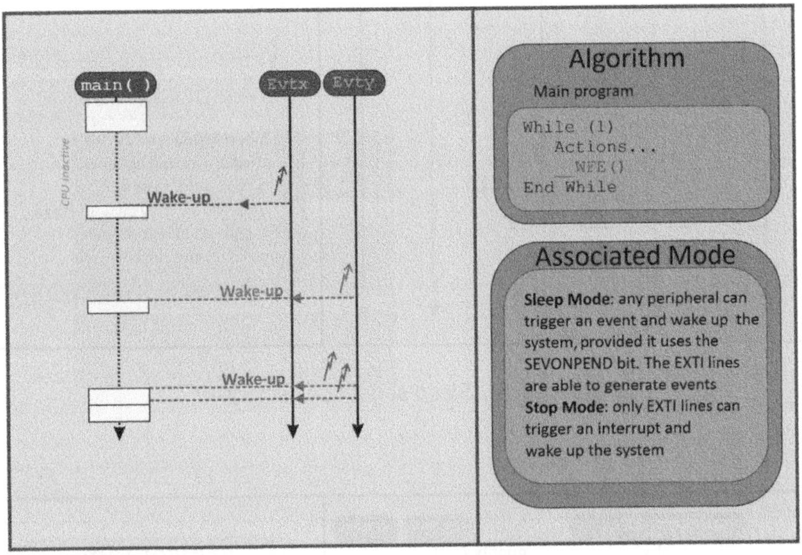

Figure 10.16. *Sleep sequence using WFE. For a color version of this figure, see www.iste.co.uk/mahout/programming.zip*

10.6.5. Standby *mode on RTC alarm*

At each alarm, the μcontroller performs a reset (Table 10.1). After the standard reboot process, the SBF (*StandBy Flag*) bit helps to direct the program toward two different actions depending on the previous state: either a program section called *Prg_Reset* (SBF = 0) or a program section *Prg_StandBy* (SBF = 1) (Figure 10.17).

10.7. Guiding thread example for *Low Power* mode

10.7.1. *Problem to solve*

The air conditioner remote control unit is inactive most of the time. The system should wake up every 30 min. It must then execute a specific program that consists of:

– transmit information to the central unit: send the local temperature, send the previous setpoint and request the new temperature setpoint;

– update the air conditioner temperature setpoint via infrared;

– go back to sleep.

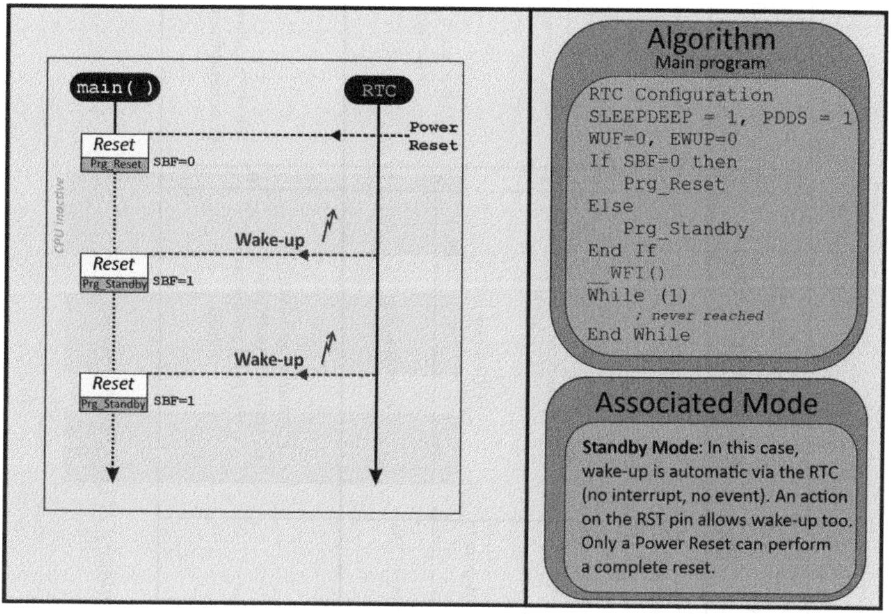

Figure 10.17. *Sequence*

The entire code example will be called MainTask().

During the inactivity period, the remote control unit must consume as little power as possible.

Finally, if the user removes the batteries or presses the nRST button, the remote control unit resets to factory settings. The associated function will be called FactoryReset().

10.7.2. *Proposed solution*

– *Choice of Low Power mode*: We choose *Standby* mode, as it is the most suitable for energy savings.

Low Power mode	Input Type Run → Low Power	SLEEPONEXIT	DEEPSLEEP	PDDS	Comments	Output Mode Low Power → Run	SEVONPEND	Comments
Sleep Mode CLOCK CPU: off NVIC: on Periph : on POWER Periph: on	WFI	0	0	0	Immediate entry	• Any interrupt	0	Device whose interrupt has sufficient priority
	Sleep on exit	1	0	0	Entry at the end of the lowest-priority active interrupt			
	WFE	0	0	0	Immediate entry unless an event has occurred	• EXTI event • Any interrupt	0	Use only *events*, otherwise it's better to work with WFI
						• Interrupt transformed into an event via SEVONPEND	1	NVIC must not be configured
Stop Mode CLOCK CPU: off NVIC: on Periph: off POWER	WFI	0	1	0	Immediate entry	• EXTI Interrupt	0	On the return it is necessary to reconfigure the clock
	Sleep on exit	1	1	0	Entry at the end of the lowest-priority active interrupt			
	WFE	0	1	0	Immediate entry unless an event has occurred	• EXTI event		
Standby Mode CLOCK CPU: off NVIC: off Periph: off POWER Periph : off	WFI or WFE	0	1	1	Immediate entry WUF must be reset to 0	• RCT Alarm (with EWUP=0), • Pin WKUP (with EWUP=1), • Pin Reset (in any case) • IWDG	0	RTC Clk: LSE or LSI only The SBF bit allows to differentiate a Power Reset from a Standby wake up.

Table 10.2. *Summary of Low Power modes*

– *Managing the 30-min sleep period*: To handle this 30-min duration, we use the RTC. It can be clocked by either the LSI clock signal or by the LSE signal. For better accuracy, LSE is recommended since it is a precise 32,768 kHz quartz oscillator. In this case, it is necessary to:

- set the LSEON bit (RCC_BDCR) to 1;

- wait for the oscillator to stabilize by polling the LSERDY flag (RCC_BDCR).

However, we prefer the LSI clock (no external component required). Indeed, the 30-min period is not critical, so the low precision of the LSI RC time base can be tolerated. Furthermore, one could imagine that the central unit sends the exact time at the moment of the information request, allowing the RTC to be adjusted accordingly. Thus, similarly to the LSE, it is necessary to:

- set the LSION bit (RCC_CSR) to 1;

- wait for the oscillator to stabilize by polling the LSIRDY flag (RCC_CSR).

– *Factory reset management*: Exiting *Standby* mode, as well as a power loss or a *System Reset* (*via* nRST), systematically leads to the program restarting through a reset process (see section 10.3). Therefore, it is necessary to distinguish these reset sources to determine the appropriate actions to take.

To do this, we use the SBF (*StandBy Flag*) bit to determine if the previous state was *Standby* mode. However, pressing the nRST button is also a wake-up source from *Standby* mode. Therefore, it is necessary to check the PINRSTF (RCC_CSR) bit to clearly distinguish between the two cases: a normal wake-up via the RTC or a user action, such as removing the batteries or pressing nRST.

The architecture of the program will be as follows:

– configure RTC with LSI;

– configure *Standby* mode;

– if SBF = 1 and PINRSTF = 0 (previous state was *Standby* and it was not an nRST action):

- SBF = 0,

- MainTask(),

- switch to *Standby*;

– otherwise (nRST or Power On Reset):

- PINRSTF = 0,

- FactoryReset(),

- switch to *Standby*.

Code example 10.1 presents the code for such a solution.

```
int main(void)
{
/****************************************/
/* RTC 30mn Configuration using LSI      */
/****************************************/
/* Access backup domain*/
  RCC->APB1ENR|=RCC_APB1ENR_BKPEN|RCC_APB1ENR_PWREN;
  PWR->CR|=PWR_CR_DBP;
/* start LSI = 40kHz*/
  RCC->CSR|=RCC_CSR_LSION;
  while((RCC->CSR&RCC_CSR_LSIRDY)==0);
/* select LSI for the RTC and enable RTC*/
  RCC->BDCR&=~RCC_BDCR_RTCSEL;
  RCC->BDCR|=RCC_BDCR_RTCSEL_LSI;
  RCC->BDCR|=RCC_BDCR_RTCEN;
/* Enable RTC write access */
  while ((RTC->CRL&RTC_CRL_RTOFF)==0);
  RTC->CRL|=RTC_CRL_CNF;
/* Configure 30mn timing */
  RTC->PRLH=0;
  RTC->PRLL=40000-1;
  RTC->ALRH=0; /* ALRH: ALRL = 1799 for 30mn overflow */
  RTC->ALRL=1800-1;
  RTC->CNTH=0;
  RTC->CNTL=0;
/* Exit RTC configuration mode */
/* Apply previously written register values */
  RTC->CRL&=~RTC_CRL_CNF;
  while ((RTC->CRL&RTC_CRL_RTOFF)==0);
/* enable RTC for wake-up and not Wkup Pin */
  PWR->CSR&=~PWR_CSR_EWUP;

/****************************************/
/* LowPower mode = Standby configuration */
/****************************************/
  PWR->CR|=PWR_CR_CWUF; /* Clear the WUF source flag */
  SCB->SCR|=SCB_SCR_SLEEPDEEP; /* DeepSleep (Stop or Standby) */
  PWR->CR|=PWR_CR_PDDS; /* Power Down Deep Sleep (Standby) */

/****************************************/
/* Wake-up code...                       */
/****************************************/
/* SBF test flag */
  if (((PWR->CSR&PWR_CSR_SBF)==PWR_CSR_SBF) && ((RCC->CSR&
      RCC_CSR_PINRSTF)==0))
  {
    /* Clear "previous state = StdBy" flag */
    PWR->CR|=PWR_CR_CSBF;
    MainTask(); /* Launch main task */
```

```
    __wfi();      /* Enter Standby mode */
  }
  else
  {
/* Reset PINRST to 0 to allow MainTask execution
        on next RTC overflow */
    RCC->CSR|=RCC_CSR_RMVF;
    FactoryReset(); /* Perform factory reset */
    __wfi();         /* Enter Standby mode */
  }
}
```

Code 10.1. *Application using Standby mode*

Appendix

Technological Elements

This appendix is intended for those who have no knowledge about the electronic implementation in a μcontroller. Although they are incredibly complex today, we think it would be useful to provide some basic technological reminders, ranging from the transistor to the flip-flop, including truth tables of the most commonly encountered logic functions.

Finally, note that in this short appendix, we use the same symbols as those used throughout the book. There are other ways to represent them.

A.1. Basic building block: the MOS transistor

A μcontroller consists of millions of MOS (metal oxide semiconductor) transistors. These components have three terminals called G (gate), D (drain) and S (source). There are two types of MOS transistors: NMOS and PMOS (Figure A.1).

This is the smallest electronic component in a logic circuit and therefore in a μcontroller. Figure A.2 illustrates the decomposition from a purely technological perspective.

In the digital context, the MOS transistor can be seen as a resistance R_{DS} between the drain and source (measured in ohms), which is a function of the voltage between the gate and the source: V_{GS} for an NMOS and V_{SG} for a PMOS. These voltages are referred to as control voltages.

In a digital circuit powered entirely between 0 and V_{DD} (in the case of the STM32, $V_{DD} = 3.3\text{V}$ or V):

For a color version of all the Codes in this chapter, see www.iste.co.uk/mahout/programming.zip

– If $V_{GS} = V_{DD}$ for an NMOS ($V_{SG} = V_{DD}$ for a PMOS), $R_{DS} = R_{DSon} \approx 0$ (switch closed, "on").

– If $V_{GS} = 0$ for an NMOS ($V_{SG} = 0$ for a PMOS), $R_{DS} \approx \infty$ (switch open, "off").

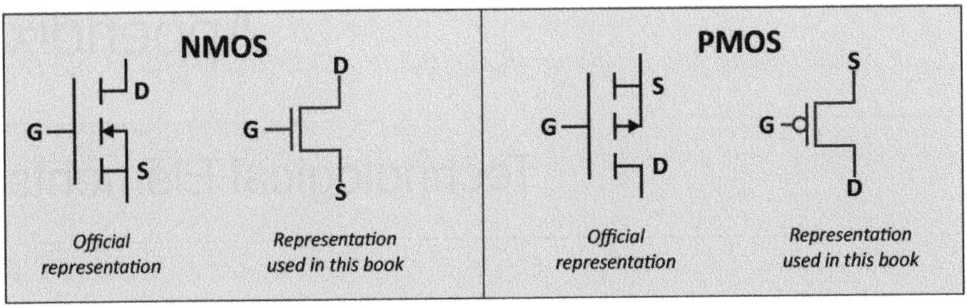

Figure A.1. *MOS transistors*

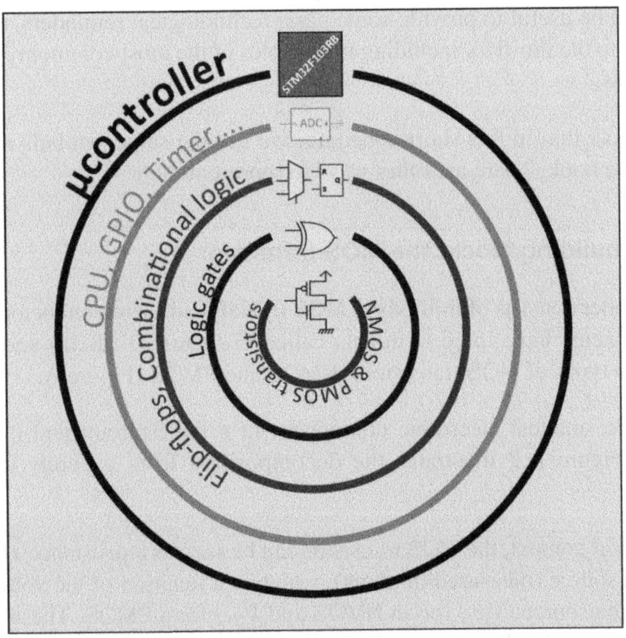

Figure A.2. *Technological decomposition of a μcontroller*

Figure A.3 shows the evolution of the resistance R_{DS} as a function of V_{GS} for an NMOS. For a PMOS, the curve is similar, with V_{SG} replacing V_{GS}.

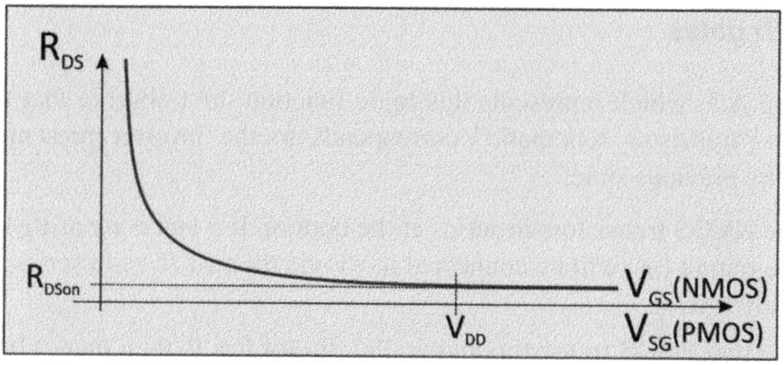

Figure A.3. *Evolution of R_{DS} as a function of V_{GS} for an NMOS and V_{SG} for a PMOS. For a color version of this figure, see www.iste.co.uk/mahout/programming.zip*

A.2. Combinational logic

A.2.1. *CMOS inverters*

The "C" in CMOS stands for *complementary*, indicating that such an inverter is built using both NMOS and PMOS transistors. Note that this will also be the case for all other logic gates presented later. Figure A.4 illustrates the implementation of this inverting function. We observe:

– If $x = V_{DD} \Rightarrow V_{GS\_NMOS} = V_{DD}$ and $V_{SG\_PMOS} = 0$. The output y is therefore 0V since the resistance R_{DS} of the NMOS is zero (or nearly so), whereas the R_{DS} of the PMOS is infinite.

– If $x = V_{DD} \Rightarrow V_{GS\_NMOS} = 0V$ and $V_{SG\_PMOS} = V_{DD}$. The output is therefore V_{DD}.

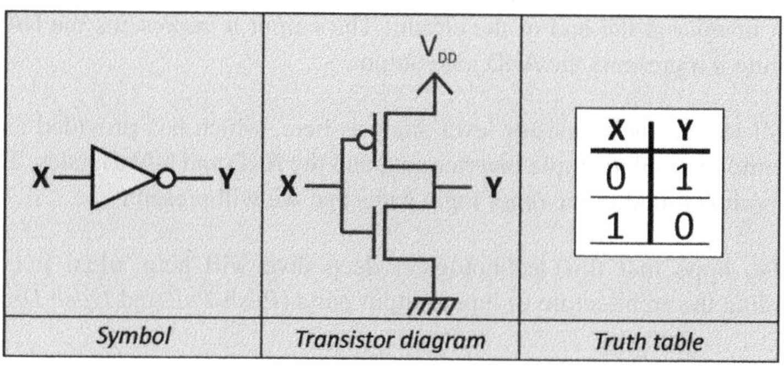

Figure A.4. *Inverter (NOT) $y = \overline{x}$*

A.2.2. *AND gates*

In Figure A.5, which represents this logic function, first observe that the second state of the "transistor schematic" corresponds to the inverter presented earlier. Regarding the previous state:

– For the NMOS transistors in series at the bottom, if a and b are at V_{DD}, then the intermediate output (y') will be connected to 0V via the two R_{DS} in series, which are approximately 0 Ω.

– For the two PMOS transistors in parallel, if a or b is 0, then one or both will be conducting since V_{SG} is then equal to V_{DD} (with R_{DS} values approximately 0 Ω).

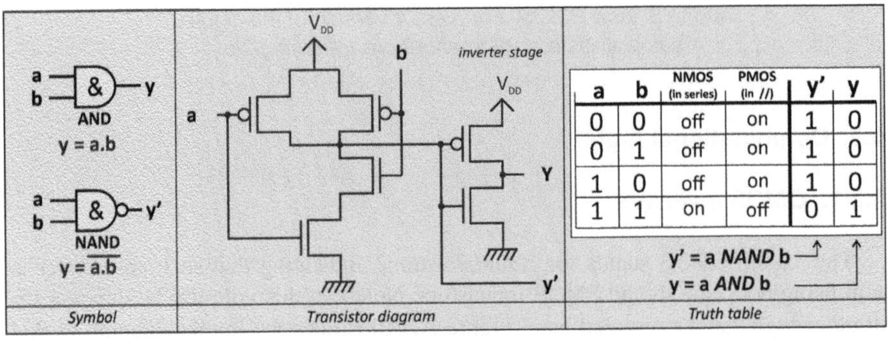

Figure A.5. *AND and NAND gates*

The right side of the figure considers each possible case, and ultimately provides the truth tables.

Technologically, the NAND gate is simpler than the AND gate since it does not require an inverter at the end of the circuit. The output y' represents the NAND gate output, while y represents the AND gate output.

We will stop at the transistor-level analysis here, which has provided an insight into the complexity of a simple inverter gate and the AND and NAND gates. The same type of circuit is found in the other logic gates that we will present.

We also hope that this technological deep dive will help when it comes to understanding the architecture of input/output ports (*Push-Pull* and *Open Drain*).

A.2.3. *OR gates*

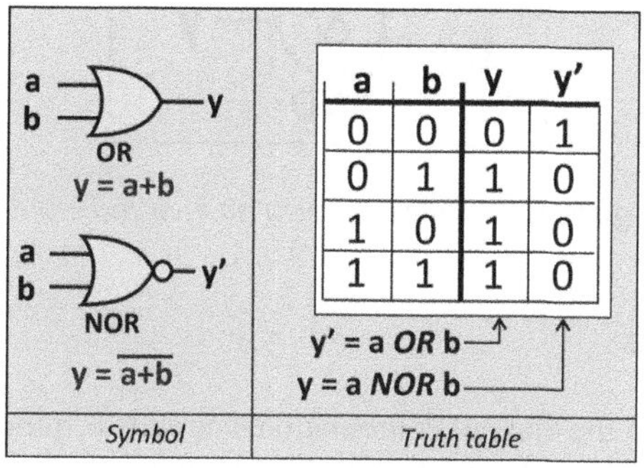

Figure A.6. *OR and NOR gates*

A.2.4. *XOR gates*

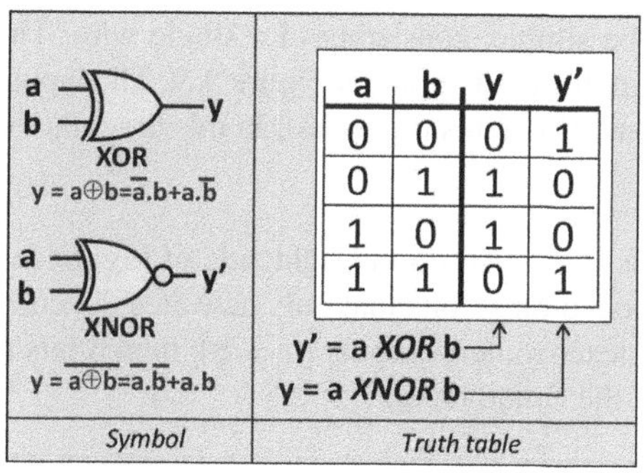

Figure A.7. *XOR and XNOR gates*

A.2.5. *Inversion formalities for logic gates*

For notational simplicity, symbols may be used that include inversion (rather than introducing separate inversion gates). We have already seen this with the classic AND, OR and XOR gates, where inversion was represented by a circle at the output.

The same can be done at the input. Thus, a circle at the input of a gate represents its inversion, as shown in Figure A.8. This is an AND gate where the second input (b) is inverted. The equation here is $y = a.\bar{b}$.

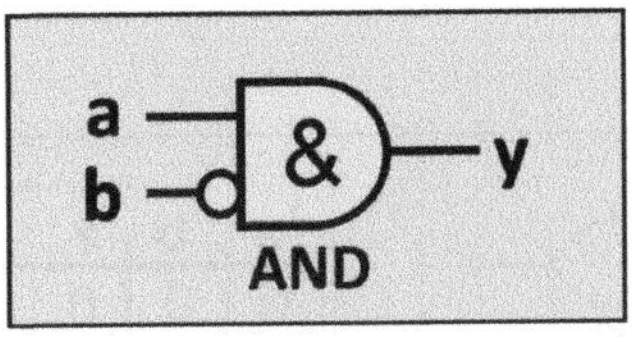

Figure A.8. *AND gate with an inverted input*

A.2.6. *Multiplexers*

The last element in the class of combinational circuits is quite special. It should be seen as a logical signal switch based on a control input:

– The number n of inputs in a multiplexer can be greater than 2.

– The inputs can be buses.

– The number N of bits required for the control signal is related to the number of inputs in the multiplexer by: $n = 2^N$.

The n inputs can be simple, consisting of a single wire. The multiplexer is then symbolized as shown in the left diagram of Figure A.9. The inputs can also correspond to data buses, consisting of p wires (or p bits). In this case, the output signal will also be a p-bit bus signal.

This second case is illustrated on the right side of Figure A.9. The control signal (Cmde) is a value encoded on N bits that only activates the corresponding input. For example, if the multiplexer routes 8 inputs ($n = 8$), then 3 bits ($N = 3$) are required to encode the value of the Cmde input.

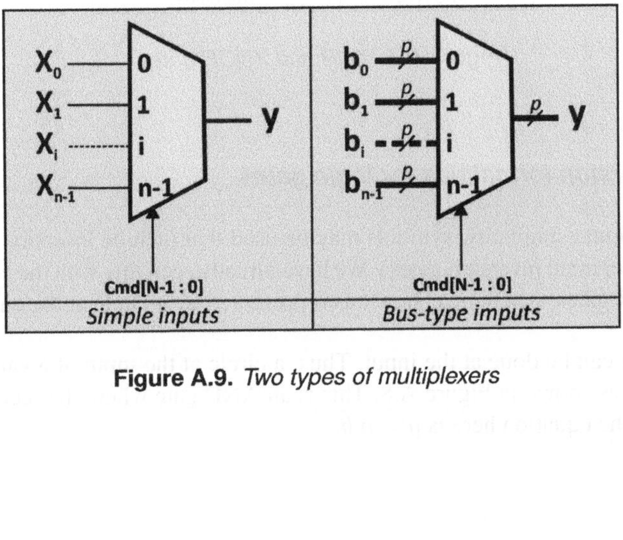

Figure A.9. *Two types of multiplexers*

A.3. Sequential logic

This section deals with electronic devices and logic functions whose outputs depend not only on the current inputs (as in combinational logic circuits), but also on their previous state. Therefore, there may be one or more memory states.

Within this large family, it is important to distinguish:

– *asynchronous* sequential circuits, which do not have a clock;

– *synchronous* sequential circuits, whose output changes are synchronized with a clock.

A.3.1. *(Asynchronous) RS flip-flops*

An RS flip-flop can be constructed using two NOR gates, as illustrated in Figure A.10. The R input is called the *reset* input, while the S input corresponds to the *set* action.

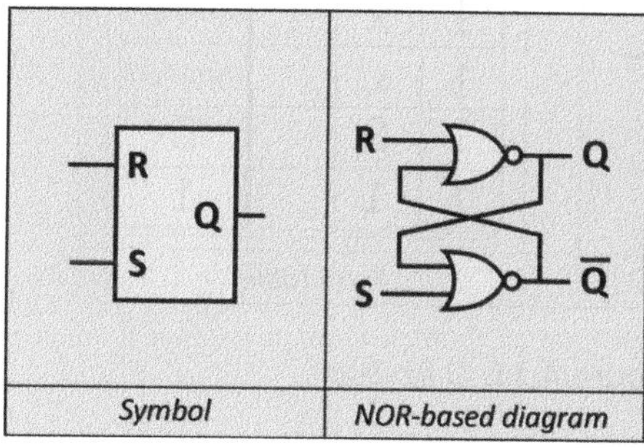

S (set)	R (reset)	Q
0	0	unchanged
0	1	0
1	0	1
1	1	0

Truth table

Figure A.10. *RS flip-flop*

Let us detail the different operating cases:

– case $S = 0$, $R = 1$: $Q = 0$ (according to the NOR truth table: as soon as one input is 1, the NOR output is 0);

– case $S = 1$, $R = 0$: $\overline{Q} = 0$ (according to the NOR truth table), so $Q = 1$;

– case $S = 0$, $R = 0$: this is the memory state, noted as *unchanged* in the truth table:

- if $Q = 0$ and $\overline{Q} = 1$ just before, Q remains at 0,

- if $Q = 1$ and $\overline{Q} = 0$ just before, $\overline{Q}$ remains at 0, and Q remains at 1 as well;

– case $S = 1$, $R = 1$: $Q = \overline{Q} = 0$. This case is, a priori, absurd, which is why it is grayed out in the figure. Indeed, it corresponds to a simultaneous request to set the output Q to both 0 and 1. Therefore, this combination is sometimes labeled as "impossible". However, this combination is entirely conceivable. The value of the output Q depends on the technology used to implement the RS flip-flop. We have shown that if the flip-flop is built using two NOR gates, then this combination results in Q being 0. This is referred to as an RS flip-flop with priority reset.

A.3.2. *(Synchronous) D flip-flops*

As the title suggests, this flip-flop has a clock input. This is symbolized by a small triangle (Figure A.11). The flip-flop has a fundamental input, labeled D. The output Q copies the value of D at the rising edge of the clock Clk. The En (*Enable*) input validates the mechanism. If En equals 0, then nothing occurs and the output remains unchanged.

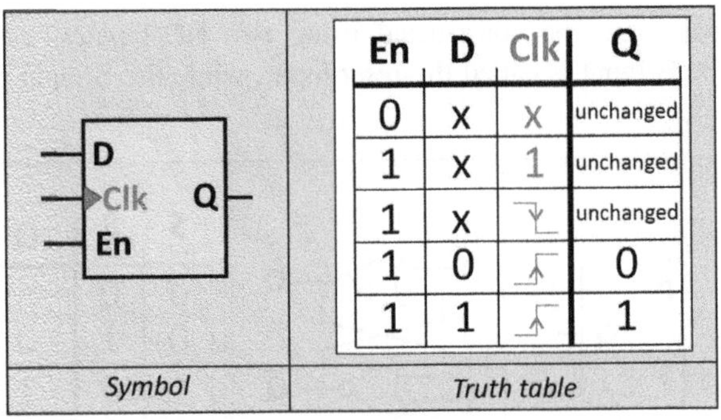

Figure A.11. *D flip-flop*

A.3.3. *Register*

The register is the fundamental building block of μcontroller programming. Ultimately, regardless of the language, programming consists of transferring data from one register to another (considering that memory can be viewed as a group of registers), and/or processing these data using the CPU.

Figure A.12 presents, as an example and for simplicity, a register composed of 4 bits. Typically, the register's input is connected to the data bus, allowing it to see all the data intended for any other register. An address decoding system (which is therefore combinational) sets the En bit to 1 if the address corresponds to the register in question, which allows for the effective writing of the register.

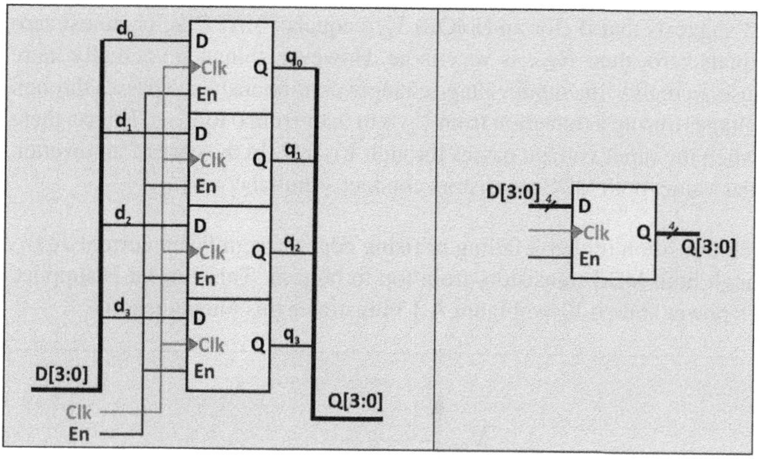

Figure A.12. *4-bit register based on D flip-flops*

A.4. Power dissipation in CMOS technology

The issue of energy is very important when it comes to choosing a μcontroller, as well as in the way it is programmed. To understand the power dissipation aspect of a CMOS-based logic circuit, it is common to refer back to the "transistor" diagram of an inverter gate (Figure A.4), and to rely on the characteristics of an NMOS and a PMOS (Figure A.3).

When X equals 1, the NMOS is conducting and the PMOS is blocked. The logic block imposing the level 1 on the X input does not consume any current. Indeed, the input of a MOS transistor is a capacitor for which $I_C = C\frac{dV_C}{dt}$, as a reminder, where V_C is the voltage across the capacitor (here V_{GS} or V_{SG}), C is the capacitance of the transistor's input capacitor (often denoted by C_{gs}) and I_C is the current flowing through the capacitor. Therefore, if the logic level equals 1, then V_{GS} typically equals 3.3V. Since this voltage remains unchanged, $\frac{dV_C}{dt} = 0$, which means the current is zero. From the output perspective, this inverter will drive another logic gate that itself is seen as a capacitor. No current will be supplied to this gate as long as the logic level remains stable (either 1 or 0). Provisional conclusion: a CMOS-based logic circuit does not consume any power as long as the logic levels do not change[1].

What happens when the logic levels do change?

1 However, note that if the logic output is on an I/O pin and drives an LED, then clearly the circuit consumes power.

Figure A.3 suggests that if (for an NMOS) V_{GS} equals V_{DD}, R_{DS} is almost zero and if V_{GS} equals zero, then R_{DS} is very large. However, things are actually more nuanced because, in reality, the input voltage changes continuously and passes through all possible voltages during a transition from V_{DD} to 0, or from 0 to V_{DD}. Hence, there is a moment when the input voltage passes through $V_{DD}/2$. In the case of an inverter, at this particular value, both MOS transistors conduct simultaneously.

During each transition (either a falling or rising edge), a significant current I_{VDD} will flow through both MOS transistors from top to bottom. This current is supplied by the circuit's power source V_{DD}. Figure A.13 illustrates this phenomenon.

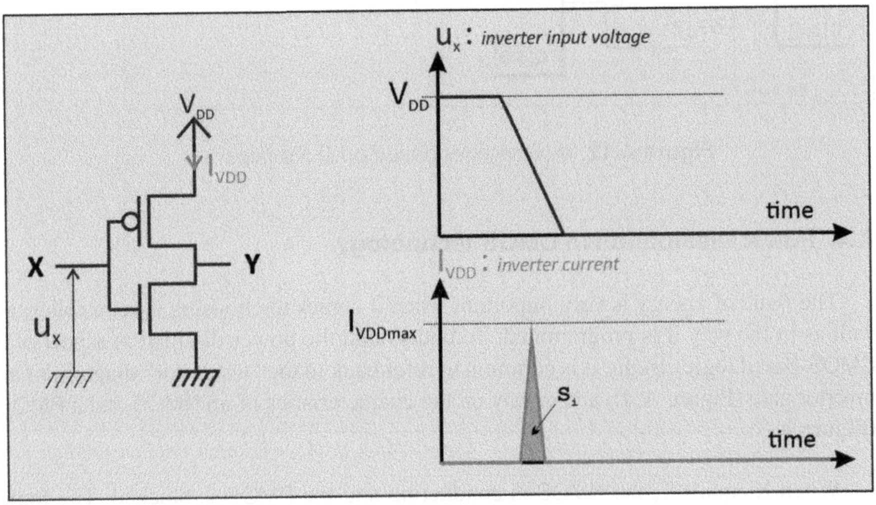

Figure A.13. *Power consumption of a CMOS inverter*

We can consider (to simplify the reasoning) that the shaded area denoted by S_i is constant during each switch of a logic gate. If we now apply a periodic square wave signal with frequency F to an inverter gate, we then obtain the voltage and current evolution curves that are shown in Figure A.14.

The power dissipated by the power supply equals:

$$P = \frac{2}{T}\int V_{DD}\times I_{VDD}dt = \frac{2V_{DD}}{T}\int I_{VDD}dt = 2V_{DD}\times F\times S_i$$

The factor S_i is specific to the technology and remains constant. Therefore, more simply, we can write:

$$P = K\times F$$

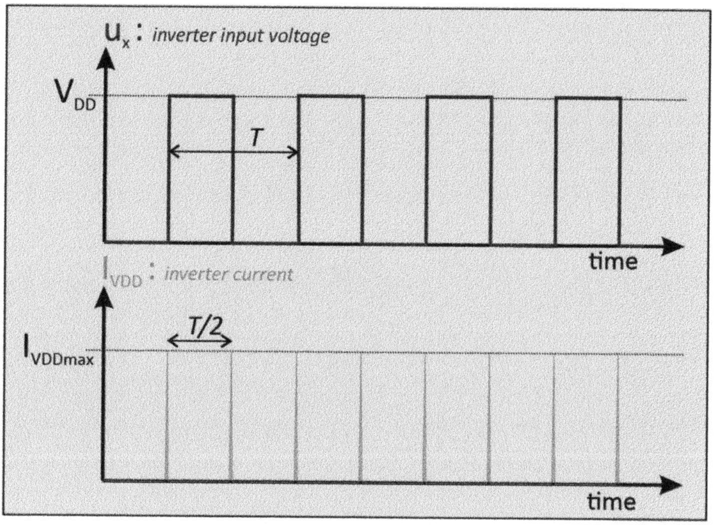

Figure A.14. *Power consumption of a CMOS inverter driven by a square wave signal*

where K is a constant, F is the frequency of the input signal, and P is the power dissipated by an inverter gate.

Therefore, we can conclude that the power dissipated by a μcontroller is:

– proportional to the frequency of the logic signals involved;

– proportional to the number of logic gates and elementary flip-flops involved.

Therefore, STmicro©'s strategy is clearly to:

– provide the ability to slowdown clocks;

– disable any clock for any unused peripheral by default.

References

Mahout, V. (2011). *Programmation en langage d'assemblage - ARM Cortex-M3*. Hermes Science Publications, Paris.

STMicroelectronics (2011). RM0008 – Reference Manual – STM32F101xx, STM32F102xx, STM32F103xx, STM32F105xx and STM32F107xx advanced ARM-based 32-bit MCUs [Online]. Available at: www.st.com.

STMicroelectronics (2012). PM0075 Programming Manual – STM32F10xxx Flash Memory Microcontrollers [Online]. Available at: www.st.com.

STMicroelectronics (2013). PM0056 – Programming Manual [Online]. Available at: www.st.com.

STMicroelectronics (2015). Datasheet des STM32F103x8 et STM32F103xB [Online]. Available at: www.st.com.

Index

G, H

I, L

M, N

O, P

R, S

T, U

V, W

Other titles from

ISTE

in

Computer Engineering

2025

CHIKH Azeddine
Systemic Approach to Categorizing and Modeling Requirements

TANEJA Ashu, KUMAR Abhishek, LIMKAR Suresh Vishnudas, OUAISSA Mariya, OUAISSA Mariyam
Driving Innovation through AI and Digital Twin for 6G Powered Sustainable Ultra Smart Cities

TANEJA Ashu, KUMAR Abhishek, LIMKAR Suresh Vishnudas, OUAISSA Mariya, OUAISSA Mariyam
6G Urban Innovation: AI and Digital Twin for Next-Gen Sustainable Cities

2024

CHAKRABORTY Rajdeep, GHOSH Anupam, KUMAR MANDAL Jyotsna, CHOUDHURY Tanupriya, CHATTERJEE Prasenjit
Smart Edge Computing: An Operation Research Perspective (International Perspectives in Decision Analytics and Operations Research Set – Volume 2)

HOMÈS Bernard
Fundamentals of Software Testing (2nd edition, revised and updated)

JERBI Abdessalem
Discrete-Event Simulation: Concepts and Production in Arena

PRADHAN Devasis, KUMAR SAHU Prasanna, MYO TUN Hla, CHATTERJEE Prasenjit
Artificial and Cognitive Computing for Sustainable Healthcare Systems in Smart Cities
(International Perspectives in Decision Analytics and Operations Research Set – Volume 3)

2023

CHOUDHURY Tanupriya, KHANNA Abhirup, CHATTERJEE Prasenjit, UM Jung-Sup, BHATTACHARYA Abhishek
Blockchain Applications in Healthcare: Innovations and Practices
(International Perspectives in Decision Analytics and Operations Research Set – Volume 1)

PAI G A Vijayalakshmi
A Textbook of Data Structures and Algorithms 1: Mastering Linear Data Structures
A Textbook of Data Structures and Algorithms 2: Mastering Nonlinear Data Structures
A Textbook of Data Structures and Algorithms 3: Mastering Advanced Data Structures and Algorithm Design Strategies

2022

HOMÈS Bernard
Advanced Testing of Systems-of-Systems 1: Theoretical Aspects
Advanced Testing of Systems-of-Systems 2: Practical Aspects

MEHTA Shikha, TIWARI Sanju, SIARRY Patrick, JABBAR M.A.
Tools, Languages, Methodologies for Representing Semantics on the Web of Things

SIDHOM Sahbi, KADDOUR Amira
Systems and Uses of Digital Sciences for Knowledge Organization
(Digital Tools and Uses Set – Volume 9)

ZAIDOUN Ameur Salem
Computer Science Security: Concepts and Tools

2021

DARCHE Philippe
Microprocessor 4: Core Concepts – Software Aspects
Microprocessor 5: Software and Hardware Aspects of Development, Debugging and Testing – The Microcomputer

DELHAYE Jean-Loïc
Inside the World of Computing: Technologies, Uses, Challenges

HARDIN Thérèse, JAUME Mathieu, PESSAUX François,
VIGUIÉ DONZEAU-GOUGE Véronique
Concepts and Semantics of Programming Languages 1: A Semantical Approach with OCaml and Python
Concepts and Semantics of Programming Languages 2: Modular and Object-oriented Constructs with OCaml, Python, C++, Ada and Java

MKADMI Abderrazak
Archives in The Digital Age: Preservation and the Right to be Forgotten (Digital Tools and Uses Set – Volume 8)

TOKLU Yusuf Cengiz, BEKDAŞ Gebrail, NIGDELI Sinan Melih
Metaheuristics for Structural Design and Analysis
(Optimization Heuristics Set – Volume 3)

2020

DARCHE Philippe
Microprocessor 1: Prolegomenes – Calculation and Storage Functions – Models of Computation and Computer Architecture
Microprocessor 2: Core Concepts – Communication in a Digital System
Microprocessor 3: Core Concepts – Hardware Aspects

DUVAUT Patrick, DALLOZ Xavier, MENGA David, KOEHL François, CHRIQUI Vidal, BRILL Joerg
Internet of Augmented Me, I.AM: Empowering Innovation for a New Sustainable Future

LAFFLY Dominique
TORUS 1 – Toward an Open Resource Using Services: Cloud Computing for Environmental Data
TORUS 2 – Toward an Open Resource Using Services: Cloud Computing for Environmental Data
TORUS 3 – Toward an Open Resource Using Services: Cloud Computing for Environmental Data

LAURENT Anne, LAURENT Dominique, MADERA Cédrine
Data Lakes
(Databases and Big Data Set – Volume 2)

OULHADJ Hamouche, DAACHI Boubaker, MENASRI Riad
Metaheuristics for Robotics
(Optimization Heuristics Set – Volume 2)

SADIQUI Ali
Computer Network Security

VENTRE Daniel
Artificial Intelligence, Cybersecurity and Cyber Defense

2019

BESBES Walid, DHOUIB Diala, WASSAN Niaz, MARREKCHI Emna
Solving Transport Problems: Towards Green Logistics

CLERC Maurice
Iterative Optimizers: Difficulty Measures and Benchmarks

GHLALA Riadh
Analytic SQL in SQL Server 2014/2016

TOUNSI Wiem
Cyber-Vigilance and Digital Trust: Cyber Security in the Era of Cloud Computing and IoT

2018

ANDRO Mathieu
Digital Libraries and Crowdsourcing
(Digital Tools and Uses Set – Volume 5)

ARNALDI Bruno, GUITTON Pascal, MOREAU Guillaume
Virtual Reality and Augmented Reality: Myths and Realities

CARDON Alain
Beyond Artificial Intelligence: From Human Consciousness to Artificial Consciousness

HOMAYOUNI S. Mahdi, FONTES Dalila B.M.M.
Metaheuristics for Maritime Operations
(Optimization Heuristics Set – Volume 1)

JEANSOULIN Robert
JavaScript and Open Data

PIVERT Olivier
NoSQL Data Models: Trends and Challenges
(Databases and Big Data Set – Volume 1)

SEDKAOUI Soraya
Data Analytics and Big Data

SALEH Imad, AMMI Mehdi, SZONIECKY Samuel
Challenges of the Internet of Things: Technology, Use, Ethics
(Digital Tools and Uses Set – Volume 7)

SZONIECKY Samuel
Ecosystems Knowledge: Modeling and Analysis Method for Information and Communication
(Digital Tools and Uses Set – Volume 6)

2017

BENMAMMAR Badr
Concurrent, Real-Time and Distributed Programming in Java: Threads, RTSJ and RMI

BOUHAÏ Nasreddine, SALEH Imad
Internet of Things: Evolutions and Innovations
(Digital Tools and Uses Set – Volume 4)

HÉLIODORE Frédéric, NAKIB Amir, ISMAIL Boussaad, OUCHRAA Salma, SCHMITT Laurent
Metaheuristics for Intelligent Electrical Networks
(Metaheuristics Set – Volume 10)

MA Haiping, SIMON Dan
Evolutionary Computation with Biogeography-based Optimization
(Metaheuristics Set – Volume 8)

PÉTROWSKI Alain, BEN-HAMIDA Sana
Evolutionary Algorithms
(Metaheuristics Set – Volume 9)

PAI G A Vijayalakshmi
Metaheuristics for Portfolio Optimization: An Introduction using MATLAB®
(Metaheuristics Set – Volume 11)

REYES-GARCIA Everardo
The Image-Interface: Graphical Supports for Visual Information
(Digital Tools and Uses Set – Volume 3)

REYES-GARCIA Everardo, BOUHAÏ Nasreddine
Designing Interactive Hypermedia Systems
(Digital Tools and Uses Set – Volume 2)

SZONIECKY Samuel, BOUHAÏ Nasreddine
Collective Intelligence and Digital Archives: Towards Knowledge Ecosystems
(Digital Tools and Uses Set – Volume 1)

2016

BLUM Christian, FESTA Paola
Metaheuristics for String Problems in Bio-informatics
(Metaheuristics Set – Volume 6)

DEROUSSI Laurent
Metaheuristics for Logistics
(Metaheuristics Set – Volume 4)

DHAENENS Clarisse, JOURDAN Laetitia
Metaheuristics for Big Data
(Metaheuristics Set – Volume 5)

LABADIE Nacima, PRINS Christian, PRODHON Caroline
Metaheuristics for Vehicle Routing Problems
(Metaheuristics Set – Volume 3)

LEROY Laure
Eyestrain Reduction in Stereoscopy

LUTTON Evelyne, PERROT Nathalie, TONDA Alberto
Evolutionary Algorithms for Food Science and Technology
(Metaheuristics Set – Volume 7)

MAGOULÈS Frédéric, ZHAO Hai-Xiang
Data Mining and Machine Learning in Building Energy Analysis

RIGO Michel
Advanced Graph Theory and Combinatorics

ZELM Martin, DOUMEINGTS Guy, MENDONÇA Joao Pedro
Enterprise Interoperability: in the Digitized and Networked Factory of the Future

2015

BARBIER Franck, RECOUSSINE Jean-Luc
COBOL Software Modernization: From Principles to Implementation with the BLU AGE® Method

CHEN Ken
Performance Evaluation by Simulation and Analysis with Applications to Computer Networks

CLERC Maurice
Guided Randomness in Optimization
(Metaheuristics Set – Volume 1)

DURAND Nicolas, GIANAZZA David, GOTTELAND Jean-Baptiste, ALLIOT Jean-Marc
Metaheuristics for Air Traffic Management
(Metaheuristics Set – Volume 2)

MAGOULÈS Frédéric, ROUX François-Xavier, HOUZEAUX Guillaume
Parallel Scientific Computing

MUNEESAWANG Paisarn, YAMMEN Suchart
Visual Inspection Technology in the Hard Disk Drive Industry

2014

BOULANGER Jean-Louis
Formal Methods Applied to Industrial Complex Systems
Formal Methods Applied to Complex Systems: Implementation of the B Method

EXPOSITO Ernesto, DIOP Codé
Smart SOA Platforms in Cloud Computing Architectures

GARDI Frédéric, BENOIST Thierry, DARLAY Julien, ESTELLON Bertrand, MEGEL Romain
Mathematical Programming Solver based on Local Search

KRICHEN Saoussen, CHAOUACHI Jouhaina
Graph-related Optimization and Decision Support Systems

LARRIEU Nicolas, VARET Antoine
Rapid Prototyping of Software for Avionics Systems: Model-oriented Approaches for Complex Systems Certification

LAURAS Matthieu, ZELM Martin, ARCHIMÈDE Bernard, BÉNABEN Frédérick, DOUMEINGTS Guy
Enterprise Interoperability: Interoperability for Agility, Resilience and Plasticity of Collaborations

OUSSALAH Mourad Chabane
Software Architecture 1
Software Architecture 2

QUESNEL Flavien
Scheduling of Large-scale Virtualized Infrastructures: Toward Cooperative Management

RIGO Michel
Formal Languages, Automata and Numeration Systems 1: Introduction to Combinatorics on Words
Formal Languages, Automata and Numeration Systems 2: Applications to Recognizability and Decidability

SAINT-DIZIER Patrick
Musical Rhetoric: Foundations and Annotation Schemes

TOUATI Sid, DUPONT DE DINECHIN Benoit
Advanced Backend Code Optimization

2013

ANDRÉ Étienne, SOULAT Romain
The Inverse Method: Parametric Verification of Real-time Embedded Systems

BOULANGER Jean-Louis
Safety Management for Software-based Equipment

DELAHAYE Daniel, PUECHMOREL Stéphane
Modeling and Optimization of Air Traffic

FRANCOPOULO Gil
LMF — Lexical Markup Framework

GHEDIRA Khaled
Constraint Satisfaction Problems: CSP Formalisms and Techniques

GOVAERT Gérard, NADIF Mohamed
Co-Clustering: Models, Algorithms and Applications

LANDRAGIN Frédérick
Man–Machine Dialogue: Design and Challenges

LUCAS Laurent, LOSCOS Céline, REMION Yannick
3D Video: Models, From Capture to Diffusion

ROCHANGE Christine, UHRIG Sascha, SAINRAT Pascal
Time-Predictable Architectures

WAHBI Mohamed
Algorithms and Ordering Heuristics for Distributed Constraint Satisfaction Problems

ZELM Martin, VAN SINDEREN Marten, FERRAIRA PIRES Luis, DOUMEINGTS Guy
Enterprise Interoperability: Research and Applications in the Service-oriented Ecosystem

2012

ARBOLEDA Hugo, ROYER Jean-Claude
Model-Driven and Software Product Line Engineering

BLANCHET Gérard, DUPOUY Bertrand
Computer Architecture

BOULANGER Jean-Louis
Industrial Use of Formal Methods: Formal Verification
Formal Methods: Industrial Use from Model to the Code

CALVARY Gaëlle, DELOT Thierry, SÈDES Florence, TIGLI Jean-Yves
Computer Science and Ambient Intelligence

MAHOUT Vincent
Assembly Language Programming: ARM Cortex-M3 2.0: Organization, Innovation and Territory

MARLET Renaud
Program Specialization

SOTO Maria, SEVAUX Marc, ROSSI André, LAURENT Johann
Memory Allocation Problems in Embedded Systems: Optimization Methods

2011

BICHOT Charles-Edmond, SIARRY Patrick
Graph Partitioning

BOULANGER Jean-Louis
Static Analysis of Software: The Abstract Interpretation

CAFERRA Ricardo
Logic for Computer Science and Artificial Intelligence

KORDON Fabrice, HADDAD Serge, PAUTET Laurent, PETRUCCI Laure
Distributed Systems: Design and Algorithms
Models and Analysis in Distributed Systems

LORCA Xavier
Tree-based Graph Partitioning Constraint

RIDHA MAHJOUB A.
Progress in Combinatorial Optimization: ISCO2010

TRUCHET Charlotte, ASSAYAG Gerard
Constraint Programming in Music

VICAT-BLANC Pascale, GOGLIN Brice, GUILLIER Romaric,
SOUDAN Sébastien
Computing Networks: From Cluster to Cloud Computing

2010

AUBRUN Christophe, SIMON Daniel, SONG Ye-Qiong
Co-design Approaches for Dependable Networked Control Systems

AUDIBERT Pierre
Mathematics for Informatics and Computer Science

BABAU Jean-Philippe, BLAY-FORNARINO Mireille, CHAMPEAU Joël, ROBERT Sylvain, SABETTA Antonino
Model Driven Engineering for Distributed Real-Time Systems: MARTE Modeling, Model Transformations and their Usages

BOULANGER Jean-Louis
Safety of Computer Architectures

SIGAUD Olivier, BUFFET Olivier
Markov Decision Processes in Artificial Intelligence

MONMARCHÉ Nicolas, GUINAND Frédérick, SIARRY Patrick
Artificial Ants

SOLNON Christine
Ant Colony Optimization and Constraint Programming

2009

FOURNIER Jean-Claude
Graph Theory and Applications: with exercises and problems

GUÉDON Jeanpierre
The Mojette Transform: theory and applications

JARD Claude, ROUX Olivier H.
Communicating Embedded Systems: Software and Design

LECOUTRE Christophe
Constraint Networks: Techniques and Algorithms

2008

BANÂTRE Michel, MARRON Pedro Jose, OLLERO Anibal, WOLITZ Adam
Cooperating Embedded Systems and Wireless Sensor Networks

MERZ Stephan, NAVET Nicolas
Modeling and Verification of Real-time Systems: Formalisms and Software Tools

PASCHOS Vangelis Th.
Combinatorial Optimization and Theoretical Computer Science: Interfaces and Perspectives

WALDNER Jean-Baptiste
Nanocomputers and Swarm Intelligence

2007

BENHAMOU Frédéric, JUSSIEN Narendra, O'SULLIVAN Barry
Trends in Constraint Programming

JUSSIEN Narendra
A to Z of Sudoku

2006

BABAU Jean-Philippe, CHAMPEAU Joël, GÉRARD Sébastien
From MDD Concepts to Experiments and Illustrations – DRES 2006

HABRIAS Henri, FRAPPIER Marc
Software Specification Methods: An Overview Using a Case Study

MURAT Cécile, PASCHOS Vangelis Th.
Probabilistic Combinatorial Optimization on Graphs

PANETTO Hervé, BOUDJLIDA Nacer
Interoperability for Enterprise Software and Applications: Proceedings of the Workshops and the Doctorial Symposium of the Second IFAC/IFIP I-ESA International Conference: EI2N, WSI, IS-TSPQ 2006

2005

GÉRARD Sébastien, BABAU Jean-Philippe, CHAMPEAU Joël
Model Driven Engineering for Distributed Real Time Embedded Systems

PANETTO Hervé
Interoperability of Enterprise Software and Applications: Workshops of the INTEROP-ESA 2005 International Conference (EI2N, WSI, ISIDI and IEHENA 2005)

Printed and bound by CPI Group (UK) Ltd, Croydon, CR0 4YY
13/09/2026
14961048-0008